CONTOURS OF
OLD TESTAMENT THEOLOGY

Bernhard W. Anderson
with the assistance of Steven Bishop

Fortress Press
Minneapolis

Cover design: Brad Norr Design
Interior design: Peregrine Graphics Services

Scripture quotations are from the following translations:
The New Revised Standard Version Bible, copyright © 1989 by the Division of Christian
Education of the National Council of the Churches of Christ in the United States. Used by
permission.

The Revised Standard Version of the Bible, copyright © 1946, 1952, and 1971 by the
Division of Christian Education of the National Council of Churches. Used by permission.

The New International Version of the Holy Bible, copyright © 1973, 1978, 1984 by the
International Bible Society. Used by permission of the Zondervan Publishing House. All
rights reserved. The "NIV" and "New International Version" trademarks are registered in the
United States Patent and Trademark Office by the International Bible Society. Use of either
trademark requires the permission of the International Bible Society.

The New English Bible, copyright © 1961, 1970 by the Delegates of the Oxford University
Press and the Syndics of the Cambridge University Press. Reprinted by permission.

The New Jerusalem Bible, copyright © 1985 by Darton, Longman & Todd, Ltd. and
Doubleday, a division of Bantam Doubleday Dell Publishing Group, Inc. Reprinted by
permission.

The TANAKH: The New Jewish Publication Society Translation According to the
Traditional Hebrew Text, copyright © 1985 by the Jewish Publication Society. Used by
permission.

The Revised English Bible, copyright © 1989 by the Oxford and Cambridge University
Presses. Used by permission.

Library of Congress Cataloging-in-Publication Data
Anderson, Bernhard W.
      The contours of Old Testament theology / Bernhard W. Anderson ;
   with the assistance of Steven Bishop.
            p.   cm.
      Includes bibliographical references and index.
      ISBN 0-8006-3074-2 (alk. paper)
      1. Bible. O.T.—Theology.   I. Bishop, Steven.   II. Title.
   BS1192.5.A53   1999
   230'.0411—dc21   99-10518
                                                                                      CIP

The paper used in this publication meets the minimum requirements of American National
Standard for Information Sciences—Permanence of Paper for Printed Library Materials,
ANSI Z329.48-1984.

Manufactured in the U.S.A.   AF 1-3074
     03   02   01   00   99   1   2   3   4   5   6   7   8   9   10

To George Ernest Wright

Colleague in
Biblical Archaeology
and
Biblical Theology

CONTENTS

PREFACE

This book is addressed primarily to the church: the believing and worshiping community. It is an introduction to biblical theology of the Old Testament, intended mainly for theological students, ministers, religious educators, missionaries, and laypersons who seek a better understanding of the biblical foundations of Christian faith.

The approach proposed here reflects my teaching experience over a period of years at the Theological School of Drew University, Princeton Theological Seminary, and the Boston University School of Theology. This period, the second half of the twentieth century, witnessed the aftermath of World War II, the turbulent sixties with the "death of God" and crisis in biblical theology, the theological crosscurrents of the seventies, and the beginning of the so-called postmodern period in the eighties and nineties. The outline of this Old Testament theology, tested in these cascading experiences, had taken shape penultimately at the climax of my teaching at Princeton Theological Seminary, as indicated by the course summary of 1982 found in Appendix 1.

The reader will not be surprised to hear in these pages echoes of what I have written in *Understanding the Old Testament* (4th ed., 1987; paperback revision, 1997), which also considers theological matters, though in a story/history context. While such a general introduction would be helpful, it is not prerequisite for this theological study.

The biblical quotations in this work are taken from the NRSV unless otherwise noted. My own translations are marked BWA.

It is evident from these pages that I am a debtor to many theologians, especially the two theological giants of the century, Walther Eichrodt and Gerhard von Rad. Also I have been profoundly influenced by Jewish philosophers and theologians: Martin Buber, Franz Rosenzweig, Emil Fackenheim, Abraham Joshua Heschel, and especially my good friend and former colleague, Will Herberg, with whom portions of this book have been discussed in vigorous table conversations. Above all I am indebted to my inspiring teacher, James Muilenburg, who was able to interweave creatively the elements of historical study, archaeological research, stylistic (rhetorical) criticism, and biblical theology.

Further, I am very grateful to my students and colleagues in theological schools who have joined me in wrestling with the issues of biblical theology, and to many people in the churches who have helped me to understand the Bible better: the Harvard-Epworth Methodist Church in Cambridge, Massachusetts; the United Church of Christ, Middlebury, Vermont; the United Methodist Church of Merced, California; the Presbyterian Church of Sunnyvale, California; St. Andrew Presbyterian Church, Aptos, California; a conference of ministers gathered at Yanzei University, Seoul, South Korea—to mention a few.

Especially I want to express thanks to my assistant, Steven Bishop, who did graduate work with me at the Boston University School of Theology. His perceptive advice and editorial skill have been immeasurably helpful in bringing this work to fruition. In addition, my thanks go to the staff of Fortress Press, particularly to Beth Wright, whose editorial skill has enhanced the quality of this work.

This book is dedicated to my colleague in biblical archaeology and biblical theology, the late G. Ernest Wright (see Appendix 2: "The Relevance of Biblical Archaeology to Biblical Theology"). Before his untimely death he encouraged me to keep at the task of biblical theology. I have continued the work, though taking a different path from the one he would have blazed.

Bernhard W. Anderson
September 25, 1998

ABBREVIATIONS

AB	Anchor Bible
ANET	J. B. Pritchard, ed., *Ancient Near Eastern Texts Relating to the Old Testament,* 3d ed. 1969
BA	*Biblical Archaeologist*
BR	*Biblical Research*
BRev	*Bible Review*
CBC	Cambridge Bible Commentary
CBQ	*Catholic Biblical Quarterly*
HBT	*Horizons in Biblical Theology*
HSM	Harvard Semitic Monographs
HTR	*Harvard Theological Review*
IB	G. A. Buttrick, ed., *Interpreter's Bible,* 12 vols., 1953–56
IDB	G. A. Buttrick, ed., *Interpreter's Dictionary of the Bible,* 4 vols., 1962
IDBSup	Supplement to *Interpreter's Dictionary of the Bible*
Int	*Interpretation*
IRT	Issues in Religion and Theology
JAOS	*Journal of the American Oriental Society*
JBL	*Journal of Biblical Literature*
JES	*Journal of Ecumenical Studies*
JSOT	*Journal for the Study of the Old Testament*
JSOTSup	JSOT Supplement Series
KJV	King James (Authorized) Version
NEB	New English Bible
NIV	New International Version
NJB	New Jerusalem Bible
NJPSV	New Jewish Publication Society Version
NRSV	New Revised Standard Version
OBT	Overtures to Biblical Theology
OTL	Old Testament Library
OTM	Old Testament Message
QR	*Quarterly Review*
RB	*Revue biblique*
REB	Revised English Bible
RelSRev	*Religious Studies Review*
RSV	Revised Standard Version
SBM	Stuttgarter biblischer Monographien
SBT	Studies in Biblical Theology
SJT	*Scottish Journal of Theology*
TToday	*Theology Today*
ZAW	*Zeitschrift für die alttestamentliche Wissenschaft*
ZTK	*Zeitschrift für Theologie und Kirche*

Preliminary Considerations

"These things
[in the Old Testament]
were written down
for our instruction,
upon whom the end
of the ages has come."

1 CORINTHIANS 10:11

1. THE OLD TESTAMENT
IN THE CHRISTIAN BIBLE

The Task of Biblical Theology

Theology is faith seeking understanding.[1] Standing within the circle of faith, a theologian articulates and elaborates the faith of the believing and worshiping community so that members of the community, or others interested, may understand who God is, God's relationship to the world and all that is in it, and the unfolding purpose of God from creation to consummation.

When this definition is applied to the Bible, which in the Christian community consists of both Old and New Testaments, the question immediately arises: what is faith?

The writer of the Epistle of Jude (v. 3) speaks of "the faith that was once for all entrusted to the saints." Here *the faith* (with a definite article) means "a clear system of teachings"[2]—a body of doctrine that was packaged and delivered to the community. This view reflects the situation of the church at the end of the apostolic age when it became necessary to have a creedal "rule of faith," or essential affirmations of faith, for the purpose of maintaining the identity of the community in the world and defending the gospel against novel teaching (e.g., Gnosticism).

In the Bible, with the major exception of this passage in the Epistle of Jude, faith is generally a *relationship* between human beings and God. To be sure, faith is nuanced in various ways. In the New Testament faith centers in Jesus Christ, who reveals God and introduces a new age. In the Old Testament faith is steadfast reliance on God amid the uncertainties and insecurities of life. "The righteous live by their faith [*emunah*]" (Hab. 2:4), that is, by faithful trust and waiting in hope for God's purpose to triumph. This vital faith finds expression in essential affirmations, such as the sole power of God (as in the Shema, Deut. 6:4), but it is weakened, if not eclipsed, when congealed into belief in doctrines.

When faith is understood in this dynamic, relational sense, the task of the biblical theologian is something other than organizing and systematizing doctrines. Biblical theologians engage in the difficult task of "beating the crust back into the batter," to borrow a figure of speech; that is, they seek to go behind the later incrustations of doctrine to the living experience of faith with all of its ambiguities, temptations, and struggles. This task requires that the theologian take into account the various ways that faith finds expression in the language of religious imagination: in poetry, story, and patterns of symbolism. Faith is not bound by literalism on the one hand or by historicism on the other, but seeks to understand how

---

1. In a classical definition, *fides quaerens intellectum* (Anselm). See the introduction to systematic (dogmatic) theology by Daniel L. Migliori, *Faith Seeking Understanding* (Grand Rapids: Eerdmans, 1991).

2. *The New Jerome Biblical Commentary*, ed. Raymond E. Brown et al. (Englewood Cliffs, N.J.: Prentice-Hall, 1990), 918.

3

words and events are charged with sacred meaning so that they become, as Abraham Joshua Heschel put it, "hyphens" connecting heaven and earth, God and humanity.[3] Theology of this sort is nearer to art than to science, to imaginative portrayal than to prosaic discourse. It appeals to the poet within us, as "deep calls unto deep" (Ps. 42:7). To comprehend God's relationship to the world and God's activity within it, writes Patrick Miller as he reflects on theological trends of the past decades, "it may be that our most helpful language will turn out to be located in poetic speech and in images that belong more to poetry and story than to philosophical analysis."[4]

The Old Testament as Canonical Scripture

Old Testament theology is a Christian discipline. Since the dawn of Christianity, "Old Testament" (Old Covenant) has been the standard label for the Scriptures that the early Christian community inherited from ancient Israel. The term indicates that the early Christian movement began in the heart of Judaism, that the pristine Christian proclamation was based on the Jewish Scriptures (called the Law and the Prophets), and that the two communities of faith belong together, as Paul argued effectively in Romans 9–11, sharing a common Bible and therefore a common story.[5]

The language "old covenant" (testament) is reminiscent of a famous prophecy in the book of Jeremiah (31:31-33) about two epochs: the time of the old Mosaic covenant, which ended in human failure; and the time of the new covenant, when the divine *torah* (law, teaching) will be written on the heart and there will be such personal knowledge of God that religious teaching will no longer be necessary. In Jeremiah's prophecy the issue is eschatology, the relation between the old age and the new, not between two bodies of Scripture.

The Jewish community located at Qumran on the shores of the Dead Sea (end of third century B.C. to A.D. 70) thought of itself as a community of the new covenant. Believing that the new age was about to come, these covenanters (probably Essenes) searched Jewish Scriptures for prophecies that were going to be fulfilled. Similarly, the early Christian community considered itself a community of the new covenant. In their own way Christians also read Jewish Scriptures with the conviction that the anticipated age of the new covenant had already dawned through the life, death, and resurrection of Jesus, the Messiah (Christ). It was appropriate, then, that in the second century, when Christians compiled their own writings, they labeled them the Scriptures of the new covenant, to distinguish

3. Abraham Joshua Heschel, *God in Search of Man: A Philosophy of Judaism* (New York: Farrar, Straus and Cudahy, 1955), 244.

4. From the concluding paragraph of an editorial, "Revisiting the God Who Acts," *TToday*, 54, no. 1 (1997) 5.

5. See my essay, "The Bible as the Shared Story of a People," in *The Old and the New Testaments: Their Relationship and the "Intertestamental" Literature*, ed. James H. Charlesworth and Walter P. Weaver (Valley Forge, Penn.: Trinity Press International, 1993), 19–37.

them from the Scriptures of ancient Israel. Thus the church has a bipartite canon, a two-volume book of Scriptures: the Old Testament and the New Testament.

Old Testament/Hebrew Bible
In recent years the Christian title "Old Testament" ("Old Covenant") has been paralleled with, or even superseded by, the neutral description "Hebrew Bible." This "renaming of Scripture" is generally practiced in academic circles (e.g., American Academy of Religion, Society of Biblical Literature), but it has also crept into Christian worship services, where a reading from the "Old Testament" is sometimes introduced by: "Listen to a reading from the Hebrew Bible."[6]

At best, this retitling of Scripture expresses an irenic, ecumenical spirit. Too long has the contrast between the "old" and the "new" fostered an anti-Semitism that has resulted in vicious hostility and terrible genocide. Christianity does not supersede Judaism; indeed, Jesus did not come to "destroy" Israel's Scriptures but to "fulfill" them (Matt. 5:17), to "complete" them. To its credit, the new nomenclature, "Hebrew Bible," attempts to respect Judaism as a religion in its own right, not an error that Christianity came to correct. Also, this noncommittal language may express an openness to Islam, which includes portions of the "Old Testament" in the Koran. It is significant that three great religions—Judaism, Christianity, and Islam—trace their roots to Abraham, the great ancestor of the faithful.

Often, however, this "politically correct" language is influenced by the reductionist view that the sacred writings of the Bible are only historical documents that must be interpreted in the context of ancient culture, specifically that of the ancient Near East. So viewed, the Old Testament is not interpreted "confessionally," as the inspired canonical books of a community of faith, but as literature that reflects "the religion of Israel," which, in turn, is part of the history of ancient religions. The great scholar Hermann Gunkel, who did so much to awaken a poetic appreciation of the Hebrew Bible through the use of form criticism, maintained that the biblical interpreter must view the religion of Israel in the wider context of the literature of surrounding peoples, such as the Babylonians and Egyptians. In his poetic universalism, biblical theology, with its concern for Israel's distinctive theological witness, was abandoned in favor of the history of Israelite religion.[7]

Problems in Renaming Scripture
The term "Hebrew Bible," however, is not satisfactory for a number of reasons. First, this label refers to the original language in which most of these writings were composed: Hebrew. A comparable designation for the "New Testament" would be "Koine Greek Scriptures." Designating these Scriptures by language gets us into

---

6. See the forceful article by William Johnson Everett, "Renaming Scripture," *Christian Century* 114, no. 30 (1997) 965–66, who challenges Christians to think theologically about this change in language.

7. On Gunkel's romanticism, see my introductory essay to the translation of Martin Noth's *A History of Pentateuchal Traditions* (Englewood Cliffs, N.J.: Prentice-Hall, 1972), especially xviii–xx.

difficulties. Not all of the Hebrew Bible is written in Hebrew: some is written in Aramaic (parts of the books of Ezra and Daniel). Moreover, the Hebrew Bible, as we can see from the translation of the Jewish Publication Society (NJPSV), excludes a number of writings found in the Catholic Christian Bible (sometimes called the Old Testament Apocrypha) that help to fill in the gap between the restoration of the Jewish community under Ezra and Nehemiah (fifth century B.C.) and the later rabbinical and Christian periods.

Second, the term is unsatisfactory because the early Christian church adopted for its Scripture the Greek Bible known as the Septuagint, a translation that began in Alexandria, Egypt, in the third century B.C. The Septuagint included not only the Hebrew Bible (preeminently the Law and the Prophets) but also writings that came to be called "apocryphal" (Protestant) or "deuterocanonical" (Catholic). At the time of the Reformation some parts of the Christian community (Lutherans, Calvinists) declared that only the books included in the Jewish Bible were canonical Scripture, and regarded the extra "apocryphal" books as useful for edification.

Third, the Christian Bible often has a different order of books. For instance, in the Hebrew Bible the book of Ruth is located in the third section (Writings), sandwiched between Proverbs and Song of Songs, whereas in the Christian Bible, influenced by the order of the Septuagint, it is found among the historical books (called Former Prophets in Jewish tradition), adjacent to the book of Judges. Also, the "minor prophets," Zechariah and Malachi, are located at the very end of the Old Testament just before the New Testament, whereas the Hebrew Bible concludes with 1–2 Chronicles, which belongs to the Writings.

The difference in the sequence of books may have theological significance.[8] On the basis of the arrangement of the Hebrew Bible some have argued that the Hebrew canon bears witness to "the disappearance of God." In the first part (Torah or Pentateuch) God is a primary actor and many miracles occur, but by the time one reaches the last part (the Writings) God scarcely appears (e.g., in Chronicles, Ezra-Nehemiah) or not at all (as in Esther). The disappearance of God is allegedly connected with humanity's coming of age, even at the terrible cost of "the death of God."[9]

If this is the canonical witness of the Hebrew Bible (which is doubtful), the Old Testament of the early Christian church (the Septuagint) makes just the opposite witness. There the last books (the Twelve Minor Prophets) express an eschatological expectancy of the Day of the Lord, when God will come in majesty and power to establish a new age on earth. The location of the prophets at the end of the Old Testament was appropriate in a community that announced that Jesus came to fulfill the hopes and expectations of Israel's prophets.

---

8. See James A. Sanders, "'Spinning' the Bible: How Judaism and Christianity Shape the Canon Differently," *BR* 14, no. 3 (1998) 23–29. He discusses how the different scriptural canons arose and the hermeneutical implications of the differences between them.

9. Richard Elliot, *The Disappearance of God: A Divine Mystery* (Boston: Little, Brown, 1995). Reviewed by Ronald S. Hendel, *BR* 12, no. 1 (1996) 17.

Finally, the retitling of Scripture, despite the intention to avoid the view that Christianity supersedes Judaism, may result in too sharp a separation between the Jewish and the Christian communities. After the Holocaust we want to be sure that Judaism has its own integrity as a religion and that, along with Christianity and Islam, it receives equal legal protection and social recognition. But this separation can be carried too far. Christianity and Judaism belong closely together in the elective purpose of God; therefore, the Old Testament cannot be torn out of the Christian Bible. "From the Christian perspective the literary separation of the two testaments," writes William J. Everett, "undermines the very core of Christian faith. The New Testament simply doesn't make any sense apart from the Old, and we need to say so every week in the way we worship."[10]

Thus for theological reasons it is best to avoid the term "Hebrew Bible" and speak of either Jewish Scriptures (Jewish usage) or the Old Testament (Christian usage). Some people, believing that "old" and "new" are prejudicial (the new is supposedly better), suggest shifting to First and Second Testaments. But it is doubtful that this innovation will become established. In my judgment, Christians should not be hesitant to use their own canonical language in Christian worship services and in intramural theological discussions.

Early Christian Scripture

Before the Christian community published this two-part canon of sacred writings, it had no scriptures of its own. It had only the received Scriptures of the Jewish people, divided into three major parts: Torah, Prophets, and Writings. The third part, the Writings, was not yet completed in the first century A.D., but one of its major components was the book of Psalms, which was used in synagogue worship. Indeed, this book was so important that the third part of the Jewish canon could be referred to simply as "the Psalms." Philo of Alexandria, who died about the middle of the first century, spoke of "the Law, the Prophets, and the Psalms."[11] The same usage is found in Luke's Gospel, from the late first century, which refers to "the Law of Moses, the Prophets, and the Psalms" (Luke 24:44).

The latter reference is in Luke's beautiful story of two disciples walking from Jerusalem to a nearby village, Emmaus. They were sad about the crucifixion of their leader, and disillusioned about the hope that he was the Messiah of Israel; but as they walked, so the story goes, they were joined by a stranger who interpreted the recent events in the light of Israel's scriptures, "beginning with Moses and all the prophets" (v. 17). The stranger proved to be Jesus, who declared that these things had happened "in order that everything written about me in the law of

10. Everett, "Renaming Scripture," 966.

11. *De Vita Contemplativa*, cited by Nahum Sarna, *BR* 9, no. 4 (1993) 32–40. See also the prologue to the Wisdom of Ben Sira (in the Protestant Apocrypha) which refers to the teachings given "through the Law and the prophets and the other books," showing that at this time the third part of the Hebrew Bible (Writings) was still open-ended. Ben Sira's grandson translated the work from Hebrew to Greek ca. 130 B.C.

Moses, the prophets, and the psalms must be fulfilled." We read (v. 45): "Then he opened their minds to understand the scriptures."

This story indicates two things. First, the Scriptures of Israel do not prepare readers for the event of the crucifixion of God's Messiah and, the other side of that event, his victorious resurrection from the dead. There is a profound discontinuity between the witness of the Old Testament and Jesus' crucifixion and resurrection. These events were surprising, and in a sense unexpected and unbelievable. But second, the disciples were persuaded to believe that, in a profound sense, the Jesus story was part of "the great story and plot of all time and space," as Amos Wilder puts it.[12] In a Christian rereading of Israel's Scriptures it was indeed "necessary" (Greek *dei*) for Jesus to suffer as he did before his vocation was crowned with victory (Luke 24:26). This event was not accidental but belonged somehow to the unity of God's redemptive purpose. The surprising novelty of all of this did not cancel out the expectations of the prophets.

Written for Our Instruction

Hence, early Christians insisted that the Bible they read, that is, the Torah, the Prophets, and the Psalms, did not belong exclusively to the Jewish community; it belonged to them too. They could say, as did Paul, that "these things were written down for our instruction upon whom the end of the ages has come" (1 Cor. 10:11). Or as Paul puts it succinctly toward the conclusion of his Epistle to the Romans: "For whatever was written in former days was written for our instruction, so that by steadfastness and by the encouragement of the scriptures we might have hope" (Rom. 15:4).

Even today in the Christian communion service worshipers often join in the "Great Thanksgiving" to God "for the goodness and love which you have made known to us in creation, in the calling of Israel to be your people, in your Word spoken through the prophets, and above all in the Word made flesh, Jesus your Son." Creation, Israel, the prophets, Jesus Christ—that is the sequence of the great story.

Early Christians, then, seized the Jewish Bible and made it their own. Indeed, whenever the word "scripture(s)" (*graphe, graphai*) occurs in the New Testament it refers, almost without exception, to the Jewish Bible. That is probably true of the famous statement in 2 Tim. 3:16: "All scripture is inspired by God and is useful for teaching, for reproof, for correction, and for training in righteousness." Here the scriptures of Israel are regarded as "God-breathed" on the analogy of Gen. 2:7, where God breathes vitality into the first human being.

In sum: the "Old Testament" is an essential part of the Christian Bible. It was "canonical" Scripture long before the discussions of the second century produced a list of authoritative Christian writings. Even today this part of the Christian Bible is—or should be—used in worship, preaching, and education. It is also consulted when formulating Christian doctrine (e.g., creation) or when seeking guidance on ethical issues (e.g., questions of social justice).

---

12. Amos N. Wilder, *The Language of the Gospel* (New York: Harper & Row, 1964), 64.

2. The Relative Independence of the Old Testament

Early Christians, we have seen, regarded the scriptures of Israel as their scriptures too, in which they perceived the unfolding purpose of God since creation and in which they found clues to the identity of Jesus of Nazareth. But this appropriation of the Old Testament proved to be difficult. For the Christian church the Old Testament has a somewhat alien character. This has shown up in various ways down through the centuries, beginning with early attempts to reject these scriptures as non-Christian and coming into the present, when many Christians sense the Old Testament to be a problem. This part of the Bible is sometimes written off as "pre-Christian" literature, because of its ancient views of God or outdated moral injunctions.

The truth of the matter is that the Old Testament has a relative independence in the Christian Bible. That is why it is possible for Christians to speak of "Old Testament theology," as something relatively distinct from "New Testament theology." A better designation would be "biblical theology of the Old Testament," a formulation that implies the essential relationship between the Old and New Testaments in the Christian Bible.[1]

Relationship between the Testaments

The relationship between the two testaments is one of continuity and discontinuity. In dealing with the Old Testament, the church has often fallen into one of two extremes.

The first extreme has been to overemphasize discontinuity. In this view the "new" has superseded the "old"; hence the "old" must be regarded as antithetical, preparatory, provisional, inferior. That was the view of Marcion in the second century, who went so far as to say that the Old Testament presents the revelation of "the strange God," different from the God revealed in Jesus Christ. His view, though regarded at the time as a heresy, was echoed by the church historian Adolf Harnack in the twentieth century. In his book *Marcion: The Gospel of a Strange God*, Harnack declared that in the second century the church rightly refused to reject the Old Testament, that in the sixteenth century the retention of the Old Testament was a fateful necessity that the Reformation was not yet able to escape, but that in the period since the nineteenth century the inclusion of the Old Testament in the Christian canon is the sign of "a religious and ecclesiastical

---

1. See the title of Brevard Childs's work, *Biblical Theology of the Old and New Testaments: Theological Reflection on the Christian Bible* (Minneapolis: Fortress Press, 1992). The distinction between Old Testament and New Testament theology in the context of biblical theology goes back to G. L. Bauer in works written at the beginning of the nineteenth century.

paralysis."[2] The New Testament theologian Rudolf Bultmann came very close to this position in his view of the significance of the Old Testament for Christian faith. He maintained that the Old Testament provides only a "preunderstanding" for the Christian gospel, in the sense that it shows human inadequacy and failure that, when taken seriously, prepare one to receive the grace of God in Jesus Christ.[3]

The other extreme is to minimize the distinction between the testaments and to regard the Old Testament as leading directly to the New. This view is held, for instance, by Hartmut Gese, who regards the New Testament as part of a continuing stream of tradition that flows through the whole Christian Bible.[4] This view is espoused in another way by Wilhelm Vischer, who finds Jesus Christ hidden in the Old Testament.[5] For instance, Jacob's nocturnal wrestle with a stranger at the ford of the Jabbok River (Gen. 32:22-32) is understood to be an encounter with the Lord Jesus Christ incognito.

"These views," as Petr Pokorny observes rightly, "run the risk of defrauding the Old Testament of its relative autonomy, in which it could also remain the Bible of the Jews, and of relativizing the unique features of the Christian message."[6] He goes on to say: "the New Testament was canonized neither as a substitute for the Jewish Bible, nor as its continuation, but as its counterpart." In short, it has a relative independence. Not an absolute independence, please understand, but a relative one, like that of two partners when joined in matrimony. Or, to shift the figure, the Christian Bible is like an antiphonal choir, in which both testaments stand vis-à-vis each other, joining in praise to the God who is creator and redeemer.

Letting the Old Testament Speak for Itself
One of the implications of this view of the relationship between the testaments is that, if we are faithful to Scripture, we are obligated to let the Old Testament speak with its own voice, even though that means interpreting passages differently than New Testament authors do. For instance, we must free texts like Genesis 2–3 from questionable interpretations that emphasize the subordination of women to men, as in 1 Tim. 2:12-15: "I permit no woman to teach or to have authority over a man; she is to keep silent. For Adam was formed first, then Eve." This view does not do justice to the Old Testament narrative. For when it is read on its own as "a tale that is being told," or a process of creation that takes place in dramatic episodes, the

2. English translation by John E. Steely and Lyle D. Bierma (Durham, N.C.: Labyrinth, 1989) of Adolph Harnack, *Marcion: Das Evangelium vom fremden Gott* (2d ed.; Leipzig: J. C. Hinrichs, 1924).

3. See the lead essay by Bultmann, "The Significance of the Old Testament for the Christian Faith" (trans. B. W. Anderson), in the symposium that I edited, *The Old Testament and Christian Faith* (Philadelphia: Westminster, 1969), 8–35. Elements of the present discussion have been drawn from my introduction there, pp. 1–7.

4. Hartmut Gese's thesis, set forth in a German essay, "Erwägungen zur Einheit der biblischen Theologie," *ZTK* 67 (1970) 417–36, is cited and summarized by Petr Pokorny, "The Problem of Biblical theology," *HBT* 15, no. 1 (1993) 90–91.

5. See his essay, "Everywhere the Scripture Is about Christ Alone," in *Old Testament and Christian Faith*, ed. Anderson, 90–101.

6. Pokorny, "Problem," 91.

relation between the sexes in God's original creation is one of mutuality, not sub-ordination, as Phyllis Trible has perceptively shown.[7]

Of course, in the Christian community it is proper to regard Scripture as a whole in a christological perspective, but this does not mean forcing particular texts to bear witness to Jesus Christ or to carry a Christian meaning. That the Old Testament must be allowed to maintain its own voice, and the New Testament too, is stressed in Brevard Childs's canonical approach to the Christian Bible. Though the Old Testament is promise and the New Testament is fulfillment, he writes, the Old Testament has not lost "its vertical, existential dimension which as scripture of the church continues to bear its own witness within the context of the Christian Bible."[8]

Admittedly, it is difficult in the community of faith to allow the Old Testament this relative independence. I was once called on to respond to a paper by Matatiahu Tsevat on "Theology of the Old Testament—a Jewish View."[9] He admitted the novelty of his presentation, for in Jewish circles "Old Testament theology" is almost unheard of—something like "the zoology of a unicorn," as he put it. He argued, however, that the Old Testament should be allowed to speak for itself independently, rather than being ancillary to the Talmud[10] (or we Christians might add, to the New Testament). At one point he used a marvelous illustration: the conveyor belt that one takes in some airports (e.g., Chicago's O'Hare), connecting both ends of a long passageway. It is easy enough to take it in one direction, he says, for "the Talmud understands itself to be a continuation and sup-plement of the Old Testament." But if one wants to reverse the direction, and move from the Talmud (Christians, read: "from the New Testament") to the Old Testament, it demands incredible exertion. It is well nigh impossible.

Yet what is almost impossible should be attempted. This is also the view of another Jewish scholar, Jon Levenson. In his important study of biblical theology, Sinai and Zion, Levenson takes his stand firmly within the Jewish community, with the result that he makes numerous references to rabbinical commentary and some critical remarks about the New Testament, especially Paul's interpretation of the law. In the introduction to this work he writes: "I make no claim that Rabbinic Judaism offers the correct understanding of the Hebrew Bible. Talmudic religion is different from its biblical ancestor . . . but the change is more evolutionary than revolutionary." He concludes: "The ultimate measure of success or failure adopted here, however, is not conformity to the Jewish tradition, but whether or not the reading proposed is true to the biblical texts themselves."[11]

7. See Phyllis Trible, "A Love Story Gone Awry," in God and the Rhetoric of Sexuality, OBT (Minneapolis: Fortress Press, 1978), chap. 4.

8. Childs, Biblical Theology, 77–78.

9. See his essay and my response in HBT 8, no. 2 (1986) 33–50, 51–59, respectively.

10. The Talmud is a large body of Jewish law and commentary that evolved during the period A.D. 200 to approximately the mid-sixth century.

11. Jon Levenson, Sinai and Zion: An Entry into the Jewish Bible (Minneapolis: Winston, 1985), 4.

That is a goal worth striving for: to give an interpretation that is "true to the biblical texts themselves" so that this body of literature (the Jewish Scriptures, the Old Testament) may speak with its own voice in a relatively independent way.

Continuity/Discontinuity

It is precisely this relative independence that we Christians must grant the Old Testament in the Christian Bible. There is a chasm between the two testaments, one that can be bridged only by those who are able to make the confession Peter made at Caesarea Philippi: that Jesus (whom the reader knows to be the crucified and resurrected one) is God's Messiah, the Christ (Mark 8:27-30). That christological confession establishes a deep discontinuity with Israel's Scripture and, at the same time, a deep continuity in the purpose of God. The discontinuity is expressed in the Gospel of Matthew: "You have heard that it was said to those of ancient times, . . . but I say to you . . ." (Matt. 5:21-22, 27). The continuity is expressed in the same Gospel: "Do not think that I have come to abolish the Law or the Prophets; I have come not to abolish, but to fulfill" (Matt. 5:17).

This hermeneutic (or mode of interpretation) of continuity/discontinuity will result, on the one hand, in a critical assessment of the Scriptures of the Old Testament. Some of this literature has been superseded in God's ongoing purpose, for instance, the practice of holy war or the sacrificial system of the temple. On the other hand, this hermeneutic will enable the church to understand that the Old Testament has its own positive theological witness that often supplements and perhaps even corrects the New Testament witness. Some theological dimensions in the Old Testament are taken for granted in the New, such as creation theology or the prophetic message of social justice. Both testaments are theologically necessary to each other if the church is to hear in the human words of the Bible the word (revelation) of God.

The Coexistence of the Jewish and Christian Communities

This whole question of the relation between the Old and New Testaments demands that we come to terms with the coexistence of the Jewish and Christian communities in the mystery of God's purpose. Too often the downplaying of the Old Testament has been connected with anti-Semitism, which should have no place in Christianity, although tragically it has persisted down through history. A special kinship exists between Christianity and Judaism—more so than in the case of Islam, which also traces its spiritual ancestry to Abraham.

One of the outstanding attempts to deal with the kinship between the Jewish and Christian communities was that of the political philosopher Eric Voegelin in his five-volume study, *Order and History*. In this work he addressed the question many people raised during the twentieth century—probably the most violent in human history—of whether "the created order of society, in one way or another, corresponds to an underlying order of the universe."[12] It is highly significant that Voegelin laid the foundation for his massive study by turning to the Old Testament, or more specifically to the phenomenon of ancient Israel in the context of the religions of the surrounding world.[13] He was not concerned with Israel as a political state or with the religion of Israel but with Israel as the bearer of "revelation" that provides a key to understanding the search for order in human history.

Voegelin maintained that Israel's exodus from Egypt was not just a political event in world history but an exodus from a symbolic world that enabled ancient empires, like that of Egypt, to see themselves as belonging to a cosmic order. Gods and humans, cosmos and history, the heavenly order and earthly empire, were bound up in one compact whole. Israel, however, broke from this "cosmological symbolism" and achieved a sense of "transcendence," that is, an awareness of the rule of God that cannot be identified with the political order or anything "worldly." The revelation of the transcendent God and God's created order, expressed in the symbolism of the biblical language, came to inspired persons, beginning especially with Moses, whose souls were so attuned to God and God's cosmic kingdom (rule) that they represented a new type of human being in world history.

According to Voegelin, God's revelation came at a great cost, which he described as a "mortgage" of Israel's mundane existence on the transcendent rule of God, as evidenced in attachment to an ethnic group (the people Israel) and a promised land (the land of Israel). As long as this mortgage was in effect, God's revelation could not achieve the universal implications anticipated in the call of Abraham (Gen. 12:1-3). In Christianity, however, this mortgage was liquidated, so to speak, and the promises to Israel were extended to all people (not just the chosen people) on the whole "earth" (not just the "land" of Israel).

Here we find a bold attempt to deal with a fundamental theological subject: divine revelation. Even those who do not share Voegelin's philosophical presuppositions will be allured by the author's treatment of religious symbolism, particularly the symbolism of biblical language. To this matter we shall return again and again.

The thorny problem, however, is the proposed understanding of the relationship between the Jewish and Christian communities of faith. It is ironic that Voegelin, for whom revelation to Israel is the foundation and starting point, comes out with a negative assessment of the future of Israel in God's purpose. As a Christian, he finds much that is true and good in the Old Testament, but these

---

12. Peter L. Berger, *A Rumor of Angels: Modern Society and the Rediscovery of the Supernatural* (rev. ed.; New York: Doubleday, 1990), 60–61.

13. Eric Voegelin, *Order and History*, vol. 1: *Israel and Revelation* (Baton Rouge: Louisiana State Univ. Press, 1956). See my review essay, "Politics and the Transcendent: Voegelin's Philosophical and Theological Exposition of the Old Testament in the Context of the Ancient Near East," *The Political Science Reviewer* 1 (Fall 1971) 1–29; revised and updated version in *Eric Voegelin's Search for Order*, ed. Stephen A. McKnight (Baton Rouge: Louisiana State Univ. Press, 1978), 62–100.

benefits are only partially valid because of the "mortgage"—the attachment of God's revelation to the concrete realities of this world: ethnic identity, a nation state, life on the land. Hence, just as Israel made an exodus from "cosmological civilization" under Moses, it must—owing to its inescapable involvement in the mundane sphere—engage in an "exodus from itself." It is the destiny of Israel to die and to be superseded by the universal revelation of God in Jesus Christ, in whom the promises to Abraham are extended to all peoples.[14]

The Mystery of Divine Election

In my judgment, there is a better way to view Jewish-Christian relationship, and correspondingly the relation between the Old and New Testaments. The particularity of God's revelation to the ethnic group Israel and the universal outreach and inclusivity of the Christian community need not conflict. The vocations of the two communities—one to be the people of the Torah and the other to be an inclusive community that knows no boundaries (see Gal. 3:28)—are complimentary in God's purpose. That view was set forth in Franz Rosenzweig's classic, *The Star of Redemption*.[15] At the center of the Jewish community is the fire of God's holy presence (cf. Exod. 3:2: "the bush burned, yet it was not consumed"); in the other community the rays of the fire reach outward into the whole world (cf. John 1:9: "the true light that enlightens everyone").

That view, I believe, is consonant with Paul's agonized discussion of the relation between the two communities in the face of Israel's rejection of Jesus as the Messiah (Christ). The statement that "all Israel will be saved" (Rom. 11:26) does not mean that the Jewish community of faith will make "an exodus from itself" and that all Jews will be Christianized. Rather, Paul grapples with the "mystery" (Rom. 11:25) of God's election that includes both Jews and Gentiles in "the Israel of God" (Gal. 6:16). God is faithful to the promises made to the ancestors of Israel and extends the meaning and power of those promises to all who have faith, those who are true children of Abraham (see Romans 4). The eschatological realization of God's purpose that "all Israel will be saved" is a mystery hidden in the grace of God. It is that mystery that prompts the apostle to exclaim at the conclusion of his anguished and not altogether consistent discussion:

> O the depth of the riches and wisdom and knowledge of God! How unsearchable are his judgments, and how inscrutable his ways!
>
> —Rom. 11:33

14. Voegelin, *Israel and Revelation*, 144, 315, 506. See further my essay, "Israel and Revelation," *BR* 13, no. 5 (1997) 17, 46–47, from which some of this discussion is taken. Also my essay presented to the Second International Conference on Voegelin's Work, held at the University of Manchester (July 1997), "Revisiting Voegelin's *Israel and Revelation* after Twenty-five Years."

15. English translation by William W. Hallo (New York: Holt, Rinehart and Winston, 1971) of Franz Rosenzweig, *Der Stern der Erlösung* (1930). See further Aaron L. Mackler, "Universal Being and Ethical Particularity in the Hebrew Bible: A Jewish Response to Voegelin's *Israel and Revelation*," *Journal of Religion* 79, no. 1 (Jan. 1999), 19–53.

This is the mystery to which our subject, the relation between the testaments, pertains. The Jewish and Christian communities belong together as closely as twins in the womb of God's creative purpose. In a deep sense both communities belong to Israel, the people of God (cf. Gal. 6:16). They have in common a Bible, the shared history of the People of God, which provides the basis for creative dialogue.[16] They differ—and probably will differ till the end of time—over the question of the climax of the story: whether the pilgrimage of God's people leads through the Jewish Scriptures to the Talmud and a continued life of messianic expectancy, or whether that pilgrimage leads through the Old Testament to Jesus, the Christ, who came not to destroy but to fulfill the Law and the Prophets.[17]

16. See the important book edited and introduced by Fritz A. Rothschild, *Jewish Perspectives on Christianity* (New York: Crossroad, 1990). The book presents the views of five Jewish thinkers on the relation of Christianity to Judaism, including Leo Baeck, Martin Buber, Franz Rosenzweig, Will Herberg, and Abraham J. Heschel, each of whom is introduced by a Christian theologian. Note my introduction to the essay by Will Herberg, my friend and former colleague, "Judaism and Christianity: Their Unity and Difference."

17. These words echo the concluding paragraph of my *Understanding the Old Testament* (4th ed.; Englewood Cliffs, N.J.: Prentice-Hall, 1986), 643.

3. Old Testament Theology in the Twentieth Century

Before venturing into a treatment of biblical theology of the Old Testament, let us pause to consider what has been going on in this field, especially in the twentieth century.

For centuries there was no separate discipline of biblical theology; rather, the issues of biblical theology were dealt with in the context of church dogmatics or the system of Christian doctrine. A modern example of this would be Karl Barth's multivolume *Kirchliche Dogmatik* (*Church Dogmatics*), which, when dealing with the various rubrics of doctrine (e.g., the doctrine of creation), gives extended treatment to the biblical witness on the subject.[1]

Some biblical theologians insist that the only way to do biblical theology is to organize the discussion according to the rubrics of doctrinal theology, which are broadly: God, humanity, salvation, eschatology. This approach has been stoutly defended by Robert Dentan, among others, in his *Preface to Old Testament Theology*.[2]

In the discussion of methodology—how to go about doing biblical theology—a fundamental question is the meaning of the preposition "of" in "theology of the Old Testament." Is there a theology of (subjective genitive) the Old Testament, one that is intrinsic to the Old Testament itself? Or is there a theology related to, or in accord with, the Bible that is the product of theological reflection from a Christian standpoint? Brevard Childs's *magnum opus*, *Biblical Theology of the Old and New Testaments* (1992), is compatible with a dogmatic approach, as evident from some of the chapter titles in the final section entitled "Theological Reflection on the Christian Bible." These chapters include "The Identity of God," "God the Creator," "Covenant, Election, People of God," and "Reconciliation with God."

The Rise of Biblical Theology

The rise of biblical theology as a discipline separate from dogmatic theology is usually traced back to the inaugural lecture in 1787 of Johann Phillip Gabler at the University of Altdorf, Germany, "A Discourse on the Proper Distinction between Biblical and Dogmatic Theology and the Correct Delimitation of Their Boundaries."[3] In this lecture Gabler declared that the two disciplines differ because

---

1. Karl Barth, *Kirchliche Dogmatik*, 5 vols. in 14 (Zurich: Evangelische Verlag, 1932–1970); *Church Dogmatics*, 5 vols. in 14, trans. G. W. Bromiley, et al. (Edinburgh: T & T Clark, 1936–1977).

2. Robert C. Dentan, *A Preface to Old Testament Theology* (New Haven: Yale Univ. Press, 1950); this approach is elaborated in idem, *The Knowledge of God in Ancient Israel* (New York: Seabury, 1968).

3. The English translation from the Latin is by J. Sandys-Wunsch and L. Eldridge, "J. P. Gabler and the Distinction between Biblical and Dogmatic Theology," *SJT* 33 (1980) 133–58. See Rolf P. Knierim, "On Gabler," in *The Task of Old Testament Theology* (Grand Rapids: Eerdmans, 1995), 495–556.

each uses a different method: the biblical theologian uses a historical approach, while the systematic theologian has a didactic interest, to give teaching (doctrine) to the church.

The first step for the biblical theologian, according to Gabler, is to consider the historical context (period, authorship, social circumstance); the next step is to compare the various historical texts to see where they agree or disagree; the final step is to sift out what is historically incidental from what is timelessly true. It is this "pure biblical theology," freed from what is temporary and passing, that the dogmatic theologian uses in setting forth teaching for the church. Thus biblical theology stands over against dogmatic theology, the one being basically historical and the other doctrinal.

Gabler raised a new question, but he was unable to give a constructive answer that stood the test of discussion. In his search for ideas that are timelessly and universally valid, he was too much under the influence of the rationalism of the Enlightenment. In retrospect it is evident that his groundbreaking essay only opened up the question of what biblical theology is and the method appropriate to the discipline.[4]

History of Salvation
A creative attempt to take seriously the historical character of Scripture was made by Johann Christian Hoffmann (1810–1877). He espoused the view that the Bible presents a "history of salvation" (*Heilsgeschichte*), that is, an unfolding drama of God's saving purpose, manifested in crucial events. Hoffman was influenced by the "federal" or "covenant" theology of John Koch, or Cocceius (d. 1669), one of the early Protestant theologians. In his *Summa Doctrinae de Foedere* (Summation of Covenant Doctrine) Hoffman insisted that people should cease turning to the Bible for proof texts (*dicta probantia*) to support doctrine; rather, they should study the dramatic movement of the Bible as a whole. For him the Bible presents a series of revelatory stages, a history of redemption, extending from creation to consummation. The canon of the Bible, in this view, is dynamic in the sense that it is based on the sequence of sacred history, the story of "the marvelous deeds of God."

This dramatic understanding of the Bible, which is reflected to some degree in my study guide, *The Unfolding Drama of the Bible*,[5] has had considerable influence in the twentieth century. It is defended, above all, by the New Testament theologian Oscar Cullmann in his book *Salvation in History*.[6] Although he avoids using the term

4. See Ben C. Ollenburger, "Old Testament Theology: A Discourse on Method," in *Biblical Theology: Problems and Perspectives: In Honor of J. Christiaan Beker*, ed. Steven J. Kraftchick et al. (Nashville: Abingdon, 1995), 81–103.

5. First used in the Student Christian Movement of the 1950s and 1960s, later published in several recensions. The version published by Fortress Press (1988) is still in circulation. This study guide is strongly influenced by historical criticism.

6. Oscar Cullmann, *Salvation in History*, trans. S. G. Sowers (New Testament Library; London: SCM, 1967).

"history of salvation" (*Heilsgeschichte*), he maintains that the Bible portrays a series of events that the biblical authors regarded as revealing the saving presence of God in human history—not history in general, but the special history reported in the Bible.

Theology of Divine Presence
A creative attempt to deal with biblical theology as a whole, including both Old and New Testaments, is the fascinating work by Samuel Terrien, with its elegant title *The Elusive Presence*. Terrien maintains that "it is the distinctiveness of the Hebraic theology of presence rather than the ideology of the covenant which provides a key to understanding the Bible."[7] The biblical theology of God's presence is rooted in the cult (community worship) and finds expression in symbolism that appeals to both the "mystical eye" (God's "glory") and "the ethical ear" (God's "name"). Both types of symbolism are necessary to express what is fundamental in both testaments: the real presence of the holy, transcendent God who is both revealed and hidden (Isa. 45:15). This study, which has not received the attention it deserves, is important for biblical theologians who want to take seriously the symbolic, poetic, aesthetic dimensions of Scripture.[8]

Two Major Old Testament Theologies

The question of whether there is a theology that can be derived from the Old Testament itself is answered in the affirmative, but in quite different ways, by the two great Old Testament theologians of the twentieth century, the Swiss theologian Walther Eichrodt and the German theologian Gerhard von Rad. In their separate ways they broke with the liberal view that had emerged since the Enlightenment that in the Bible one can trace a spiritual growth or evolution from the primitive level of Mosaic religion to the "ethical monotheism" of the prophets and the New Testament. This "modern use of the Bible" was popularized by Harry Emerson Fosdick (1878–1964), minister of Riverside Church in New York City, who maintained that "abiding experiences"—relevant even today—underlie the "changing categories" of the biblical development.[9]

Eichrodt's Covenant Theology
Eichrodt defined the task of Old Testament theology by raising a question: "How to understand the realm of Old Testament belief in its structural unity and how, by examining on the one hand its religious environment and on the other its essential coherence with the New Testament, to illuminate its profoundest meaning."[10]

---

7. Samuel Terrien, *The Elusive Presence: Toward a New Biblical Theology* (San Francisco: Harper & Row, 1978), p. xxvii.

8. See my later treatment of covenantal patterns of symbolism, chapters 4ff.

9. Fosdick's writings include *The Modern Use of the Bible* (New York: Macmillan, 1924), and *A Guide to Understanding the Bible* (New York: Harper and Bros., 1938).

10. Walther Eichrodt, *Theology of the Old Testament*, trans. J. A. Baker, 2 vols., OTL (Philadelphia: Westminster, 1961–67), 1:31.

This definition indicates two fundamental concerns. First, Eichrodt wanted to understand the Old Testament in the context of the cultural environment of the ancient Near East. To appreciate this interest we must consider the situation in which he found himself as a biblical interpreter. When he wrote (in the early 1930s), Old Testament theology was overshadowed by study of the religion of Israel, which in turn was viewed in the wider context of the history of religions (*Religionsgeschichte*). There was much excitement about the rediscovery of the literature of ancient cultures, for example, the excavation of the palace of Ashurbanipal at Nineveh (from the late sixth century B.C.) that yielded the Babylonian story of the flood (Gilgamesh Epic) and the Babylonian creation epic (*Enuma Elish*).[11] Also, beginning in 1928 new light was thrown on the religion of Israel by the discovery of the Ras Shamra tablets, Canaanite mythological texts dating from the fourteenth century B.C.[12] It became increasingly clear that the Old Testament was part and parcel of the literature of the ancient world. Eichrodt attempted to revive the task of Old Testament theology by demonstrating that something unique was going on in ancient Israel—not just a general historical-cultural development but a special movement of divine revelation.

Another concern was to understand the Old Testament's "essential coherence" with the New. Eichrodt wanted to let the Old Testament speak in its own way, but also to show that its message is consistent with that of the New. He insisted that the Old Testament has a relative independence, but that it belongs within the canonical context of the Christian Bible.

What, then, is the witness of the Old Testament that was unique in its ancient cultural environment and coherent with the message of the New Testament? Eichrodt maintained that the dominant thrust of the Old Testament was the inbreaking of the kingdom of God into ancient Israel and its dynamic movement toward the manifestation of God's dominion in Jesus Christ. In this sense, the Bible as a whole discloses a history of salvation—a movement of divine redemption, evidenced in God's entrance into the historical arena to call and constitute a people and, through that people, to lead toward the time when God's kingdom would come on earth as it is in heaven.

Furthermore, Eichrodt maintained that the theologian can take a "cross-section" (*Querschnitt*) of this dynamic development at any point in the historical process in order to explore the Old Testament's structure of belief and to perceive its integrity vis-à-vis the religions of the environment. Just as a logger can cut through a tree and study the structure of its growth, so the theologian can study the "cross-section" that shows the "inner shape" or consistent structure manifest in its development. The faith of Israel is not a miscellaneous assortment of beliefs, nor is it only a process of growth and development. Rather, it manifests a structural

---

11. For translations of both of these stories, see *ANET*, 42–44 and 72–99. A popular version, quite accessible to the general reader, is David Ferry, *Gilgamesh: A New Rendering in English Verse* (New York: Farrar, Straus and Giroux, 1992).

12. See *ANET*, 129–55.

unity or theological integrity that is fundamentally the same in all historical stages. Eichrodt's approach is *synchronic* ("happening together," like notes struck simultaneously in a musical chord), though he also attempted to do justice to the *diachronic* dimension ("happening through time," like the successive notes of a scale). In his view Old Testament theology does not concentrate on growth or evolution (e.g., the growth of the idea of God) but on "structural" features that remain the same in all historical periods.

Finally, Eichrodt maintained that when a cross-section is taken, the structure of the "log," visible at any place that one chooses to make a cut, is covenantal, that is, it manifests relationship between God and people. He was not concerned to lift up a particular covenant (e.g., Abrahamic, Mosaic, Davidic) or to study the uses of the term "covenant" (*berith*); rather, he wanted to stress the relational character of the faith of ancient Israel. The Old Testament does not deal with God as a separate subject (theology) or with Israel as a separate subject (anthropology); rather, theology and anthropology belong together, in relationship. Hence the importance of the copula "and": God *and* Israel, God *and* the world, God *and* human being—the major captions of his work.

Here, then, we find an attempt to deal with the dynamic (historical) and the structural (systematic), the diachronic and the synchronic. In this view the Old Testament discloses a movement in time toward the New Testament revelation (a history of redemption), but the faith of Israel, the people of God, maintains its identity and integrity during the whole movement.

This impressive proposal was instrumental in bringing about a revival of interest in Old Testament theology. But the question was quickly raised and debated: Can the whole Old Testament be brought under the umbrella of "covenant"? There are actually several covenant "theologies" in the Old Testament, as we shall see; and not all the literature of the Old Testament belongs in any kind of covenantal framework (e.g., wisdom literature such as Job, Proverbs, and Ecclesiastes). Furthermore, Eichrodt's attempt to discover "structural unity" was unsuccessful; there is too much variety and diversity to allow for that. Nevertheless, his emphasis on the *relational* character of Old Testament theology was a salutary contribution that we need to retain. The Jewish philosopher Abraham Joshua Heschel said something similar from his perspective: revelation is not the disclosure of God's nature or essence but of God's "relation to history."[13]

Von Rad's Story-telling Theology

We turn now to the second major Old Testament theologian of the twentieth century, Gerhard von Rad. His monumental work, *Old Testament Theology*, came out in two volumes: *The Theology of Israel's Historical Traditions* (1962) and *The Theology of*

---

13. Abraham Joshua Heschel, *God in Search of Man: A Philosophy of Judaism* (New York: Farrar, Straus and Cudahy, 1955). See further my essay, "Coexistence with God: Heschel's Exposition of Biblical Theology," in *Abraham Joshua Heschel: Exploring His Life and Thought*, ed. John C. Merkle (New York: Macmillan, 1985), 47–65, especially 53–58.

Israel's Prophetic Traditions (1965). This work represents a radical departure from Eichrodt's presentation.

Von Rad criticized Eichrodt's work for not doing justice to the character of the Old Testament itself. It was too structural, too systematic, and not sufficiently dynamic and historical. Consonant with this criticism, he advocated a new methodology, one that uses form criticism and the history of traditions. Form criticism is a method that studies the literary form of scriptural units in their social setting (e.g., a poem for an enthronement ceremony; cf. Psalm 2). Tradition history is a method that studies the expansion, combination, and reinterpretation of literary units (poems, stories, law codes, oracles, proverbs, etc.) from their original formulation in oral tradition until the final formation of the tradition as the received Scriptures.[14]

His method was set forth in his programmatic essay, "The Form-Critical Problem of the Hexateuch," in which he tried to account for the simplicity of Israel's early confession of faith, found in the so-called little historical credo (Deut. 26:5-10), and the greatly expanded elaboration of its content in the Hexateuch as a whole.[15] In his view the final literary composition (Hexateuch) was the end result of a history—a history of traditions. It is this history that the theologian must take seriously—not events in a history of Israel or even events in a "history of salvation," at least in the old sense, but a history of traditions, that is, history of the interpretation and reinterpretation of the core confession of faith.

Thus von Rad's method is diachronic. The Old Testament, he said, is by and large a history book that, in all its diversity, bears witness to the history of Yahweh with his people. It presents the unfolding drama of the divine purpose with Israel from its beginnings until the coming of the Son of Man. This "history," however, is not ordinary history, as John Bright and Martin Noth have written, but a history of traditions, in which an early Israelite confession of faith was constantly being reinterpreted in new situations. Past tradition was always being contemporized in new times, new circles, new ways; and this went on continuously until finally the process of reinterpretation reached its climax in the New Testament.

Accordingly, the task of the Old Testament theologian is to "retell" the story just as Israel told and retold it. "Event," von Rad said with a critical eye toward Eichrodt and all systematicians, "has priority over logos." In this history of traditions there are many breaks, many new starts, many disconnected testimonies. There is no systematic unity, but diversity, variety, multiplicity. Indeed, he went so far as to say that the attempt to find anything in the Old Testament that gives it theological integrity or unity is misguided. Here we are dealing with a process, a movement, a history of traditions that has no "center" (*Mitte*). The process reaches

14. See definitions of "form criticism" and "canonical criticism" in my *Understanding the Old Testament* (abridged 4th ed.; Englewood Cliffs, N.J.: Prentice-Hall, 1997), 487–88, 578.

15. In Gerhard von Rad, *The Problem of the Hexateuch and Other Essays*, trans. E. W. Trueman Dicken (New York: McGraw-Hill, 1966), 1–78.

its culmination in Jesus Christ, who is the center of the Bible (obviously this means the Christian Bible).

This, too, is a magnificent presentation. For a brief time it swept the field until the demise of the "biblical theology movement" around 1970 (approximately the time of Brevard Childs's book, *Biblical Theology in Crisis*). Several problems emerged in the course of discussion. For one thing, von Rad made a sharp distinction between "actual history" and "story of faith." Theologically, he was concerned not with events in history but with a history of traditions, reconstructed according to the method of form criticism. Also, von Rad was not very clear about what gave Israel a distinctive theological integrity and sense of identity over against the environment. He spoke about "the inner connection (*Zusammenhang*) of Old Testament speech about God," but surely this coherence cannot be explained only on the basis of a history of traditions. Moreover, von Rad seemed to deny that the Old Testament speaks with an independent theological voice, even within the Christian canon. Apart from Jesus Christ, he said, the Old Testament has no theological center or integrity, and belongs only to the history of Israel's religion. It is with words to this effect that his *Old Testament Theology* closes.[16]

The Future of Old Testament Theology

So, where do we go from here? As a student humorously asked, "Is there life after *Heilsgeschichte?*"

Walter Brueggemann begins an essay on "Futures in Old Testament Theology" with the observation: "The only two things sure about Old Testament theology now are: 1. The ways of Walther Eichrodt and Gerhard von Rad are no longer adequate. 2. There is no consensus among us about what comes next."[17]

Brueggemann's Bipolar Theology

Among scholars of a younger generation Brueggemann has taken the lead in addressing the problems and possibilities of producing an Old Testament theology in the "postmodern" climate of biblical studies, that is, in the period after the domination of the eighteenth-century Enlightenment.[18] In advance of the recent appearance of his own major opus, *Theology of the Old Testament*,[19] he wrote several

16. Gerhard von Rad, *Old Testament Theology*, trans. D. M. G. Stalker, 2 vols. (New York: Harper & Row, 1962–65), 2:428–29.

17. Walter Brueggemann, *Old Testament Theology: Essays on Structure, Theme, and Text*, ed. Patrick D. Miller (Minneapolis: Fortress Press, 1992), 111. The flux and ferment in the Old Testament field is well described and analyzed by Leo G. Perdue, *The Collapse of History: Reconstructing Old Testament Theology* (Minneapolis: Fortress Press, 1994).

18. A helpful introduction to postmodern philosophy and its impact on Christian theology is *A Primer of Postmodernism*, ed. Stanley J. Grenz (Grand Rapids: Eerdmans, 1996). See also Allan Megill, *Prophets of Extremity: Nietzsche, Heidegger, Foucault, Derrida* (Berkeley: University of California Press, 1985).

19. Walter Brueggemann, *Theology of the Old Testament: Testimony, Dispute, Advocacy* (Minneapolis: Fortress Press, 1997).

preliminary essays that give some indications of how a "new" Old Testament theology should be conceived.

To begin with, he proposes that the biblical theologian should "accept a mode probably more appropriate to our cultural moment of scattering and our intellectual moment of hermeneutical self-knowledge." We should be realistic about the breakdown of any consensus in biblical studies and about the inescapability of a hermeneutical perspective. This is no time, he avers, for "a grand design" that "includes and accounts for everything," such as attempted in the monumental works of Eichrodt and von Rad.[20]

Specifically, this means that "we might cease to ask about a *center* for Old Testament theology and ask about boundaries, edges, limits, parameters, within which faith proceeds and beyond which it may not legitimately go." Unlike Childs, who, as we shall see, declares that the canon of Scripture sets the boundaries, Brueggemann proposes a sociological criterion: "cultural embrace" and "cultural criticism." By this he means that "in every issue [under discussion] one may ask the extent to which Israel borrows, appropriates, coheres with the general practice of the ancient Near Eastern culture and the extent to which it makes its own distinctive statement out of its own concrete experience, which has the effect of transforming cultural forms and values."[21] From these statements it is clear that Old Testament theology must take seriously the religions of the ancient Near East, which in this discussion are designated "the common theology."

Old Testament theology, he says, will be "bipolar"; it will reflect the tension between texts that serve to "legitimate structure" (the common theology) and those that, by "embracing pain," challenge the established order (Israel's distinctive witness). It is not that the theologian selects one or the other: either those texts that legitimate order (creation theology in this sense) or those that express the pain of oppressed minorities; rather, it is the interaction of the two that constitutes the dynamic of Old Testament theology.[22]

Now that Brueggemann's monumental *Theology* has appeared, we can appreciate the fulfillment to which these preliminary remarks point. To begin with, despite his criticisms of historical criticism, as a child of the Enlightenment he is profoundly under its influence when he concentrates on the "multiplicity" and "density" of Old Testament texts. This book could only have been written by one who had been subjected to the analytical dissection of historical criticism.

Two major movements in biblical criticism provide the lens, so to speak, through which Brueggemann views the Old Testament. The first is rhetorical criticism, the child of form criticism; the second is sociology, a relative newcomer on the scene of biblical criticism.

20. Walter Brueggemann, "Futures in Old Testament Theology," in *Old Testament Theology*, 114.

21. Ibid., 114–15.

22. This bipolar dialectic is discussed in his two lead essays on Old Testament theology in *Old Testament Theology*: "A Shape for Old Testament Theology, I: Structure Legitimation," 1–21; and "A Shape for Old Testament Theology, II: Embrace of Pain," 22–44.

The Hermeneutic of Language

Rhetorical criticism is a method that concentrates on the art of expressive speech found in biblical texts. Form criticism had concentrated on literary units and their "setting in life" (e.g., the "covenant lawsuit," Hebrew *rib;* cf. Jer. 3:4-13); rhetorical criticism goes beyond this into a study of the language itself: its style, structure, symbolism, assonance, and so on.[23] Brueggemann takes a step further: for the Old Testament theologian "speech is the reality to be studied," for speech creates the world in which God is presented. The theological task is not to seek some reality behind the text, for instance, a historical event that may have happened, or even the Being of the God who transcends the reality of the text. Rather, the theologian studies Israel's speech about God in biblical texts in their multiform variety. The question is simply and profoundly, "What is said?"—Israel's testimony in words.[24]

At the outset of this new venture in Old Testament theology, Brueggemann pays tribute to the influence of Paul Ricoeur, an outstanding philosopher of the twentieth century. In Ricoeur's philosophy of language, the basic question is one of epistemology, that is, "How do we know?"[25] He rejects the view, dominant since the philosopher René Descartes (1596–1650), that human beings are thinkers who cogitate an external world that can be rationally (mathematically) measured, historically explained, and subjected to scientific control. This rationalism, summed up in Descartes's *cogito ergo sum* (I think, therefore I am), underlies the modern scientific world. It is manifest, for instance, in so-called historical criticism that subjects biblical texts to rational analysis and historical verification. Instead, Ricoeur advocates a mode of interpretation (hermeneutic) that relies more on the imagination. A biblical text (say, a narration, a prophecy, a hymn of praise) "opens onto a world, the biblical world, or rather the multiple worlds" portrayed in diverse kinds of biblical literature. The task is not to understand the intention of biblical authors, or to penetrate the ancient historical situation out of which the texts came, but to hear the "testimony" of the text, which has a poetic function in that it projects a "new world of being," different from "the world of ordinary experience." The reader is invited to enter and "inhabit" the new world of the Bible and thereby to find a new being.[26] "The Bible is one of the great poems of existence," says Ricoeur, and therefore like any great literature offers a new being; but it is also unique in that it brings one to the limits of discourse about God and to "the name of the unnameable."[27]

23. A great pioneer in this field was James Muilenburg, "Form Criticism and Beyond," a presidential address to the Society of Biblical Literature, *JBL* 88 (1969) 1–18. A magnificent example of the use of this method is found in Phyllis Trible's study of Genesis 1–3 in *God and the Rhetoric of Sexuality*, OBT (Philadelphia: Fortress Press, 1978).

24. Brueggemann, *Theology of the Old Testament*, 118–20.

25. For a summary of Ricoeur's philosophy of language, see the introduction to Ricoeur's essays, *Figuring the Sacred: Religion, Narrative, and Imagination*, ed. Mark I. Wallace (Minneapolis: Fortress Press, 1995) 1–32.

26. Paul Ricoeur, "Toward a Hermeneutic of the Idea of Revelation," *HTR* 70 (1977) 27–33.

27. Ibid., 26. See further my discussion of the name of God, chapter 6.

Sociology and the Bible

Another major influence in Brueggemann's *Theology* is the sociology of knowledge, which views human language as expressing the interests and values of a social group or, in the Marxist version, the group that holds power. Under the influence of Norman Gottwald, who proposed a quasi-Marxist dialectic of the conflict between those who have power and those who are oppressed by the power holders, Brueggemann perceives that the dynamic of Old Testament theology is found in this bipolarity. Gottwald, to whom he is indebted, has attempted to translate theology into sociology without remainder. In his view "Yahweh" means "the historically concretized, primordial power to establish and sustain social equality." "Chosen people" means "the distinctive self-consciousness of a society of equals created in the intertribal order and demarcated from a primarily centralized and stratified surrounding world." And so on.[28]

Sociology of this kind helps to understand the "bipolar" dynamic of Old Testament theology: the conflict between "cultural embrace" and "cultural criticism." Brueggemann wants to avoid the reduction of theology to sociology. He declares that God is not only "in the fray" (the social process) but "above the fray" (beyond the reach of sociological analysis). "The poets and narrators in Israel," he says, "do, in fact, speak the mind of God [*sic*]," who is beyond the historical process. Yet "biblical artists enter into the struggle in which God is involved," whether to be the god of common theology who sanctions order or to be the God who acts with liberating power and does what is new and unexpected.[29] Although Brueggemann wants to emphasize both order and novelty, structure and protest, one gets the impression that "the word of God" is spoken most authentically in those texts that deal with "the embrace of pain," that is, the cries of those who lack power.

This sociological approach, influenced by the Marxist dialectic of power and powerlessness, can have a heuristic value, enabling us to notice theological dimensions that otherwise might be overlooked. This sociology calls our attention to the problem of faith and ideology, an issue that we must wrestle with from time to time. Sociological method, however, has its own limitations. It may enable us to see how God is "in the fray," but it offers little help in understanding how God, who is "above the fray," speaks a word of revelation. If the Bible is the Word of God in some sense for a community of faith, it surely contains more than "a rumor of angels," that is, hints of divine transcendence.[30]

Testimony and Trial

To organize his theological exposition of the Old Testament, Brueggemann adopts the metaphor of the court trial before the nations, found centrally in the poetry of

---

28. Norman Gottwald, *The Tribes of Yahweh: A Sociology of the Religion of Liberated Israel, 1250–1050 B.C.E.* (Maryknoll, N.Y.: Orbis, 1979), 692. See my review in *TToday* 38 (April 1981) 107–8.

29. Brueggemann, "Shape, I," in *Old Testament Theology*, 19.

30. In *Rumor of Angels* (rev. ed.; New York: Doubleday, 1990) the sociologist Peter Berger explores the question of whether sociology can reach beyond its own methodological limitations. The results are not encouraging for the theologian.

Second Isaiah (cf. Isa. 41:1—42:4). This trial has three elements: (1) Israel makes its core testimony, grounded primarily on the God of the exodus who liberates from bondage; (2) Israel and the nations make a countertestimony about the God who upholds order and grants fertility; and (3) this dialectic prompts Israel, as an advocate for Yahweh, to make a new theological witness.

In his elaboration of this metaphor, Brueggemann invites us to break out of past theological categories and to view the witness of the Old Testament in an entirely new way. This creative proposal will no doubt prove to be a powerful ferment as a new century begins.

Like its predecessors, this bold theological venture raises questions for theological discussion. First, there is a basic methodological question: how does one ascertain the "core testimony" in the context of the "multiple worlds" presented by texts of the Old Testament? Brueggemann, of course, knows well the rich diversity of the Old Testament; nevertheless he speaks of "Israel's characteristic speech about God," "the usual modes of speech," "consensus testimony."[31] In describing what is allegedly Israel's "normative" testimony, Brueggemann draws widely on Old Testament texts without giving a clear criterion for selection.

Brueggemann attempts to deal with this methodological problem by appealing to a "grammar of faith," which starts with God as the subject (verbs), moves to the objects that are transformed (nouns), and includes adjectives that portray the character of the God who acts. This approach, however, is questionable when one considers that the meaning of a theological sentence depends on the context in which it functions (e.g., Deuteronomistic, Priestly, Davidic).[32]

Second, Brueggemann "brackets out all questions of historicity," such as "what happened" or the historical circumstances that prompted the testimony.[33] The court "cannot go behind the testimony to the event"; it has to take the testimony as "the real portrayal."[34] Here the analogy of a trial seems to break down, for generally the court seeks factual evidence other than the testimony (e.g., DNA tests, ballistics tests, fingerprints). There is a problem here, I believe, that cannot be resolved by "bracketing out" historicity.[35] The dimension of "facticity and historicity," as Will Herberg emphasized, cannot be ignored theologically.[36] Surely a

31. Brueggemann, *Theology of the Old Testament*, 122–30.

32. This contextual approach to Old Testament theology (which we are following in this book) is also suggested by Philip Peter Jenson, *Graded Holiness: A Key to the Priestly Conception of the World*, JSOTSup 106 (Sheffield: JSOT Press, 1992). He speaks of a "conceptual approach" (p. 214) based on "groups of texts which reflect a distinctive set of concerns and a relatively unified outlook (e.g., the prophets, the Deuteronomic history, the Priestly writing, the wisdom writings). These tend to reflect the predominance of a certain style of writing or genre (e.g., cultic law), and a particular social setting (e.g., the priesthood)."

33. Brueggemann, *Theology of the Old Testament*, 118.

34. Ibid., 120–21.

35. See Appendix 2, "The Relevance of Biblical Archaeology to Biblical Theology: A Tribute to George Ernest Wright."

36. Will Herberg, *Faith Enacted as History* (Philadelphia: Westminster, 1976), 156–60.

Christian theologian has to deal in some way with the factuality of the crucifixion, to say nothing of the reality of the resurrection.

Third, it is questionable whether Brueggemann does justice to the fact that Old Testament theology is in a special sense a Christian discipline, as the designation "Old Testament" suggests. He seems to feel that the so-called Old Testament stands by itself, independent of the Jewish and Christian communities, and therefore may be understood in its own right with the method of modern rhetorical criticism.[37] But this does not do justice to the canonical status of these writings in the Jewish and Christian Bibles. This literature is inseparably related to a community of faith, "the people of God," that produced it and interpreted it during its historical pilgrimage. In the mysterious grace of God the Christian community, along with the Jewish, belongs to the Israel of God (Gal. 6:17). In the future, new light may break forth as these two communities of faith engage in dialogue about the meaning of the Scriptures they hold in common.[38]

Finally, in Brueggemann's theological exposition the question of "revelation" comes to the fore. He does not say that the biblical testimony *reveals* God, but that the testimony is adjudged to be truthful and is *taken as* revelation. "That is, the testimony that Israel bears to the character of God is taken by the ecclesial community of the text as reliable disclosure about the true character of God."[39] More clarity is needed on the identity of this "ecclesial community of the text" (the jury) in which the testimony *becomes* revelation. Brueggemann concludes his *Theology* with a ringing challenge to this community, wherever it is present, to engage the theological claims of the biblical testimony and to reorder its life according to "the world of Yahweh."[40]

In conclusion, Brueggemann maintains that new revelation occurs, and will occur, through the dialectical conflict between Israel's core testimony of God's saving power and the countertestimony of God's maintenance of order. In the face of countertestimony, which also claims to be true, the court has to decide what is the truth. The question of the true linguistic portrayal of God is debatable, and a final verdict has not been reached. In the great court trial, "the waiting is long and disconcerting, because other gods are sometimes most formidable. And the jury only trickles in—here and there, now and then."[41]

37. This is a legitimate objection of Dennis T. Olson, "Biblical Theology as Provisional Monologization: A Dialogue with Childs, Brueggemann and Bakhtin," *Biblical Interpretation: A Journal of Contemporary Approaches* 6 (1998) 162–80.

38. See the discussion of the election of Israel, chapter 2.

39. Brueggemann, *Theology of the Old Testament*, 121. See his n. 9, where he comments on what it means "to take something as reality."

40. Brueggemann, "Moving Toward True Speech," in ibid., 743–50.

41. Ibid., 750 (the final sentences of the book).

4. An Experimental Approach to Old Testament Theology

This period of uncertainty, if not confusion, in the biblical theology field is a good time to experiment with various approaches. That is what I am offering: an experiment in Old Testament theology. This experiment, however, is based on "laboratory tests" in teaching Old Testament theology, a course I began teaching at Princeton Theological Seminary in 1968. At first I started gingerly with a course on "Motifs of Old Testament Theology" (echoing a course taught by my esteemed teacher, James Muilenburg).[1] Over the years I gradually became bolder, until eventually I actually titled a course "Old Testament Theology" or, as at Boston University School of Theology, "Biblical Theology of the Old Testament."

From Analysis to Synthesis

Looking back over the past thirty years, it is evident that a revolution has been going on. There has been a shift from attempts to explore the earliest phases of Israelite tradition, whether by isolating putative literary sources or preliterary forms of oral discourse, to an emphasis on the final canonical shape of the biblical "books" or larger scriptural units (e.g., Pentateuch).[2]

In the former period the important word was "tradition," an English term that encompasses both "that which was handed down" (content or *traditum*) and "the transmission of what was received" (process or *traditio*). Gerhard von Rad, who dominated the discussion, subtitled his theological work: "A Theology of Israel's Traditions." He was not really concerned with the final canonical shape of biblical books. Admittedly, in the preface to his commentary on Genesis he quoted approvingly the observation of the distinguished philosopher of Judaism, Franz Rosenzweig, that the sign "R," used to designate "redactor," must not be underrated; the sign should really signify *Rabbenu,* which in Hebrew means "our master," for we are dependent on the editor who has given us the Scriptures in their final form.[3] But von Rad was basically concerned with the process of tradition—the transmission and appropriation of materials handed down—not the final redactional or canonical formulation. Similarly, James Sanders emphasized the "canonical process" in which the received tradition, as appropriated in new situations in the history of the people of God, became "adaptable for life."[4]

---

1. See my tribute to Dr. Muilenburg, "A Teacher Like Elijah," *BR* 14, no. 1 (1998) 16.

2. See Rolf Rendtorff, "The Importance of the Canon for a Theology of the Old Testament," in *Canon and Theology,* OBT (Minneapolis: Fortress Press, 1993), 46–56.

3. Gerhard von Rad, *Genesis,* trans. John Marks, rev. ed., OTL (Philadelphia: Westminster, 1972), 42.

4. This attractive view, which suggests a hermeneutic for the appropriation of the sacred tradition today, is set forth in such writings as *Torah and Canon* (Philadelphia: Fortress Press, 1972),

My writings reflect this shift in scholarly emphasis—"from analysis to synthesis."[5] Under the influence of my teacher, James Muilenburg, I came to appreciate the literary study of the Old Testament, as advocated especially by Hermann Gunkel, the founder of form criticism and the subsequent shift to "rhetorical criticism."[6] And having studied under von Rad, I was much influenced by the history of Israelite traditions, beginning with the early oral period. Indeed, I took the time to translate Martin Noth's study of the history of the transmission of pentateuchal traditions.[7]

Brevard Childs's Approach

A decisive turning point was reached in 1970 with the publication of Brevard Childs's *Biblical Theology in Crisis*.[8] Childs showed the weaknesses of a biblical theology resting on the revelation of God in historical events. During the days of the so-called biblical theology movement (just after World War II), this view had been set forth preeminently by George Ernest Wright in his monograph *God Who Acts*, in which he took a stand against a doctrinal approach and emphasized historical recital, that is, the narrative of God's acting in the world.[9] Childs was critical of any attempt to base biblical theology on objective historical events (the Albright school), and he extended his criticism to history in the sense of "history of traditions" (Noth, von Rad, and others). He insisted that there must be "a still more excellent way."

Canon and Biblical Theology
The even better way, in Childs's view, involves taking seriously the final form of the tradition, not just as it is shaped by redactors but as set forth in the canon of biblical books that the community of faith accepts as authoritative. Against his critics, he insists that emphasis on the canon does not mean a flat interpretation of Scripture, which lacks the dynamic of a diachronic movement. The interpreter, he declares, must take seriously the "depth dimension," that is, the stages of

Canon and Community (Philadelphia: Fortress Press, 1984), and "Adaptable for Life: The Nature and Function of Canon," in *Magnalia Dei: The Mighty Acts of God. Essays on the Bible and Archaeology in Memory of G. Ernest Wright*, ed. Frank M. Cross Jr. et al. (Garden City, N.Y.: Doubleday, 1976), 531–60; see my extended review of Sanders's contribution in *RelSRev* 15 (1989) 97–100.

5. See, for instance, my essay, "From Analysis to Synthesis: The Interpretation of Genesis 1–11," *JBL* 97 (1978) 23–29.

6. See Muilenburg's monumental essay, "Form Criticism and Beyond," *JBL* 88 (1969) 1–18.

7. Martin Noth, *A History of Pentateuchal Traditions*, trans. Bernhard W. Anderson (Englewood Cliffs, N.J.: Prentice-Hall, 1972; repr. Chico, Calif.: Scholars Press, 1981). See now *The History of Israel's Traditions: The Heritage of Martin Noth*, ed. Steven L. McKenzie and M. Patrick Graham, JSOTSup 182 (Sheffield: Sheffield Academic Press, 1994).

8. Brevard S. Childs, *Biblical Theology in Crisis* (Philadelphia: Westminster, 1970).

9. Wright, *God Who Acts*, SBT 1/8 (Chicago: Regnery, 1952). Wright's valid concern for the acts of God—not just the word(s) of God—has been considered anew by Patrick D. Miller, "Revisiting the God Who Acts," *TToday* 54, no. 1 (1997) 1–5.

development that took place in the long period before the tradition was given its final scriptural form. However, the purpose of studying the depth dimension through source criticism, form criticism, tradition history, and redaction criticism is not to recover the theological interpretation that lies behind the present text but to understand the Bible in its final canonical shape. "One can better appreciate a symphony," he says in this connection, "if one has been trained to recognize the contribution of each of the various musical instruments involved."[10]

Childs's exposition of biblical theology is governed by the following considerations:

1. In the canon of the Christian Bible, Old and New Testaments are bound together christologically, that is, each bears witness to the God revealed in Jesus Christ.

2. This interrelationship of the Testaments respects the discrete witness of both. The Old Testament, specifically, has a quasi-independent status in the canon.

3. When turning to the discrete witness of the Old Testament, Childs follows a historical outline as far as possible, that is, from Genesis through Ezra. Thus he discusses theologically, in conversation with biblical scholars: "Creation," "From Eden to Babel," "Patriarchal Traditions," "Mosaic Traditions," "The Possession of the Land and the Settlement," "The Tradition of the Judges," "The Establishment of the Monarchy," "The Divided Kingdom," "Exile and Restoration." When this chronological outline runs out, he turns to special materials: "Prophetic," "Apocalyptic," "Wisdom," and "Psalms."

4. After treating the discrete witness of the New Testament following a similar chronological sequence ("The Church's Earliest Proclamation" to "The Post-Pauline Age"), Childs turns to "theological reflections on the Christian Bible," considering in parallel the Old Testament witness and that of the New Testament. Here he abandons historical sequence and turns to a topical discussion: "The Identity of God," "God the Creator," "Covenant, Election, People of God," "Christ the Lord," "Reconciliation with God," and so on. One can see clearly that, in Childs's view, biblical and dogmatic theology are closely related.

This is truly a monumental work that will be discussed for years to come. For two decades I have struggled with Childs's canonical approach, finding in it things to agree with and to differ over. On the positive side, it has been a major influence in moving me to concentrate on the final form of the Scriptures that we have received. Also, I welcome the insistence that the Old Testament has a relatively independent place in the Christian Bible, although I would emphasize more the dialectic of continuity/discontinuity between the Testaments.[11] My major difficulty is that this approach, being so close to dogmatic theology, does not give sufficient theological attention to the "discrete witness of the Old Testament," and especially to the pattern of symbolism that governs literary units in their final

---

10. See Brevard Childs, *Biblical Theology of the Old and New Testaments* (Minneapolis: Fortress Press, 1992), "Methodological Problems," 104–6, quotation, 105.

11. See above, chapter 2.

form (e.g., Pentateuch, Deuteronomistic history). As noted above, biblical theology finally turns out to be a discussion of theological topics. Perhaps there is another way that follows more closely the Old Testament canonical structure.

Hermeneutical Considerations

The following presentation also begins by taking a firm stand in the community of faith known as the church. At the same time, I give due consideration to the way the Jewish community reads this common Bible and, from time to time, engage in Jewish-Christian dialogue.[12] There is a great deal of affinity between this presentation of Old Testament theology and the "entry into the Jewish Bible" given by Jon Levenson in *Sinai and Zion*.[13]

In this venture, I recognize that the Old Testament contains a diversity of materials that resists being pressed into a coherent, structural unity (the weakness of Eichrodt's approach). Nevertheless, theological understanding is aided by an organization of the diverse materials, rather than just reading the Bible "from cover to cover." Other organizations may be helpful too, such as the work of Christoph Barth, *God with Us*, which is organized in a sequence of narrative statements, "God Created Heaven and Earth," "God Chose the Fathers of Israel," "God Brought Israel out of Egypt," and so on.[14]

Also, I recognize that invariably we read the past through the lens of our own experience or categories. We are sociolinguistic beings who want to bring the past into *our* world and appropriate it on our terms. This epistemological limitation, however, does not justify a deliberate reading of the past through a particular lens (as in the case of some liberation theologies); it only warns us to be deliberate about allowing the past, in so far as possible, to speak to us with its own voice, rather than being ventriloquists who project our voice onto the Bible. We must allow the Old Testament to be a different, even an alien, voice that speaks to us from another world of discourse.

Moreover, as Karl Rahner[15] has well said, the interpreter must have a poetic sense that yields to and appreciates biblical imagery if she or he is to hear in the Bible "the Word of God." This view is echoed in Walter Brueggemann's Yale Lectures on Preaching, in his introductory essay, "Poetry in a Prose-Flattened World," where he effectively quotes Walt Whitman:

> *After the seas are all cross'd, (as they seem already cross'd,)*
> *After the great captains and engineers have accomplish'd their work,*
> *After the noble inventors, after the scientists, the chemist, the geologist, ethnologist,*

12. See Rolf Rendtorff, "Toward a Common Jewish-Christian Reading of the Hebrew Bible," chap. 4 in *Canon and Theology*.

13. Jon D. Levenson, *Sinai and Zion: An Entry into the Jewish Bible* (Minneapolis: Winston, 1985).

14. Christoph Barth, *God with Us: A Theological Introduction to the Old Testament* (Grand Rapids: Eerdmans, 1985).

15. Karl Rahner, *More Recent Writings*, trans. Kevin Smyth, Theological Investigations 4 (Baltimore: Helicon, 1966), 363.

> *Finally shall come the poet worthy of that name,*
> *The true son of God shall come singing his songs.*[16]

Singing a new song (Ps. 96:1) requires avoiding, on the one side, the Scylla of literalism and, on the other, the Charybdis of historicism. The texts of the Bible
invite us into a world—a real world—that is construed by poetic imagination.
Therefore, we shall give due attention to the covenantal patterns of symbolization
(Priestly, Mosaic, Davidic) that govern Old Testament books or blocks of material (e.g., the book of Isaiah, the Chronicler's history).

God's Covenants with Israel

Accordingly, let's start with a clue found in the New Testament, specifically Paul's
discussion of the relation between the Jewish and Christian communities in the
economy of God's purpose in Romans 9–11. In a context where Paul expresses sad-
ness that his own people, the Jews, do not accept Jesus as God's Messiah, he lists
seven historic privileges that belonged to Israel as the people of God:

> They are Israelites, and to them belong the adoption, the glory, the covenants, the
> giving of the law, the worship, and the promises; to them belong the patriarchs,
> and from them, according to the flesh, comes the Messiah, who is over all, God
> blessed forever. Amen.[17]
>
> —Rom. 9:4-5

This is a very solemn statement, as indicated by the concluding "amen." Its solem-
nity is heightened by Paul's use of the term "Israelites" (rather than "Jews")—the
ancient sacral term for Israel as the people of God (Gen. 32:28). He lists seven pre-
rogatives of Israel—eight if one counts the last statement that the Messiah sprang
out of Israel.[18]

1. Sonship, that is, Israel was adopted or elected as God's son, according to
important Old Testament passages: Exod. 4:22; Deut. 14:1; Hos. 11:1.

2. The glory, or "glorious presence." This refers to the resplendent manifestation of God's presence (*kabod*, "glory") during the wilderness wanderings (Exod.
16:10; 40:34) or in the Jerusalem temple (1 Kgs. 8:10-11; Ezekiel 10; etc.).

3. The covenants—the Abrahamic (Genesis 17), Mosaic (Exod. 19:5; 24:1-4;
renewed at Shechem, Joshua 24), and the Davidic (2 Samuel 7; Psalm 89). Some
manuscripts read singular, *diatheke*, in which case the reference would probably be
to the Mosaic covenant. But most translations render the plural *diathekai*.

---

16. See Walter Brueggemann, *Finally Comes the Poet: Daring Speech for Proclamation*, especially the
introduction, "Poetry in a Prose-Flattened World" (Minneapolis: Fortress Press, 1989) 1–11. The
lines are from Walt Whitman's "Passage to India," 5:101–5, in *Leaves of Grass* (New York: New
American Library, 1954), 324.

17. The last words could be punctuated, "who is God over all, forever praised," as in NIV.

18. See the discussion by J. A. Fitzmyer in *New Jerome Biblical Commentary*, ed. Raymond E.
Brown et al. (Englewood Cliffs, N.J.: Prentice-Hall, 1990), 856.

4. The giving of the law: the revelation of God's will, as given to Moses (e.g., Ten Commandments in Exodus 20 and Deuteronomy 5).

5. The worship, that is, the cult—worship in the tabernacle or the temple, where God chose to be present as "the Holy One in your midst." The book of Psalms is the book of worship for the praises of Israel.

6. The promises—primarily the promises made to Abraham (land, posterity, relationship with God that would benefit other peoples), although promises of grace were also made to Moses and to David (Deut. 18:18-19; 2 Sam. 7:11-16).

7. The patriarchs, that is, the ancestors of Israel who were invited into special relationship with God, so that God was known as the God of Abraham, Isaac, and Jacob (Exod. 3:6). The Israelites, Paul could say (Rom. 11:28), were loved by God on account of the patriarchs.

Thus election, promises, covenant, law, God's holy presence in the midst of the people, as they gathered in the temple for worship—these are some of the major subjects of the Old Testament. Instead of taking these up one by one, I propose an organization according to the major covenants with Israel: the Abrahamic, the Mosaic, the Davidic.

The term "covenant" (Hebrew *berith*) points to a fundamental reality in Israel's experience: God's special relationship with the people. After a thorough review of the controversial discussion of this subject, especially since the time of the founder of modern biblical criticism, Julius Wellhausen (from 1878 to 1918), E. W. Nicholson concludes that "covenant" expresses "the distinctiveness of Israel's faith":

> So, far from being merely one among a wide range of terms and ideas that emerged, flourished, and had their day, "covenant" is a central theme that served to focus an entirely idiosyncratic way of looking at the relationship between God and his chosen people, and indeed, between God and the world. As such it deserves to be put back squarely on the agenda for students of the Old Testament.[19]

Our interest will fasten not on covenant itself but on a *pattern of symbolism*—or perhaps one should say, a theological perspective—that is expressed in each of the covenants. Each covenant, considered in its scriptural context, nuances in symbolic terms what it means to live in the presence of the holy God, who has entered into special relationship with the people Israel.

Covenant Trajectories
Now, it so happens that each of these covenants is dominant in a major block of Old Testament literature (see fig. 1). The Abrahamic covenant is fundamental in the Tetrateuch (or Pentateuch, i.e., Tetrateuch plus the last verses of Deuteronomy), which reached its final form at the hands of Priestly writers. The Mosaic covenant is dominant in Deuteronomy, which serves as a preface to the historical work Joshua through 2 Kings (Former Prophets, or Deuteronomistic history). The

19. E. W. Nicholson, *God and His People: Covenant and Theology in the Old Testament* (Oxford: Clarendon, 1986), v.

Davidic covenant is dominant in the major book of the Writings, the book of Psalms, as well as in the Chronicler's history (1 and 2 Chronicles).

FIGURE 1. *God's Covenants with Israel*

	PRIMARY SCRIPTURAL CONTEXT	BIBLICAL FIGURES	MAJOR PROPHET
Abrahamic Covenant[20]	Pentateuch in final Priestly form	Abraham and Sarah	Ezekiel
Mosaic Covenant	Deuteronomy, Deuteronomistic history	Moses, Aaron, and Miriam (cf. Mic. 6:4)	Hosea, Jeremiah
Royal Covenant	Book of Psalms, 1–2 Chronicles	David	Isaiah

Thus the three major figures in Old Testament tradition are Abraham (add Sarah), Moses (add Aaron and Miriam), and David the great king, Yahweh's anointed, who was regarded as the prototype of the Messiah to come.

It is also significant that major prophets were influenced by each of these theological perspectives: Ezekiel by the Priestly theology of the tabernacling presence of the holy God in the midst of the people; Jeremiah by the Mosaic covenant as expressed supremely in the book of Deuteronomy; and Isaiah by Zion theology with its salvific institutions of temple and kingship.

After exploring these theological perspectives, we shall see how the great catastrophe of the fall of Jerusalem and the destruction of the temple affected each and precipitated a profound theological crisis. In this period, the time after the crucial event of 587 B.C., the tragedy of Israel called into question the covenantal relationship between God and people and precipitated the problem of theodicy, or the justice of God, as expressed in the skeptical wisdom literature, Ecclesiastes and Job. In this period of suffering and change, when the foundations of Israel's faith were shaken, torah came to be identified with wisdom, an independent movement in Israel that originally was sponsored by the royal court. Prophecy, as represented by the great classical prophets (e.g., Amos, Hosea, Jeremiah), moved into apocalyptic, as evident from the book of Isaiah and late prophetic writings such as Haggai and Zechariah.

The Pentateuch and the Abrahamic covenant, the Deuteronomic history and the Mosaic covenant, the books of Psalms and Chronicles and the Davidic covenant: in these major blocks of literature we find three dominant covenantal

20. This is a broad way of describing the ancestral covenant made with Abraham, Isaac, and Jacob. Remember that in the final Priestly form of the Pentateuch the Abrahamic covenant embraces and supports the Mosaic covenant found in the book of Exodus; see Exod. 2:14 and references to "the God of your ancestors, the God of Abraham, of Isaac, and of Jacob" (Exod. 3:6, 13, 16, etc.).

perspectives. Owing to the gravity of the problem of evil, however, each of these perspectives was tried in the balance and found wanting, prompting a movement from torah to wisdom, and from prophecy to apocalyptic.

Finally, we shall see how these theological perspectives converge in the New Testament, though it is not my task to give a detailed discussion of New Testament theology. The Christian community celebrates God's apocalyptic triumph in Jesus Christ—over all the powers of sin, darkness, death, and anything that threatens to separate people from the love of God known in Jesus Christ. In the last analysis, Jesus Christ is hailed as prophet, the one who stands in the Mosaic tradition like Jeremiah; as priest, the one who, standing in the Abrahamic tradition, is acclaimed as a priestly mediator between the holy God and human beings (Epistle to the Hebrews); and as king, that is, the Son of God of the Davidic tradition.

In this exposition of God's covenants with Israel we shall be influenced by the shape of the canon, considering first the Pentateuch, then the Former Prophets (Joshua through 2 Kings), then the major prophets who are associated with particular theological perspectives, and finally the Writings, chiefly the book of Psalms and the Chronicler's history, which reflect Davidic (or "Zion") theology. The movement from torah to wisdom, evident in the book of Psalms, allows us to explore other books in the Writings (wisdom literature: Proverbs, Ecclesiastes, Job), with some consideration of wisdom writings outside the Hebrew Bible (Wisdom of Ben Sira, Wisdom of Solomon). The movement from prophecy to apocalyptic allows us to consider the book of Isaiah in its final form and writings that lie at the boundary of the New Testament in the Christian Bible: Zechariah and Malachi.

Theology and Imagination
While this presentation is organized, as much as possible, according to the canonical sequence of the books of the Old Testament, we shall also be influenced by historical and sociological considerations. Each covenantal perspective belongs to a particular historical and social setting. The Priestly perspective belongs to the priestly order of the Jerusalem temple, perhaps dating into the period of the monarchy (around the middle of the eighth century according to Jacob Milgrom),[21] though it was given its final shape during the exile. The Deuteronomic perspective reaches back into the period of the northern kingdom (the capital, Samaria, fell in 722 B.C.), though it was given its final expression in and around the reform of Josiah on the eve of the fall of Judah (587 B.C.). The Davidic covenant belongs to the time of the Davidic kingdom, inaugurated by David and Solomon and surviving throughout the prophetic period and beyond (reflected in the book of Isaiah as a whole).

These covenantal perspectives represented the symbolic world of particular social circles and reflected the tragic reality of Israel's historical experience before

21. "On the Parameters, Date, and Provenance of P," *Leviticus 1–16* (Anchor Bible 3; New York: Doubleday, 1991).

and after the fall of Jerusalem in 587 B.C. But the symbolic power of the language transcends the social location and the historical circumstances in which it was originally expressed and was released with new power when the tradition became *scripture* for the community of faith.[22]

The task of the biblical theologian is to enter and understand the biblical world(s) construed by imagination. When the symbolism finds an echo in our poetic response, as "deep calls to deep" (cf. Ps. 42:7), the Bible may speak today with the power of the Word of God.[23]

A Meditation

ROBERT: What did you mean when you said that St. Catherine and St. Margaret talked to you every day?

JOAN [of Arc]: They do.

ROBERT: What are they like?

JOAN (suddenly obstinate): I will tell you nothing about that: they have not given me leave.

ROBERT: But you actually see them; and they talk to you just as I am talking to you?

JOAN: No: it is quite different. I cannot tell you: you must not talk to me about my voices.

ROBERT: How do you mean? Voices?

JOAN: I hear voices telling me what to do. They come from God.

ROBERT: They come from your imagination.

JOAN: Of course. That is how the messages of God come to us.[24]

22. See further my essay, "Biblical Theology and Sociological Interpretation," *TToday* 42 (1985) 292–306.

23. On the role of imagination in biblical understanding, see the "hermeneutic of language" advocated by Paul Ricoeur, discussed above, chapter 3.

24. George Bernard Shaw, *Saint Joan* (1924), scene 1.

Part I
Yahweh, the Holy One of Israel

For I am God, and no mortal
the Holy One in your midst.

HOSEA 11:9b

5. The Experience of the Holy

In the last section of the introduction I raised the question: Where do we go from here? The hermeneutical issues are so complex, and the disagreements are so great, that only the bravest, or perhaps the most foolhardy, dare to enter the fray.

Methodological Requirements

If one attempts a theology *of* (subjective genitive) the Old Testament[1] there are several methodological requirements:

1. We must find a valid starting point in the midst of the multiplex literature of the Old Testament in its tripartite division: Torah, Prophets, Writings.

2. From that starting point, we must ascertain the fundamental witness that remains constant throughout various mutations, from the final text back to early stages of tradition.

3. We must do justice to the diversity of Israel's theological expressions and at the same time show the integrity of the faith of Israel in relation to the religions of antiquity.

4. We must show that this theological exposition stands in continuity and discontinuity with the New Testament.

When one considers the scope and magnitude of the task, it is appropriate to say in the words of the psalmist, "Such knowledge is too wonderful for me; it is high, I cannot attain unto it!" (Ps. 139:6, KJV)

Seeking a Starting Point

In past generations some theologians have sought a "center" in the Old Testament: perhaps a central theme such as God's redemptive action (based on the exodus) or the dominion (kingdom) of God (based on Israel's experiment with monarchy). This search has been in vain; the Old Testament does not have a center in the same sense that Jesus Christ is the center of the New Testament. Nevertheless, it is important to consider what part of the Old Testament is central, in the sense of being fundamental to Israel's theological understanding.

When the matter is put this way, there cannot be serious doubt about the part of Scripture that the Jewish community regards as central. The Torah (Pentateuch) is central and primary. At this point, I believe, we stand on solid rock, though all else around may be shaky ground. To be sure, the Christian community tends to shift from the Torah to the Prophets, from Mosaic law to prophetic promise.[2] But the community that shaped the Israelite traditions as "Scripture," according to a tri-

---

1. On the distinction between *theology of* and *theology about* the Old Testament, see above, chapter 3.

2. See Hans von Campenhausen, *The Formation of the Christian Bible*, trans. J. A. Baker (Minneapolis: Fortress Press, 1972).

partite canonical structure, recognized the primacy of the Torah or the Penta-teuch. Other scriptures (Former and Latter Prophets, Writings) surround this canonical center in concentric circles (see fig. 2) and, in an extended sense, could be regarded as belonging also to Torah (as in John 10:34, which quotes Ps. 82:6 as "written in your law").[3]

FIGURE 2. *The Jewish Scriptures (Tanakh)*

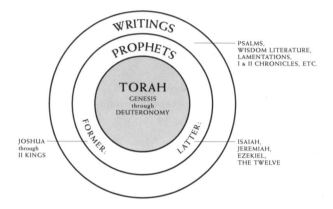

The canonical primacy of the Torah was certified in the period of the restora-tion when, under the leadership of Ezra, it became the constitutional basis of the Jewish community (ca. 400 B.C.). From this time on, the Torah was authoritative as canonical Scripture. Whatever may have been the history of the traditions before, it was in this final form that the Torah was normative for faith and practice.

Admittedly, it is tempting to shift the emphasis to some other part of Scripture: to the prophets who preached "let justice roll down"; or to wisdom literature, which resonates with modern intellectual struggles; or to the book of Psalms, which is basic for worship and private devotions (sometimes the book of Psalms is bound up in an edition with the New Testament). But if we are to find what is "cen-tral" or "foundational" in the Old Testament, we must lay aside our predilections and ascertain the theological witness of Israel within this primary context, the Torah (Pentateuch).

The Holy One of Israel

When we turn to this central part of the canon, it is evident that what is basic is Israel's witness to divine revelation: the self-disclosure of the Holy One (*qadosh*) so that the people may call on (worship) God by the personal name, YHWH (Yahweh, usually translated "the Lord"). At the fountainhead of Israel's sacred tra-

---

3. See Ronald E. Clements, *Old Testament Theology: A Fresh Approach* (Atlanta: John Knox, 1978), Chapter 5, "The Old Testament as Law."

dition and pervading the literature of the Old Testament is this witness to the revelation of God, the Holy One. In a very early poem (probably eleventh century B.C.), the Song of the Sea, Yahweh is praised as "glorious in holiness."

> *Who is like you among the gods, O Yahweh?*
> *Who is like you, glorious in holiness,*
> *awesome in praise, doing wonders?*
> —Exod. 15:11 (BWA)

Centuries later, in the eighth century, the prophet Hosea expressed the meaning of God's presence with the people:

> *For I am God [ʾel] and not a mortal man [ʾish],*
> *the Holy One [qadosh] in your midst.*
> —Hos. 11:9b (RSV)

"God is holy," emphasized Ernst Sellin, a leading Old Testament theologian of a former generation; "herein we touch on that which constitutes the deepest and innermost nature of the God of the Old Testament."[4]

In Israel's tradition holiness is associated with the name of YHWH (Yahweh). This is evident in the formula of God's self-identification, "I am Yahweh, your God" (e.g., Exod. 3:20; Lev. 18:2). "The Old Testament," wrote Walther Zimmerli, a major Old Testament theologian, "holds fast to the identity [Selbigkeit] of God which it knows under the name Yahweh. Throughout all change it firmly maintains that this God, Yahweh, wants to deal with his people, Israel."[5] This is a helpful contribution that throws light on "the constancy and persistence of Israel's rendering of God."[6] Israel's relation to the holy God, named Yahweh, remains a theological constant in the midst of change and diversity.

Hence it is not just faith in "God" that distinguishes Israel, but rather faith in God known and worshiped under the name "Yahweh." "The true divine name, to which all others are secondary, is Yahweh," observed Ludwig Koehler.[7] He cited statistics: this personal name appears more than 6,700 times; the nearest competitor is the general term ʾelohim, occurring some 2,500 times, which means "God," or sometimes "gods." In short, Yahweh is the name that Israel invokes in lament, thanksgiving, and hymnic praise in the Psalter, with the exception of the so-called Elohist Psalter (Psalms 42–83), which prefers the general term Elohim. The first petition of the Lord's Prayer is that God's "name" may be hallowed, that is, set apart as holy.

---

4. Ernst Sellin, *Theologie des Alten Testaments* (Leipzig: Quelle & Meyer, 1936), 19; quoted by John Gammie, *Holiness in Israel*, OBT (Minneapolis: Fortress Press, 1989), 3.

5. Walther Zimmerli, *Old Testament Theology in Outline*, trans. David E. Green (Louisville: John Knox, 1978), 14.

6. The language is that of Walter Brueggemann, editor's foreword to John Gammie, *Holiness in Israel*, x.

7. Ludwig Koehler, *Old Testament Theology*, trans. A. S. Todd (Philadelphia: Westminster, 1957), 36, 41.

Holiness in the History of Religions

The self-disclosure of God, symbolized by the giving of the personal name Yahweh, occurs in the general context of the experience of the holy and thus in the context of what Israel has in common, to some degree, with other religions. "The concept of holiness," observes Dale Moody, "is the ground on which all religions meet."[8] To use a musical analogy, here we find the "ground bass" (*basso ostenato*), a term for "a musical phrase repeated while the upper voices pursue their courses, sometimes improvised."[9] In other words, holiness is the primary datum of Israel's knowledge of God that is reflected and refracted in various traditions: priestly, prophetic, and sapiential.[10] Holiness is the fundamental tone that sounds through the whole range of the literature of the Old Testament.

This is not a new discovery. The point was stressed years ago by J. Hänel in his book, *Die Religion der Heiligkeit* (*The Religion of Holiness*, 1931), and has been seconded by other Old Testament theologians.[11] Hänel's pathbreaking book in the Old Testament field was influenced by the monumental work of Rudolf Otto, *Das Heilige*, which appeared in English translation as *The Idea of the Holy*.[12] In fact, it is rumored that the systematic theologian Paul Tillich once remarked that the three most important books on religion in the twentieth century were Albert Schweitzer's *Quest for the Historical Jesus*, Karl Barth's *Epistle to the Romans*, and Rudolf Otto's *Idea of the Holy*.

Writing from the standpoint of the history of religions, Otto maintained that all religions, especially the religions of antiquity, give expression to a sense of mystery, that is, "feelings of the non-rational and numinous" or "the sheer absolute wondrousness that transcends thought."[13] To this dimension of mystery and wonder he gave the term "the numinous" (from Latin *numen*, "divine spirit or power"). Otto's work has been carried further by other studies in the phenomenology of religion (or "comparative religion"), especially Mircea Eliade's examination of hierophanies or "manifestations of the sacred" in various cultures.[14]

---

8. Dale Moody, *Word of Truth* (Grand Rapids: Eerdmans, 1981), 94.

9. For music appreciators, a good example is Pachelbel's "canon."

10. This is shown by Gammie, *Holiness in Israel*.

11. Johannes Hänel, *Die Religion du Heiligkeit* (Gutersloh: C. Bertelsmann, 1931). Of the various scholars cited in Gammie's book (p. 3), I should like to draw attention especially to the Dutch theologian who has influenced me a great deal, Th. C. Vriezen, *An Outline of Old Testament Theology* (2d ed.; Oxford: Oxford Univ. Press, 1970; Dutch original, 1949), 149–62. "The holiness of God," writes Vriezen (p. 151), "is the central idea of the Old Testament faith in God." See his discussion of God's holiness, 149–62.

12. Rudolf Otto, *The Idea of the Holy*, trans. John W. Harvey (2d ed.; New York: Oxford Univ. Press, 1950). First published in German in 1922. The German title should strictly be translated as "Holiness" or "The Sense of the Holy," for the holy, in Otto's view, cannot be reduced to a concept.

13. Ibid., 72.

14. See, for instance, Mircea Eliade's book, *Patterns in Comparative Religion*, trans. R. Sheed (Cleveland: World, 1963; French original, 1948).

The Overwhelming Mystery

According to Otto, the sense of the holy (the wonderful, the aweful, the numinous) has two aspects: dread and fascination. One is drawn to the mystery and at
the same time repelled by it, as in the case of Moses' experience at the burning
bush (Exodus 3). Similarly in the story of the theophany at Mount Sinai (Exodus
19) the people are drawn to the mystery of the sacred mountain, but they stand
back in fear and dread lest they be consumed by divine holiness.

Fascination and dread, however, are human *responses* to the peculiar nature of
the holy. In Otto's view, the holy is not just mystery described by such words as
"the ineffable, the wholly other, the transcendent." Even more fundamentally the
holy is power that Otto describes as:

- awefulness, plenitude of power which evokes a sense of dread
- overpoweringness, plenitude of being, absolute unapproachability
- urgency, vitality, will, force, movement, excitement, activity, energy; [meta-
  phorically a] consuming fire.[15]

Otto further states that already in the Bible there are attempts to "rationalize"
the mystery, that is, to convert it into a theological concept (such as the idea of
God) or into ethical values (as in "ethical monotheism"). But these conceptualiza-
tions and rationalizations cannot destroy the sense of the holy that erupts again
and again in the presence of the *mysterium tremendum*, as in the book of Job (the voice
from the whirlwind). The sense of the holy is "beyond our categories of appre-
hension and comprehension, and causes the radical disablement of metaphor."[16]
The holy God is veiled in mystery and is even "beyond good and evil," all our
moral categories. Perhaps on this level there is common ground between Jews/
Christians and Buddhists, who, though not usually using the word "God," believe
that the truly Real is beyond conceptualization and therefore approachable only
through meditation.[17]

A possible weakness of Otto's book is that it can be understood as reducing
holiness to a state of consciousness, that is, the holy is viewed solely from the subjective, anthropological side.[18] Read this way, the work could be taken to support
Schleiermacher's emphasis on "feeling" (*Gefühle*), which accounts for the polemic
against it in neo-orthodoxy (e.g., Karl Barth). But this objection must be weighed
against Otto's contention that these feelings are human responses to manifestations of numinous divine power. In any case, in the ancient world, and clearly in

---

15. See Gammie's précis of Otto's study, *Holiness in Israel*, 5.

16. David R. Blumenthal, *Facing the Abusing God: A Theology of Protest* (Louisville: West-
minster/John Knox, 1993), 23.

17. See the report on the Kentucky meeting for dialogue between Buddhists and Christians,
"Divergence, Convergence: Buddhist-Christian Encounters," *Christian Century* 113, no. 29 (1996)
964–73.

18. A caveat of Gerhard von Rad, *Old Testament Theology*, trans. D. M. G. Stalker, 2 vols. (New
York: Harper & Row, 1962–65), 1:205.

Israel, the holy was experienced as power that breaks into the human world, threatening existence and arousing both fascination and dread. Holiness is not a quality, or a state of consciousness, but is power—highly active, energetic, dynamic, even threatening.

Earthquake, Wind, and Fire

A classical illustration of the manifestation of the holy in Israel is the portrayal of the theophany at Mount Sinai, in connection with the issuing of the Ten Commandments (Exod. 19:16—20:21) and the making of the covenant (19:3-9; 24:3-8). Here holiness is tremendous power manifest in a fierce mountain storm. "There was thunder and lightning," the mountain was enveloped in a thick cloud, a loud trumpet blast filled the air, causing the people to tremble (19:16; 20:18). The narrator says that God, veiled in a cloud, descended to the mountaintop "in fire," causing the mountain to shake with seismic tremors (19:18). The presence of God on the mountaintop charged the whole mountain with dangerous power, like high-voltage electricity; hence the people were warned not to approach it or touch it lest many of them die (19:21-22). Indeed, Moses was instructed to set bounds so that the people would not come near, "otherwise Yahweh will break out against them" (19:24; also 19:12-13). So terrified were the people at the ominous display of God's holiness that they asked Moses to go up into the mountain and speak with God and then come back to them with a message, "but do not let God speak to us, or we will die" (19:18-19).

In the story of Moses' call and commission (Exodus 3), the presence of God is symbolized by fire: a bush that burns yet is not consumed. The appropriate response was for Moses to remove his sandals, for the presence of God made the very ground on which he was standing sacred. In other contexts, God's holiness makes objects so sacrosanct that one cannot look on them (Num. 4:18-20) or touch them without suffering harmful effects (Exod. 19:12). Holiness attaches especially to the ark, regarded as the throne seat on which God is invisibly seated (1 Sam. 4:6), and therefore inspires fear when escorted into the city of Beth-shemesh: "Who is able to stand before the Lord, the holy God?" (1 Sam. 6:20). Thus the holy manifests *itself* (in German *das Heilige* is neuter) as power—power that breaks into the human world with shattering force, like fire or electricity, with positive or negative effects.

This elemental sense of the holy is, in large measure, alien to the modern, secular world. The closest modern persons may come to this experience is the ontological awareness of the wonder of being, a dimension that Abraham Joshua Heschel explores in his writings.[19] He appeals to the basic human sense of the sublime, manifest in spontaneous awe and radical amazement.

---

19. Especially *God in Search of Man* (New York: Farrar, Straus and Giroux, 1955).

Awe enables us to perceive in the world intimations of the divine, to sense in small things the beginning of infinite significance, to sense the ultimate in the common and the simple; to feel in the rush of the passing the stillness of the eternal.[20]

Moreover, scientists, like Albert Einstein, who contemplate the vast immensities of celestial space and of the atomic world find themselves overwhelmed by a sense of wonder. Einstein wrote:

> The most beautiful thing we can experience is the mysterious. It is the source of all true art and science. He to whom this emotion is a stranger, who can no longer pause to wonder and stand rapt in awe, is as good as dead: his eyes are closed. This insight into the mystery of life, coupled though it be with fear, has also given rise to religion.[21]

It is more difficult, however, for modern people to understand the holy as "primal energy"—divine or demonic power that breaks into the human world created by our language and symbols. The holy is literally "out of this world," to use a well-worn expression. When it invades the human world defined by our language, our customs, our thought—everything that is "familiar"—it excites the response described by Otto: dread and fascination, awe and wonder.

A Sound of Sheer Silence

Many people, ancient and modern, turn to the quiet aspects of nature to find symbols of the divine, as in the case of Pharaoh Akhenaton's beautiful "Hymn to the Aton"—the sun disk that symbolizes the beneficent rays that lavish the earth with light and life. This beautiful Egyptian poem seems to have influenced the composition of Psalm 104, one of the great creation poems of the Bible.[22] Also the Egyptian view is reflected in Psalm 19, which exclaims that "the heavens declare the glory of God" in an inaudible anthem and which portrays divine beneficence in the daily circuit of the sun.

Israel's poets, however, turn not just to serene metaphors but to violent ones: the fierce mountain storm that breaks the cedars of Lebanon (Psalm 29); the roaring of a lion that fills people with terror (Amos 1:2); an awesome day when people will flee to the mountains and caves from the display of divine majesty (Isa. 2:12-21); a whirlwind out of which God speaks (Job 38). The presence of God is disturbing, upsetting, awe-ful.

---

20. Ibid., 75. See my essay on Heschel's biblical theology: "Coexistence with God: Heschel's Exposition of Biblical Theology," particularly the section on "The Sense of the Holy," in *Abraham Joshua Heschel: Exploring His Life and Thought*, ed. John C. Merkle (New York: Collier Macmillan, 1985), 49–52.

21. Albert Einstein, quoted in an unpublished essay on "The Miracle and Mystery of Life" by Joyce Starr Griswold (1998).

22. I discuss briefly Psalm 104 and its Egyptian parallel in my study book on the Psalms, *Out of the Depths* (Philadelphia: Westminster, 1983; rev. ed. forthcoming, 2000), 44–45. The whole Egyptian poem is found in *ANET*, 369–71.

Otto properly describes the experience of the holy as having a daunting or threatening character: "wrath" is the code word for this aspect of the divine character. Divine "wrath" is daunting especially to those who perceive nothing in the divine but goodness, gentleness, love, support—as a loving father or friend. The holy, however, cannot be domesticated or humanized; it remains a stranger in our world. There is a sense in which God is known as an enemy, before being known as a friend.[23] Walther Eichrodt observes pointedly that if Christianity surrenders the fundamental awareness of God as "power before whom the creature cannot stand," "of the opposition between God and his creatures," it would then lose "that note of absolute urgency without which the Gospel entrusted to it can never be other than unthinking and superficial."[24]

In the Elijah story, which presents Elijah as a kind of second Moses, the Sinai theophany is interpreted in a new way. According to the narrative context, in the ninth century B.C. Elijah had fought valiantly to preserve Israel's religious tradition based on the covenant at Sinai. But he was up against a power establishment embodied in a tyrannical queen and a pusillanimous king. Discouraged and exhausted, the prophet fled for his life into the southern wilderness (1 Kings 19). There in a cave (reminiscent of the cave experience related in the exodus story, Exod. 33:17—34:8) he witnessed a display of God's holiness in a fierce mountain storm, powerfully portrayed in Mendelssohn's oratorio *Elijah*.

In this case, however, the narrator emphasizes that God was *not* in the earthquake, *not* in the wind, *not* in the fire. These demonstrations of divine power were only a prelude to the real theophany. Whereas at Sinai (or Horeb) God spoke to Moses "in thunder" (Exod. 19:19), this time God spoke in "a soft murmuring sound" (NJPSV), or "a gentle whisper" (NIV), or—perhaps the best translation—"a sound of sheer silence" (NRSV). "When Elijah heard it" (the sound of silence), he stood at the entrance to the cave, where he heard the divine question: "What are you doing here?" and the divine imperative to take part in the political struggle. According to this story, God's holy power does not crush human freedom but addresses it, as happened at the "burning bush" when Moses was sent as an agent of God's purpose.

The Face of God

In summary, holiness belongs essentially to the divine, whether experienced in Israel, Canaan, or elsewhere. It is the Wholly Other, which exceeds everything worldly: all human conceptuality, all moral categories, all metaphors. It is the power that belongs to "the very essence of deity." It may be more fundamental in

---

23. A statement attributed, I believe, to Alfred North Whitehead.

24. Eichrodt, *Old Testament Theology*, trans. J. A. Baker, 2 vols., OTL (Philadelphia: Westminster, 1961–67), 1:276–77. See his discussion of "The Holiness of God," 270–82. It is strange that it took Eichrodt 270 pages to reach this fundamental dimension of Old Testament theology.

the Godhead than the personal traits that are emphasized in biblical tradition.[25] The new element in Israel's experience of the holy, however, is that the holiness is associated primarily with the name of Yahweh. The holiness that breaks into the human world, exciting wonder and dread, is not impersonal power but has a personal "face" or character. Thus the Torah, our starting point, brings us to the primary confession that the God whom Israel worships is "the Holy one in your midst" (Isa. 12:5-6). The name of Yahweh, the God of Israel, is *qadosh* (holy). Throughout the Old Testament we hear the amazing announcement that this holy power is also saving power; it is not only transcendent but immanent, dwelling "in our midst." In the book of Isaiah, a poet hears God's word:

> *Thus says the high and holy one*
> *who inhabits eternity, whose name is Holy:*
> *"I dwell in the high and holy place,*
> *and also with those who are contrite and humble in spirit,*
> *to revive the spirit of the humble,*
> *and to revive the heart of the contrite."*

> —Isa. 57:15

25. Blumenthal, in *Facing the Abusing God*, maintains, however, that "God has two essential attributes: holiness and personality" (p. 7 and chaps. 2 and 3). Whether "personality" is *essential* to God's being is a philosophical question that will come up later.

6. The Name of God

I-Thou Relationship

Holiness is not impersonal power, "It," but is manifest as "Thou," signified by a personal name, Yahweh, which people use in the "I-Thou" relationship of prayer and worship. Walther Eichrodt, an eminent twentieth-century Old Testament theologian, writes:

> "Holy" is the epithet deemed fittest to describe the divine Thou whose nature and operations are summed up in the divine Name; and for this reason it comes to mean that which is distinctively characteristic of God, that which constitutes God's nature.[1]

This is perhaps the most amazing thing that Israel has to say to the world: the Holy is not just power—the awesome power manifest in the storm, "earthquake, wind, and fire," but is power manifest in relationship with people, saving power and ethical concern. The wonder of this "I-Thou" relationship, to echo the title of Martin Buber's classic,[2] is celebrated by a psalmist who, beneath the starry sky, is overwhelmed with the realization that the Creator, who controls the vast universe, is mindful of, cares about, the existing person.

> *When I look up at your heavens, the work of your fingers,*
> *at the moon and the stars you have set in place,*
> *what is a frail mortal, that you should be mindful of him,*
> *a human being, that you should take*
> *notice of him?*

Ps. 8:3-4 (REB)

The Giving of God's Name

In the final edition of the Pentateuch, produced by Priestly theologians, great stress falls on the name Yahweh, as the Holy One of Israel, the creator and redeemer. The Priestly writers presented a *toledoth* (generations) history, from the time of creation to the Mosaic period. They schematized the history as a history of covenants: Noachic, Abrahamic, Mosaic,[3] each period being characterized by a particular divine epithet:

- From creation to Abraham: Elohim (God)
- From Abraham to Moses: El Shaddai (God Almighty)
- From Moses on: Yahweh (the Lord)

---

1. Walther Eichrodt, *Theology of the Old Testament*, trans. J. A. Baker, 2 vols., OTL (Philadelphia: Westminster, 1961–67), 1:274.
2. Martin Buber, *I and Thou*, trans. R. G. Smith (Edinburgh: T. & T. Clark, 1937).
3. See the discussion of the Priestly periodization of history in chapter 10.

Thus in a Priestly passage, we read:

> God also spoke to Moses and said to him: "I am the Lord [Yahweh]. I appeared to Abraham, Isaac, and Jacob as God Almighty [El Shaddai], but by my name "The LORD" [Yahweh] I did not make myself known to them.
>
> —Exod. 6:2

This is the cultic name that the people are to use in worship. To praise God, as we know from the book of Psalms, is to "call upon the name of Yahweh," in lament (Ps. 116:4) or in thanksgiving (Ps. 116:13).

The Priestly writer inherited and interpreted one strand of Old Epic tradition that traced the cultic practice to the time of Moses (contrary to Gen. 4:26b). Remember the story told in Exodus 3, about Moses' experience of the holy at a mountain in the wilderness. The narrator says that when Moses encountered "God" (Elohim), he was told that he was standing on holy ground and should take off his sandals as a gesture of reverence. When asked the name of the deity, he was told in a somewhat evasive manner that he should lead the Hebrew slaves out of Egypt in the name of the god, Yahweh (translated "The Lord").

It is doubtful that the passage means to say that the name Yahweh was unknown and unused in the time before Moses. According to traditions in the book of Genesis, the name Yahweh was used in the pre-Mosaic period; indeed, one strand of tradition traces the usage of the divine name all the way back into the primeval history, to the time of Enosh (Gen. 4:26b: "At that time people began to invoke the name of the Lord [YHWH]"). The Priestly writers, however, are concerned about the beginning of the cult, the service of worship. YHWH (the Lord) is the cultic name that the people are to use when invoking God.

Here we are not concerned with archaeological questions: Where did this divine name come from? What does the name in itself mean? Was the name also found outside Israel? These questions, which belong to the history of religions, have been debated for many years. Rather, our interest is theological: What does it mean for God to have a personal name?

The Name in Relationship

Start at the level of ordinary human relationships. "What's in a name?" That is the question Juliet asks in Shakespeare's tragedy, *Romeo and Juliet* (Act 2, Scene 2): "What's in a name? A rose by any other name would smell as sweet!" The answer, of course, is that everything is in a name: the name signifies personhood, identity. "The name is the soul [self]," observed Johannes Pedersen.[4] To be nameless is to have no identity. The greatest tragedy that could befall anyone would be to be stripped of his or her name, to be reduced to a number, a cipher (e.g., a Social Security number). The astounding witness of the Old Testament is that the holy

---

4. Johannes Pedersen, *Israel: Its Life and Culture,* trans. Aslaug Moller, 4 vols. printed in 2 (Oxford: Oxford Univ. Press, 1926–40), 1–2:245–59.

God is not nameless but has a personal name, so that worshipers may call on this God in prayer, using the language of "Thou."

Paraphrased in more philosophical language: God does not remain as Being: being-in-itself, metaphysical reality and power; rather, God is known as being-in-relationship, being with identity, being that is identified with a people. The name of Yahweh signifies the being of God turned toward a people with personal concern and ethical demand. God chooses to have identity, to enter into relationship with the finite and the human, to be "God with us" or "God in our midst." Accordingly, Israel does not build altars to an unknown God, but to the God who is known personally and therefore is to be both feared and trusted.

It would be fruitless theologically to try to understand the significance of God's giving a personal name by exploring the sounds and letters of the word "Yahweh" itself (a causative verbal form, "he causes to be"),[5] or even the cryptic etymology of the tetragrammaton in Exod. 3:13-15, 'ehyeh 'asher 'ehyeh (I am who I am). The name Yahweh cannot be understood by exploring its etymology, any more than the name of any person—your name or mine—can be understood by analyzing its constituent elements. Just as a person's name belongs to his or her life story and loses its meaning when abstracted from that narrative context, so God's name, Yahweh, belongs essentially to the story or history in which the Holy One broke into the world of slaves with redeeming and demanding power.

That is how it is in the book of Exodus: the name of God is given in connection with an event in which God's holiness was manifested as saving power, as suggested in the condensed narrative: "I am Yahweh your God who brought you out of the land of Egypt" (Exod. 20:1). The prophet Hosea speaks in the name of this saving God:

> Yet I have been Yahweh your God
> ever since the land of Egypt;
> you know no God but me,
> and besides me there is no savior.
> —Hos. 13:4

Reverence for the Name

In the story of the burning bush, the divine name is not given openly and directly in answer to the people's request ("What is his name?" Exod. 3:13), but only indirectly in a wordplay on the tetragrammaton ("I am who I am"). The narrator seems to suggest hesitance, a holding back, in giving the divine name, for when God's name (identity) is known it might be used wrongly, even to gain power over God, as in the story of Jacob's nightlong wrestle with a stranger, God incognito (Gen. 32:29).

5. Construed as a Hiphil (causative) form of the verb *hwh*, the etymology would be "He causes to be what is" (or what happens), that is, the one who is creator and lord. Frank M. Cross argues that originally the word was part of a cultic sobriquet, Yahweh Sabaoth, "He who creates the heavenly armies"; see his "Yahweh and 'El," *Canaanite Myth and Hebrew Epic: Essays in the History of the Religion of Israel* (Cambridge: Harvard Univ. Press, 1973), 44–75.

The reticence about disclosing God's name, and thus making God accessible in human language, must be taken with the utmost theological seriousness. There is a sense in which God is nameless, beyond all human "naming" in language, even our highest thoughts and loftiest metaphors (see Isa. 55:8-9). Imagination cannot really "image" God; it can only point to the holy God, who is beyond human language, even though God chooses to speak through human words.

Paul Ricoeur observes that the Bible is not only "one of the great poems of existence," which invites us into a new being like other great literature, but also it is a unique poem "because all its partial forms of discourse are referred to that Name which is the point of intersection and the vanishing point of all our discourse about God, the name of the unnameable."[6] In an essay on "Naming God," Ricoeur remarks that God is "the being whom humanity cannot really name, that is, hold at the mercy of our language."[7]

Mystics, both Jewish and Christian, acknowledge "the inexpressible transcendence of God, the ineffable infinity of the divine." Speaking of a medieval mystical philosopher, church historian Paul Rorem writes that

> the Dionysian author stays on the edge of transcendence, audaciously straining language and thought, resorting finally to negation and silence, all in the effort to point beyond ourselves, our best words and highest thoughts, to something wholly other, the *mysterium tremendum*.[8]

This is the great biblical paradox: that the God who is beyond naming chooses to be known by name.

As a sign of reverence for God, and to avoid any profanation of God's name, rabbis later connected the vowels of *adonai* (Lord) with the sacred consonants (YHWH), indicating thereby that this substitute form of address was to be read whenever the tetragrammaton is written. The translators of the King James Version did not understand this literary convention but read the given consonants and the substitute vowels together, with the resulting hybrid form "Jehovah."[9]

This attitude of reverence, expressed in honoring God's name, is certainly appropriate in prayer and worship. One of the Ten Commandments (Exod. 20:7) stipulates that in the covenant community "you shall not take the name of YHWH your God in vain" (or "make wrongful use of" the name, NRSV). Paul Tillich, the distinguished theologian and philosopher, once observed that we feel a kind of "sublime embarrassment" when we say "God"; indeed, "the presence of the divine in

---

6. Paul Ricoeur, "Toward a Hermeneutic of the Idea of Revelation," *HTR* 70 (1977), 27–33, quote from 26. See above, chapter 3.

7. Ricoeur, "Naming God," in *Figuring the Sacred: Religion, Narrative, and Imagination*, trans. David Pellauer, ed. Mark I. Wallace (Minneapolis: Fortress Press, 1995), 228.

8. From a paper by Paul Rorem (March 25, 1998, Princeton Theological Seminary) on a sixth-century Neoplatonic philosopher-theologian called Pseudo-Dionysius (to distinguish him from the real one mentioned in Acts 17), "Empathy and Evaluation in Medieval Church History and Pastoral Ministry: A Lutheran Reading of Pseudo-Dionysius," p. 14.

9. For further discussion of "Jehovah" and the synagogue usage "the Lord," see chapter 8.

the name demands a shy and trembling heart."[10] The profanation of God's name, as Tillich also points out, is not just a matter of speech. God's name is wrongfully used, as prophets insisted, whenever it is invoked to support social injustice or to serve national interests (Jer. 7:3-4). The holiness of God means that God is beyond all the phenomena of this world. God cannot be captured in human conceptualization or mobilized to serve human interests. God is "the elusive Presence."[11]

God's Self-Revelation

What is at stake in the giving of God's name, then, is revelation—the disclosure of God's identity and the manifestation of God's presence. This brings us to one of the thorniest problems of biblical theology: the relation between story and history. Is God's presence given in a story that is spun out of poetic imagination and is essentially fictitious? Or is God's presence manifest in a history, in the down-to-earth suffering and liberation of slaves that in some degree is open to historical criticism?

Today many theologians have given up on the notion of the revelation of God in history.[12] History, when studied scientifically (as scholars attempt to do in universities), does not disclose God or anything "supernatural." Ernst Troeltsch, a leading theologian of the nineteenth century, casts his long shadow over modern biblical study. The theologian who uses a historical method, he observed, can reach at best only historical probability (not certainty) and can understand past events—even those claimed to be unusual or miraculous—only in terms of analogies familiar in the present. In this view, the study of history brings us only to the awareness of historical relativity, not to the God who transcends the relativities of human society.[13]

Revelation as Event

In view of this prevailing historical skepticism, Jewish philosophers such as Martin Buber and Emil Fackenheim seem to be "voices crying in the wilderness." In his little book *God's Presence in History*,[14] Fackenheim bases philosophical reflection on a Jewish midrash, which states that at the very beginning of the biblical tradition

10. Paul Tillich, "The Divine Name," *Christianity and Crisis* 20 (1960–61) 55–58. In this sermon he spoke of a threefold embarrassment—of tact, of doubt, and of awe.

11. Samuel Terrien, *The Elusive Presence*; see especially the discussion of "The Disclosure of the Name" (Exod. 3:1—4:17), 109–19.

12. See Leo G. Perdue, *The Collapse of History: Reconstructing Old Testament Theology* (Minneapolis: Fortress Press, 1994). In his *Theology of the Old Testament* Walter Brueggemann "brackets out" questions of historicity; see above, chapter 3. On the retrieval of the idea of revelation see Mark I. Wallace, *The Second Naiveté: Barth, Ricoeur, and the New Yale Theology* (Macon, Ga.: Mercer Univ. Press, 1990), especially 111–25.

13. See Garret E. Paul, "Why Troeltsch? Why Today? Theology for the 21st Century," *Christian Century* 110, 20 (1993) 676–81.

14. Emil L. Fackenheim, *God's Presence in History: Jewish Affirmations and Philosophical Reflections* (New York: New York Univ. Press, 1970).

something happened at the Red Sea that was more marvelous than Ezekiel's visions of wonderful similitudes of God. There the women "saw what Isaiah, Ezekiel, and all the other prophets never saw." He continues: "The Midrash insists that not messengers, not angels, not intermediaries, but God himself acts in human history— and he was unmistakably present to a whole people at least once."[15]

Note the language: "at least once." Fackenheim does not claim that God is at work everywhere, or that God's footprints are visible on the sands of time. He does not advocate a *Heilsgeschichte*, a history of salvation traceable in the Bible. Rather, he is impressed with the mystery that lies at the root of Jewish tradition.

> How can historical explanation come to an arbitrary halt in order to accept the Inexplicable—the presence of God. God it seems, must be expelled from history by the modern historian, just as [God] is expelled from nature by the modern scientist.[16]

The result is, he writes, that neither modern Jewish nor modern Christian theologians can affirm God's real presence in history but, at most, God's providence over it.

Attempting to understand the mystery of the sea, which is enshrined in ancient poetry and story, Fackenheim says that those involved in the event did not interpret it as a miracle but experienced it as one, as an act of God. Following the lead of Martin Buber's discussion,[17] he insists that the event was a "natural-historical" event that, however, had another dimension. "Those present at the Red Sea," he continues, did not *infer* their God from the natural-historical event in an attempt to explain it by a God-hypothesis. Rather, their experience was fundamentally an "abiding astonishment," a sense of wonder that proved to be a turning point in the life of a people. Except for this abiding astonishment, the Sole Power would not be present, but only a freakish event that needed explanation. But "at that hour"— a fateful hour in the destiny of a people—Israel experienced holiness breaking into the world. The result was, as we can see in the unfolding tradition, "Israel wonders and keeps on wondering" as this crucial event is recalled and reenacted.

At the source of the Israelite tradition and manifest in the whole of Israel's Scriptures is theological wonder, a sense of the holy. God is not a phenomenon of our world or even comprehensible within worldly categories. The Holy is the completely Other, the Unfamiliar, the Strange. If the holy God intrudes into the human world, from the outside so to speak, the divine presence will be experienced as wonder that excites both dread and fascination, both fear and trust. Israel testifies that once—at least once—the holy God, the Sole Power, was manifest in this world, and that the name of this Power is Yahweh, the Holy One, *qadosh*.

At one point in his discussion of "revelation" through the Bible, Paul Ricoeur warns against a narrow "theology of the word" that is concerned only with "word

15. Ibid., 4.
16. Ibid., 4–5.
17. See my discussion of Buber's view in *The Living Word of the Bible* (Philadelphia: Westminster, 1979), 58–59.

events": "God's mark is in history before being in speech. It is only secondarily in speech inasmuch as this history itself is brought to language in the speech-act of narration."[18]

The biblical story of God's revelation to Israel is based—in some degree—on *real* events that happened in the experience of an ancient people. This has to be affirmed even though we cannot settle such questions as, "What happened at the Reed Sea?" The attempt of scholars like John Bright or Martin Noth to write a history of Israel is a meaningful enterprise, even though the historical events are elusive and can never be proven scientifically.[19] The Bible presents a realistic narrative, rooted in concrete experiences, not one that is completely spun out of the imagination. Therefore, the theologian has to reckon with the activity of God in the world, echoing the fundamental concern of George Ernest Wright's famous monograph, *God Who Acts*. In this view, religious language does not "create" reality, as in so-called postmodern linguistic theory, but is a "response to the reality of divine activity" in the world.[20]

Revelation as Word

God's revelation, however, was not only eventful but word-ful. It was a speech event, expressed in the symbolism of language.

This is evident in the story of the victory at the Reed Sea, which a critical historian, Martin Noth, regards as the "bedrock" of the exodus tradition. To the earliest stage of this tradition belongs the ancient Song of Miriam. In contrast to the later Song of the Sea (Exod. 15:1-18), Miriam—not Moses—is the primary actor and interpreter.[21]

> *Sing to Yahweh, triumphant is he,*
> *horse and rider he has hurled into the sea.*
> —Exod. 15:21 (BWA)

The salvation at the sea was not just a historical experience, as Buber and Fackenheim maintain, but it was at the same time a speech event—one that was given linguistic expression in Miriam's inspired song. The verbalization of the experience is fundamental, for we would not hear about the historical event, and celebrate it in abiding wonder, were it not for Miriam's song and the accompanying story.

18. Ricoeur, "Hermeneutic of Revelation," 6–7.

19. See Appendix 2, "The Relevance of Biblical Theology to Biblical Archaeology."

20. See Margaret S. Odell's perceptive review of Leo G. Perdue's contributions to Old Testament theology, "History or Metaphor," *RelSRev* 24, no. 3 (1998) 241–45. She specifically contrasts G. E. Wright's view of language as a witness to "the reality of divine activity" with the postmodern view of language as "a human exercise in creating worlds" (p. 244). See the discussion of Paul Ricoeur's hermeneutic of language, above, chapter 3.

21. See my essay, "The Song of Miriam Poetically and Theologically Considered," in *Directions in Biblical Hebrew Poetry*, ed. Elaine Follis, JSOTSup 40 (Sheffield: JSOT Press, 1987), 285–96; also Phyllis Trible, "Bringing Miriam out of the Shadows," *BR* 5, no. 1 (1989) 14–25, 34.

If this was true at the earliest stage of tradition, it is more so in the final literary stage that we have received from the hands of Priestly editors. The revelation of God, identified by the name Yahweh, is not a distant event that historians attempt to recover. It is an event enshrined in the symbolic language of the story as it unfolds in the Torah, especially in the book of Exodus.

In the community of faith, which receives and passes on this story, people know God through what is written, "scripture." Scripture testifies to revelation in words as well as events. In a profound sense Scripture is the Word of God. It must be added immediately, however, that Scripture is the word of God in human words—words that arise out of, and are shaped by, ancient culture and by the social life of the Israelite people. God condescends to speak to us not in the tongues of angels but in human language with all its strengths and weaknesses.[22] God's word is incarnate, so to speak, in human language.[23]

God's Presence in the World

In summary, the Old Testament bears witness to God's presence in the world, particularly in an I-Thou relationship with the people Israel. To portray God's presence, the language of poetic imagination is used, as we shall see in later chapters that deal with covenant patterns of symbolization (Part II). God's revelation, however, does not belong to an imaginary world but occurs in a real world of suffering and joy, of hardship and hope. It belongs to the historical world in which ancient Israel lived and, in a profound sense, the world of violence, oppression, and tragedy in which we live. Biblical theologians must deal with the activity of God in the world and—the reverse of the same coin—with the words of God (cf. Jer. 1:9, "words"). God's revelation in Jesus Christ is manifest in both actions and words in the New Testament as well.

If God is really and truly present in the world, theological problems inevitably arise. Religions and philosophies that are essentially otherworldly, like the gnostic cults of the ancient Hellenistic world, do not have to cope with God's incarnation in the concrete realities of the human world. Religions and philosophies that are atheistic, such as Buddhism, which normally does not speak of God or creation, do not have to struggle with the apparent absence of God in times of suffering and change (see the laments of the book of Psalms). Because Israel took seriously the revelation of God's presence in this world, through act and word, it had to face in a unique way the problem of "theodicy," the justice of God in the face of a world of violence and suffering. Therefore, we shall turn in due course to this existential problem that touches the "existence" of every person who comes into the historical world (see Part III: "Trials of Faith and Horizons of Hope").

22. See the subsequent discussion of God's "condescension" or "accommodation," chapter 8.

23. See Terence E. Fretheim and Karlfried Froehlich, *The Bible as Word of God in a Postmodern Age* (Minneapolis: Fortress Press, 1998).

7. The Characterization
of Yahweh

We have seen that the God revealed to Israel is not an ineffable, inscrutable, unknowable "It" but a "who," as expressed narratively in many ways, for example, "God who brought Israel out of Egypt," "God who created heaven and earth." God, the Holy One, chooses to have identity, to be an I in relation to a Thou, to know and to be known. God has a name and gives that name to the people so that they may address God in prayer, though in doing so God takes the risk that the name will be used in vain. Knowing the name, people will try to make God part of their world, to use God to support their nation or their purposes, in short, to make Yahweh "our God" in a possessive sense. As Walther Zimmerli puts it, the danger is the "cage of a definition."[1]

In this I-Thou relationship, Yahweh's character is made known to the people. The English word "character" is a rich term with a variety of meanings: it may refer to a person's pattern of behavior; it can mean a distinctive trait or attribute (from the basic meaning of Greek *charaktein*, "to engrave"); or it can refer to a person in a play, story, or novel, that is, a character.

God as Actor in a Drama

Since Yahweh's name is given in the context of a story centering in the exodus of slaves from Egypt, it is tempting to emphasize the last meaning indicated. The Bible presents Yahweh as a character in a story or drama, and in this literary sense Yahweh is the God who acts, to recall the title of a little book by George Ernest Wright written in the days of the biblical theology movement.[2]

This approach is proposed by Dale Patrick in an intriguing book, *The Rendering of God in the Old Testament*.[3] He describes himself as a refugee from the biblical theology movement with its excessive emphasis on God's activity in history. He believes that one can preserve the concerns expressed in "God's mighty acts in history" by moving from history to story. Thus he proposes to revitalize biblical theology with a paradigm drawn from "drama and the other mimetic arts." The two "governing concepts" of this paradigm are "characterization" and "dramatic action."

> By characterization I mean the representation of personages in such a way that they engage an audience's imagination, in essence causing us to entertain their existence

---

1. Walther Zimmerli, *Old Testament Theology in Outline*, trans. David E. Green (Atlanta: John Knox, 1978), 20–21.
2. Wright, *God Who Acts*, SBT 1/8 (Chicago: Regnery, 1952). See above, chapter 4.
3. Dale Patrick, *The Rendering of God in the Old Testament*, OBT (Minneapolis: Fortress Press, 1981).

as living individuals. By dramatic action is meant the representation of deeds and occurrences within a spaciotemporal framework, exhibited in such a way that the audience enters in as participant.[4]

Accordingly, he proceeds to "characterize" God, the actor in the biblical drama.

This is a fascinating book, because it helps the reader to take the Bible seriously as *literature*. Others, also under the influence of new literary criticism, argue that attempts to go behind the text (circumstances of composition, authorship, etc.) are illegitimate. The power of a Shakespearian play depends not on its accurate portrayal of historical realities or even its historical "referent," but on the way it creates an imaginary world and draws us into the dynamic of the plot. One can go a step further and say that the "characters" in the drama have reality only in the context of the story. That is true, for instance, in John Fowles's *The French Lieutenant's Woman*. The author tells us that he creates the characters and lets them have a life of their own. Similarly, so it is argued, the biblical narrators present God as a character in a story, a *dramatis persona*.

This view is set forth in a very interesting way by Harold Bloom in *The Book of J*, where the author—a professor of English literature at Yale University—argues that the Yahwist Epic (the J source of historical criticism) characterizes Yahweh vividly as an impish, mischievous, unpredictable, contradictory character. But this wonderful character is only an actor in a story, allegedly composed by a woman! In another recent book, *God: A Biography*, Jack Miles maintains that the structure of the Hebrew Bible, viewed strictly as a literary work, provides the basis for writing a history of the "character" called God.[5]

This approach has intriguing possibilities for interpretation. For one thing, it enables us to appreciate the bold anthropomorphisms of Scripture: Yahweh is like a human being, with eyes, ear, nose, mouth, hands, feet, and so on. It can even be said that God "laughs" (Ps. 2:4) and that God "rested and was refreshed" (Exod. 31:17). Moreover, Scripture is replete with more subtle anthropomorphisms and anthropopathisms: Yahweh thinks, regrets, decides, loves, hates, remembers, and so on. The ascription of human traits to Yahweh is appropriate in a story in which Yahweh is an actor, who enters into relation with human beings on the stage of history. So viewed, the Bible has at least the inspirational power of a Shakespearian drama or other great literature.

But a disturbing question lurks in this narrative approach. Is Yahweh only a figment of the literary imagination, an actor who has reality only in the story? This seems to suggest a form of Docetism, a heretical view in early Christianity that regarded God's revelation in Jesus Christ as only an imaginary appearance, not a flesh-and-blood reality. Brevard Childs's criticism of narrative theology, and specifically Dale Patrick's approach, exposes the problem: "Only in the final chapters

---

4. Ibid., 2.

5. Harold Bloom, *The Book of J* (New York: Grove Weidenfeld, 1990); Jack Miles, *God: A Biography* (New York: Knopf, 1995).

does he attempt, in a somewhat tortuous manner, to relate his literary characterization of God to the problem of God's reality."[6]

The God of the Bible is not a mere "character" in a drama. The reality of the holy God is prior to, and transcends, the story that expresses it. "Holy" describes the being of God, the essential nature of deity. A Jewish theologian, David Blumenthal, maintains that holiness and personality are the two "essential attributes" of God's being.[7] To ascribe "personality" to God, however, presents difficulties, unless this is a way of saying that God is known personally.

In dealing with this difficult subject, an analogy from our interpersonal relations may be helpful. I cannot probe into the innermost being of another but can only know that person—his or her "personality" or "character"—in a relationship expressed in words and deeds. Analogically, we can know the mystery of God's being only as God chooses to be known in relationship with us.[8] As Walther Eichrodt appropriately observes: "'Holy' describes the character of God as it has been made known to this people."[9] Such knowledge is covenantal or relational knowledge, symbolized by the disclosure of God's name (nature, identity).

Manifestation of God's Character

Another meaning of "character," as noted above, is a person's "pattern of behavior." In this sense God's character is manifest in God's dealings with the people Israel.

This behavioristic meaning is brought out in a striking passage, Exod. 34:5-9. It is found in the context of the portrayal of the "root experiences" of biblical tradition, that is, as Emil Fackenheim puts it, the "saving experience" (exodus) and the "commanding experience" (Sinai).[10] In this passage Yahweh is represented as proclaiming the sacred name, Yahweh—of "calling upon the name of Yahweh," to use the liturgical formula (Ps. 116:12-13).

Consider the story in Exodus 33 and 34. Moses wants to know whether Yahweh will really accompany this people into the future, a people who so easily betray God and take God's name in vain, as illustrated in the story of the golden calf. He wants to know God's "ways," that is, how God acts in relation to this fickle people. First, Moses says, "show me your ways," and he receives the answer that God's presence (*panim*, "face") will go with him (33:14-15). Then he requests: "show me your glory," and receives the response that Yahweh's goodness (*tub*) will be displayed to him and that God will proclaim before him the name Yahweh (33:18-19).

---

6. Brevard Childs, *Biblical Theology of the Old and New Testaments* (Minneapolis: Fortress Press, 1992), 19.

7. Blumenthal, *Facing the Abusing God: A Theology of Protest* (Louisville: Westminster/John Knox, 1993).

8. For this analogy I am grateful to my friend, Victor Nuovo, Professor of Philosophy Emeritus, Middlebury College.

9. Walther Eichrodt, *Theology of the Old Testament*, trans. J. A. Baker, 2 vols., OTL (Philadelphia: Westminster, 1961–67), 1:273.

10. Emil Fackenheim, *God's Presence in History* (San Francisco: Harper Torchbook, 1970).

In the story Moses' concerns are appropriate because God has chosen to step out of the mystery of holiness and to enter the human world, to be present as the Holy One in Israel's midst. Yet this people, just having entered into covenant with their saving God, have taken the name of God in vain by "making gods" that belong to their world. How can this people live in the presence of the holy God? And how can the holy God be with and go with this people into the future? This is the force of the requests: show me now your "ways," or show me now your "glory." Thus, according to the story, Yahweh promises to display the divine "goodness" and to proclaim the name Yahweh before Moses.

The narrator goes on to say that Moses is placed in a cave (see the Elijah story, 1 Kgs. 19:11-13)[11] so that he can see Yahweh only "in passing"—from behind, not in a direct face-to-face encounter. Later (after an editorial transition) we hear the proclamation in ancient liturgical language (Exod. 34:6-9), echoed in various contexts in the Old Testament (e.g., Ps. 103:8-9). The ancient confession of faith is a description of Yahweh's character.

> The Lord, the Lord [Yahweh, Yahweh], a God merciful and gracious, slow to anger, and abounding in steadfast love [ḥesed] and faithfulness, keeping steadfast love [ḥesed] for the thousandth generation, forgiving iniquity and transgression and sin, yet by no means clearing the guilty, but visiting the iniquity of the parents upon the children and the children's children, to the third and fourth generation.
>
> —Exod. 34:6-9

Here it is clear that Yahweh's holiness—the power of deity—is not manifest arbitrarily or capriciously. To be sure, Yahweh is characterized by "wrath," a manifestation of divine holiness. As expressions of holy power, God's actions cannot be comprehended in rational categories,[12] and sometimes seem to defy understanding in terms of a covenantal relationship,[13] as shown in the archaic story of Yahweh's attempt to kill Moses, the covenant mediator, on the way to fulfill his mission (Exod. 4:24-26). Israel's prophets proclaimed that the holy God shows hostility toward human beings and their way of life.[14]

Nevertheless, in the proclamation of God's name we hear that Yahweh is "slow to anger." Indeed, Yahweh is trustworthy: Yahweh is "rich in" or "abounds in" steadfast love and faithfulness (rab ḥesed weʾemeth), or as NEB translates, is "ever constant and true." See the magnificent poetic expression of the themes of Yahweh's "overflowing wrath for a moment" and Yahweh's "everlasting love" in Isa. 54:9-11.

11. Compare the Elijah story, 1 Kgs. 19:11-13, discussed above, chapter 5.

12. Recall Rudolf Otto's observation that divine wrath is a manifestation of God's holiness, above, chapter 5.

13. A point made effectively by Walter Brueggemann, "Unexpected Radicality," in *Theology of the Old Testament: Testimony, Dispute, Advocacy* (Minneapolis: Fortress Press, 1997), 280–82.

14. See, e.g., Ezekiel's message of "divine wrath and mercy," in chapter 16 below.

Yahweh's Faithfulness

In this characterization of Yahweh, the Holy One, we find one of the most important theological terms in the Old Testament: *hesed*. It is very difficult to render into English, as evidenced in the various translations: "mercy" (KJV), "steadfast love" (NRSV), "love" (NIV), "kindness" (NJPSV). "Loyalty" is probably the best translation, as evidenced by the adjacent term "faithfulness." "Loyalty and faithfulness" is a hendiadys, a figure of speech in which two words, connected by a conjunction, connote a single idea.

Here Yahweh's relation to the people is described in terminology drawn from interpersonal relationship. The relationship could be a political covenant or "treaty," such as the treaties made between ancient Hittites and their vassal states (to be considered in chapter 18). Or it could be a covenant of friendship, such as the "sacred covenant," literally "a covenant of Yahweh," between David and Jonathan (1 Sam. 20:8).

Following Katharine Sakenfeld's treatment of the term, *hesed* refers not to a relationship in which parties are strictly equal (peers), but rather to relationships in which one party is "superior" in the sense of having more power or influence because of social position.[15] As long as Jonathan had the superior position as the king's son, it was his obligation as a friend to help David escape from Saul's wrath; but Jonathan made David promise that when their roles were reversed and David rose to power, David would manifest loyalty (*hesed*) to him (1 Sam. 20:12-17). David's obligation of friendship lasted even beyond Jonathan's death (2 Sam. 9:1, 2, 7).

Such loyalty, according to Sakenfeld, is not a virtue but rather an obligation—something to be done, which accounts for the emphasis on "faithfulness in action": to do, to maintain, to love *hesed* (Mic. 6:8). Moreover, we must not think of noblesse oblige—people of high standing behaving nobly toward inferiors, for example, the rich giving condescendingly to the poor. Rather, loyalty arises from the relationship itself, not from external law or social custom. One is free to be loyal or not to be loyal, even though the weaker party may have no other source of help.

It is significant that this term, which describes a human relationship that is strong and steadfast, is used to describe the relation between the holy God and the people. Yahweh, the holy God, acts with freedom, is not bound by any necessity (cf. Exod. 33:19: "I will have mercy on whom I will have mercy, and I will have compassion on whom I will have compassion"). In freedom God makes a commitment to the people, and is free to keep or terminate the relationship. But Yahweh is trustworthy, rich in *hesed*. God's faithfulness is firm, not fickle; it is steadfast, not capricious. This term comes close to the meaning of the New Testament term *charis*, "grace." Later we shall see how this important theological term is nuanced

---

15. Katharine Doob Sakenfeld, *Faithfulness in Action: Loyalty in Biblical Perspective*, OBT (Minneapolis: Fortress Press, 1985). See also Gordon R. Clark, *The Word "Ḥesed" in the Hebrew Bible*, JSOTSup 157 (Sheffield: JSOT Press, 1993).

in the major covenantal perspectives of the Old Testament: the Abrahamic, the Mosaic, and the Davidic.

Yahweh's Wrath

Yahweh's loyalty, however, is not indulgent love or what might be called "cheap grace." To be sure, Yahweh "forgives iniquity and sin," but Israel's betrayal of the relationship evokes divine judgment, though—as we have seen above—on a limited, terminating basis. Yahweh visits the sins of the parents on the children only to the third and the fourth generation, that is, a contemporary generation (parents, children, grandchildren—who may be living at the same time as an extended family). Yahweh's anger is holy anger, but it is brief; it does not cancel out Yahweh's "loyal love," which continues unbroken through generations without number.

> For a brief moment I abandoned you,
>   but with great compassion I will gather you;
> in overflowing wrath for a moment
>   I hid my face from you,
> but with everlasting love I will have compassion on you,
>   says the LORD [Yahweh], your Redeemer.
> —Isa. 54:7-8

The meaning of divine faithfulness is beautifully expressed in Ps. 103:6-13, a passage that echoes the ancient liturgical proclamation of the name of God quoted above (Exod. 33:6-9).

One of the great teachings of Israel's prophets is that God is characterized by divine *pathos*.[16] Unlike the deity of some Greek philosophers (e.g., Aristotle), God is not apathetic—above and beyond human suffering and historical tragedy—but is "pathetic" or, to use a better English word, "compassionate." God's faithfulness includes concern for and identification with our human condition, but—in the face of manifestations of injustice or violence—it also has the dimension of anger and hatred, as many of the prophets declared.

> I hate, I despise your festivals,
>   and I take no delight in your solemn assemblies.
>   . . .
> Take away from me the noise of your songs;
>   I will not listen to the melody of your harps.
> But let justice roll down like waters,
>   and righteousness like an everflowing stream.
> —Amos 5:21-24

To summarize: holiness is not one special characteristic of God among others, but is manifest in all of Yahweh's ways. Wrath and compassion, judgment and forgiveness are dimensions of Israel's experience of "the Holy One in your midst."

---

16. This is the thesis of Rabbi Abraham Joshua Heschel's magnificent book, *The Prophets* (New York: Harper and Row, 1962).

Notice the words of the psalmist: "But there is forgiveness with you, so that you may be feared [RSV 'revered']" (Ps. 130:4).

Guided by the biblical witness, a biblical theologian does not start with the concept of personality and say that God is a glorified personality. Rather, one begins with the holiness of God, whose reality is beyond our world, our existence, our categories, and from that starting point goes on to affirm that God's relationship to us is expressed in personal terms, even in the familial terms of parent and child.

> *How can I give you up, Ephraim?*
> *How can I hand you over, O Israel?*
>   . . .
> *My heart recoils within me;*
>   *my compassion grows warm and tender.*
> *I will not execute my fierce anger;*
>   *I will not again destroy Ephraim;*
> *for I am God and no mortal,*
>   *the Holy One in your midst,*
>   *and I will not come in wrath.*
>   —Hos. 11:8-9

Contrary to Marcionites, ancient and modern, there is no antithesis between divine wrath and divine mercy; rather, both are comprehended in the experience of the presence of "the Holy One" in our midst.[17]

17. This applies not just to the Old Testament but also to the whole Bible. A statistician has calculated that one-sixth of all the references to divine "wrath" are found in the New Testament.

8. Yahweh and the Gods

One of the tasks of Old Testament theology, as noted earlier, is to show the distinctiveness or integrity of Israel's faith in relation to the religions of the environment. There has been such tremendous advance in the study of the history of religions in the twentieth century, beginning particularly with the work of Hermann Gunkel,[1] that any theologian who ignores the religions of antiquity may be charged with theological irresponsibility. The tremendous contributions of archaeological research, such as the discovery of ancient Babylonian literature and of the Canaanite texts from ancient Ugarit, make this task unavoidable. These contributions have been highlighted in such journals as *Biblical Archaeological Review* and *Bible Review*.

Also, we have seen that the distinctive testimony of the Torah is the self-disclosure of the Holy One in the concrete historical experience of a people, Israel, and that this revelation occurs in the context of the religions of the ancient world. Israel's knowledge of God, under the personal name Yahweh, was given within the general human experience of the holy. According to the tradition, Yahweh is not a different god from the God of ancestral and primeval times, but the same God who is henceforth known and served in a different way in the Israelite cult (Exod. 6:2-3).[2]

Yahweh and the Worship of El

It is striking that the name of the people of God, *yisra'el*, contains the theophorous element *'el*, the name of the high god of the Canaanite pantheon. Indeed, the earliest reference to the Israelite people outside the Bible is in the so-called Merneptah Stele (ca. 1220 B.C.), in which an Egyptian monarch celebrated in exaggerated language his victories over various peoples: Israel is desolate, its seed is not.[3] One would expect the name of the Israelite confederacy to be linked with the element Yah, as in the case of other names like Elijah (My God is Yahweh) or Micaiah (Who is like Yahweh?). This El-name seems to indicate that the revelation of the Holy One under the name Yahweh is related to, or founded on, the previous worship of El in Canaanite culture.

Some of the old El titles are preserved and emphasized in Israelite tradition, for example, El Shaddai (Gen. 17:1; Exod. 6:2), usually translated "God Almighty," or El Elyon (Gen. 14:18-20), usually translated "God Most High."

---

1. See the brief treatment of the work of Hermann Gunkel (1862–1932) in my "Introduction" to Martin Noth's *A History of Pentateuchal Traditions* (Englewood Cliffs, N.J.: Prentice-Hall, 1972; repr. Chico, Calif.: Scholar's Press, 1981), xviii–xx.

2. See discussion of the name of God in chapter 6 above.

3. *ANET*, 378.

With an ecumenical outreach, Israel has simply taken over these ancient Canaanite epithets and identified them with Yahweh. A good illustration is the curious story in Genesis 14, which, according to literary critics, stands outside the major pentateuchal traditions. On his return from a skirmish with four kings in the Valley of Salt (Dead Sea), Abram paused at Jerusalem, a Canaanite stronghold at that time, and Melchizedek, the priest-king of Salem (Jerusalem), blessed him in the name of *'el 'elyon,* "creator of heaven and earth." This title "creator" (*qoneh*) is used of El in the Ugaritic texts, where the high god is called "creator of creatures." According to the story, Abram responds to Melchizedek's blessing in the name of "Yahweh, creator of heaven and earth" (Gen. 14:22), that is, by identifying Yahweh with El and thus bringing creation theology into the worship of Yahweh.

The Incomparability of Yahweh

One theme used in Israel's praise is that no other god can be compared with Yahweh. It is found, for instance, in the Song of the Sea, by general agreement one of the oldest poems in the Old Testament. The poet exclaims,

> *Who is like you, O* LORD *[Yahweh], among the gods?*
> *Who is like you, majestic in holiness,*
> *awesome in splendor, doing wonders?*
> —Exod. 15:11

Similar ascriptions of praise are found elsewhere in poetic literature, for instance in Deut. 33:26, which affirms that there is none like the God of Jeshurun ("upright one," a poetic Hebrew title for the people of Israel); also Ps. 89:5-8, which states that there is no god like Yahweh in the heavenly council.

In these texts, devotees regard Yahweh as superior to other gods. Language like this, also found in texts from ancient Mesopotamia and Egypt, represents the extravagance of adoration. In the Hymn to the Moon God, for instance, the worshiper says: "O Lord, who is like you, who can compare with you?"[4] Indeed, sometimes the same worshiper could ascribe incomparability to different gods, perhaps like a suitor who says the same sweet things to different objects of affection. This only goes to show that ancient Israelite poets were influenced by the poetic conventions of surrounding religions in ascribing praise to Yahweh.

Israel's borrowing from ancient religions can be traced in other areas: for instance, the appropriation of the old myth of the battle of the creator god with the powers of chaos, the theme of the kingship of God in the heavenly council, the notion that Zion is the center of the earth, and so on. From very early times, Israel's language of faith was influenced by Canaanite culture and religion.

---

4. *ANET*, 383. See also the Hymn to the Moon God, Sin, quoted below.

But it is going too far to say that Israel was essentially a breakaway Canaanite cult and that there were no essential differences between Yahweh and the gods of Canaanite culture.[5] There are affinities, yes, but also major differences.

Mythopoetic Language of Faith

The major advance in our understanding of the religions of Israel's environment has been the realization that these religions were not crudely primitive, as caricatured by earlier interpreters, but were very sophisticated and, in some respects, profound. For one thing, the religions of the ancient world employed mythopoetic language to express the experience of the divine. This was stressed years ago in a book by scholars at the University of Chicago entitled *Before Philosophy*, later reissued under the title *The Intellectual Adventure of Ancient Man*.[6] Mircea Eliade and other students of comparative religion have shown that myth provides poetic language for expressing the experience of the divine.[7]

Also, in these religions the experience of the holy was expressed not in the language of "It" (mysticism) but in the I-Thou language of prayer. This is evident when one turns to the prayers and hymns collected in what is commonly known as "the Bible of the Ancient Near East," *Ancient Near Eastern Texts Relating to the Old Testament*, edited by J. B. Pritchard. A beautiful example is a hymn to the moon god named Sin.[8]

> *O Lord, decider of the destinies of heaven and earth, whose word no one alters,*
> *Who controls water and fire, leader of living creatures, what God is like thee?*
> *In heaven who is exalted? Thou! Thou alone art exalted.*
> *On earth who is exalted? Thou! Thou alone art exalted.*

Finally, the high gods and goddesses were regarded as powers who upheld order in society in the face of the ever-threatening forces of chaos. They were arranged in a hierarchy, an orderly system, with the high god El presiding over the council of the gods. These gods dealt with all the concerns of human life: fertility of the soil, political security, military adventures, life in the household, wisdom and the arts, and so on. It is not surprising that Israel drank deeply at the wells of ancient religions.

---

5. See the book by Mark S. Smith, with its intriguing title, *The Early History of God* (San Francisco: Harper & Row, 1990), where this view is maintained.

6. Henri A. Frankfort, et al., *Intellectual Adventure of Ancient Man: An Essay on Speculative Thought in the Ancient Near East* (reprint ed., Chicago: University of Chicago Press, 1977).

7. For instance, his books *Cosmos and History: The Myth of the Eternal Return* (San Francisco: Harper & Row, 1954) and *The Sacred and the Profane: The Nature of Religion* (San Francisco: Harper & Row, 1961).

8. "Hymn to the Moon-God," *ANET*, 386.

Yahweh as the Sole Power

The distinctiveness of the Yahweh faith becomes evident when one considers the two characteristic features of the religions of antiquity and how Israel responded. The first of these is polytheism; the second, sexuality in the divine realm.[9]

That the religions of the ancient world were essentially polytheistic needs no demonstration. By contrast, the faith of Israel, at least in its mainline expression, was based on a fierce devotion to Yahweh. The first commandment of the Decalogue reads: "You shall have no other gods before [or besides] me" (Exod. 20:3); and the second commandment rejects the ancient practice of representing a god in a visual image or icon: "You shall not make for yourself an idol" in the form of anything in heaven, on earth, or the water under the earth (i.e., the whole creation). It would be excessive to claim that these are expressions of strict monotheism, although W. F. Albright used them to argue for Mosaic monotheism.[10] This incipient monotheism did not come to full expression until later in the poems of so-called Second Isaiah composed during the exile (e.g., Isa. 45:18). At the first, however, Israel confessed out of their own historical experience that Yahweh is the Sole Power and that the people are to worship Yahweh solely, as demanded in the Shema ("Hear").

> Hear, O Israel! The LORD [Yahweh] is our God, the LORD [Yahweh] alone. You shall love the LORD [Yahweh] your God with all your heart and with all your soul and with all your might.
>
> —Deut. 6:4-5 (NJPSV)

Israel is to have a single, not a divided, religious loyalty.

Yahweh's Jealousy

The reason for this demand for wholehearted devotion to Yahweh is evident in one of the aspects of Yahweh's "character" or "characteristics," as indicated in explanatory words added to the Second Commandment: "For I, the LORD [Yahweh] your God, am a jealous [zealous] God" (Exod. 20:5). Indeed, in another version of the covenant law it is said that Yahweh's name (or character) is Jealous.

> You shall worship no other god, for the LORD [Yahweh] whose name is Jealous (*qanna'*), is a jealous God (*'el qanna'*).
>
> —Exod. 34:14

This term *qanna'* is difficult to translate adequately.[11] It refers to Yahweh's energetic power and therefore could be translated "zeal," as at the conclusion of Isa. 9:7: "The zeal of the LORD [Yahweh] of hosts will do this." Also, it refers to the

---

9. In this discussion I have been influenced by a lecture given by my Princeton Seminary colleague, J. J. M. Roberts.

10. W. F. Albright, *From the Stone Age to Christianity* (2d ed.; Baltimore: John Hopkins Univ. Press, 1957).

11. On Ezekiel's use of the term, see below, chapter 16.

intensity of Yahweh's claim on the people and therefore could be translated "jealousy." However one renders it, this divine characteristic—like "wrath" or "forgiveness"—is an expression of divine holiness in the world that excites "fear" or reverence. As Gerhard von Rad remarks: "Zeal and holiness are in fact only different shaded expressions of one and the same characteristic of Yahweh."[12]

According to an old tradition embedded in Joshua 24, the ancestors of Israel were polytheists. Terah, the father of Abraham and Nahor, "served [worshiped] other gods" (Josh. 24:2). Joshua exhorts the people to "put away the gods that your ancestors served beyond the River and in Egypt," and to "serve the LORD [Yahweh]" wholeheartedly (24:14). In this narrative context the reason for exclusive devotion is also based on the character of Yahweh: Yahweh "is a jealous God" (24:19) who, in the case of defection, will display consuming wrath. In the world many "gods" compete for human loyalty, but for Israel there is only one divine power—the Sole Power who has broken into the world with saving power and demanding will.

God and the Heavenly Council
Before leaving the subject of polytheism, let us consider a major metaphor that Israel adopted to portray Yahweh's relation to the gods of the surrounding world. These gods were considered to be members of the heavenly council, over which Yahweh, the supreme God, presided as king (as in 1 Kgs. 22:19-23). This is probably the meaning of the "plural of majesty" in Gen. 1:26, "Let us make . . .": Here God is speaking to the heavenly council. This administrative council is called the council of the *bene 'elohim*, the "sons of God" or the "heavenly beings," as in the hymn of praise to Yahweh, the high God, in Psalm 89.

> *Let the heavens praise your wonders, O LORD [Yahweh],*
> *your faithfulness in the assembly of the holy ones.*
> *For who in the skies can be compared to the LORD [Yahweh],*
> *who among the heavenly beings is like the*
> *LORD [Yahweh],*
> *a God feared in the council of the holy ones,*
> *great and awesome above all that are around him?*
> —Ps. 89:5-7

The mythical language is retained in other psalms:

> *For Yahweh is a great God,*
> *and a great King above all gods.*
> —Ps. 95:3; also 103:19-20

The book of Job, one may recall, opens with a scene in the heavenly council where "the heavenly beings" or "sons of God" convene before the high God (Job 1:6).

12. Gerhard von Rad, *Old Testament Theology,* trans. D. M. G. Stalker, 2 vols. (New York: Harper & Row, 1962–65), 1:205. See his valuable discussion of this term, 203–12.

The metaphor of the heavenly council is used in different ways. In Deut. 32:8-9 we are told that Yahweh, the sovereign of the council, assigns other gods the oversight of the provinces of various peoples but reserves Israel as "Yahweh's own portion." This is one way to deal with the many gods: to put them under Yahweh's administrative sovereignty.

Another use of this motif is found in Psalm 82, where the high god El (here identified with Yahweh),[13] presides over the divine council and indicts the gods for failing to administer justice, with the result that the foundations of the earthly social order are shaking. The divine King renders a judgment that strips the gods of their divinity:

> I say, "You are gods,
>   children of the Most High, all of you;
> nevertheless, you shall die like mortals,
>   and fall like any prince."
> —Ps. 82:6-7

Here the other gods are divested of divinity and Yahweh alone is hailed as the ruler who upholds justice in the earth.

The metaphor also appears in the prophecy of Second Isaiah, which begins with the announcement of the heavenly King, Yahweh, in the heavenly council (Isa. 40:1) that Israel, having suffered for their sins, will have a future in the forgiving and comforting grace of God. In this prophecy the poet declares that the other gods are only idols, who pale into powerless artifacts before Yahweh, the universal sovereign of the nations and the creator of the ends of the earth (e.g., 40:18-20; 45:20-22). Here we stand firmly on the ground of the monotheism that was characteristic of Judaism at the time of the beginnings of Christianity.

Sexuality in the Divine Realm

We turn now to the second major feature of ancient religions: sexuality in the divine realm. Not only were there many deities, organized in a pantheon, but every major god was paired with a goddess. In the Canaanite pantheon, the high god El, the father of the gods, had his female counterpart, Asherah; Baal, the god of storm and fertility, was related to his consort Ashtarte (Ishtar); and so on. In Israel, at least in the mainline tradition represented in the Old Testament, this sexual model was rejected. Yahweh had no wife or consort. To be sure, outside the land of Israel, in the Jewish colony at Elephantine, Egypt, Yahweh seems to have had a consort, Anath, according to the Elephantine papyri of the fifth century B.C.

---

13. At least this interpretation is proper in the context of the so-called Elohistic Psalter (Psalms 43–83), where Elohim has often been substituted for Yahweh. Simon B. Parker argues, however, that originally, before this interpretation "was pressed upon the psalm" contextually, Yahweh was one of the gods, under the presidency of El or Elyon (Ps. 83:18), who protested that his colleagues (gods of the nations) were governing unjustly ("The Beginning of the Reign of God: Psalm 82 as Myth and Liturgy," *RB* 102 [1995] 532–59).

Archaeological investigation seems to indicate that, at least in popular religion, there was worship of the mother goddess in Canaan too,[14] which should not surprise us in view of polemical passages like Jer. 7:18 (the queen of heaven). If so, most evidences of this masculine-feminine relationship have been edited out in the process of the formation of the scriptural tradition. The statement of the Shema, "Yahweh is our God, Yahweh alone" (Deut. 6:4), implies that Yahweh has no female partner.

Yahweh versus Baal

Indeed, there was a special animus against one aspect of Canaanite culture: the worship of Baal and Astarte (Ishtar), the Lord and the Lady. As we know from the Ras Shamra literature, there was a Canaanite mythos (story) about the relations between Baal and his sister/consort, the maiden Anath. In the judgment of many scholars this story was dramatized or acted out in cultic rituals, which signalized the end of the old year and the springtime of a new year.

The prophet Jeremiah was especially critical of Baal religion, maintaining that Israel's turning from Yahweh to Baal was the supreme expression of the people's betrayal of the covenant loyalty. This is evident in a rehearsal of the Israelite story:

> I brought you into a plentiful land
> to eat its fruits and its good things.
> But when you entered you defiled my land,
> and made my heritage an abomination.
> The priests did not say, "Where is the LORD [Yahweh]?"
> Those who handle the law did not know me;
> the rulers transgressed against me;
> the prophets prophesied by Baal,
> and went after things that do not profit.
>
> —Jer. 2:7-8

Specifically, Jeremiah criticized family members for joining in making cakes for Ishtar, the Queen of Heaven—the mother goddess worshiped in the ancient world (Jer. 7:18).

In a world of religious tolerance and syncretism, one wonders why Israel's interpreters were so hostile to Baalism. One reason, sociological in nature, is that Baal religion was tied up with the city-state culture against which the Israelites revolted in the period of the judges and later. Elijah's contest against Baal, in the famous scene on Mount Carmel (1 Kings 18),[15] was in part a political struggle against the Phoenician mercantile economy that threatened Israel under the influence of the aggressive queen, Jezebel. Strict allegiance to Yahweh, the God of Sinai (1 Kings 19), gave Israel a sense of social identity. Another reason for

14. See William Dever, *Recent Archaeological Discoveries and Biblical Research* (Seattle: University of Washington Press, 1990), 128–66.

15. See the discussion of this passage above, chapter 5.

opposition may have been ethical in nature. Israelites, with their strict family ethic, reacted against "the iniquity of the Amorites" (Gen. 15:16), manifest in practices that they found abhorrent.[16] Finally, Israel's interpreters preferred metaphors for God derived from the political arena: king, judge, divine warrior, shepherd (often a term for leaders), prophet. In these metaphors the basic issue is not masculine-feminine relationship; indeed, a man or a woman could perform these roles, as in the case of a judge, Deborah (Judges 4–5), or Miriam, a prophet (Exod. 15:21-22); rather, these metaphors suggest a social role in a covenant or "treaty" between God and people.

Despite the animosity toward Baal and the mother goddess, Israel took over much from the very religion that the prophets opposed, including the feminine dimension of Baal's goddess. This is evident especially in the book of Hosea, where the myth of the sacred marriage is transferred to the relation between Yahweh the husband and Israel the wife (chaps. 1–3). Moreover, Israel's poets made use of the feminine or "womb" dimension to express Yahweh's compassionate nature and nurturing care.[17] Numerous other instances of motifs of Baal religion were appropriated and applied to Yahweh, for example, the epithet "rider of the clouds" (Ps. 68:4); the identification of Zion with the summit of Mount Zaphon, Baal's Olympic home on Mount Cassius, north of Ugarit (Ps. 48:1); and the slaying of the mythical monster Leviathan, "the fleeing, twisting serpent" (Isa. 27:1), which echoes the very language of the Baal epic.[18]

Nevertheless, one cannot escape the masculine way in which Yahweh is portrayed. Many of the images are masculine: divine warrior, shepherd, king, father, lord. In Hebrew Yahweh is described with masculine pronouns and verbs. Yahweh's masculinity is forcefully emphasized in such passages as:

> I, I am He
> *who blots out your transgressions for my own sake,*
> *and I will not remember your sins.*
> —Isa. 43:25

The Lord, Jehovah

Some of this masculinity has been unnecessarily introduced into biblical translations, and much of that has been corrected in recent renderings, especially the New Revised Standard Version (1989). A special example of this is the substitution

16. See "the detestable ways of the nations" listed in Deut. 18:9-13. Whether Canaanite religion advocated ritual prostitution (the acting out of the sacred marriage between Baal and his consort in a temple) is not certain. See Phyllis Bird, "Male and Female He Created Them: Gen. 1:27b in the Context of the Priestly Account of Creation," *HTR* 74 (1981) 129–59 (reprinted in *Missing Persons and Mistaken Identities: Women and Gender in Ancient Israel*, 123–54, OBT [Minneapolis: Fortress Press, 1997]).

17. In prophetic speech "the womb is a basic metaphor of divine compassion" (e.g., Hosea 11; Jer. 31:20); on female imagery see Phyllis Trible, "Nature of God in the Old Testament," *IDBSup*, 368–69.

18. See my essay, "The Slaying of the Fleeing, Twisting Serpent," in *From Creation to New Creation*, OBT (Minneapolis: Fortress Press, 1994), chap. 12.

of "the Lord" (Hebrew ʾadonai) for the personal name Yahweh, which the Christian church has adopted from the Jewish synagogue. In Jewish tradition the name was regarded as being so holy that it should not be uttered with human lips, lest one take the name of God in vain. Accordingly, the rabbis punctuated the consonants of the tetragrammaton (YHWH) with the vowels of ʾadonai, a plural of majesty meaning "lord." When consonants and vowels, so punctuated, are read together the result is "Jehovah." The hybrid form was used in early Bible translations and is still used in some circles, for example, Jehovah's Witnesses. This rendering survives in some of our hymns, such as "The Lord Jehovah Reigns" or "Guide Me, O Thou Great Jehovah." Most Bible translators, however, follow the synagogue practice: accept the Qere (what is vocalized) and say "the Lord" (ʾadonai), not the Kethib (what is written), the sacred tetragrammaton.

This solution, however, has problems. For one thing, "The LORD" is a title, not a personal name; it is as though my wife were to speak of or to me as "the professor" or "the reverend," rather than addressing me by name. Furthermore, the title is emphatically masculine. In the English language this may not be immediately evident, for "lord" echoes aristocratic language that is rather archaic; we do not use "lord," and the counterpart, "lady," any more. To us the language may sound lofty, solemn, majestic. It suggests God's sovereignty over the whole world and all creation. But in other languages the substitute for the sacred name has a shockingly masculine ring. For instance, the hymn "Holy, Holy, Holy" begins this way in Spanish:[19]

> Santo! Santo! Santo!
> Señor omnipotente . . .

No wonder that some religious bodies in the United States have debated whether to use the substitute for the name in worship!

In dealing with this problem, several options are available. (1) Whenever possible use the word "God," a practice followed in the so-called Elohistic Psalter, Psalms 43–83. Notice that Psalm 53 is practically the same as Psalm 14, except that it uses "God" (ʾelohim) instead of the sacred name. (2) Boldly use Yahweh, as does the Jerusalem Bible. As a compromise, the Book of Common Prayer retains Yahweh at only two places: Pss. 68:4 and 83:18. Also it retains "hallelujah," instead of translating "praise the LORD." (3) Use the hybrid term "Jehovah," which at least has the advantage of being a name, not a title, and is solemn and unusual.

In my judgment it is best for the church to abandon the synagogue practice. The Elohistic Psalter offers a recommendation for liturgical practice today: whenever possible use "God" instead of "The LORD." Another possibility is to use "The Holy One," "O Holy One," a usage for which there is ample biblical (e.g., Hos. 11:9b) and rabbinical precedent.

19. See the New Methodist Hymnal (Nashville: United Methodist Publishing House, 1989), no. 65. Some of this discussion is taken from my editorial, "Moving Beyond Masculine Metaphors," BR 10 (1994) 22, 57–58.

God's Condescension

Such attempts to minimize the masculinity of Yahweh are, however, only Band-Aids that in the final analysis do not cure the problem. It is helpful to call attention to feminine dimensions of Scripture that have been overlooked or covered up in the past, and we can be grateful to feminist interpreters for bringing these passages to light.[20] Yet one can only go so far in this direction; attempts to produce a gender-neutral lectionary result in jarring translations that, in the experience of some, divert attention from the worship of God to a language problem. The familiar John 3:16 is rendered this way in an "inclusive version": "For God so loved the world that God gave God's only Child, so that everyone who believes in that Child may not perish but may have eternal life."[21]

In the final analysis one has to come to terms with the masculinity of Yahweh. The Bible cannot be "depatriarchalized," to use a jawbreaker that I think Phyllis Trible coined. Here we face a problem that must be dealt with theologically—not sociologically or literarily.

In my judgment the problem must be understood in terms of Israel's fundamental witness: the inbreaking of the Holy One, known by the name Yahweh, into the world that is defined by human language, human customs, human ways of thinking. Sexuality does not belong to the holy God. God is neither male nor female, nor is God both male and female (in which case one would use the pronoun He/She). God's holiness transcends the distinctions, the divisions, the definitions of the human world. Yet when God chooses to be God in relation to a people, that self-disclosure occurs under the limitations of the human world. It occurs under the limitations of patriarchal society, for that was the kind of society that prevailed in ancient Israel and in the rest of the ancient world—for that matter, in much of the world today. It occurs under the limitations of human language, and in this case under the limitations of the Hebrew language, with its masculine-feminine grammar. It occurs under the sociological limitations of Israelite society, with its conceptions of holy war, its family structure, its geographical location, its mythopoetic view of the world. If God were not manifest under these limitations, God could not be known and could not establish relationship with a people.

Some of the great scriptural interpreters of the past, for instance, the church father John Chrysostom (ca. 344/354–407), spoke of God's accommodation to a humanity limited by its language and social relations. The Greek word for it was *synkatabasis* and the Latin was *accommodatio*—terms that refer to God's "stooping," as

---

20. See Cullen Murphy, "Women and the Bible," *Atlantic Monthly* 272 August 1993, 39–64; idem, "The Bible According to Eve," *U.S. News and World Report* (Aug. 10, 1998) 46–52. Also Alice L. Laffey, *An Introduction to the Old Testament: A Feminist Perspective* (Minneapolis: Fortress Press, 1988); Alicia Suskin Ostriker, *Feminist Revision and the Bible* (Oxford: Blackwell, 1993).

21. *The New Testament and Psalms: An Inclusive Version*, ed. Victor Roland Gold et al. (Oxford: Oxford Univ. Press, 1995). See the review by Gail R. O'Day, "Probing an Inclusive Scripture," *Christian Century* 113 (July 3–10, 1996) 692–94.

it were, to meet human beings at their own level, just as a parent gets down on the floor and "lisps" to a child.[22] This view is echoed in the foreword to the *New Jerome Biblical Commentary*, where the editors speak of "the marvelous condescension of God in transmitting His word in human language."[23]

One should not, however, take God's concession to human limitations, for the sake of being God-with-us, to establish norms that endorse patriarchal society, sanction war as a political strategy, or validate prescientific views of the universe. God's revelation cannot be trapped within the limitations of human language. When we were children, we spoke, reasoned, and acted like children (see 1 Cor. 13:11), but now that we are mature and enlightened—and for Christians that means being "mature in Christ"—we are no longer bound by earlier limitations.[24]

I think, therefore, that the desire to use inclusive language in the church has theological support; for the God whom we worship is beyond sexuality. To be sure, the language of the Bible is privileged; and the canon of Scripture is something given. It would be a mistake to try to rewrite the Bible in modern terms, or to recast the canon so that it contains other books than those given to us. The Bible is the Word of God in human words, to cite the traditional formulation, and it is our task to read the Bible in its own idiom so that, as the Holy Spirit guides, we may hear God speaking to the people of God today.

22. See Ford Lewis Battles, "God Was Accommodating Himself to Human Capacity," *Int* 31 (1977) 19–38, especially 22–26.

23. *The New Jerome Biblical Commentary*, ed. Raymond E. Brown et al. (Englewood Cliffs, N.J.: Prentice-Hall, 1990), xv, quoting the encyclical *Dei verbum*, 13.

24. On the question of masculine/feminine relationships in the whole Bible, Old and New Testaments, see the helpful discussion by Samuel Terrien, *Till the Heart Sings: A Biblical Theology of Manhood and Womanhood* (Philadelphia: Fortress Press, 1985).

9. The People of God

We have seen that the exposition of Old Testament theology begins with the self-disclosure of the holy God who chooses to enter into relationship with a particular people. This community is to be God's "treasured possession out of all the peoples" (Exod. 19:5) and to be the agent through whom divine blessing is mediated to other families of the earth (Gen. 12:3).

The God of Israel

The name of this people is "Israel." In a secondary sense the term, both in biblical times and today, may be used of a political state (e.g., the northern kingdom of Israel or the modern state of Israel). Sometimes the term "nation" (*goy*) is used, as in the divine promise to Abraham (Gen. 12:2), the "eagles' wings" passage (Exod. 19:5-6), and the "little historical credo" (Deut. 26:5)—usages that probably reflect the nationhood at the time of David. But "Israel" is primarily a sacral term that refers to a community of faith, "the people [Hebrew *'am*] of Yahweh" who are bound together by various ties (kinship, language, territory), but fundamentally by a religious devotion.[1] Yahweh is "the God of Israel," and Israel is "the people of Yahweh," as we read in the ancient poem in Judges 5 called "the Song of Deborah," dating from the premonarchic period.

> *The mountains quaked before the* LORD *[Yahweh], the One of Sinai,*
> *before the* LORD *[Yahweh], the God of Israel.*
> > —Judg. 5:5; cf. v. 11

The designation of the people as "Israel" goes back to two centuries before David, the time of the "judges" (1200–1000 B.C.). This is evident not only from the Song of Deborah, just quoted, but also from the earliest reference to this people outside the Bible, in the victory stele of Pharaoh Merneptah (ca. 1220 B.C.).[2] In view of contemporary political realities, one must emphasize that this ethnic group was called "Israel" long before it became a nation-state.

During the early monarchy Israelite storytellers projected back to the premonarchic era, or even before into the ancestral period, the ideal unity of the people as a twelve-tribe confederation, symbolized by the twelve stones in the middle of the Jordan River (Josh. 4:8-9) or the twelve pillars at the foot of Sinai (Exod. 24:4). In the final form of the Pentateuch this pan-Israelite consciousness is reflected in the stories of the ancestors, especially Jacob who, during a crucial encounter with God at the ford of the Jabbok River, received the new name Israel (Gen. 32:22-32). These stories are not straightforward history but narrative portrayals of the ups and downs of faith as the people of God, represented by their

---

1. See Ronald E. Clements, "The People of God," chap. 5 of *Old Testament Theology: A Fresh Approach* (Atlanta: John Knox, 1978).
2. On the Merneptah stele, see above, chapter 8.

ancestors, move toward the horizon of God's promised future.

This people, then, is defined primarily by relation to the God who is manifest in the "root experiences" of exodus and Sinai. Yahweh is the liberating God "who brought you out of the house of bondage" (Exod. 20:1). Yahweh is the commanding God, the "One of Sinai" (Judg. 5:5), who makes known the divine will according to which the people are to live. This God speaks in relational language: "I will be your God and you shall be my people." The formula "your God . . . my people" recurs again and again in narrative, prophetic oracles, and psalms of praise. In a profound sense, which transcends political boundaries and divisions, Paul could speak of the Christian community as being essentially related to, and indeed part of, "the Israel of God" (Gal. 6:16). Those who have the faith of Abraham are his true descendants, children of Abraham and Sarah (Rom. 4:13-25).[3]

People of the Covenant

In the Bible the primary term for expressing the relationship between God and people is "covenant." After much scholarly discussion, it has become evident that covenant is a fundamental reality in the religion of Israel.[4] The Hebrew term *berît* seems to have the root meaning of "bond, fetter," indicating a binding relationship; and the Greek term *syntheke* also suggests the idea of "binding, putting together." Another term used in the New Testament, *diatheke*, means "will, testament," pointing more to the obligatory or legal aspect of a covenant.

The theological significance of covenant, however, cannot be determined by the etymology of the Hebrew word. As in the case of words we use today, meaning is determined by use or function in particular contexts. One cannot just consult a dictionary; one has to know how a word is used in a context. Moreover, the importance of "covenant" cannot be determined by counting occurrences of the term, for the context implies the relationship even when the specific word is not used. Word count is not particularly helpful. It would be wrong to estimate the importance of the church in the Gospel of John by counting the number of times *ekklesia* occurs in the Greek text. Moreover, when we move from a historical study of Israel's traditions to an examination of the Torah in its final form, it is clear that the heart of the Pentateuch is God's covenant at Mount Sinai that summoned the people Israel, grateful for their liberation from bondage, to respond by living in obedience to God's commands. As evident in the structure of the Pentateuch, God's covenant with Israel is central and fundamental. Ronald Clements has stated the matter forcefully:

> It is from within this literary perspective that we see that the concept of covenant between God and Israel is central to the Old Testament, even though the idea of covenant may not always have been used with comparable frequency through all ages of Israelite-Jewish religion.[5]

3. See above, chapter 1.
4. See E. W. Nicholson, *God and His People* (Oxford: Clarendon, 1986).

In the light of this "canonical" approach we see that "the Pentateuch is a covenant literature." Clements continues:

> When therefore we speak of an Old Testament, with the word "testament" arising, by way of the Latin *testamentum*, as translation of the word "covenant" (Hebrew *berît*), this is in all essentials entirely appropriate. The Old Testament is a covenant literature because it recounts as its focal point the making of the covenant between God and Israel, and central to its structure is the presentation of the demands that fall upon Israel as a consequence of this covenant.[6]

God's Covenants with Israel

As we have seen earlier, the theologian Walther Eichrodt took the word "covenant," understood in the broad sense of "relationship," as the organizing principle of his great work on Old Testament theology. There is much truth in his covenantal approach, which emphasizes the copula "and": God *and* Israel, God *and* the world, God *and* the individual.[7] In the Old Testament, however, the term "covenant" does not have a single meaning, nor is it a theological umbrella that covers everything (the metaphor is noticeably absent, for instance, in wisdom literature). Indeed, there are several covenants between God and Israel, to say nothing of the universal, ecological covenant with Noah, embracing all peoples, all nonhuman creatures, and the earth itself (Genesis 9). As noted previously, Paul apparently recognized this plurality of covenants when at the beginning of his important discussion of the relation between the two communities, Jewish and Christian (Romans 9–11), he said: "They are Israelites, and to them belong . . . the covenants" (Rom. 9:4).[8]

In this study I propose to concentrate on three covenants: the Abrahamic covenant set forth classically in Genesis 17; the Mosaic covenant found in the book of Exodus and elaborated in Deuteronomy; and the Davidic covenant formulated in 2 Samuel 7 and echoed in the book of Psalms (e.g., Psalms 89, 132) and the Chronicler's Work (1–2 Chronicles). Each of these great figures of Israel's history—Abraham, Moses, David—stands for one of three ways of formulating or symbolizing the relationship between God and people.[9]

These three covenants are each covenants of grace, for they rest on the gracious initiative and superior status of the divine covenant maker. A parity covenant, or covenant between equals, does not make sense, for God and human beings are not on the same level. To claim equality with God, or even to be like God, is the height of presumption or sin, as we are told in the paradise story (Gen. 3:5). The difference between God and human beings is emphasized in a crucial passage in the book of Hosea: "I am God, not a human being, the Holy One in

---

5. Clements, *Old Testament Theology*, 119.
6. Ibid.
7. See the discussion of Eichrodt's covenantal theology, above, chapter 3, pp. 18–20.
8. In the above discussion (chapter 4) I noted that some textual witnesses read singular "covenant" here, but the plural is accepted by most translators.
9. See the discussion above, chapter 4.

your midst" (Hos. 11:9). If the holy God enters the world and establishes relationship with human beings, the divine-human relationship will be one of *ḥesed*, to recall our previous discussion, that is, a relationship based on the gracious commitment and spontaneous loyalty of the stronger party to the weaker.

Each of these three covenant formulations symbolizes the relationship between God and people in a different manner. Each exhibits a particular theological accent, a distinctive symbolic vista. Yet all of them are necessary for expressing the presence and activity of the holy God in the midst of the people.

Lest there be any misunderstanding, I should state again that in this discussion I do not understand "covenant" as a theological concept. Rather, a covenant formulation is a pattern of symbolization, a linguistic gestalt, or—to use an expression of Walter Brueggemann—an "imaginative construal."[10] The Scriptures that deal with these covenantal perspectives are artistic writings—story, poetry, song— that invite us into a literary "world," in which the relationship between God and people is expressed in the language of imagination. This artistic construal, however, does not mean that God appears in an imaginative world, rather than in the flesh-and-blood world of historical reality, as Docetists later supposed regarding God's revelation in Christ. To be sure, God is present in Israel's concrete history, in the "root experiences" of exodus and Sinai; but God's holy presence in Israel's historical experience is expressed in symbolic language, in covenantal formulations that appeal to our religious imagination.

Dialectical Contradictions

In *God's Presence in History*, Emil Fackenheim helps us to understand our theological task. In the community of faith, he points out, the people reenact the "root experience" of the presence of the Holy God in our midst with a sense of immediacy and personal involvement. They relive the experience in the celebration of worship, or they act it out in their daily lifestyle. The Bible is not fundamentally a book of theology but an "unfolding drama" in which we are invited to be coactors with God. The task of the theologian, however, is to stand back from immediate involvement and reflect on the "root experience"; "and the moment such reflection occurs," says Fackenheim, "it reveals the root experience to be shot through with at least three all-pervasive, dialectical contradictions."[11]

The first dialectical contradiction is divine transcendence and divine immanence (or "involvement"). How can the God who is beyond this world, and therefore unlimited in power, be involved in the limitations of the human world? The second dialectical contradiction is divine sovereignty and human freedom. God's power is so great that it could overwhelm and crush human freedom. How then can a manifestation of God's holy presence issue in a call to decision and respon-

10. See Walter Brueggemann's Lyman Beecher Lectures, *Finally Comes the Poet: Daring Speech for Proclamation* (Minneapolis: Fortress Press, 1989).

11. Emil Fackenheim, *God's Presence in History: Jewish Affirmations and Philosophical Reflections* (New York: New York Univ. Press, 1970), 16–19.

sibility? The third contradiction is between the universal sovereignty of God over all history and creation and the particularity of God's revelation to Israel. How can the Sole Power manifest at the Reed Sea be the God of all peoples?

Of course, beneath all of these polarities is the problem of evil, which came to be expressed as the problem of theodicy. How can the God who is transcendent but involved, all-powerful yet granting human freedom, universal but active with liberating power in the life of a people—how can this God tolerate the evil that we perceive in history and nature? As we shall see, all of Israel's covenant theologies—Abrahamic, Mosaic, Davidic—proved to be inadequate in the face of the enormity of the problem of evil that impacted Israel with shattering force in the time of the destruction of Jerusalem and the exile of the people (587 B.C. and later).

In our theological reflection we shall discover that these dialectical contradictions, or paradoxes, are evident in each of the three construals of God's covenant with the people. These paradoxes are present in each covenantal perspective; yet each one gives special expression to one of the polarities.

1. The Abrahamic covenant deals with the relation between the universal and the particular. The God who is holy, who is creator of the cosmos and the Lord of all being, human and nonhuman, is known to and through a particular people—the descendants of Abraham and Sarah.

2. The Mosaic covenant deals with the relation between God's sovereignty and human freedom: the God who has all power in heaven and earth, who holds the whole cosmos in almighty grasp, calls people to decision and to responsible partnership with God.

3. The Davidic covenant deals with the mystery of divine transcendence and immanence: the God who is far off, the high and Holy One who inhabits eternity, is near to the humble and the contrite, and indeed is Immanuel, "God with us."

It is tempting to choose just one of these covenantal perspectives; some liberation theologians, for instance, are critical of the Davidic covenant and favor the Mosaic perspective. But in the Old Testament all of these covenantal perspectives interact and are interrelated. In the final analysis, all are necessary for expressing the relationship between God and people.

Thus diversity of theological perspective is not something that a theologian seeks to overcome by imposing unity on diverse materials; rather, scriptural pluralism helps us to deal with the paradoxes or "dialectical contradictions" inherent in the experience of the presence of the holy God in the midst of a people. In this sense, *e pluribus unum* (out of many, one) is still a good motto for a biblical theologian.[12]

---

12. See John Goldingay, *Theological Diversity and the Authority of the Old Testament* (Grand Rapids: Eerdmans, 1987), who considers several ways of seeing that the various voices of the Old Testament are not in opposition to each other but belong together.

PART II
YAHWEH COVENANTS
WITH THE PEOPLE

A. THE ABRAHAMIC COVENANT

Yahweh appeared to Abram and said to him:
"I am El Shaddai [God Almighty];
walk before me and be blameless!
I will establish my covenant
between me and you,
and I will make you exceedingly fruitful!"

GENESIS 17:2 (BWA)

10. The History
of God's Covenants

When one seeks to understand the theological perspectives of the Bible, much is to be said for starting at the beginning, with the book of Genesis, and following the canonical sequence. Of course, many readers have bravely tried this approach and have often gotten bogged down, usually in the book of Leviticus. The main reason for lack of theological excitement is that many readers fail to grasp the total context in which the books function.

Theological Context

The importance of context is evident when one turns to the first canonical unit of the Old Testament, the Pentateuch or Torah. In the Priestly perspective that governs the Torah, especially the first four books, the unfolding narrative is punctuated by three divine covenants, each of which is termed an "everlasting covenant" (*berît 'olam*).[1] Each covenant has its own character and scope; and each prepares for, and provides the foundation for, the next. By dividing the biblical narrative into successive periods, characterized by a special covenant, Priestly writers provide an imaginative vision of a history that sweeps from the dawn of creation to the climactic revelation at Mount Sinai, when God condescended to "tabernacle" in the midst of the people. Read in this "periodized history," the individual narratives have a fuller, larger meaning.[2]

A Periodized Covenant History

Let us survey the marvelous theological vista presented in the history of God's covenants (see fig. 3).

Period I
  The first period extends from creation to the end of the primeval history (Genesis 1–11). Like other ancient traditions,[3] the period is divided in two by a catastrophic flood, an event that marks the transition from the antediluvian times

---

1. The book of Deuteronomy, except for the last chapter, does not belong essentially to the Priestly history but serves as a bridge to the ensuing Deuteronomistic history (Joshua through 2 Kings). See further my discussion of "The Priestly Point of View," in *Understanding the Old Testament* (abridged paperback 4th ed.; Englewood Cliffs, N.J.: Prentice-Hall, 1997), 454–65.

2. On the Priestly periodization of history, see Frank M. Cross, "The Priestly Work," in *Canaanite Myth and Hebrew Epic: Essays in the History of the Religion of Israel* (Cambridge: Harvard Univ. Press, 1973), 298–300.

3. For instance, the Sumerian King List, which goes back to the second millennium B.C., begins with an antediluvian preamble that is followed by a list of kings who ruled "after the flood." See *ANET*, 265.

FIGURE 3. *The Priestly Periodization of History*

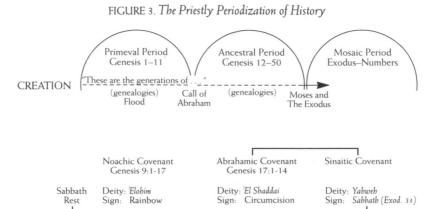

to the times "after the flood" (Gen. 10:1). The account of the covenant with Noah and his family after the flood, in Gen. 9:1-17, is one of the important theological passages in the book of Genesis, comparable to the Priestly creation story (Gen. 1:1—2:3) and to the account of the covenant with Abraham and Sarah (Genesis 17), passages to be considered later.

The Noachic covenant is specifically designated as a *berît 'olam*, an "everlasting covenant" or covenant in perpetuity (Gen. 9:16). This is a covenant of "grace alone" (*sola gratia*) because its permanence is based solely on God's pledge, guaranteed by a solemn divine oath, and therefore is not conditioned or threatened by human behavior. Notice that the flood story ends with Yahweh's covenantal promise that never again would such a catastrophe strike the earth, even though "the inclination of the human heart is evil from youth" (Gen. 8:21).

Moreover, the Noachic covenant is a universal covenant that embraces all human beings—the descendants of Noah and his wife. This covenant is not made exclusively with Israel, the people of God, but with "all peoples that on earth do dwell," as we sing in a well-known doxology. Further, it is an ecological covenant that includes the whole nonhuman creation ("every living creature of all flesh," Gen. 9:15) and the earth itself (9:13). This universal covenant, which demands reverence for life, both animal and human, has tremendous implications for global ethics today, as we shall see (chapter 11).

Period II

The second period in the history of God's covenants extends from Abraham to Moses, the mediator of the Sinai covenant. Here the biblical story moves from the general to the specific, from humanity and the whole earth (*'erets*) to the people

Israel and the land given to Israel (*erets yisra'el*). As we shall see in greater detail (chapter 12), this is a promissory covenant that looks toward the future, guaranteeing the promise of a great posterity, the grant of the land of Canaan, and the presence of God, who may be invoked by the personal name Yahweh.

Viewed in Priestly perspective, the Mosaic covenant does not supersede previous covenants. The universal Noachic covenant provides the ecumenical context for the particular covenant with the ancestors of the people Israel: Abraham, Isaac, and Jacob. Moreover, the Mosaic covenant does not replace the Abrahamic covenant but is based on it, just as the Abrahamic covenant presupposed the Noachic covenant. Indeed, God's special revelation in the time of Moses is regarded as an endorsement or fulfillment of the Abrahamic covenant, which God "remembered" when the descendants of Jacob were oppressed in Egypt (Exod. 2:24; cf. Lev. 26:45). It was "the God of the ancestors" who spoke to Moses at the burning bush, assuring him that God had not forgotten the promises of old and that God had "come down" to rescue the people from slavery and to lead them into the land promised, "a land flowing with milk and honey" (Exod. 3:1-12).

Period III

In Priestly perspective, the Sinai covenant, within which the people live and worship, is regarded as "an everlasting covenant" (Exod. 31:16). Indeed, the whole cultus introduced at Sinai is the God-given means of grace that enables a holy people to live in the presence of the holy God on a holy land. As set forth in the book of Leviticus, sacrifices are provided for the expiation of sin and reconciliation with God (see later, chapter 14).

Thus the goal toward which this covenant history moves, from the beginning of creation, is the tabernacling of the holy God in the midst of a worshiping community or "congregation" (*edab*). The people Israel are bound to God in an "everlasting covenant," or "a commitment for all time" (Lev. 24:8, NJPSV). Under the influence of the Mosaic covenant, to be considered later (part II.B, chapters 17–22), the everlasting covenant, on the human side, has a conditional element. The people may "break" this covenant by spurning God's commandments and therefore suffer divine judgment (Lev. 26:15); but *if* the people confess, and make amends for, their iniquity and that of their ancestors, Yahweh will stand by the everlasting commitment made to the ancestors.

> Yet for all that, when they are in the land of their enemies, I will not spurn them utterly and break my covenant with them; for I am the LORD [Yahweh] their God; but I will remember in their favor the covenant with their ancestors whom I brought out of the land of Egypt in the sight of the nations, to be their God; I am the LORD [Yahweh].
>
> —Lev. 26:44-45

Covenant Signs

In the movement of the covenant history, the three covenants are accompanied by three signs. (1) The rainbow of the Noachic covenant (a universal phenomenon after a storm) signifies that the whole realm of nature and of animal and human life are embraced within God's promise. (2) Circumcision is required in the Abrahamic covenant as a sign of membership in the covenant community. This rite is binding only on males, though the covenant itself is made with a family, headed by Abraham and Sarah. Female circumcision, still practiced today in some parts of the world, is not sanctioned. (3) The Sabbath of the Sinaitic covenant (Exod. 31: 12-17), anticipated in the "sabbath rest" at the end of the creation story, is the sign of the Sinai covenant. Thus in a beautiful *inclusio* or envelope construction, the Sabbath climax of the Sinai story recalls and recapitulates the beginning at creation and binds the whole scheme together.

> Therefore the Israelites shall keep the sabbath, observing the sabbath throughout their generations, as a perpetual covenant [*berît ʿolam*]. It is a sign forever [*leʿolam*] between me and the people of Israel that in six days the LORD [Yahweh] made heaven and earth, and on the seventh day he rested, and was refreshed.
>
> —Exod. 31:16-17

Theological Nuances

Also, in Priestly perspective each of these covenant periods is characterized by a special theological emphasis. In the period from creation to Abraham, the narrator uses the general name for deity, *elohim,* in order to stress God's cosmic and worldwide sovereignty. Thus the biblical story opens with "In the beginning Elohim. . . ."[4] In the period from Abraham to Sinai, the characteristic divine epithet is El Shaddai, as at the time of the Abrahamic covenant:

> The LORD [Yahweh] appeared to Abram, and said to him: "I am God Almighty [*el shaddai*]; walk before me, and be blameless."
>
> —Gen. 17:1

The divine promise "to be God to you and your offspring after you" in an everlasting covenant (Gen. 17:7) anticipates the revelation at Sinai when God is present to the people, known and invoked by the personal name that signifies the I-Thou relationship.

> God [*elohim*] also spoke to Moses and said to him: "I am the LORD [Yahweh]. I appeared to Abraham, Isaac, and Jacob as God Almighty [*el shaddai*], but by my name 'The LORD' [YHWH] I did not make myself known to them."
>
> —Exod. 6:2-3

Thus the biblical narrator presents a wonderful vista of three periods, characterized by three covenants, three signs, and three divine names. The whole story from creation to Sinai is anchored in the worship of God who is creator and redeemer.

---

4. The statement in Gen. 4:26b, "At that time [the time of Adam's grandson] people began to invoke the name of Yahweh," comes from an Old Epic tradition that Priestly editors have appropriated and allowed to stand, despite its tension with their overall presentation.

In the primeval history the final Priestly editors have reworked an Old Epic tradition (the sources J and E of historical criticism), bringing it into the periodized history that moves in a succession of covenants toward the Sinai realization of God's plan. At four crucial points editorial interpreters have presented distinctively Priestly passages that, like the pillars of a vast bridge, connect creation with the Sinai revelation (see fig. 4).

FIGURE 4. *Priestly Pillars*

CREATION	NOACHIC COVENANT	ABRAHAMIC COVENANT	SINAI THEOPHANY
Gen. 1:1—2:3	Gen. 9:1-17	Gen. 17	Exod. 25–32, 35–40; Lev. 1–17; Num. 1–10

The hand of the Priestly interpreters is especially heavy in the exodus and Sinai materials, for in their view this is the climax toward which the whole history moves: the tabernacling presence of the holy God in the midst of the people.

Levels of Meaning

In their theological presentation Priestly theologians have handed on what they received, the Old Epic tradition. How this epic tradition arose is a question that, properly speaking, lies beyond the bounds of Old Testament theology. By the time the tradition was edited by Priestly editors, it had undoubtedly received *literary* form. As a result of the incorporation of the epic account into the Priestly framework, stories found in the history of God's covenants have several levels of meaning. Echoes of voices of the past are heard in the final canonical rendition, and one must take these into account in theological interpretation.

As an illustration, consider the story of the testing of Abraham in Genesis 22.[5] The Old Epic story deals with the problem of human faith: How can one believe God's word of promise when all the evidence, humanly speaking, seems to deny any possibility of fulfillment? At first, Abraham and Sarah have no child: Sarah is barren. Yet Abraham believes (puts his faith in) God's promise, despite lack of evidence (15:1-6). Then, when the couple finally have a child in their old age, God strangely asks that this son, the only link to the future fulfillment of the promise of a great posterity, be placed on the altar of sacrifice.

Modern women reading this story are perplexed, and men should be too, by the fact that Sarah, Abraham's wife, is completely left out of the story. Abraham does not even consult her about the strange command to offer up *their* son as a sacrifice, but strikes out on his own.[6] This is a shocking weakness of the story, from

5. See my essay, "Abraham, Friend of God," *Int* 42 (1988) 353–66.
6. See Cullen Murphy, "Women and the Bible," *Atlantic Monthly* 272 (August 1993) 39–64, especially 39–45, 48, 50–55, 58, 60, 62–64.

our point of view. The story is told from a patriarchal vantage, evident in part by the fact that the family line is traced through the firstborn son, Isaac. Considering the story from its own presuppositions, however, the intention is to portray the ambiguities and perplexities of the experience of faith. The narrator leads the reader into the dimension of the absurd. The God who gives the promise of a future actually asks that the bridge from the present to the future—Abraham's only son—be destroyed, to show that Abraham's faith is in God, not in the promise itself.

Priestly interpreters, however, are more interested in the theological (objective) aspect of the divine promise than in the experiential (subjective) dimension of faith. To Abraham and Sarah God has made an irrevocable promise of land and posterity, guaranteed by a covenant oath based on God's holiness. Just as the land was given to them as an "everlasting possession," one that cannot be taken away despite historical developments, so God has made a binding commitment to the ancestors and their descendants. Israel will have a future, despite all evidence to the contrary.

Therefore, at the beginning of the exodus story Priestly interpreters observe, in connection with Pharaoh's attempt to reduce the Israelite population and even to exterminate the people, that God "remembered" the covenant with Abraham, Isaac, and Jacob. Despite the ups and downs of human experience, the ambiguities and perplexities of faith, the everlasting covenant with Abraham and Sarah stands firm. God's covenant is "a commitment for all time" (Lev. 24:8, NJPSV).

The Priestly Torah in a Nutshell

To summarize: In the Priestly view, the successive periods of revelation were marked by a sequence of names for the deity. In the first era, with its ecumenical horizon, the deity was known as *'elohim* ("God"). In the second period, the deity was known to Abraham by the special name *'el shaddai* (often translated "God Almighty"). Not until the third (Mosaic) period was the cultic name (*YHWH*) introduced (Exod. 6:2-3)—a name so holy that it must not be taken in vain, so ineffable that no layperson could pronounce its sacred syllables. Thus the disclosure of the sacred name, at the very climax of God's historical design, inaugurated a new and special relationship between God and Israel. In this Priestly view the goal toward which everything moves is the constitution of Israel as a cultic community (*'edah*)—a community called to serve God by following the laws that order life and worship. In short, Israel is a holy people living in the presence of the holy God. The Priestly view of the historical movement from Creation through a succession of covenants to the realization of the divine purpose is illustrated in figure 3, "The Priestly Periodization of History" (p. 82).[7]

---

7. This summarizing paragraph and figure 3 are from my *Understanding the Old Testament*, 4th ed. abridged, by Anderson, B.W., © 1998. The figure is reprinted by permission of Prentice-Hall, Inc., Upper Saddle River, N.J.

11. Creation and the Noachic Covenant

The first segment of the periodized history of God's covenants (Genesis 1–11) sets before us the spacious vista of creation. The story extends from the creation of heaven and earth (the universe) to the near return of the earth to primeval chaos in the time of the flood, then on to the new beginning afterward, signalized by God's universal covenant with humankind, nonhuman creatures, and the earth itself (Genesis 9). In its present form this primeval history—better, primeval story—is a preface to the special history/story that begins with Abraham and Sarah.

That the God whom Israel worships is the creator of heaven and earth is the fundamental doctrine that Christianity received from Judaism and that both communities of faith announce to the world. The doctrine received its classical formulation in the so-called Priestly creation story (Gen. 1:1—2:3), and is elaborated in hymns of praise (Psalms 33, 104), prophetic doxologies (Amos 5:8-9; Isa. 40:21-26, 28), and wisdom reflection (Prov. 8:22-31).

Creatio ex Chaos

According to the Genesis creation story, God created the universe by executive command, without any resistance or struggle. Moreover, God created out of chaos. The earth was once *tohu wabohu*, a "vast waste" (REB) or "formless void" (NJB). The expression in Gen. 1:2 refers to primeval disorder, which persists even after God's creative work wrought order and harmony (a matter to which we shall return later). The view of *creation ex nihilo*, set forth in late Jewish writings (e.g., 2 Macc. 7:28) and early Christian doctrine, is not supported explicitly by the biblical text.

The formulation "creation out of chaos" is influenced by the mythopoetic view of creation, found in ancient myths.[1] In my judgment, the use of the chaos motif in the biblical story does not justify the view that originally the Creator had "mastery" only over chaos and that God will not have complete sovereignty until the eschatological consummation.[2] That view may be supported by a putative early version of the biblical story that was influenced by the Babylonian myth of the creator's battle with the powers of chaos. In the final biblical form of the creation

---

1. See the classic work of Hermann Gunkel, "The Influence of Babylonian Mythology Upon the Biblical Creation Story," translated and abridged in *Creation in the Old Testament*, ed. B. W. Anderson, IRT 6 (Minneapolis: Fortress Press, 1984), chap. 1. Also my work, *Creation versus Chaos: The Reinterpretation of Mythical Symbolism in the Bible* (Minneapolis: Fortress Press, 1987).

2. This view is advocated by Jon Levenson, *Creation and the Persistence of Evil* (San Francisco: Harper & Row, 1988). See, however, my essay, "The Persistence of Chaos in God's Creation," *BR* 12, no. 1 (1996) 19, 44, which is used in part in this discussion.

story, however, despite vestigial remains of the old myth, the prevailing view is that God creates in absolute sovereignty.

One should note that at no point does the biblical narrator equate chaos with evil. Rather, chaos is primeval disorder symbolized by turbulent waters and uncreated darkness. Order and chaos belong to the creation that, as a whole, the Creator perceives to be "very good" (Gen. 1:31). Since chaos persists, it is proper to say that God continues to create, inviting human beings, made in the divine image, into the ongoing creative process. The Genesis portrayal is compatible with a new revolution in science in which the Newtonian view of a static, ordered cosmos is superseded by that of a complex, dynamic universe in which order and chaos belong together.[3]

Furthermore, in the mythopoetic view the triumphant Creator establishes boundaries for the chaos that continues. According to the magnificent creation poem, Psalm 104, which in some respects parallels the Genesis creation story, the poet uses the mythical language rather freely to portray God "rebuking" and driving back the restive, insurgent waters of chaos and assigning them their place in the orderly scheme of creation. In Genesis 1, by contrast, there is no resistance; the chaotic element is completely in God's control. Creation by the word, indicated by the command execution formulae ("God said . . . and it was so"), expresses God's absolute sovereignty (see Psalm 33). Israel's witness to the sole sovereignty of God and the essential goodness of God's creation led inevitably to the problem of God's justice (theodicy), an issue to which we shall return when treating wisdom literature (Ecclesiastes and Job).

Creation in the Beginning

Some translators tone down the familiar translation of Gen. 1:1, "in the beginning God created the heavens and the earth," by construing these words as part of a temporal clause that leads up to the main sentence in either v. 2 or, more likely, v. 3. So translated, the text may be taken to refer to a process of creation, not an absolute beginning. This translation has some support by analogy with other ancient creation texts (e.g., the Babylonian creation epic, which begins with a temporal clause, "When above, . . ." Akkadian *enuma elish*). Translators vacillate on this matter. On the one hand, in the RSV, for instance, the first word of the Hebrew Bible (*berēʾshith*) is construed to refer to a definite, absolute beginning ("In the beginning God created the heavens and the earth"; cf. John 1:1), but the NRSV regards this as part of a temporal clause ("In the beginning when God began to create . . ."). On the other hand, the NEB translates the opening words of Genesis as a temporal clause, "When God began to create, . . ." whereas the successor REB reverts to the traditional translation. Both translations of the Hebrew are grammatically possible. But stylistic study of the Genesis creation story favors taking

---

3. James Gleick, *Chaos: Making a New Science* (New York: Penguin, 1987). "To some physicists chaos is a science of process rather than state, of becoming rather than being" (prologue, p. 3).

the first words of the Bible as an absolute declarative sentence, as in the Greek Bible (Septuagint), our earliest hermeneutical witness.[4]

Discussions of creation and science must take into account differences of language. The Genesis storyteller uses language metaphorically, drawing deeply on ancient mythopoetic views; by contrast, scientific accounts use language that aims for exact description. Though using different kinds of language, the scientist and the theologian have common interests. Some maintain that the "big-bang" theory, which holds that the universe was created in a fiery explosion at a sharply defined instant some sixteen billion years ago, is compatible with the Genesis creation story, which opens by portraying the beginning of creation in a cosmic flash of light.[5]

The Wonderful Order of Creation

The picture presented in the Priestly creation story is one of symmetrical order and esthetic harmony. All of God's creatures, from the sun and moon that measure the times to the animals that creep on earth, have a particular function in the wondrous whole. Something marvelous happens during the second part of the creation drama: the emergence of biological life (*nephesh hayyah*, "living being[s]," 1:20), characterized by the capacity to move in a particular medium (water, air, land) and to reproduce its kind or species. The highest form of *nephesh hayyah*, according to the story, is 'adam, constituted sexually as "male and female." As in the case of animals (1:22), the primary purpose of heterosexuality is reproduction: "Be fruitful, multiply. . . ." God's blessing releases the sexual fertility that makes future generation of species possible.

In a sense, there is equality between human and nonhuman creatures in God's creation. Both are *nephesh hayyah*, living being (1:20; 2:7, 19); both are heterosexual creatures who receive a blessing to reproduce their kind (1:22, 28); both share the same earthly habitat and depend on earth's regularities and resources; and both are valued in God's sight. Yet equality of status before God does not mean equality of position and responsibility. To quote the well-known words from George Orwell's *Animal Farm*, "All animals are equal, but some animals are more equal than others." In the biblical story, the being who is "more equal" than other earth creatures is 'adam, "human being" or humankind.

Made in the Image of God

The creation story reaches a climax with God's solemn resolution, announced in the heavenly council ("Let us . . ."), to do something special.

---

4. See my essay, "A Stylistic Study of the Biblical Creation Story," reprinted in *From Creation to New Creation*, OBT (Minneapolis: Fortress Press, 1994), chap. 3.

5. See my essay, "Theology and Science: Cosmic Dimensions of the Creation Account in Genesis," in *From Creation to New Creation*, chap. 6.

> Let us make 'adam [humanity] in our image, after our likeness,
> and let them have dominion
>   over the fish of the sea,
>   over the birds of the air,
>   over the cattle and over all wild beasts,
>   and over all crawling things that move on the earth.
>   —Gen. 1:26 (BWA)

In the execution of this resolution, God creates humankind as "male and female," showing that both sexes share the divine image. Their special status in God's creation entitles them to exercise a special task. Therefore, immediately after the creation of "male and female" in God's image, they are given a divine blessing that empowers them to have dominion together over the earth.

> Be fertile, multiply,
>   fill the earth and subdue it!
> Rule over the fish of the sea,
>   over the birds of the air,
>   and over every living creature that moves
>   on the earth.
>   —Gen. 1:28 (BWA)

Here it is clear that the primary purpose of sex is procreation, as in the case of nonhuman creatures. Sex for pleasure in an I-Thou relationship is not mentioned, though other biblical texts suggest that this is also an aspect of the goodness of God's creation (e.g., the Song of Songs). In the Genesis story, the expansion of human population through sexual procreation is a manifestation of human dominion over the earth. By contrast, in the Babylonian Atrahasis myth from the eighteenth century B.C., the gods are disturbed by the threat of growth in the human population and seek to place limits on it.[6]

The Genesis text was written for a time when overpopulation was not a problem. The command to "be fruitful, multiply, and fill the earth," the first commandment in the Bible, has been fulfilled, for today there is scarcely a habitable spot on earth that lacks human beings. Today the exercise of human dominion requires the commandment to restrain population growth and save the planet for posterity.[7]

The expressions "image of God" and "likeness of God" occur only in the Priestly recension of the primeval history (but cf. Isa. 40:18). These terms refer primarily to function or role. They indicate that 'adam is created to be God's *representative* on earth, just as a child represents the parent on a family estate. A helpful parallel usage occurs in ancient Babylonian and Egyptian texts that describe the king

---

6. On the limitation of population growth in the Atrahasis Myth, see Norbert Lohfink, S.J., "The Future: Biblical Witness to the Ideal of a Stable World," in *Great Themes from the Old Testament*, trans. R. Walls (Edinburgh: T. & T. Clark, 1982), 183–201.

7. See Bill McKibben, "The Case for Single-child Families," *Christian Century* 115, no. 15 (1998) 498–504, adapted from his book *Maybe One: A Personal and Environmental Argument for Single-Child Families* (New York: Villard Books, 1998).

in similar language. For instance, in an Egyptian text the deity addresses Pharaoh Amenophis III:

> You are my beloved Son, produced from my members,
> my image which I have established on the earth.
> I have made you rule the earth in peace.[8]

Here the emphasis is on the king's role in the royal office, his function ex officio. Analogously, in the biblical texts the image is not something *in* human nature (reason, will, conscience, immortal soul), but refers to the bodily, social *role* of 'adam, consisting of male and female. Viewed in this perspective, 'adam is not an autonomous being, at liberty to rule the earth arbitrarily or violently. On the contrary, human dominion is to be exercised wisely and benevolently so that God's dominion over the earth may be manifest in care for the earth and in the exercise of justice.

The theme of human dominion over the works of the Creator is echoed in the exquisite Psalm 8. Looking up at the night skies, where the stars twinkle like diamonds and the moon shines in queenly splendor, this poet marvels that God, who created the heavenly bodies, is actually concerned about tiny human beings and, more than that, draws them into God's cosmic administration, giving them dominion over "the works of [God's] hands."

> When I look up at your heavens, the work of your fingers,
> at the moon and the stars you have set in place,
> what is a frail mortal, that you should be mindful of him,
> a human being, that you should take notice of him?
> Yet you have made him little less than a god,
> crowning his head with glory and honour.
> You make him master over all that you have made.
> —Ps. 8:3-6 (REB)

This "coronation" does not give human beings license to violate God's creation or to misuse its resources; rather, they are called to be God's vice-regents in the earthly sphere of divine sovereignty.

The modern notion of a split between nature and history, which is said to be the basis of the subjection or exploitation of nature for human purposes,[9] receives no support from the biblical creation story. What we regard as two discrete spheres, history and nature or material and spiritual, are one realm in God's creation. Therefore, the creatures of the natural world take part in praising God (Ps. 98:7-9: "the floods clap their hands" and "the hills sing together for joy"), even

---

8 . Ancient texts are quoted and discussed in my essay, "Human Dominion over Nature," reprinted in *From Creation to New Creation*, chap. 7.

9. This thesis is set forth in a famous essay by Lynn White Jr., "The Biblical Roots of Our Ecological Crisis," which first appeared in *Science* 155 (1967) 1203–7; I discuss it in "Human Dominion over Nature," chap. 7 in *From Creation to New Creation*.

as nature is involved in the human tragedy (see the flood story) and "groans in travail" with human beings (Rom. 8:22-23).[10]

The Corruption of God's Creation

In the book of Genesis, creation is not presented as an independent "doctrine" but belongs in the context of an extended story that moves from the beginning toward the fulfillment of God's purpose for all creatures and the whole creation. In this narrative perspective, creation is embraced within God's covenant, specifically the Noachic covenant.

The primeval history displays a structure and movement that, like other ancient versions of mythical beginnings, proceeds from creation to flood to a new beginning after the flood. The major divisions are "before the flood" and "after the flood" (10:1). The continuity of history from the primeval history into the ancestral history is indicated by the sequence of genealogies (the so-called begats). Five times in the primeval history and five in the ancestral story the unfolding narrative of Genesis is punctuated with the recurring formula, "these are the generations of. . . ."[11] The formula occurs first at the introduction to the story of paradise (Gen. 2:4a), suggesting that this is the real beginning of the primeval history. The Priestly creation story, which stands apart from this scheme, shows that the presuppositions for the human story and the history of nature are given in God's original creation.

Those materials that are generally accredited to the Priestly tradition do not mention a "fall" of human beings or a "fall" of nature. After the creation, the divine image continued to characterize human beings (Gen. 5:1-2). By incorporating episodes from Old Epic tradition into their presentation (Genesis 2–3; 4; 6:1-4), however, Priestly theologians have given a realistic picture of the world in which we live. The world does not manifest unambiguously the goodness and harmony of God's creation; rather, it has been corrupted by human violence, as stated in the introduction to the Priestly reworking of the old flood story.

> Now the earth was corrupt in God's sight, and the earth was filled with violence. . . .
> And God said to Noah, "I have determined to make an end of all flesh, for the earth is filled with violence because of them."
>
> —Gen. 6:11-13 (RSV)

In the reworking of the tradition, "violence" (*hamas*) is illustrated in vignettes from Old Epic tradition: disobedience in the garden of Eden, murder in the first family, Lamech's lust for blood revenge, the heavenly beings who forcibly seized human maidens and had intercourse with them. All of this indicates that there is a tragic

---

10. See Rosemary Radford Ruether, *Gaia & God: An Ecofeminist Theology of Earth Healing* (San Francisco: HarperSanFrancisco, 1992), chap. 1.

11. See Frank M. Cross Jr., "The Priestly Work," in *Canaanite Myth and Hebrew Epic: Essays in the History and Religion of Israel* (Cambridge: Harvard Univ. Press, 1973), 293–325.

dimension in human life. The misuse of the freedom that God has given to creatures, particularly to human beings, has resulted in broken relations: between
human beings and God, within the human family, and between social groups. If
this is to be called "sin," it is not the transgression of specific laws set down in a
code, but a perversion of the human will that results in corruption of the goodness
of God's creation.

The narrator portrays corruption that affects "all flesh" as widespread, even universal. Violence is, as it were, a disease contaminating all creatures, animal and
human, that share the earthly *oikos* or habitat. As we know all too well from the
tragic twentieth century, probably the most violent in the history of humanity, this
disorder not only affects the social order but also permeates the animal world and
pollutes the environment. Power corrupts.

In the primeval history it is not suggested that violence is rooted in "nature"—
in the nonhuman world. In the natural realm, of course, there is great violence:
earthquake, wind, and fire; disease and pestilence; or as in evolutionary theory,
"nature red in tooth and claw." Perhaps, as Byron Bangert suggests, "what manifests
itself as natural evil in this world is the chaotic, the unformed, the still disordered
that God has yet to shape and fashion and coordinate with the existing creation."[12]

In other words, chaos persists in God's creation and God continues to create.
The biblical story, however, does not mention this violent face of nature. Even the
flood itself, which may be reminiscent of a natural calamity caused by the ram-
paging waters of the Tigris and Euphrates Rivers, is regarded as a sign of the severity of God's judgment, not the caprice of nature. The biblical story makes an
uncomfortable point: the violence that corrupted "all flesh" is traced to God's
noblest creatures, who were made in the image of God. In creating human beings
with an independent will and with creative freedom, God risked the potential
chaos that results from human violence.

God's Mistake

The flood story opens with the arresting announcement that God has made a mistake and resolves to start over.

> The LORD [Yahweh] saw that the wickedness of humankind was great in the earth,
> and that every inclination of the thoughts of their hearts was only evil continually.
> And the LORD [Yahweh] was sorry that he had made humankind on the earth, and
> it grieved him to his heart.
>
> —Gen. 6:5-6

This statement challenges us to think more deeply about God's "almighty" power.
The greatest limitation to God's sovereignty is human freedom, fundamentally
unpredictable and uncontrollable. In a sense God acts experimentally, waiting to
see what the human response will be. As the older KJV put it, God "repents"

12. Byron C. Bangert, "Why Owls Matter, Mosquitoes Bite, and Existence Remains a Mystery:
A Case for *Creatio ex Chaos*," QR 15 (Winter 1995–96) 421.

(*niham*).[13] In other words, God's will is not an inexorable fate or an unalterable necessity, but is flexible, changeable, open to the future. According to the flood story, the Creator resolves to wipe the slate clean and start all over, saving a remnant of humans and animals to provide seed for a new generation. Of course, incipient in this mass destruction of the innocent along with the guilty is the problem of the justice of God (theodicy), which Abraham later articulated in his expostulation with God on the eve of the holocaust of Sodom and Gomorrah (Gen. 18:22-33).

A New Creation

In the final priestly version of the story the flood marks a radical new beginning, indeed a new creation that corresponds to the original creation. This is evident when one reads the creation story and the flood story side by side. There are numerous affinities, even in language. In the creation story the earth is created out of watery chaos; in the flood story the *mabbul* threatens a return to the *tohu wabohu* of Gen. 1:2. In the creation story God pushes the waters back so that the dry land (earth) may appear; in the flood story God causes a wind to blow over the watery expanse with the result that the earth begins to green again. In the creation story God blesses human beings with fertility; after the flood God blesses them and gives the same imperative: "Be fruitful and multiply" (9:1, 7). Other correspondences and affinities could be added. The new beginning is like the original beginning, only with a major difference. In this case, God deals not with primeval disorder (chaos) but with the disorder created by the misuse, or abuse, of human freedom.

The Noachic covenant, then, is a *covenant of creation*.[14] First, it is universal. The storyteller indicates this by saying that God made this covenant with the family of Noah, regarded as representatives of all humankind. Moreover, it is ecological. The narrator indicates this by saying that God made this covenant with the earth, pledging to preserve the constancies of nature ("Seedtime and harvest, cold and heat, summer and winter, day and night") as long as the earth lasts (Gen. 8:22). Above all, it is a covenant of grace—an "everlasting covenant" (*berît 'olam*), one that lasts indefinitely because it is predicated not on human actions or anything finite, but on God's free and gracious commitment to the whole creation.

The Ethic of the Noachic Covenant

The Noachic covenant provides the basis for a global ethic. For one thing this covenant stresses the universality of God's grace: all creatures are embraced within

---

13 . Depending on the context, the Hebrew verb *niham* means to have a change of mind, repent, regret, as in Jeremiah's parable of the potter and the clay, Jer. 18:1-12. See my essay, "When God Repents," *BR* 12 (1996) 21, 44.

14. See my essay "Creation and the Noachic Covenant," in *From Creation to New Creation*, chap. 9.

God's mercy and care, without any exception. We are apt to place limitations and to draw distinctions, along ethnic, religious, national, or other divisive lines. But the Noachic covenant speaks of God's inclusive grace, the sign of which is the rainbow that may be seen by all peoples after a storm.

Furthermore, the Noachic covenant emphasizes reverence for the mystery of life, symbolized by the blood. Permission is given to human beings to slaughter meat for food, but with appropriate reserve and reverence (Gen. 9:4-5). Their God-given freedom does not entitle them to kill for sport or to destroy whole species. The nonhuman creation is not there simply for humans to use or exploit. Animals too are precious in God's sight, and this valuation may extend to trees, flowers, and other parts of "nature." In short, human beings are caretakers of God's creation. As we have seen, this is what is involved in being made in the image of God: to rule the earth in wisdom, justice, and compassion so that the rule of God may be manifest in human actions.

Finally, the Noachic covenant stresses the dignity of human beings, those creatures who have a special place in God's creation because they are made in the image of God, a theme that is repeated in this context (Genesis 6). This rules out the violence of murder (as specifically stated in 9:5-6); but the Noachic principle could be extended to include other forms of violence, such as genocide, warfare to obtain land or to enslave others, child abuse, domestic battering—the list could go on. Suffice it to say that the Noachic covenant provides a theological basis for ethical obligation in a pluralistic world.

God's Covenant Commitment
Thus the primeval history moves in a vast sweep from creation, through a catastrophe that threatened the earth with return to precreation chaos, to a new beginning or new creation that lies beyond tragedy. In this narrative context, the biblical narrators portray the greatness and misery of human beings, but always in the awareness of the sovereignty of God, whose power is flexible and whose love is steadfast. The biblical storytellers and poets are realists. Human beings do have the terrible power to pollute the earth with their lifestyle. They do have the capacity for violence to the degree that the earth may be threatened with a return to chaos. This is the precarious possibility of human history, as we have sensed in the violent twentieth century. Nevertheless—and this "nevertheless" is rooted in the Noachic covenant—the Creator remains committed unconditionally to the creation in an everlasting covenant. An eschatology, or hope for future consummation, is incipient in the flood story. For the Creator moves human history from potential chaos toward a new age in which the relations between human beings, nonhuman creatures, and their environment will be reordered. The rainbow is a sign of the purpose of God that overarches history from creation to new creation.

Significantly, the Noachic covenant had special meaning in the aftermath of the fall of Jerusalem in 587 B.C., when people had experienced the violence of destruction and the dislocation of exile from homeland. A poet, writing in the time of "the eclipse of God" (Martin Buber's phrase), declared that the "hiding of God's face [presence]" was only momentary. God's "covenant of peace" endures forever, despite the vicissitudes of history.

> For this is like the days of Noah,
>   when I swore that the waters of Noa
>   would never again cover the earth.
> So now I have sworn not to be angry with you,
>   never to rebuke you again.
> Though the mountains be shaken
>   and the hills be removed,
> Yet my unfailing love [hesed] for you will not be shaken,
>   nor my covenant of peace be removed,
>   says the LORD [Yahweh], who has compassion on you.
>   —Isa. 54:9-10 (NIV)

In Christian perspective, the Noachic covenant belongs to a history of God's covenants that leads up to the "everlasting covenant" made through the blood (sacrifice) of Jesus Christ (Heb. 13:20). Christ's covenant of peace does not supersede the Noachic covenant: it is built upon it, as the temple atop the graduated levels of a ziggurat rests on a broad foundation.

Creation and Global Witness

The New Testament makes surprisingly few references to God's creation of the universe. This paucity is not to be explained by saying that the Christian gospel shifts from creation to redemption, as Marcion argued in his deviant reinterpretation of the gospel in the second century; rather, creation is presupposed as a fundamental witness of the Scriptures that the church shared with the Jewish people. Paul's preaching to the Gentiles presupposed some knowledge of the Hebrew Scriptures on the part of sympathizers with Judaism. As Robert Bellah says, even when Paul preached to "the biblically illiterate Athenians" in his famous address on the Areopagus as portrayed in Acts, he spoke of "God who made the world and everything in it, [God] who is Lord of heaven and earth" (Acts 17:24) and in this sense Paul "had to convert [hearers] to Judaism before he could convert them to Christianity."[15] In the early centuries, so church historians tell us, the Christian church relied on Jewish theologians whose monotheistic faith was rooted in the doctrine of creation.

The part of the Christian Bible that has often proved to be most difficult—the Old Testament—actually has strategic importance in the church's witness to the world. The so-called Old Testament (or Hebrew Bible) is the common Bible shared by Jews and Christians, and to some degree by Muslims as well. Within the Christian canon, the Old Testament has a relatively independent place, as we have seen (chapter 2). Hence, in making its witness to the world, the church can appeal

---

15. Robert N. Bellah, "At Home and Not at Home: Religious Pluralism and Religious Truth," *Christian Century* 112, no. 13 (1995) 423–24.

to the Old Testament without having to regard it christocentrically as a book that points not just to Christ (the Messiah) but to *Jesus* Christ. Theology of creation, to which the Old Testament bears witness, is common ground on which the religions of the world—at least some of them—may stand together, in dialogue and, perhaps in some sense, in worship.[16]

It is noteworthy that in the Psalms of God's kingship (Psalms 47, 93–99), to be considered later (chapter 24), the nations are invited to praise God in ecumenical worship. The basis of this global witness is creation faith.

> *Declare [God's] glory among the nations,*
>   *his marvelous works among all the peoples.*
> *For great is the LORD, and greatly to be praised;*
>   *he is to be revered above all gods.*
> *For all the gods of the peoples are idols,*
>   *but the LORD [Yahweh] made the heavens.*
> —Ps. 96:3-5

16. The last two paragraphs are extracted from my "Creation Theology as a Basis for Global Witness," published by the General Board of Evangelism and Global Ministries, United Methodist Church (New York: UMC, 1999), Mission Evangelism Series #2. The original address (1996) was represented at the Fisher Lecture at the Claremont School of Theology.

12. The Promissory Covenant with Abraham

In the history of God's covenants the second in the sequence is the covenant made with Abraham and Sarah, the ancestors of the people of God, Israel. This covenant looms large in the period of biblical Judaism, beginning with the Second Temple, that is, the postexilic era of reconstruction. Moreover, it is very important for understanding the early Christianity that emerged out of Judaism. At the beginning of the Gospel of Luke it appears in the Benedictus, spoken by the father of John the Baptist:

> *Thus [God] has shown the mercy promised to our ancestors,*
> *and has remembered his holy covenant,*
> *the oath that he swore to our ancestor Abraham,*
> *to grant us that we, being rescued from the hands of our enemies,*
> *might serve him without fear, in holiness and righteousness before him all our days.*
>
> —Luke 1:72-75

An Everlasting Covenant

Like the Noachic covenant, the Abrahamic covenant is designated as an "everlasting covenant" (*berît 'olam*), a covenant in perpetuity. This covenant has perpetual validity and can never be abrogated precisely because it is based solely on God's firm commitment—God's faithfulness (*hesed*) or "steadfast love."

Therefore it is a covenant of *sola gratia*, grace alone. Later we shall study another covenant, the Mosaic, that is also a covenant of grace but is conditional in character (chapter 17). The Mosaic covenant emphasizes the call to human decision and the fateful results of the exercise of human freedom. By contrast, the Abrahamic covenant is unilateral in the sense that it is based on God's loyalty, which endows the relationship with constancy and durability, not on the people's response, which is subject to human weakness and sin. This covenant is sealed by God's solemn oath (as stated in the Benedictus), an oath based on God's holiness or essential being.

The unilateral character of this covenant is stressed in Genesis 17, a passage from Priestly tradition. According to this crucial text, God—here known as El Shaddai, "God Almighty"—takes the initiative to enter into covenant relationship with Abraham and Sarah and their descendants. The language is very theocentric. God resolves to "establish [set up] my [God's] covenant" as an "everlasting covenant," which will stand in perpetuity because it is grounded in God's holy will. Circumcision is not a condition but a sign of membership in the covenant community, and is binding only on males. Other members of the family—women and children—are obviously included. Individuals may fail to "keep the covenant" by not submitting to this rite of admission, but God's covenant with the community represented by the family of Abraham and Sarah stands forever.

In delineating this special covenant between God and people (Genesis 17), Priestly theologians have built on an older tradition found in Gen. 15:7-21, where the word "covenant" (*berît*) appears for the first time in the ancestral history. This curious episode, apparently from Old Epic tradition associated with the southern place Mamre, near Hebron, defies understanding. Abraham is portrayed as securing some animals and birds and then cutting them in two. At sunset a deep sleep falls on him; while in this trancelike state, a smoking fire pot and a flaming torch (symbolizing God's participation) pass through the bloody corridor between the pieces. The passage is so archaic that its ancient meaning has almost completely eroded away. Notice, however, that in this eerie covenant-making rite, during which God made a pledge under solemn oath, the patriarch was in a passive state, asleep. The covenant was made unilaterally by God; Abram was a passive recipient.

A Covenant of Promise
This strange account in Gen. 15:7-21 also indicates that the Abrahamic covenant was promissory. This covenant is characterized by the giving of promises, not the imposition of obligations.

Notice the context. The account belongs to the history of the promise that begins in Genesis 12 with God's command to Abram to leave his home country and to go toward a horizon that God would open before him. To the ancestor of Israel three promises are given. First, God will make of him a great "nation." The use of the term "nation" (*goy*, as in 18:18) rather than the fundamental term "people" (*'am*), apparently reflects the nationalism of the early monarchy, when this tradition was given written form.[1] Second, God promises to give his descendants the land of Canaan—the first reference in the Bible to the so-called promised land.[2] Third, through this people blessing would be mediated to all the broken and scattered families of the earth. It is uncertain whether the verb should be translated as a passive, "be blessed," suggesting that blessing will overflow from Abraham's people to other nations, or as a reflexive, "bless themselves," meaning that the nations will bring blessing on themselves by invoking the God of Abraham.

In any case, the promise to Abraham is seen in the horizon of God's worldwide purpose (see Rom. 4:10-25). The narrative background is the primeval history that ended in failure, signified by the abortive building of the Tower of Babel and the scattering of human beings (Gen. 11:1-9). Having failed to achieve justice and peace in the primeval history (see Gen. 6:5-8 and 8:21), God intends to use

1. In "'People' and 'Nation' of Israel," *JBL* 79 (1960) 157–63, E. A. Speiser argues that ancient Israelite tradition speaks of "the people of Yahweh" (e.g., Exod. 15:13; Judg. 5:11), not "the nation of Yahweh."

2. For a discussion of the promise of land, see my essay, "Standing on God's Promises: Covenant and Continuity in Biblical Theology," in *Biblical Theology: Problems and Perspectives*, ed. Steven J. Kraftchick et al. (Nashville: Abingdon, 1995), 145–54.

another strategy: to call a people for a special service (cf. Exod. 19:5-6). Later in the unfolding story this theme reappears in connection with the Sinai covenant. "The whole earth" belongs to God, yet God selects this people, Israel, as "my treasured possession" so that they may serve God as "a priestly kingdom and a holy nation" (Exod. 19:5-6, echoed in 1 Pet. 2:4-5).

Faith and Doubt

Today it is sometimes supposed that genuine faith leaves no room for doubt. This popular view finds no support in the ancestral history, where Abraham, the father of the faithful, has "the courage to doubt," or perhaps one should say "the faith to doubt."[3] With the exception of the story of the testing of Abraham in Genesis 22, where Abraham seems completely submissive, Abraham is the representative of faith that boldly seeks understanding (especially in Gen. 18:16-33).

Genesis 15 portrays two episodes in which Abraham expresses doubts about two of God's promises. First, how can he know that he will have a great posterity when he has no son (15:1-6)? There is no tangible evidence to support the divine word. Sarah seems unable to give him a son, and so far his head steward, Eliezer, is slated to inherit his estate. The story goes that one night as he looked up into the starry sky God reaffirmed the promise, saying that his posterity would be as innumerable as the stars. Then comes a crucial text, much discussed in Christian circles (see Rom. 4:16-25; Jas. 2:18-26), which NJPSV translates:

> And because he put his trust in the LORD [Yahweh], He reckoned it to his merit.
>
> —Gen. 15:6

Sometimes the key verb is translated "believed" (NRSV). This is not, however, the kind of belief that rests on rational argument or conclusive evidence; it is the belief that is appropriate to a relationship, as when one says: "I believe my friend," that is, put my trust in him or her. The evidence does not come first; rather, faith comes first, then seeks for understanding that weighs evidence.

In the second episode, Abraham again expresses doubt about God's promise of land. How can he know that he will possess it (Gen. 15:8)? The evidence for the validity of this promise was pretty slim, even nonexistent. At that time the land was under the control of powerful Canaanite city-states, and the whole social system was under the hegemony of great empires, especially that of Egypt. The descendants of Abraham and Sarah were sojourners in the land, living on the fringes of the political and social establishment. When it came to burial of the dead, according to a story in Genesis 23, Abraham had to negotiate with Hittites to buy a parcel so that the ancestors could, at least in death, claim a portion of the promised land.

---

3. For the former see the book by the Scottish theologian Robert M. Davidson, *The Courage to Doubt: Exploring an Old Testament Theme* (London: SCM, 1983). The latter is the title of a book by my good friend and former colleague at Colgate University, M. Holmes Hartshorne (Englewood Cliffs, N.J.: Prentice-Hall, 1963).

In the story Abraham's question about the validity of the land promise is not answered by presenting evidence, but only by the strange covenant rite, considered previously, in which God submits to an oath and thereby certifies that the promise is true. For a long time the descendants of Abraham and Sarah will be "aliens in a land that is not theirs," indeed, they will be oppressed as slaves for centuries (Gen. 15:13-17). In the long interim between promise and fulfillment, the people must live by faith. Only in retrospect will they have a faith that understands the working of God's purpose in the tangled events of history.

This covenant of promise does not free one from obligation; indeed, in the parallel chapter 17 God summons Abraham to "walk before me and be blameless" (*tamim*, i.e., a whole person, a person of integrity). The covenant recognizes Abraham's integrity and responsibility. The emphasis falls, however, on the giving of promises, not laws. No wonder that Paul, in his proclamation of God's unconditional grace displayed in Jesus Christ, went back before the Mosaic covenant of obligation to the Abrahamic covenant of promise (Romans 4). Abraham was held up as the great representative of that faith which is a trusting response to God's word of promise.

The Threefold Promise

Genesis 17 is one of the most important theological discourses in the Old Testament. This chapter sets forth the divine promises that are guaranteed to the people in the Abrahamic covenant of grace. As in the Old Epic tradition found in Gen. 12:1-7, the promises here are threefold.

First Promise (cf. Gen. 12:2)
Abraham and Sarah will have numerous descendants. Indeed, by a Hebrew wordplay on the patriarch's name, Abraham is to be "the father of a multitude of nations" (see 17:4). Furthermore, the promise is made that Sarah will be a "mother of nations; kings of peoples will come from her" (see v. 17). This assurance of the fruitfulness of the people of God is picked up later by a prophetic poet during the period of the exile, when it seemed that Israel was barren and had no future:

> Look to the rock from which you were hewn,
>   and to the quarry from which you were dug.
> Look to Abraham your father
>   and to Sarah who bore you;
> for he was but one when I called him,
>   but I blessed him and made him many.
>   —Isa. 51:1-2

Second Promise (cf. Gen. 12:3)
This covenant assures God's special relationship to, and presence with, the people of Abraham and Sarah, for El Shaddai (God Almighty) promises to "be God to you and to your descendants after you." This promise points forward to the Priestly

passage in Exod. 6:2-9, where El Shaddai discloses the proper name of God that signifies relationship to, and presence with, the people:

> *I am Yahweh . . . and I will take you to be my people,*
> *and I will become your God, and you shall know*
> > *that I am Yahweh.*
> > > —Exod. 6:7 (BWA)

In this view, the people of God is a worshiping community that is allowed to know God's personal name (identity, character) and therefore to be in an I-Thou relationship. To worship God is to "call upon the name of Yahweh" in times of distress, as in psalms of lament (Ps. 116:4) or to "call upon the name of the Lord" in times of deliverance from trouble, as in psalms of thanksgiving.[4] In a song of thanksgiving, a poet says:

> *What shall I give back to Yahweh*
> > *for all his benefits to me?*
> *I will lift the cup of salvation,*
> > *and call on the name of Yahweh.*
> > > —Ps. 116:12-13 (BWA)

Third Promise (cf. Gen. 12:6-7)

The Abrahamic covenant is connected essentially with the land, the geographical dimensions of which are already stipulated in Gen. 15:18-21. The language is that of a formal, legal grant: "I will give to you, and to your offspring after you, the land where you are now an alien, all the land of Canaan, for a perpetual holding" (17:8; see also 48:4). In strong legal terms, the perpetual covenant (*berît 'olam*) assures the claim on the land as a "perpetual holding" (*a huzzath 'olam*).

This "covenant of grant," Moshe Weinfeld observes, is analogous to the royal grant widely practiced in the ancient world. In this legal arrangement the donor, usually in recognition of past loyalty, binds himself unilaterally by oath to give property permanently.[5] So in this case the grant of the land is based on Yahweh's oath, is given in recognition of Abraham's past loyalty, is an irrevocable grant in perpetuity, and is unilateral, for no specific obligations are imposed. The real-estate dimension of the Abrahamic covenant is highlighted in a storytelling psalm:

> *The Lord [Yahweh] our God . . . is mindful of his covenant forever,*
> > *of the word that he commanded, for a thousand generations,*
> *the covenant that he made with Abraham,*
> > *his sworn promise to Isaac,*
> *which he confirmed to Jacob as a statute,*
> > *to Israel as an everlasting covenant,*

---

4. See above, chapter 6, and my book *Out of the Depths: The Psalms Speak for Us Today* (Philadelphia: Westminster, 1983; rev. ed. forthcoming 2000), chaps. 3 and 4.

5. Moshe Weinfeld, "The Covenant of Grant in the Old Testament and in the Ancient Near East," *JAOS* 90 (1970) 184–203.

saying, "To you I will give the land of Canaan
as your portion for an inheritance."
—Ps. 105:8-11

The real-estate dimension of the promise is fundamental and at the same time problematic, especially when one considers the "forgotten peoples" who were disinherited: the Kenites, the Kenizzites, the Hittites, and so on, who are listed in pedantic detail (e.g., Gen. 12:1-7; Exod. 3:8).[6] The problem is exacerbated in Deuteronomy, where the invading Israelites are told to "show no mercy" but to destroy the artifacts of Canaanite culture (Deut. 7:2; 12:3). The problem is mitigated somewhat by the Deuteronomic explanation that this policy would prevent the Israelites from being "ensnared" by native culture (7:25) or that God was giving the land to the Israelites not because of their "righteousness" but because of "the wickedness of these nations" (9:4). But these considerations, while helpful sociologically, offer no theological solution. We remember too well chapters of American history in which the biblical motif of the promised land was appropriated at the expense of Native Americans.

We will have to return to this major problem of biblical theology later. Suffice it to note for the present that Paul, who insists that God's promises to Israel are endorsed by Jesus Christ, reinterprets "land" in its larger sense of "earth" or "world" (Greek *kosmos*, Rom. 4:13). In this broader sense, the "meek" will inherit the earth (land). As Walter Brueggemann observes: "The good news is not that the poor are blessed for being poor, but that to them belongs the kingdom, that is, the new land." Brueggemann presents this Christian interpretation of the promise in the context of a call to the Christian community to engage in discussions with the Jewish community about "the land question," which is inextricably rooted in the common Bible (Law, Prophets, Writings) shared by both communities.[7]

Here, then, we find a distinctive covenantal perspective that casts its influence over the whole Pentateuch and indeed over the whole Bible, both Old Testament and New. To summarize:

1. The Abrahamic covenant is an "everlasting covenant" based on the sovereign will of God, not on human behavior.

2. The Abrahamic covenant is a covenant of grace, based on the unilateral initiative of the covenant maker, not the virtues of the covenant recipient.

3. The Abrahamic covenant is a guarantee of the validity of God's promises, specifically, that the people of God will be fruitful, that they will possess the land,

---

6. See my essay, "Standing on God's Promises," in *Biblical Theology: Problems and Perspectives*, ed. Kraftchick et al., 145–54, where I consider the problem of the dispossession of native inhabitants.

7. Walter Brueggemann, *The Land*, OBT (Philadelphia: Fortress Press, 1974), 190–91. He remarks (190): "While the Arabs surely have rights and legitimate grievances, the Jewish people are peculiarly the pained voice of the land [or broadly 'the earth'] in the history of humanity, grieved Rachel weeping (Jer. 31:15)."

and that they will stand in a special relation to God as a serving, worshiping people.

Hope for the Future

This promissory covenant, based on God's "steadfast love" (*ḥesed*), offers continuity into the future. It gives the people confidence as they move toward the fulfillment of the divine purpose. To be sure, on the subjective or human side, there are uncertainties, anxieties, and frustrations that are expressed in the stories from Old Epic tradition. Is God's promise of family increase credible when there is no heir (Gen. 15:1-6) or when the ancestress of Israel is past childbearing age (18:1-15)? Is the promise of land secure when the territory of future Israel hangs in the balance of Lot's decision (13:2-17) or the Canaanites occupy the land (12:6)? Isn't the promise of a future for the people of God nullified by God's demand that Abraham, in a decision of faith, lay on the altar his only son, the one who is to inherit the promises (22:1-18)?[8]

These old stories, however, now function in the context of God's everlasting covenant with Abraham and Sarah and their offspring. Despite the problems or anxieties of faith, the promises of God, endorsed by God's solemn oath, are trustworthy. God's word stands firm, even though everything else is transient (Isa. 40:8). Even when evil designs seem to prevail, as in the Joseph story, God works for good: as Joseph says to his brothers in Egypt, "Even though you intended to do harm to me, God intended it for good" (Gen. 50:19). People may live in the time of "the eclipse of God" (Martin Buber's phrase), but in the bold confidence of faith the human story moves toward the horizon of God's future for this people, Israel, and the nations who will receive blessing, or be blessed, through them (Gen. 18:18; 26:4; 28:14; cf. 50:20).

The Universal and the Particular

Before we explore the place of the Abrahamic covenant in the unfolding story of the Pentateuch, one point deserves special attention. This covenant emphasizes an important theological dimension of Israel's experience of the presence of the holy God in the world. Recall Emil Fackenheim's observation that the experience of God's saving and commanding presence in history, when reflected upon philosophically, exhibits certain tensions or polarities. One of these "dialectical contradictions" is that the God who is creator of all that is and who is the Sole Power is known in and through the particular, the historical experience of a people. In prophetic tradition this finds expression in the vision of the pilgrimage of the

---

8. See my essay, "Abraham, the Friend of God," *Int* 42 (1988) 353–66; also the summary of "Trials of Faith" in *Understanding the Old Testament* (4th ed.; Englewood Cliffs, N.J.: Prentice-Hall, 1986), 172–77; abridged paperback ed. (Englewood Cliffs, N.J.: Prentice-Hall, 1997), 156–60.

nations to Zion, from which Torah goes forth, with the result that they beat their swords into plowshares (Isa. 2:1-4; Mic. 4:1-4).[9]

Christians have a good illustration of this paradox in the Johannine teaching that Jesus is the Way, the Truth, and the Life, and that "no one comes to the Father except through me" (John 14:6). Surely this statement, and others like it (Acts 4:12), should not be construed to deny the universality of God's sway as creator and Lord of humanity or that other people may have access to God in a different way. Rather, the God who claims the community of faith through Jesus Christ is the God of all humankind; indeed, Christ is the "life" that gives light to "all people" (John 1:4). The particularity of God's revelation in Jesus Christ must be held in tension with the universality of God's sovereignty manifest, perhaps in a hidden manner, in general human experience.

This paradox, that the history of a particular people discloses the God who is truly God of all creation and all human beings, comes to expression in the Abrahamic covenant. The theological mystery is that of divine election, that is, the calling of Abraham to be the bearer of God's promises. Abraham is called "the friend of God" (Isa. 41:8); he is "known" by God in a special sense (Gen. 18:19). Yet Abraham's calling is part of God's universal purpose. Keep in mind that one of God's promises is that through Abraham's people all the families of humankind will be blessed (Gen. 12:3) or, as reformulated in the Priestly chapter 17, that Abraham and Sarah will be "the father" and "the mother" of many nations (17:5-6, 15-16). Later an anonymous prophet, who reflected on the meaning of the ancestral traditions, expressed this paradox in magnificent poetry. God speaks to the descendants of Abraham and Sarah:

> It is too light a thing that you should be my servant,
>   to raise up the tribes of Jacob
>   and to restore the survivors of Israel;
> I will give you as a light to the nations,
>   that my salvation may reach to the end of the earth.
>
> —Isa. 49:6

9. See my editorial column, "A Worldwide Pilgrimage to Jerusalem," *BR* 8 (June 1992) 14, 16.

13. The Tabernacling Presence

Owing to the literary artistry of Priestly interpreters, the Torah presents a marvelous vision of a history that extends from creation in the beginning to the revelation at Sinai, when Israel was established as a cultic community, a worshiping people. When one stops to contemplate the overall work (Genesis through Numbers), the overarching theme is theologically exciting. The Priestly Torah announces that the holy God, the creator of the universe and the sovereign of history, has graciously condescended to be present in the midst of Israel, a worshiping community.[1]

The Service of Worship

The Hebrew term for "worship" is ʿabodah, from a verb that means "serve." Worship is the service of God, and Israel, in this sense, is called to be the servant of God. Even yet we speak of worship services or "liturgy" (from Greek *leitourgia,* meaning "public service"). The prophets of Israel insisted that the service of God, properly understood, should extend beyond the confines of the temple into daily life, where God requires people "to do justice, love mercy, and walk humbly with your God" (Mic. 6:8). But none of the great prophets was against the "cult" as such. A non-cultic religion, one without forms, does not exist. Religion, when it goes beyond individual piety or otherworldly mysticism and is a community exercise, inevitably involves rituals, prayers, holy times and places, leaders, and ordination—in short, a system of worship. It is in the basic sense "cultic." Here, of course, we bracket out the popular, pejorative use of "cult" that the dictionary defines as extravagant, faddish devotion to a program or practice, for example, the cult of nudism.

The whole story that begins with creation, and is structured in a sequence of covenants (Noachic, Abrahamic, Mosaic), is an imaginative construal of a world in which God is present in the midst of a worshiping people. As Gerhard von Rad remarks: the Priestly theologians who have given us the Pentateuch in its present form are "utterly serious in wanting to show that the cult which entered history in the people of Israel is the goal of the origin and development of the world. Creation itself was designed to lead to this Israel"—that is, the people gathered at the foot of Mount Sinai as a worshiping "congregation" (ʿedah) or "assembly" (qahal). In the Greek Bible (Septuagint), these terms for the people of God are translated as *ekklesia* (church) and *synagoge* (synagogue). Early Christians, who read Israel's Scriptures in Greek, adopted the term *ekklesia* to show that they, along with the Jews of the *synagoge,* belonged to the people of God. (Notice Acts 7:38, "the church in the wilderness.")

---

1. In this chapter I draw on a lecture that I was invited to give on the Catholic rite of ordination in use at that time, "Ordination to the Priestly Order," *Worship* 42 (August–September 1968) 431–41.

God's Dwelling Place

The keynote of Priestly theology is given in connection with the Sinai revelation, the large block of priestly material that has gravitated to Mount Sinai (Exodus 25–32, 35–40; Leviticus 1–17; Numbers 1–10). Right at the beginning of this section Yahweh instructs Moses about the establishment of the cult:

> Let them make me a sanctuary, that I may dwell among them.
>
> —Exod. 25:8; see also 40:34–35

This note is echoed a few chapters later (Exod. 29:42-46) in a passage where it is said that the tent of meeting is the place where Yahweh intends to meet and speak with the mediator of the covenant, Moses.

> I will meet with the Israelites there, and it shall be sanctified by my glory; I will consecrate the tent of meeting and the altar; Aaron also and his sons I will consecrate, to serve me as priests. I will dwell among the Israelites, and I will be their God. And they shall know that I am the LORD [Yahweh] their God, who brought them out of the land of Egypt that I might dwell among them; I am the LORD [Yahweh] their God.
>
> —Exod. 29:43-46

At first glance it would seem that this announcement, that God intends to tabernacle in the midst of a people, is parallel to pagan myths about the building of a temple for the supreme deity. For instance, the Babylonian creation myth tells how Marduk wins a great victory over Tiamat and her chaotic allies, with the result that the temple of Esagila in Babylon is built for the high god. Also, in the Canaanite (Ugaritic) mythological literature a basic theme is the building of a temple for Baal to celebrate his triumph over his adversaries, River and Flood.

In the Priestly vision, however, the building of a sanctuary for Yahweh—one that prefigures the Jerusalem temple—is not part of a mythical drama. That is clear from the reference to the exodus in a passage just cited (Exod. 29:45-46). The making of the sanctuary, in this view, is part of a history/story that reaches a climax in the deliverance from Egypt. This crucial event has a prehistory that reaches back through the ancestral period into the primeval history, ultimately to creation, the absolute beginning of everything. Thus we find a historical sequence: creation, flood, ancestors, exodus, establishment of the cult at Sinai. As we have seen, the formation of Israel as a cultic community is the goal of the movement of the whole story from the very beginning.

The Sign of the Sabbath

The connection between creation and the establishment of Israel as a worshiping community is evident in the institution of the Sabbath. The creation story reaches its climax with the announcement that God "rested" on the seventh day from the work of creation (Gen. 2:2-3). To be sure, only the verb (*shabat*, "rested") is found here, not the noun (*shabbat*, "sabbath"). Nevertheless, the seventh day of rest is implied; the Sabbath is "hidden in creation." God rests, like an artist who rejoices in the execution of his design. But what is implicit in the creation story becomes explicit in the Sinai revelation, as is clear in Exod. 31:12-17, a Priestly passage. The Sabbath is the sign of an "everlasting covenant."

> It is a sign forever between me and the people of Israel that in six days the LORD [Yahweh] made heaven and earth, and on the seventh day he rested, and was refreshed.
>
> —Exod. 31:17

As we have seen previously (chapter 10), Priestly interpreters view the Mosaic covenant as an everlasting covenant that stands in sequence with the covenant of creation (Noachic) and the covenant with the ancestors (Abrahamic).

Thus a bridge is established from the sabbath rest of creation to the institution of the Sabbath at Sinai, linking the whole story together at its beginning and its climax (*inclusio*). The Sabbath is the sign of a relationship between the holy God and the people Israel, a relationship that is stable and perpetual because it is grounded in the will and purpose of the holy God, the Creator. To remember the Sabbath, and keep it holy, is to sense the mystery of God's creation and to celebrate "the Beyond in our Midst," to use a phrase of Dietrich Bonhoeffer.[2] By sanctifying this segment of time, the seventh day, all days are embraced within God's purpose. In Priestly Perspective the sharp separation of the sacred from the secular is ruled out; there is no basis for a secularism in which God is absent from social life.

Hence the Sabbath of Sinai harks back to the Sabbath "hidden in creation." Further, Israel's communion with God in worship realizes the promise made to Abraham that the time would come when El Shaddai would be "their God," God-in-relation to the people (Gen. 17:7). The making of a sanctuary is inseparable from the disclosure of the sacred name, YHWH. For when God turns toward a people, they have access to God and may call on the name of God in prayer—in lament, thanksgiving, and hymnic praise.

Priestly interpreters affirm that God's turning toward the people is evident not only in wonderful deeds, such as the deliverance from Egyptian bondage, but also in the establishment of a cult in which the people are granted fellowship with God. God has ordained the sacrificial cult as a means of grace so that the people may reach out to God in prayer, and God may reach the people with divine grace and forgiveness.[3]

The Tabernacle

In the symbolic language of Priestly theology the locus of God's presence in the midst of the people is the "tabernacle" (*mishkan*), the Priestly version of the tent of

---

2. Dietrich Bonhoeffer, *Letters and Papers from Prison*, ed. Eberhard Bethge, trans. Reginald Fuller et al. (New York: Macmillan, 1967), 182. I am grateful to Reverend Battina Kluenaman for this reference.

3. See Gerhard von Rad, *Old Testament Theology*, trans. D. M. G. Stalker, 2 vols. (New York: Harper & Row, 1962–65), 1:233–34.

meeting (*'ohel mo'ed*) of Old Epic tradition. According to the old tradition found in Exod. 33:7-11, Moses used to go out to the tent, which was pitched outside the camp, and there "Yahweh used to speak to Moses face to face, as one speaks to a friend." In Priestly perspective, however, the tent becomes an elaborate tabernacle, located not outside but in the center of the camp. There the priests—Aaron and his descendants—mediate between God and people. If God is to be at the center, in the midst of the people, then God's sanctuary must be in the center, as in the portrayal of the arrangement of the Israelite encampment (Num. 2:1-2; see fig. 5).

FIGURE 5. *Encampment of the Tribes of Israel*
Num. 3:1-31   Num. 10:11-33

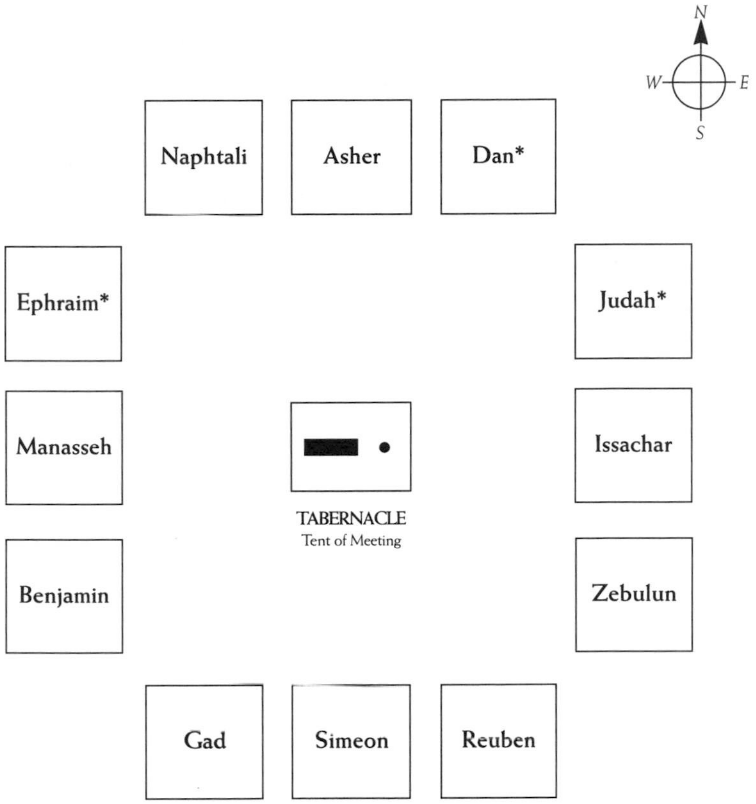

*Leading tribe of the group

It may be that, once upon a time, the two ancient cultic items—the ark and the tent—had different theological meanings. To ancient Israel, the ark—regarded as the throne-seat of Yahweh—was the sign of God's immediate and continuing presence with the people in their wars and wanderings (see the Song of the Ark, Num. 10:35-36). When the ark came into the camp, the people were "enthusiastic," literally "in God" (Greek *en + theos*, "possessed of god"), as vividly described in 1 Sam. 4:5-9. By contrast, the tent belongs to a tradition that is more reticent about affirming God's immediate presence among the people. It is a rendezvous or meeting place between Yahweh, the God of the covenant, and Moses, the covenant mediator. Yahweh does not dwell in the tent, but from time to time comes from heaven to meet with Moses and give instructions through Moses to the people.[4]

In an illuminating essay, Gerhard von Rad attempts to show that Priestly theologians combined these once separate traditions—a theology of divine presence and a theology of divine manifestation—by putting the ark inside the tent (see Exod. 26:31-35) or, oddly, on top of the tabernacle (36:14). God's presence was not a constant presence as symbolized by the ark; God did not dwell (Hebrew *yashab*) in the sanctuary; rather, from time to time God would come to tent (*shakan*) with the covenant mediator in the tent (*mishkan*) and be available to the people in prayer and worship. Attempting to do justice to both God's transcendence (tent) and immanence (ark), the two are combined symbolically: the ark is put inside the tent.[5]

Whatever may be the merit of this theory, the theological issue of transcendence and immanence is as pressing today as it was in biblical times. The holy God who is transcendent, beyond the human world, does not dwell permanently in any building; yet a call to worship usually invokes God to be present in the midst of a gathered congregation.

The Glory

One of the most important aspects of Priestly symbolism is "glory," a term that pervades the Old Testament and the New (Hebrew *kabod*, e.g., Isa. 6:3; 40:5; Greek *doxa*, John 1:14; 15:8). Hebrew *kabod* has various meanings. It basically means "weight" and thus applies to a person of weight or importance. When applied to God, it refers to God's visible manifestation, usually as radiance or resplendent light (later, the Shekinah). Only in this symbolic sense is God visible; otherwise no human being may see God (Exod. 33:20). This scene is picked up in one of our church hymns:

---

4. Frank M. Cross maintains that Priestly writers, in order to avoid the notion that the sanctuary is literally God's dwelling place, employed the archaizing technical term *shkn* (*shaken*), which in Canaanite meant "to tent" or "to lead the roving life of the tent dweller" (*Canaanite Myth and Hebrew Epic* [Cambridge: Harvard Univ. Press, 1973], 298–300).

5. Gerhard von Rad, *The Problem of the Hexateuch and Other Essays*, trans. E. W. Trueman Dicken (New York: McGraw-Hill, 1966), 103–24; idem, *Theology*, 1:234–41.

Great Father of Glory, pure Father of Light,
Thine angels adore Thee, all veiling their sight.
All laud we would render, oh help us to see,
'Tis only the splendor of Light hideth thee.[6]

In Old Epic tradition, God's visible manifestation is a luminous cloud, seen as a bright cloud by day and fire by night (Exod. 16:10). In Priestly tradition, however, God's glory is visibly manifest in, or above, the tabernacle, a prototype of the later temple (as in Isaiah's temple vision). Thus we read in Exod. 40:34:

> Then the cloud covered the tent of meeting, and the glory of Yahweh filled the tabernacle.

The narrator goes on to say that whenever this radiant cloud was taken up, the Israelites moved forward in their journey, with God going ahead of them. God's "glory" could fill the sanctuary, showing the presence of God, but God's "glory" is not confined to a holy place (Isa. 6:3), even the great temple of Jerusalem. As we shall see when dealing with the prophecy of Ezekiel, God's "glory" could leave the temple and go with the people into exile (Ezek. 10:4). The symbolism indicates that God is mobile, on the move.

In Priestly perspective this is God's world, for God has chosen to be present at the center of the community—in the tabernacle—and in this sense to tabernacle in the midst of the people. Just as the Sabbath makes all times holy, so the tabernacle sanctifies space. The land around this center, that is, the land of Israel, becomes a holy land because it is the scene of a history that reaches its climax in the creation of a sanctuary where people have access to the holy God, who is Creator and Redeemer. This sacramental view is comparable to the view in the prologue to the Gospel of John, which announces that in the beginning the divine Logos was made flesh and "tented [tabernacled] among us," enabling people of faith to behold God's glory in Jesus Christ (John 1:14; cf. 13:31, etc.).

The Mediatorial Office of the Priest

In connection with the announcement that God will dwell in the midst of the people, it is said that God designates Aaron and his sons to serve as priests in the sanctuary. God sanctifies (makes holy or sets aside) the tent of meeting or tabernacle as the divine dwelling place and consecrates the priests descended from Aaron, Moses' priestly aide, to serve at the altar (Exod. 29:43-46).

We turn, then, to a consideration of the role of priests in the Priestly theology of the Torah.[7] This is an unfamiliar subject to many modern Christians, except those in the Catholic or Episcopal churches who speak of their spiritual leaders as priests, not just ministers, pastors, or preachers. It has also become a

---

6. "Immortal, Invisible," by Walter C. Smith (1814–1908).

7. See Richard D. Nelson, *Raising Up a Faithful Priest: Community and Priesthood in Biblical Theology* (Louisville: Westminster/John Knox, 1993).

controversial subject since it seems to give no support to the ordination of women as clergy.

It is appropriate to begin with the role of Moses as covenant mediator between God and people. While interpreters in the Mosaic tradition viewed Moses as a prophet, the greatest of them all (see the conclusion to the book of Deuteronomy, 34:10-12), Priestly interpreters portrayed him in a priestly role, acting alongside his priestly brother, Aaron.

Priestly interpreters built on their knowledge of ancient tradition that portrayed Moses as covenant mediator.[8] Yahweh designates Moses as the one who is to come into the immediate presence of God and then return to speak to the people (Exod. 19:9a; cf. 34:27). Moreover, the people, standing back in fear and trembling from the awesome mountain, asked for a mediator:

> You speak to us, and we will listen; but do not let God speak to us, or we will die.
> —Exod. 20:18-21

A major prerogative of the covenant mediator is intercessory prayer, that is, representing the people before God (Exod. 32:30-32), a task that was taken up by prophets who stood in the Mosaic tradition (Jer. 15:1), and which may be performed by any minister who stands in the succession of biblical priests and prophets. In the biblical view, prayer can make a difference in God's attitude, and can even "persuade" God to alter a course of action. Human beings are not caught in fatalistic necessity before a God who is apathetic or powerless; rather, God's sovereign exercise of power is flexible and open to the future.[9]

Furthermore, Priestly tradition emphasized Moses' Levitical lineage. According to ancient tradition, Moses was born of the tribe of Levi (Exod. 2:1). Very early the Levites were set aside as a landless tribe whose "portion" was Yahweh, that is, they were set apart as priests whose task was to give torah and officiate at the altar. Recall the story in Judges 17 and 18 in which a Levite was drafted to be chaplain to the migrating Danites.

Thus the portraits of Moses the prophet and Moses the priest stand side by side in the Pentateuch, each reflecting the views of the circle that wields the brush. In Israelite society prophecy was a calling, a vocation. A person was designated as a prophet by some special experience or manifestation of God's Spirit (see Amos 7:14-15). Prophecy was characterized by spontaneity and freedom, for the Spirit is like wind: "it bloweth where it listeth [chooses]," as the KJV put it (John 3:8). By contrast, priesthood was an "office" to which a person was "ordained" or, to use more biblical language, for which an individual was "consecrated" (Exod. 29:44). There is a difference between "vocation" (calling) and "profession" (exercise of a public role), though these two tend to overlap in the modern understanding of

8. A helpful discussion of Old Epic (J and E) traditions is found in Murray Newman, *The People of the Covenant: A Study of Israel from Moses to the Monarchy* (New York: Abingdon, 1962).

9. For an excellent discussion of biblical prayer, including intercessory prayer, see Patrick D. Miller, *They Cried to the Lord: The Form and Theology of Biblical Prayer* (Minneapolis: Fortress Press, 1994); my review, *TToday* 52 (July 1995) 276–82.

ministry. Today many say that the ideal ministry is one that combines both priestly and prophetic roles.

Priestly Ordination and Succession
Exodus 29 sets forth the rite for the ordination of a person to the high priesthood. The individual was "anointed" with oil (29:7) and thus—like a king—could be considered "the Lord's anointed." Ordination, in the Priestly view, has three major aspects.

First, in this context ordination implies priestly orders, that is, a hierarchical system in which the high priest is assisted by Levitical priests of lesser rank. Indeed, the word "hierarchy" basically means, as the dictionary tells us, "a system of church government by priests or other clergy in graded ranks" or orders. Not all priests have the same rank in the administration of sacramental rites; some play a supportive role.

Second, priests were indispensable in worship services because they officiated at the altar. They did some teaching (i.e., they gave torah), but primarily they served at the altar where sacrifices were performed that were believed to be efficacious in making atonement for the people and mediating to the people the forgiving and healing grace of God (see chapter 14).

Finally, ordination provided continuity from generation to generation, as evident in the priestly lineage or succession. Indeed, the emphasis on the continuity of God's covenant purpose for the community of faith is a fundamental note of Priestly theology. This contrasts with ancient Israelite prophecy, which stressed the novelty and discontinuity of God's actions. We think of the prophets following one another in sequence, beginning with Amos, but they were relatively independent figures who arose sporadically. The notion of a prophetic "succession" is really an oxymoron. On the other hand, priests stand for order in the service of God. Just as Priestly theology envisions a providentially ordered succession of events (creation, Noachic covenant, Abrahamic covenant, Sinai revelation), so this tradition emphasizes that the cult established at Sinai was based on an ordered priestly succession.

Because of problems of succession, the history of the Israelite priesthood is a complicated matter. We find hints of the issue of priestly succession in the Old Epic tradition. Those who were invited to the covenant meal in the presence of the God of Israel on top of Mount Sinai (Exod. 24:1-2, 9-11) were Moses, Aaron, Nadab, Abihu, as well as the seventy elders. This may suggest a priestly succession, beginning with Moses.[10] In any case, this was the way the tradition was interpreted by the Priestly school. To Priestly interpreters it would not have seemed accidental that those invited to the "summit meeting" were mentioned in that order. This is evident from the Priestly genealogy found in Exod. 6:15-24, which traces a Levitical line of succession from Moses and Aaron through Aaron's third son Eleazar to Phinehas (cf. Exod. 28:11). According to Priestly tradition (Lev.

10. So Newman, *People of the Covenant*, 89.

10:1-3), Nadab and Abihu, the two older sons of Aaron, were destroyed for making an unauthorized offering, and they died childless. Hence the revised succession was: Moses, Aaron, Eleazar, and Ithamar, as in Numbers 3 (also Exod. 28:1). Also included in this line was Phinehas, the son of Eleazar (Exod. 6:25; cf. Num. 25:10-13).

Underlying these prosaic genealogical details is the view that the order of the priesthood expresses God's covenant grace, which continues with Israel in perpetuity. Indeed, it is said that God granted to the Aaronic line of priests, specifically to Phinehas, a "covenant of peace," that is, "a covenant of perpetual priesthood" (Num. 25:13-14).

Who Speaks for God?

From all of this it is clear that the Israelite priesthood was not a charismatic office, based on a gift of the Spirit or *charisma*. The priests, at least the best of them, did not want to rule out the activity of the Spirit and did not necessarily stand in opposition to the prophets. In sociological terms, however, the Priestly theology of order was an ideology, that is, a justification of the Jerusalem power establishment. It is not surprising that voices of protest are heard, at least faintly, in the evolving tradition.

A murmuring of protest is heard, for instance, in a strange incident reported in Numbers 12. Irked about Moses' marrying a Cushite woman, Miriam (the sister of Moses) joined Aaron the priest in challenging Moses' authority: "Has Yahweh spoken only through Moses? Has he not spoken through us also?" (Num. 12:2). Moses' prophetic authority was upheld, and the punishment fell only on Miriam, in the form of the outbreak of a skin disease. The story is hard to understand, especially why Miriam is treated so harshly while Aaron, the co-conspirator, gets off scot-free. Perhaps it reflects a power struggle in the community during the monarchy, especially over the charismatic role of a woman known to be a prophetess (Exod. 15:20).[11] In any case, here an ordained priest and an unordained woman join in raising the question of who speaks for God—a perennial question!

It is clear that in the Old Testament period the office of priesthood was reserved for men. When studied sociologically, the Priestly view reflects a male ordering of society. When viewed theologically, however, it is not so clear that masculinity is necessarily required for a priestly ministry. Mediation of the grace of the "everlasting covenant" is essentially tied up with the *office* of the priest, not with the person who occupies it.

In any case, priests minister along with prophets in Israel's services of worship. When prophecy ceased in Israel, it was the priests who preserved the words of the prophets so that they might be read in services of worship. The Priestly concern, as we have seen, was to stress the order of Israel's service of worship, to stand for the continuity of God's gracious presence throughout the generations, and to serve

---

11. See my editorial essay, "Miriam's Challenge," *BR* 10 (June 1994) 16.

at the altar as ministers of the everlasting covenant. Even today the priestly blessing, entrusted to Aaron and his sons (the Zadokite Jerusalem clergy), is given to a worshiping congregation:

> May God bless you and keep you,
> May God show favor upon you, and be gracious to you;
> May God bestow kindness upon you, and give you peace.
> —Num. 6:24-26 (BWA)

14. Priestly Theology
of Sacrifice and Atonement

We turn now to the priestly sacrificial system set forth in the Priestly sections of the book of Exodus: Exodus 25–31 and 35–40 and the book of Leviticus. The service of worship described here is paralleled, with some differences, in Ezekiel 40–48, which envisions the new temple to supersede the one destroyed in 587 B.C.

This part of the Old Testament is very difficult for modern readers of the Bible. After the vivid, engaging narratives of primeval history and the ancestral history and those dealing with exodus and Sinai in the first part of the book of Exodus (Exodus 1–24), what a change! Reading this material is the modern form of wandering in the wilderness. The "Leviticus syndrome," as it has been called, weakens and paralyzes the reader's resolve to go forward. Yet it is in the book of Leviticus that we find, like a diamond in the rough, the commandment, "Thou shalt love thy neighbor as thyself" (Lev. 19:18, KJV), the commandment quoted by early rabbis and by Jesus as the heart of the Torah.

Ritual and Belief

To deal with this difficult material, it may be helpful to begin with a general word about the relation between ritual and belief in a community of faith. The rituals of priestly sacrifice, though no longer practiced in Judaism or Christianity, say something essential about God's relation to the community of faith, "the people of God." Ritual is belief that is acted out by the people in corporate worship or by their representatives, the ministers or priests. In religion what is *done* in worship is sometimes more important than what is said. Actions may express convictions about God and God's relation to the people more eloquently than words or even specific theological statements.[1] Our task, then, is to find out what is expressed in the act of making sacrifices to God at an altar as depicted especially in Leviticus.

A Book of Worship

In early rabbinic Judaism the book of Leviticus was called "the priest's manual" (*torath kohanim*). It could be called more appropriately "the book of worship," since it deals not only with the function of priests but also with the laws and rituals that the laity should follow to be a holy people.[2]

There is a continuity between the books of Exodus and Leviticus. The Priestly material in Exodus tells about the making of the tabernacle and its furnishings,

---

1. See Jacob Milgrom, "Seeing the Ethical Within the Ritual," *BR* 8 (August 1992) 6; see also his major commentary, *Leviticus 1–16*, AB 3 (New York: Doubleday, 1991).

2. In addition to Milgrom's commentary on Leviticus see Israel Knohl, *The Sanctuary of Silence: The Priestly Torah and the Holiness School* (Minneapolis: Fortress Press, 1995); and Baruch Levine, *In the Presence of the Lord* (Leiden: Brill, 1974).

including priestly vestments. Leviticus 8–10 tells of the investiture and induction of the priests after the sanctuary has been completed.

An important detail, found at the beginning of this material, may easily escape attention. The whole layout, we are told, is to be made according to the "pattern" or "design" (*tabnith*) that God revealed to Moses on the mountaintop (Exod. 25:9, 40). To later interpreters this suggested a typological correspondence between the heavenly and the earthly, between transcendent reality and its shadowy replica as in Plato's philosophy, which contrasts eternal forms (the Good, True, and Beautiful) and their imperfect temporal manifestations. The Epistle to the Hebrews, which quotes the detail from Leviticus (Lev. 25:9, 40), interprets the earthly temple and its sacrificial system as "a shadow and copy of what is in heaven" (Heb. 8:5). Christ is the high priest who enters into the sanctuary of God's presence and makes the perfect sacrifice of his own blood.

One need not make this specific christological interpretation to sense that the portrayal of the temple and its sacrificial system in Leviticus leads beyond the literal sense. Speaking out of rabbinical tradition, Jon Levenson, a Jewish theologian, observes that the temple of Zion (here prefigured in the tabernacle) "represents the possibility of meaning above history, out of history, through an opening into the realm of the ideal. . . . The temple and its rites," he continues, "can be conceived as the means for spiritual ascent from the lower to the higher realms, from a position distant from God to one in his very presence."[3]

When God Draws Near

Everything in the book of Leviticus is based on the fundamental Priestly premise that the holy God has chosen to tabernacle in the midst of the people. God's intention is stated in Exod. 25:8 (discussed above, chapter 13) in connection with the description of the sacrificial system: "Let them make me a sanctuary, that I may dwell in their midst."

Thus God chooses to draw near, to be present to a worshiping people. But this raises an inescapable question: Who is worthy to stand in God's holy presence? God's drawing near may, and usually does, evoke an overwhelming sense of unworthiness, moral inadequacy, guilt. That was Isaiah's experience at the time of his call to be a prophet (Isaiah 6). In the temple he was overwhelmed with God's majestic holiness, an experience echoed in the well-known hymn, "Holy, Holy, Holy." His response to God's holy presence was a feeling of unworthiness, of utter inadequacy: "Woe is me! I am lost, for I am a man of unclean lips and I live among a people of unclean lips!" Then something strange and unexpected happened in his vision. One of the ministers in God's heavenly temple, which in his imagination corresponded to the earthly copy, took a coal from the altar, touched his lips, and said: "Your guilt has departed and your sin is blotted out." The verb translated "blotted out" (*tekuppar*) is an atonement verb, meaning to remove the effects of sin

3. Jon D. Levenson, *Sinai and Zion: An Entry into the Jewish Bible* (Minneapolis: Winston, 1985), 141.

and to restore good relations with God—in other words, to forgive. Thus Isaiah, a forgiven person, was enabled to stand in God's holy presence and offer himself in service.

Isaiah's experience in the temple helps us to understand the meaning of the sacrificial system of the book of Leviticus. The priests were obsessed with an inordinate sense of guilt and sin in the presence of the holy God. As a biblical poet said, God's holiness is a consuming fire:

> *The sinners in Zion are afraid;*
> *trembling has seized the godless:*
> *"Who among us can live with the devouring fire?*
> *Who among us can live with everlasting flames?"*
>
> —Isa. 33:14

That sense of human unworthiness is also expressed in the message of the priestly prophet, Ezekiel, who was overwhelmed with the aweful contrast between the holy God and human beings.

In the Priestly view, however, the sacrificial rituals, and preeminently the sacrifice on the Day of Atonement, the high holy day, signify God's willingness to accept, cleanse, and renew so that people may live in God's holy presence and offer themselves in the service of God. In these sacrifices the shedding of blood was held to be efficacious; for blood was regarded as the seat of the mystery of life and as such was sacred to God, the giver of life. Echoing Old Epic tradition (Gen. 9:4), Leviticus states the fundamental premise of sacrifice:

> The life of the flesh is in the blood, and I have given it to you for making atonement for your lives on the altar; for, as life, it is the blood that makes atonement.
>
> —Lev. 17:11

Sacrifice

Why the sacrifice of animals or the offering of food? In Mesopotamian religion, priestly service of worship was for the purpose of supplying the gods with what they needed, including food offered in sacrifice. Although Leviticus uses the archaic expression "the food of God" (Lev. 21:6), the whole idea of God hungering for food or savoring the odor of sacrifice is repudiated. That notion is foreign to Israel's experience of worship (see Ps. 50:20). Rather, in Priestly theology these rituals metaphorically express God's readiness to establish good relations. They are ritual ways of expressing belief in God's power to overcome the sin that distances people from God so that they may live in communion or fellowship with God.

Accordingly, in the Priestly view the sacrificial system is a means of grace that God has provided. Various sacrifices are set forth in the priestly manual in Leviticus 1–7, and in Leviticus 16 we find the ritual for the Day of Atonement (Yom Kippur), the supreme holy day.

Main Types of Sacrifice

Leviticus 1–6 presents three types of sacrifice:[4]

1. The whole burnt offering (*'olah*). This "holocaust," probably the oldest kind of sacrifice, is the only offering to God that is wholly consumed by fire on the altar. It is fundamentally an act of praise, in recognition that God is the giver of life, health, and peace.

2. The "peace offering" (*zebaḥ shelamim* or *shelem*), or as Jacob Milgrom translates, "the well-being offering," is the second type.[5] Part of this offering (suet) is offered in smoke to God, part is received by the priests, and the remainder is given to the donor for a family meal. This is a social occasion for celebrating the I-Thou covenant relationship: communion with God and fellowship with one another.

3. The "sin offering" (*ḥaṭṭaṭh*) and "guilt offering" (*asham*) belong together. The purpose of this sacrifice is to remove contamination arising from inadvertent violation of laws (e.g., those that specify the distinction between "clean" and "unclean"). The priestly manual emphasizes that this is efficacious for sins committed "unwittingly" and hidden from the community. For sins committed "with a high hand," that is, in deliberate arrogance, there is no provision in the priestly system (Num. 15:30-31).

The donor is to present these offerings "at the entrance of the tent of meeting so as to secure acceptance before the Lord [Yahweh]" (Lev. 1:3, REB). This harks back to the description of the tabernacle in Exodus 25ff., which states that in the tabernacle Yahweh comes to meet the people through the priestly mediator. The role of the priest, as we have noted, includes several functions: to give torah (or "teaching") about the tradition, to validate offerings acceptable to God, to render a decision in difficult cases, and above all to mediate God's grace and forgiveness.

At-One-Ment with God

Because these sacrifices are efficacious in overcoming the sinful distance between the people and God, they are "acceptable in your behalf as atonement" (Lev. 1:4). The Hebrew verb used here (*kipper*) means basically "to cover," and then "to make amends, expiate," and so on. It is nicely translated by our English word "atone," which goes back to an old word meaning "to be at one, in agreement." The sacrificial rituals, especially those prescribed for the Day of Atonement, express the view that God acts to "cover" or remove the effects of sin and to be "at one"—in accord—with the people; in other words, God seeks reconciliation. God provides the means of "at-one-ment" so that a sinful people may be accepted in the presence of the holy God. Like Isaiah in the temple, persons may experience the forgiveness of God, which, like a cleansing fire from the altar, touches their lives, empowering them to serve the holy God.

---

4. For a brief discussion of the various sacrifices, see Susan Rattray, "Worship," in *Harper's Bible Dictionary*, ed. Paul Achtemeier et al. (San Francisco: Harper & Row, 1985); Roland de Vaux provides a thorough discussion in *Studies in Old Testament Sacrifice* (Cardiff: University of Wales Press, 1964).

5. Jacob Milgrom, *Leviticus 1–16*.

The Mercy Seat

In the Priestly view, as we have seen, God meets with the people in the temple (the former tent of meeting) and its services. Within that sanctuary, holiness is especially intense in the innermost shrine, the Holy of Holies. In that inner sanctum is the ark, with guardian cherubim on either side, on which God was supposed to be invisibly enthroned, as reflected in an enthronement psalm:

> *The LORD [Yahweh] is king, let the peoples tremble!*
> *He sits enthroned upon the cherubim; let the earth quake!*
> —Ps. 99:1

The cover of the ark is called the *kapporeth* (described in Exod. 25:17-22), a term based on the verb for "atone" (*kipper*). In the Priestly view, this is the seat of God's holy presence in the midst of the people where God appears to make atonement, especially by the sprinkling of blood on the Day of Atonement (Lev. 16:14-16). Traditionally, the Hebrew word for "cover" has been translated "mercy seat."

> The LORD [Yahweh] said to Moses:
> Tell your brother Aaron not to come just at any time into the sanctuary inside the curtain before the mercy seat that is upon the ark, or he will die; for I appear in the cloud upon the mercy seat.
>
> —Lev. 16:2

Christian hymns have adopted and enlarged this priestly symbolism when appealing to people to "come to the mercy seat," that is, to stand before the throne of Christ and receive grace and forgiveness.

Propitiation or Expiation?

Does "atonement" in these Priestly passages involve "propitiation" or "expiation"? The difference between these two terms is very important theologically. In the former case, the view would be that God, who is angry and alienated by human sin, requires something to appease divine anger before showing favor to the sinner. The hindrance to reconciliation lies with God. By contrast, in the case of expiation the hindrance to right relationship with God lies in human sin and the obstacle is overcome by the God-provided means of grace.

One must recognize that the priests have retained traditional language that should not be pressed literally. An example is the concluding rubric: "A pleasing odor to Yahweh" (Lev. 1:9, etc.). This archaic metaphor is found in the flood story (Gen. 8:21), which states that Yahweh "smelled the pleasing odor" and vowed never again to bring such a cataclysm. The language recalls the even bolder description in the Babylonian flood story of the gods smelling the odor of sacrifice and crowding around the altar like flies. Moreover, one can find instances where the verb *kipper* is used to express appeasement, as in the case of Jacob's offer of a gift to Esau to "appease" his wrath (Gen. 32:20).

Appeasement does not, however, accord with the Priestly theology of atonement. First, in the Priestly view God is the one who provides the whole sacrificial system according to a "pattern" given on the mountain. Second, in some cases God is actually the subject of the verb *kipper:* God "makes atonement for" (2 Chron. 30:18). Finally, when God is the subject of the verb, it may mean "forgive" (Ezek. 16:63; Deut. 21:8; Ps. 78:38). This is the way the verb is used in a passage considered previously: the account of the call of Isaiah (Isaiah 6). In the temple the prophet hears the words of assurance: "Your sin is forgiven" (*kipper,* v. 7). In this case too, God is the one who takes the initiative to cancel the consequences of sin. This view seems to be expressed in Isaiah 53, which calls the servant's sacrifice an *asham,* a sin offering, that restores broken relations with God (Isa. 53:10).

In short, atonement involves "expiation," not "propitiation." In the Priestly view, God takes the initiative to overcome the barrier of human sin and provides the means of grace for restoring good relations, that is, reconciliation. It is appropriate, then, that in the Communion Service of the United Methodist Church, which once read: "He is the propitiation for our sins, and not for ours only but also the sins of the whole world," the word "propitiation" has now been changed to "expiation."

Conclusion

At the conclusion let us return to the issue raised at the beginning of this discussion: the relation between ritual and belief. These sacrificial rituals set forth in the book of Leviticus are no longer used in temple worship, whether Jewish or Christian. The forms of worship have changed, but the meaning or "belief" that they once expressed may live on in the community of faith. This is certainly true in the Christian community, which affirms, as in the Epistle to the Hebrews, that Christ's sacrifice on the cross fulfills and completes the meaning of the priestly sacrificial system of the Old Testament. His sacrifice has acted out, more compellingly than any word that may be spoken about him, the forgiving love of God that restores broken relations and empowers persons to stand confidently in God's holy presence, offering their very selves as "a living sacrifice," as Paul puts it at the beginning of Romans 12.

15. The Life of Holiness

Looking back over the ground traversed thus far: we have seen that the Priestly interpreters imaginatively construe a world in which the holy God, creator of heaven and earth, chooses to be present in the midst of the community of Israel. In the Priestly scheme, we have seen, there are three movements in the story that begins with creation and reaches a climax with the Sinai revelation. First, God creates a world of order and promises that it will never lapse back into chaos, a promise that is guaranteed by the everlasting covenant with Noah. Second, God calls Abraham and Sarah and promises them land and increase, guaranteeing this promise with an everlasting covenant. Finally, God condescends to tabernacle in the midst of the worshiping congregation (*'edah*) and provides in the Sinai covenant, also understood to be an everlasting covenant, the means of grace so that the people may live in the presence of the holy God.

A Holy People

It follows that if the people are to live in the presence of the holy God, holiness is to characterize their common life. This is the theme of the so-called Holiness Code (Leviticus 17–26):

> *You shall be holy,*
> *for I, the Lord [Yahweh] your God, am holy.*
> —Lev. 19:2, etc.

Holiness is the quality that belongs solely to God. No thing or being is holy intrinsically; God alone, the Supreme Being, is *qadosh*, "Holy One." Holiness pertains to what philosophers call God's aseity—the unconditioned essence or being of God. David Blumenthal maintains that holiness and personality are the two essential attributes of God.[1] But to ascribe "personality" to God, as I noted in an earlier connection, is problematic, for this raises the profound question as to where one draws the line between metaphor and reality. In any case, holiness is the fundamental reality of the God who is portrayed in, but transcends, metaphorical speech.

In a derivative or secondary sense things or creatures may be "made holy" (sanctified, consecrated) when they are drawn into God's sphere of holiness or when they are brought into relationship with the holy God. Thus the tabernacle or temple is holy because God chooses it to be the place of the divine presence. The land of Palestine (Canaan) becomes the Holy Land because God reserves it as the portion for the people of God, Israel. Sacrifices are holy, utensils are holy,

---

1. See David Blumenthal, *Facing the Abusing God: A Theology of Protest* (Louisville: Westminster/John Knox, 1993), "Holiness as an Attribute of God," chap. 3. See my discussion above, chapter 4.

priests are holy because these are drawn into the service of the holy God. Scripture is holy (the "Holy Bible") because it contains "the oracles of God" entrusted to the Jewish people, as Paul put it (Rom. 3:2). These things are, so to speak, taken out of the ordinary, profane realm and drawn into the realm of the sacred, the holy.

This view of separation from the ordinary world is presupposed in Numbers 1–10. Here the people of God are portrayed as making an orderly march through the wilderness. When they camp, the tribes are arranged in order around the tabernacle to safeguard its holiness, with the Levites (the priestly tribe) camped immediately around it, to protect it so that no outbreak of divine holiness (wrath) will fall on the people (Num. 1:53; 8:19; see above, fig. 5, p. 109). When they break camp and move on, the Levites are the bearers of the movable sanctuary and its holy things. In this manner we are given a graphic picture of God at the center of the community, of the Holy One in the midst of Israel (cf. Hos. 11:9b).

A Holy Land

When we turn to the Holiness Code (Leviticus 17–26), the priestly sense of the holy is extended beyond the tabernacle and its sacred area to the whole land and the people living on the land. This is the fundamental difference between the Priestly writers (P) and the Holiness Code (H, a separate, perhaps earlier source incorporated into the Priestly book of Leviticus). "The priesthood, Israel, and mankind respectively," says Jacob Milgrom, an authority on the book of Leviticus, "form three rings of decreasing holiness about the center, God."[2]

This view of "rings of decreasing holiness" makes sense when holiness is considered as divine power, not a subjective awareness of the sacred (see above, chapter 5). In the priestly view, holiness is most intense at the center—the tabernacle, especially in the most holy sanctum, beyond the curtain, containing the holy ark and its most holy cover (kapporeth), regarded as God's throne-seat.[3] From this holy center, the power of holiness extends outward in concentric waves, though decreasing in force as it reaches the periphery. Thus the whole territory of Israel, with the tabernacle (temple) at the center, is a holy land. In a larger sense, the whole earth is full of the glory of the holy God, as a heavenly choir sings in God's holy temple (Isa. 6:3).

Consecrated for Service

According to the Holiness Code, it is not just the priests who are "made holy" (sanctified, consecrated) for the service of God but also the whole people of Israel. They are called to be a holy people, separated from other nations by virtue of their relationship to the holy God. Here the Holiness Code picks up a theme found in Old Epic tradition: the people, with whom God chooses to make a covenant, are

---

2. See Jacob Milgrom, "Leviticus," in *The Books of the Bible*, ed. B. W. Anderson (New York: Scribners, 1989); also his commentary *Leviticus 1–16*, AB 3 (New York: Doubleday, 1991).

3. On the "mercy seat" see above, chapter 14.

called to be "a kingdom of priests and a holy nation" (Exod. 19:6; cf. Deut. 7:6). Building on this tradition of the holy people, New Testament writers affirm that the church is a holy nation (1 Pet. 2:9), and that it is composed of "saints" or "holy ones" (Rom. 1:7; 1 Cor. 1:2). Indeed, the author of 1 Peter, quoting the Holiness Code, says that Christian people are called to a life of holiness.

> As he who called you is holy, be holy yourselves in all your conduct; for it is written, "You shall be holy, for I am holy."
>
> —1 Pet. 1:15

In line with this, Christians confess in the Apostles' Creed that they believe in a "holy, catholic [universal] church."

If the people Israel are to be holy, they "must abide by a more rigid code of behavior than that practiced by the nations, just as the priest lives by more stringent standards than those applying to common Israelites."[4] Thus *torah* in the sense of "law" is fundamental in Priestly theology. By obeying the "statutes and ordinances" of the covenant the people show themselves to be holy. As David Blumenthal, a modern Jewish theologian, explains, *qedushah* (holiness) "is created by an act of the will," that is, of obedience to the Torah. "Through it," he goes on to say, "one dedicates an act to God. It is a function of *mitsva*, of commandment, and of the intention to fulfill that command."[5]

Contrary to extreme interpretations of the Christian gospel, the Christian is not free from, or above, the law, but is called to show a holy life by performing works of righteousness, a point made forcefully in the Epistle of James.

Holiness as Separation From

Holiness of life has two aspects: one negative and the other positive. Negatively, it means that the people of God are to be separated from other nations so as to live in special relation to God.

> Speak to the people of Israel and say to them: I am the LORD [Yahweh] your God. You shall not do as they do in the land of Egypt, where you lived, and you shall not do as they do in the land of Canaan, to which I am bringing you. You shall not follow their statutes. My ordinances you shall observe, and my statutes you shall keep, following them: I am the LORD [Yahweh].
>
> —Lev. 18:2-4

The Holiness Code, then, draws a boundary that separates Israel from other peoples. In sociological terms, a distinction is made between "us" and "them," insiders and outsiders.[6] At the conclusion of Leviticus 18 (vv. 24-29), the people are

---

4. Milgrom, "Leviticus," in *Books of the Bible*, 68.

5. Blumenthal, *Facing the Abusing God*, 25–26. See also Abraham Joshua Heschel, *God in Search of Man* (New York: Meridian, 1951), part 3.

6. The sociological dimension of separation between "us" and "them" is discussed by Simon B. Parker, "The Hebrew Bible and Homosexuality," *QR* 11, no. 3 (1991) 4–19.

told that they must keep the covenant statutes and ordinances and not commit the "abominations" practiced by the nations. The line is drawn so sharply that any person who commits one of these abominations is to be "cut off" from the people (excommunicated) and in some instances put to death.

Take a look at the commandments contained in the code. They are quite a mix.

- No member of the Israelite community or resident alien (sojourner) may eat blood; a person who eats blood shall be "cut off" from the people (17:10-16).
- Various forms of incest are prohibited: "None of you shall approach anyone near of kin to uncover nakedness" (18:6-18). Almost every society, according to anthropologists, has taboos against incest to protect the identity and vitality of the social group.
- Prohibition against sexual intercourse during a woman's menstrual period (18:29), a taboo based on revulsion at a flow of blood, for "the blood is the life of every creature" (17:14).
- Prohibition against homosexual relations between men (18:22; also 20:13). Nothing is said against lesbianism.
- Laws, also found in the Decalogue, concerning honoring parents, observing the Sabbath, prohibiting idol worship (19:3-4), stealing, bearing false witness (19:11-14).
- Prohibitions against breeding different kinds of animals, sowing a field with two kinds of seed, wearing a garment made of two different materials (19:19). Laws about sexual relations with a slave woman (19:20), against turning to mediums or spiritualists (19:31), against oppressing a resident alien (19:34).
- Shining out with a special luster is the commandment known in Christian circles as the Second Great Commandment: "You shall not take vengeance or bear a grudge against any of your people, but you shall love your neighbor [fellow Israelite] as yourself" (Lev. 19:18). It is well known that Jesus, in the parable of the good Samaritan (Luke 10:27-37), broadened the meaning of "neighbor" to refer to any human being, even an enemy.

This collection is a legal hodgepodge. Surely the same weight cannot be given to all of these laws, whether in the Jewish or the Christian community. Intended for a particular time in the history of God's people, not all of them are relevant today. Ethical discrimination is needed to determine what is central and what is peripheral, what is transient and what is of abiding value. Christian interpreters must take seriously the dialectical tension of continuity/discontinuity between the old age and the new, as Jesus expresses it in the Sermon on the Mount.[7]

---

7. Jesus has not come to destroy the Torah and Prophets, yet he also says "It was said to you of old . . . but I say . . ." See discussion above, chapter 2.

Homosexuality

Since homosexuality has become a controversial issue in our time, let us concentrate on this law. In the Holiness Code the prohibition is stated twice:

> If a man lies with a male as with a woman, both of them have committed an abomination [*to'ebah*]; they shall be put to death; their blood is upon them.
>
> —Lev. 20:13; also 18:22

This law does not occur in any other legislation in the Old Testament: the Ten Commandments in Exodus 20 and Deuteronomy 5, the Covenant Code (Exod. 20:23—23:33), or Deuteronomic Law (Deuteronomy 12–16). Sometimes it is said that the issue appears in two Old Testament narratives: the story about the wickedness of Sodom in Genesis 19, on which our word "sodomy" is based; and the "mirror story" of the rape of a Levite's concubine in Judges 19. Both of these stories, however, deal with gang rape and are not relevant to a discussion of homosexuality as such. Only in the Holiness Code does the law appear in the Old Testament.

In evaluating this law, ethicists must consider several matters. First, the law is not grounded in the Noachic creation covenant, which would give it a universal or general validity, but on God's "everlasting covenant" with the people Israel at Sinai. In the creation stories, God blesses heterosexuality ("male and female") so that species, both animal and human, may reproduce themselves. Nothing is said about homosexuality, for that is beyond the immediate concern for procreation (see above, chapter 11).

Second, the Levitical law is applicable primarily to the holy people living in the holy land. A distinguished Jewish scholar, Jacob Milgrom, argues forcefully that "the ban on homosexuality and other illicit unions [in Leviticus 18] applied solely to the residents of the holy land."

> What is the symbolism of the holy land? It is the sphere of God, like his temple in Jerusalem. In this theology, all those who live in God's extended temple—the holy land—are accountable to a higher moral and ritual standard.[8]

In the case of the Egyptians, who do not live in the holy land, "their sexual aberrations are not sins against God and, hence, not subject to divine sanctions." This interpretation, which has stirred up a lively response, is a reminder that one must understand the laws of holiness within the symbolic world that the Priestly writers have created.

Third, as we have seen, the purpose of this and other prohibitions in Leviticus is to define the boundaries between this people and the nations. Definition of boundaries came to be a big issue in the early Christian community, as illustrated by the story in Acts about Peter's vision at a time when he was dealing with Cornelius, a military man and a Gentile who was well esteemed in the Jewish community. In his vision Peter saw the heavens opened and something like a large sheet was lowered, containing all kinds of animals, "clean and unclean" or kosher

---

8. Milgrom, "Does the Bible Prohibit Homosexuality?" *BR* 9 (December 1993) 11. Milgrom draws attention to the fact that the prophet Ezekiel, who was familiar with the holiness laws, "not once [mentions] the several violations of Lev. 18, let alone homosexuality."

and nonkosher. Peter was commanded to kill and eat, but he held back, saying that he had never eaten anything regarded by Jewish laws as profane and unclean. Nevertheless he heard a voice saying: "What God has made clean, you must not call profane."

This dream gave a new interpretation of the book of Leviticus, in particular the dietary laws that define the Jewish community over against the nations, the Gentiles. When Cornelius and his entourage arrived, Peter began a discourse: "I perceive that God shows no partiality, but in every nation anyone who fears him and does what is right is acceptable to him." In other words, the Christian community is an open community that welcomes all to table hospitality. God shows no partiality.

This story indicates that in Christian circles the book of Leviticus is read with critical discrimination. Not everything is appropriated or given the same weight. If this *discrimen* applies to dietary laws, doesn't it also apply to other laws in the book of Leviticus, including those that exclude homosexuals from the holy community? The hermeneutical question is the dialectic of continuity/discontinuity in the relation between the Old Testament and the New (see below, chapter 36). There is continuity, for holiness of life is to distinguish the new people of God. But there is also discontinuity, for the separating barriers between "us" and "them" are broken down in the community that is "in Christ" (see Gal. 3:28).

Separated For

Holiness also has a positive aspect, which is evident when one turns from the prohibitions of Leviticus 18 to the prescriptions of Leviticus 19. Holiness is not just separation *from*, but separation *for*—for the service of God. According to the Holiness Code, this divine service is performed by engaging not just in ritual acts (such as sacrifices) but also in acts of justice, including what the Decalogue requires (Lev. 19:11-16). The life of holiness involves a godly life—"the imitation of God" (*imitatio Dei*), as Jacob Milgrom observes. "How can human beings imitate God?" he asks. "The answer of Leviticus 19 is given in a series of ethical and ritual commands, above which soars the command to love all persons" (Lev. 19:18)—the great commandment that is part of the Shema of Judaism.[9] And love of the neighbor is manifest in doing justice.

If we take our cue from this part of the Holiness Code, holiness of life is measured by love—love of God and love of neighbor, the two being the obverse and reverse of the same coin (see 1 John). Some groups within the church, such as the Methodists, believe that this is what the life of holiness is all about. Within the community of faith, according to this view, persons are "going on toward perfection"—wholehearted love of God and boundless love of one another. In the Sermon on the Mount (Matt. 5:48) this "perfection" is spelled out to include love of the loveless, even one's enemies (vv. 43–47). The REB translates appropriately: "There must be no limit to your goodness, as your heavenly Father's goodness knows no bounds."

9. Milgrom, "Leviticus," in *Books of the Bible*, 68.

16. Prophecy in Priestly Tradition

The message of the great, but enigmatic, prophet Ezekiel belongs essentially to the symbolic world portrayed in priestly imagination. To be sure, there are major differences between Ezekiel's vision and that of the Priestly writers (P). First, Ezekiel does not present a comprehensive view that begins with creation; indeed, creation theology has no place in Ezekiel's message. Ezekiel traces God's purpose back to the promise of land made to Israel's ancestors (20:42), specifically to Abraham (33:24) and Jacob (37:25), and above all to the time of the exodus from Egypt, when God "chose" Israel (20:5-7). Also, there are major differences between the portrayal of the temple in Ezekiel 40–48 and that of the tabernacle/temple in Exodus 25–40 and Leviticus. Literary and theological affinities are especially strong with the so-called Holiness Code (H) in Leviticus 17–26, which is closely related to Priestly tradition (P).[1] Also, there are impressive similarities to the Priestly portrayal of the revelation of Yahweh's "glory" to the people Israel at Mount Sinai (Exodus 25–40).

A Priestly Prophet

Ezekiel's theological task was to interpret the events leading up to and after the fall of Jerusalem in 587 B.C., events in which he was personally involved. His message stands primarily in Priestly tradition but overlaps with Mosaic covenant tradition (to be considered later), as evident by affinities with Jeremiah's preaching. Ezekiel is a complicated figure who cannot be put into a theological pigeonhole. Moreover, the final form of the book of Ezekiel, which is the basis for theological exposition, betrays evidences of a history of composition.

The Glory of God

In Ezekiel's imaginative construal of God's world, the key word is "glory" (*kabod*). The prophet was clearly familiar with the Priestly portrayal of the Sinai theophany in which the glory was an envelope of light, associated with the pillar of cloud and fire, that both revealed and veiled God's holy presence (Exod. 24:15-20). As we have seen, the divine glory was associated especially with the tabernacle, the successor of the tent of meeting (Exod. 40:34-38), which prefigured the temple.

Just as the glory settled over the tabernacle, so in Ezekiel's vision it settled over the cherubim that flanked Yahweh's throne-seat (the ark) in the Holy of Holies,

---

1. In his commentary *Leviticus 1–16* (AB 3; New York: Doubleday, 1991), Jacob Milgrom maintains that the P tradition, which stems from about 750 B.C., was finally shaped by Holiness Code editors (symbolized by H).

the innermost cella of the Jerusalem temple.[2] Yahweh's glory filled the temple, signifying God's presence in the midst of the people (8:4; 9:3; 10:4; 37:26-27). But God is not bound to a sanctuary; God is free to move on with the people and to display divine "glory" in unexpected and undeserving ways, a point that is made in Old Epic tradition:

> Moses said, "Show me your glory, I pray." And he [Yahweh] said, "I will make all my goodness pass before you, and will proclaim before you the name, 'The LORD' [Yahweh]; and I will be gracious to whom I will be gracious, and will show mercy on whom I will show mercy."
>
> —Exod. 33:18-19

Just as the pillar of cloud and fire lifted from the tabernacle and accompanied the people in their journey, so Yahweh's glory moved with the people into exile (Ezekiel 8-11); moreover, in Ezekiel's vision of the restoration, Yahweh will return with them to the land, at the center of which is the temple (3:12, 23; 10:4-5; etc.). The holy God is free to move with the people and to lead them into the future. Thus the glory of God is not confined to a sanctuary separated from the profane world (the tabernacle), but radiates out into the profane world (cf. Isa. 6:3). In this case the glory is manifest in a foreign land to which God has exiled the people and from which God will bring them back. Speaking of God's return with the people to their homeland along a marvelous "highway," a later poet announced:

> Then the glory of the Lord shall be revealed, and all people shall see it together.
>
> —Isa. 40:5

God's Holiness

The manifestation of God's overwhelming glory is portrayed in the vision of a marvelous throne-chariot coming out of the north—in Canaanite mythology the place of the abode of the gods (cf. Ps. 89:12; Isa. 14:13-14). In this vision, found at the beginning of the book of Ezekiel and recalled various times, divine holiness is manifest as tremendous power, symbolized by a violent windstorm and a cloud flashing with lightning. The reticent language, indicated by "something like," "as if," "as it were," shows that the prophet uses metaphors to express what transcends human language. The manifestation of divine holiness is something "out of this world"; the divine mystery is ineffable. Ezekiel's vision gave rise to "chariot" (merkabah) mysticism in later Judaism.

True to Priestly theology, the book of Ezekiel indicates that the instinctive response to the blinding glory of the holy God is an overwhelming sense of mortal weakness and human unworthiness. Ezekiel's "glimpse of God," as Katheryn Darr says appropriately regarding the prophet's response (Ezek. 1:28b), "literally

---

2. See Katheryn Pfisterer Darr, "The Book of Ezekiel: Commentary and Reflections," in *The New Interpreter's Bible*, ed. Leander Keck (Nashville: Abingdon, forthcoming), especially her treatment of "Ezekiel's Inaugural Vision and Call to Prophesy" (Ezek. 1:1—3:15).

3. Ibid.

'lays him out.'"[3] Only a word from the holy God can overcome this paralyzing reaction and empower a person born of dust to stand up and be a messenger of the heavenly King.

> [The Lord] said to me:
> O mortal ["son of man"], stand up on your feet that I may speak to you.
> —Ezek. 2:1 (NJPSV)

The expression "son of man" (*ben 'adam*), used some 93 times in the book of Ezekiel, is appropriately translated as "O mortal" in some modern versions (NJPSV, NRSV). It occurs in this sense one other time in the Old Testament:

> *What is man [`enosh] that You have been mindful of him,*
> *mortal man [ben 'adam, "son of man"] that You*
> *have taken note of him?*
> —Ps. 8:4 (NJPSV, v. 5)

Otherwise, it occurs only in an apocalyptic writing, the book of Daniel (7:13; 8:17), where it has the opposite meaning: not a man of dust (mortal) but a man from heaven (an angel), who signifies the coming kingdom of God. Likewise in the New Testament it is applied to Jesus, portrayed as an eschatological figure who introduces God's kingdom (e.g., Mark 8:31, 38).

Divine Wrath and Mercy

In the book of Ezekiel the sense of the holy is not just an awareness of the mystery of ultimate reality—the "God beyond the gods," so to speak. Holiness is manifest as overwhelming power. God's power, however, is not impersonal force like the energies of nature. The power of divine holiness is manifest as special concern for, and jealous claim upon, the people Israel, indeed, upon the nations too. Divine power expresses God's energetic will (zeal) that reacts negatively to any behavior that dishonors God's name or "being," "self" (Ezek. 36:22-32, etc.).[4] Not only is divine wrath poured out on Israel for their offenses against God, but also God becomes "jealous" for God's holy name when the nations affront God by mistreating Israel (Ezek. 39:25-29).

Some would regard Ezekiel as the Jonathan Edwards of the Old Testament, preaching sermons on "sinners in the hand of an angry God." Yet while Ezekiel often speaks of God's wrath, he insists (like Edwards, I believe) that God is merciful and compassionate. Indeed, God's acts of judgment are intended to shake the

---

4. I find great difficulty with Walter Brueggemann's attempt to translate this expression of Yahweh's holiness with our psychological term "self-regard," *Theology of the Old Testament: Testimony, Dispute, Advocacy* (Minneapolis: Fortress Press, 1997), 293–96: "The terms assume Yahweh's singular preoccupation with self, and the expectation that Yahweh will be fully honored and readily obeyed in every circumstance" (p. 293).

people out of a false way of life and bring them to a new life, to give them a "new heart." God wills life, not death, and is puzzled about why the people stay bogged down in self-destructive ways.

> Cast away from you all the transgressions that you have committed against me, and get yourselves a new heart and a new spirit! Why will you die, O house of Israel? For I have no pleasure in the death of anyone, says the Lord GOD [Adonai Yahweh]. Turn, then, and live.
>
> —Ezek. 18:31-32

Ezekiel insists that the holy God does not deal with the people arbitrarily or capriciously. Rather, the people have provoked Yahweh's holy anger or "jealous wrath" (23:25) by their own conduct: by flouting Yahweh's laws and statutes and thereby polluting Yahweh's land (38:16)—also called "the land of Israel"—with violence, bloodshed, and idolatry. In the face of all this, however, the holy God wills health and wholeness (salvation). "Like a mother who in one instance spanks her child and in the next rocks it to sleep," God will perform a miracle that brings new life to them.[5]

In the famous vision of the valley of dry bones (Ezek. 37:1-14), the prophet envisions that the dead bones—symbolic of Israel's hopeless condition in Babylonian exile—will come together, bone connected with bone (recall the famous folk spiritual), and will be resuscitated by life-giving breath (wind, spirit). This is the first reference to "resurrection" in the Bible. Here it portrays a corporate revival of a people that had lost its life and hope, not the raising up of an individual for life beyond the grave.[6]

Know That I Am God

The book of Ezekiel is an excellent example of how the significance of covenant cannot be estimated by counting the occurrences of the term *berît*. A fundamental concern of the prophet's message is *the relationship* between the holy God and the people ("my people Israel," 36:8). God's acts of judgment or of mercy are performed so that "you will know that I am Yahweh," according to the recurring refrain (7:9; 13:14; etc.), which echoes language found in the Priestly Torah (Exod. 16:12; 29:46; etc.).[7] This is the "knowing" of personal relationship. In the end, when this knowledge of God becomes genuine and inward, the covenant promise will be realized: "I will be their God, and they shall be my people" (Ezek. 36:28).

This knowledge of God, however, will not be confined to Israel but will be found among the nations, for Yahweh's appearance in Israel's history is, in some sense, a theophany to the nations.

---

5. Walther Eichrodt, *Ezekiel*, trans. Cosslett Quin, OTL (Philadelphia: Westminster, 1970), 36.
6. See further discussion of resurrection in chapter 35 below.
7. This motif, which occurs some 65 times, is explored by Walther Zimmerli, *I Am Yahweh*, trans. Douglas W. Stott (Atlanta: John Knox, 1982).

> The nations shall know that I am Yahweh, says
>   Adonai Yahweh,
> when through you I display my holiness before
>   their eyes.
>
> —Ezek. 36:23b (BWA)

A New Covenant

Ezekiel's affinities with Jeremiah suggest that he thinks in terms of the Mosaic covenant, which received special emphasis in the Deuteronomistic perspective, to be considered in the next section (chapters 17–22). Indeed, two passages (11:18-20 and 36:25-28) come very close to Jeremiah's prophecy of the new covenant (cf. Jer. 31:29-30).

> I shall give you a new heart and put a new spirit within you: I shall remove the heart of stone from your body and give you a heart of flesh. I shall put my spirit within you and make you conform to my statutes; you will observe my laws faithfully. Then you will live in the land I gave to your forefathers; you will be my people, and I shall be your God.
>
> —Ezek. 36:26-28 (REB)

In chapter 16, where Ezekiel employs the term "covenant" to express Yahweh's wooing, marrying, and elevating a beautiful young woman to be queen, despite her lust for other lovers, he is concerned primarily with a defect of the human will that prompted the people to betray the covenant loyalty. This problem of the will is central. In chapter 20, where the prophet traces Israel's election to the exodus, Ezekiel declares that there never was a time when the people were faithful in their loyalty to God. But in the future things will change, thanks to God's saving action. The last part of the book of Ezekiel is dominated by the theme of the eschatological new exodus—the new beginning for the people of God.[8]

Divine Sovereignty and Human Freedom

Ezekiel struggles with one of the paradoxes (dialectical contradictions) that arise out of the experience of the presence of the holy God in the world: that of divine sovereignty and human freedom. He seems to want to grasp both horns of the paradox. On the one hand, he insists that the people are not caught in a fatalistic situation: every person is responsible for his or her own life and is not a captive of heredity or environment, demonic forces at work in society, or any principalities or powers. Accordingly, his task is to place before the people the options and call them to repent (14:6-8; 33:10-11). God wills life, not death.

---

8. Brevard Childs discusses the influence of Exodus tradition on Ezekiel in *Biblical Theology of the Old and New Testaments* (Minneapolis: Fortress Press, 1993), 131, 171.

> Therefore I will judge you, O house of Israel, all of you according to your ways,
> says the Lord GOD [Adonai Yahweh]. Repent and turn from all your transgression;
> otherwise iniquity will be your ruin.
>
> —Ezek. 18:30

On the other hand, the prophet defends God's honor and justice by insisting that it is the people who have been unjust in their ways, not God (18:25-19; 33:17-20). People will come to understand that "it was not without good reason" that God brought disaster on Jerusalem (14:23b). If Israel has a future, it will be because of God's sovereignty, which empowers human freedom and makes possible a new beginning. God's incalculable mercy will supersede God's awesome wrath. After Israel has experienced divine judgment, God will show compassion by restoring "the fortunes of Jacob." This will happen because Yahweh is "jealous" for the divine name (39:25).

Hope for the future, then, rests on the side of God, not on the side of the people, who have consistently broken the covenant. Beyond tragedy Yahweh will ultimately establish an "everlasting covenant" (berît ʿolam) with a people who have a new heart.

> Yes, thus says the Lord GOD [Adonai Yahweh]: I will deal with you as you have
> done, you who have despised the oath, breaking the covenant; yet I will remember
> my covenant with you in the days of your youth, and I will establish with you an
> everlasting covenant."
>
> —Ezek. 16:59-60

Unlike Priestly theology, the everlasting covenant does not come at the beginning, with the promise of grace to Abraham or even the Noachic covenant of creation, but at the end, beyond the history of Israel's failure. At that time there will be a "new exodus," when Yahweh brings the people back to the land promised to their ancestors. The "glory of Yahweh" will return and fill the temple and Yahweh will dwell among the people "forever" (see 43:4-9). Indeed, the name of the city, according to the very last words of the book, will be "Yahweh is there" (YHWH shammah).

Furthermore, Ezekiel draws not only on the Mosaic covenant tradition but also on the Davidic covenant (which we will consider in chapters 23–26). In Ezekiel 37 we find assurances that a united monarchy will be restored with David, God's "servant," as king, and that God will tabernacle in their midst and will be "their God."

> They shall live in the land that I gave to my servant Jacob, in which your ancestors
> lived; they and their children and their children's children shall live there forever;
> and my servant David shall be their prince forever. I will make a covenant of peace
> with them; it shall be an everlasting covenant with them; and I will bless them and
> multiply them, and will set my sanctuary among them forevermore. My dwelling
> place shall be with them; and I will be their God, and they shall be my people.
>
> —Ezek. 37:25-27

As can be seen from this passage, the book of Ezekiel brings together major elements of Israel's religious tradition: the Priestly theology of God's sanctuary in the midst of the people, the Mosaic tradition of the exodus and Sinai revelation, and the royal theology of David as God's anointed (messiah). Ezekiel, then, provides a point of transition from the "everlasting covenant" of Priestly theology to the next sections, where we consider the conditional Mosaic covenant of Deuteronomic tradition (chapters 17–22) and the "everlasting covenant" of royal, Davidic tradition (chapters 23–26).

PART II
CONTINUED

B. THE MOSAIC COVENANT

You have seen what I did to the Egyptians, and how I bore you on eagles' wings and brought you to myself. Now therefore, if you obey my voice and keep my covenant, you shall be my treasured possession out of all the peoples.

EXODUS 19:4-5

17. At the Mountain of God

In the preceding section (II.A, chapters 10–16) we have found that in the Pentateuch the Priestly theology of the "everlasting covenant" presents a distinctive pattern of symbolization: the Creator of heaven and earth enters into special relationship with the people Israel and condescends to tabernacle in their midst. The holy God dwells in the midst of a holy people at the center of a holy land. We turn now to the Mosaic covenant perspective, as set forth preeminently in the book of Deuteronomy. Deuteronomic interpreters present a symbolic world in which God chooses to be present in the midst of the people, "going before them" in their wanderings and eventually dwelling in their midst by putting the divine name on the central sanctuary.

The central person in this "world of meaning" is Moses, the rugged figure portrayed in Michelangelo's well-known statue. In ancient tradition he was accompanied by two other persons: his brother Aaron and his sister Miriam (Mic. 6:4).[1]

Abrahamic and Mosaic Covenants

In the final form of the Pentateuch (Torah), the Mosaic covenant is subordinate to the Abrahamic. In this canonical context the Abrahamic covenant, which guarantees the promise of land and posterity, is the overarching theme within which the Mosaic covenant of law is embraced. This is evident from the fact that the book of Deuteronomy, the classical exposition of Mosaic covenant theology, is inserted into the Priestly work, just before its conclusion. In this location, the book of Deuteronomy provides the conclusion to the Priestly Torah (Pentateuch), which is actually a Tetrateuch plus the conclusion of Deuteronomy, chapter 34. At the same time it is the introduction to the historical work that follows: Joshua through 2 Kings, known as the Latter Prophets, or in scholarly terms, the Deuteronomistic history. Thus we are presented with a huge narrative, extending from creation to the conclusion of the monarchy (Pentateuch + Former Prophets).

In this canonical arrangement, the Abrahamic covenant provides the perspective within which the exodus from Egypt and the Sinai sojourn are viewed. In a Priestly passage found at the beginning of the exodus story we read that the enslaved Israelites groaned under Egyptian bondage and cried to God for help.

> God heard their groaning, and God remembered his covenant with Abraham, Isaac, and Jacob.
>
> —Exod. 2:24

The covenant later made at Sinai, as portrayed in the Old Epic tradition (Exodus 19–24), is subsumed under, or included within, the Abrahamic covenant, showing

---

1. On the overshadowing of Miriam in the present form of the tradition, see the discussion, p. 54; and Phyllis Trible, "Bringing Miriam Out of the Shadows," *BR* 5, no. 1 (1989) 14–25, 34.

that in the view of the final editors these two covenants belong together inseparably—a matter that we must explore as we go along. We have already found that in
the message of Ezekiel the two covenants (as well as the Davidic covenant to be
considered in the ensuing section II.C, chapters 23–26) are brought together.

There is good reason to believe, however, that originally, before the canonical
combination of the two covenants, the Mosaic covenant belonged to a separate
theological tradition. This tradition was especially at home in north Israel
(Ephraim), where prophets like Moses appeared, especially Samuel, Elijah, and
Hosea. This Ephraimitic provenance would explain why the northern prophet,
Hosea, speaks from the platform of Mosaic theology (exodus and Sinai covenant)
and does not refer to the Abrahamic covenant at all (see Hos. 11:1; 12:9, 13).

The Symbolic World of the Mosaic Covenant

The best way to gain an entry into the symbolic world of the Mosaic covenant is
to read the opening chapters of Deuteronomy, which purport to be Moses' final
sermon(s) to the people just before his death in full sight of the promised land and
just before the people crossed over the Jordan River to ascend what is now called
the West Bank.[2] In these chapters we find impassioned preaching to the people,
based on and elaborating the sacred story of exodus and Sinai that unfolds in the
book of Exodus, especially the Old Epic tradition found in Exodus 1–24 and
32–34.

The book of Deuteronomy presents not one sermon but three: the first in
1:6—4:40; the second in chapters 5–28; and the third in chapters 29–30. Moses is
represented as giving a retrospective view back to the "root experiences" of exodus
and Sinai for the purpose of warning the people of opportunities and dangers that
lie ahead in their further historical pilgrimage.

In the imaginative construal of this preaching we see a mountain that is the
meeting place between heaven and earth to which God descends and up which
Moses ascends. The imagery, of course, is taken from the Old Epic tradition about
the journey of the people, under Moses' leadership, to "the mountain of God"
(Sinai, Horeb), where they were to "serve" (worship) Yahweh, their liberating God
(cf. Exod. 3:12). The preaching conjures up in the people's memory the picture of
a mountain whose top flamed with fire as the holy God came down to speak to the
people through Moses, the covenant mediator. In Moses' preaching, creation—
which looms large in Priestly perspective—is reduced to an allusion:

> For ask now about former ages, long before your own, ever since the day that God
> created human beings on the earth.
>
> —Deut. 4:32

2. Still deserving attention, despite changing emphases of biblical scholarship, is George
Ernest Wright's Introduction to and Exegesis of the book of Deuteronomy in *IB* 2:311–537.
Among more recent works, see Patrick D. Miller, *Deuteronomy*, Interpretation (Louisville: John
Knox, 1990).

Attention focuses primarily on the theophany, or manifestation of God's holiness, on the mountaintop.

> Ask from one end of heaven to the other: has anything so great as this ever happened or has its like ever been heard of? Has any people ever heard the voice of a god speaking out of a fire, as you have heard, and lived? Or has any god ever attempted to go and take a nation for himself from the midst of another nation, by trials, by signs and wonders, by war, by a mighty hand and an outstretched arm, and by terrifying displays of power, as the LORD [Yahweh] your God did for you in Egypt before your very eyes?
>
> —Deut. 4:32b-34

In language reminiscent of Moses' encounter with God at the burning bush (Exod. 3:1-6), the speaker says that the holy God appeared invisibly in, and spoke out of, a consuming fire.

> To you it was shown so that you would acknowledge that the LORD [Yahweh] is God, there is no other besides him. From heaven he made you hear his voice to discipline you. On earth he showed you his great fire, while you heard his words coming out of the fire.
>
> —Deut. 4:35-36

Moses' storytelling sermon urges the people to hold that image in mind as they move into the future: the sacred mountain, where the holy God met with Moses their mediator, entered into covenant with them, and called them to obey the commandments that would make them "a people holy to Yahweh" (7:6). Israel was to remain in wonder that at the sacred mountain they heard the voice of God "out of the fire."

> You said, "Look, the LORD [Yahweh] our God has shown us his glory and greatness, and we have heard his voice out of the fire. . . . For who is there of all flesh that has heard the voice of the living God speaking out of fire, as we have, and remained alive?"
>
> —Deut. 5:24-26

In comparison with the Priestly view, which stressed the visible "glory" of God, here is a theological view that emphasizes the word(s) of God. The emphasis falls on hearing, rather than seeing.[3]

Sinai, the Mountain of God

Mount Sinai, located in the southern Sinaitic Peninsula, is one of the famous mountains of the world. Today the traditional mountain is called Jebul Musa, Arabic for "mountain of Moses." Archaeologists are by no means sure that Jebul Musa is the "mountain of God" once visited by ancient Israelites in Moses' time. But that does not really matter, because the mountain has become a powerful symbol in Israel's religious tradition, right to the present.

---

3. On seeing and hearing, see Samuel Terrien, *The Elusive Presence: Toward a New Biblical Theology* (San Francisco: Harper & Row, 1978), chaps. 3–4, 9–10.

In his book *Sinai and Zion,* Jon Levenson focuses attention on the symbolism of Mount Sinai, juxtaposing that mountain to another symbolic mountain, Zion (to which we shall turn our attention in the next section, chapters 23–26). He proposes that a study of these two symbolic mountains provides "an entry into the Jewish Bible."[4] Another engaging study by a Japanese theologian, Kosuke Koyama, describes the crossroads of the East and West in the imagery of two mountains: Fuji and Sinai.[5]

The preaching in the book of Deuteronomy is, in large part, a commentary on what happened at the sacred mountain according to Old Epic tradition found in Exodus 19–24. There we are given a vivid picture of the theophany or manifestation of the holy God that is a prelude to the making of a covenant between God and people.[6]

In this reinterpretation of the old story, Sinai symbolizes the presence of God, who is concerned for the people's distress and chooses to enter into personal relationship with them—indeed, establishes community or communion with them. "Communion," according to the dictionary, means "community of relations," even "intimate intercourse."

But here a difficulty arises. If we take seriously the holiness of God, how can there be such "communion" or "solidarity"? How can God and human beings be that close, that intimate? According to ancient tradition, "no human being can see God and live" (Exod. 33:2).

"They Beheld God, and They Ate and Drank"

To deal with this paradox—the distance and the nearness of God—let us turn to the key passage about the making of the covenant at the mountain of God: Exod. 24:1-11. Here we read that Moses and the leaders of Israel actually "saw the God of Israel" and "ate and drank" before God. This is a very ancient covenant tradition, some would say the most ancient. The passage is so archaic that it almost defies interpretation.

Scholars generally agree that this passage contains two units: one tells about a "summit meeting" on top of Mount Sinai (24:1-2, 9-11); and the other describes a covenant-making ceremony at the base of the mountain (24:3-8).

The Summit Meeting. In the first unit only Moses and leaders are invited; the people are told to keep away. Of the leaders, only Moses, the covenant mediator, is privileged to "come near"; the chiefs and elders are to "worship" from a distance. Here the stress falls on the sovereignty of God, who is enthroned above some sort of celestial pavement of sapphire (v. 10). God's holy power is not life-threatening, however; God did not harm the leaders, but "they saw God and ate and drank."[7]

---

4. Jon D. Levenson, *Sinai and Zion* (Minneapolis: Winston, 1985).

5. Kosuke Koyama, *Mount Fuji and Mount Sinai: A Critique of Idols* (Maryknoll, N.Y.: Orbis, 1985).

6. On the manifestation of God's holiness, see above, chapter 5.

7. See E. W. Nicholson, "They Saw God and Ate and Drank," in *God and His People: Covenant and Theology in the Old Testament* (Oxford: Clarendon, 1986), 121–33, who theorizes that despite God's holiness, they continued to eat and drink normally.

This refers apparently to some sort of celebration in God's presence, perhaps a sacred meal (cf. Gen. 26:6-30 and 31:43-50).

The Service at the Base of the Mountain. The second unit is quite different. Here the leaders are not mentioned; attention focuses on Moses, who conducts a covenant service at the base of the mountain that includes sacrifices. The distance of God is overcome; God and people are brought near in covenant community, symbolized by the power of blood dashed upon the altar and upon the assembly.

While the first unit ends with a mystical vision of God, an ecstatic rapture perhaps, the second emphasizes God's solidarity with the people and the people's responsibility to obey covenant laws as a sign of their relationship to God.

What is the relationship between these two units, the banquet on top of the mountain and the service at the base of the mount? Rabbinical commentators have struggled with this question, one rabbi suggesting, for instance, that the sacrifices at the base of the mountain provided the food for the communion meal at the top.[8] Some scholars try to cut the Gordian knot in one blow by severing these units from the present context and reading them separately. But this is inadequate. To be sure, these are independent traditions, somewhat different in content, yet in the final textual arrangement they belong together. Like the creation and paradise stories at the beginning of the Bible (Genesis 1–3), these units supplement and illuminate each other.

Notice the final form of the tradition: the covenant ceremony at the base of the mountain, which portrays God's solidarity with the people and the people's covenant responsibility, is sandwiched within the story of the meeting at the summit, which portrays the sovereignty and holiness of God, who is the cosmic host at a banquet. What does this tell us theologically about communion with God?

For one thing, this communion does not dissolve into mystical vision, as in some religions ancient and modern. Like Isaiah in the temple, the leaders "see" the cosmic King seated on a heavenly throne (Isa. 6:5b), yet God's sovereignty is not overwhelming. God's holiness is not destructive but creative; it does not negate human freedom but calls one to partnership with God and to the exercise of covenant responsibility, that is, obedience of God's will as expressed in the Ten Commandments. The blood of the covenant, dashed upon the altar and spread out upon the congregation, sacramentally unites the holy God with a holy people.

This text, in its present form, brings the reader before two of the great paradoxes of Israel's experience of the presence of God in history: the sovereignty of God, whose service is "perfect freedom," as Christians say in a traditional prayer;[9] and, as we sing, the "Lord of all being, who is throned afar," is also near, indeed, bound in relationship with the people of the covenant.[10]

---

8. Ibid., 131.

9. As Walter Brueggemann puts it, in Israel's testimony there is a profound "disjunction" between the powerful sovereignty of Yahweh and Yahweh's solidarity with the people. See his discussion of "The Disjunctive Rendering of Yahweh," in *Theology of the Old Testament* (Minneapolis: Fortress Press, 1997), 268–75.

10. See the hymn, "Lord of All Being, Throned Afar."

18. Salvation and Obligation

The symbol of "the mountain of God," where God meets with the people in a theophany of earthquake, wind, and fire, and enters into covenant relation with them, does not stand by itself. In the book of Deuteronomy it belongs to a larger pattern of symbolization that is characteristic of the Mosaic covenant.

Covenant and Treaty

One of the major advances in biblical studies in the twentieth century has been the discovery that the Mosaic covenant is analogous to a type of ancient treaty (or covenant) known as the "suzerainty" or overlord treaty, best illustrated in treaties found by archaeologists in the archives of the Hittite capital located in Asia Minor (modern Turkey). The Hittites, who reached the height of their power about 1400 B.C., regulated relationships between their state and their vassals or client states by a treaty arrangement that has six component parts. To review what has become widely known:

- First comes a preamble in which the covenant maker identifies himself: his name, titles, position of authority.
- Second, there is a review of the previous history of relations between the Hittite king and the vassal, stressing the overlord's beneficent actions that should elicit gratitude and fidelity.
- Third, there is a statement about continuing good relations, based on mutual faithfulness to conditions agreed upon.
- Fourth, the treaty sets forth specific stipulations (laws), especially the requirement that the vassal is not to have an independent foreign policy.
- Fifth, the gods of heaven and earth are invoked as witnesses, and in addition there is an appeal to natural phenomena such as mountains, seas, heaven, and earth.
- Finally, the treaty concludes with the sanctions of blessing and curse: blessing that would result from the protection of the overlord (political security, economic well-being, etc.), and curses in the form of every conceivable disaster that would result from disobedience.[1]

Many interpreters have been impressed with the affinity between the suzerainty treaty and the Mosaic covenant form, and a large literature has arisen on this subject.[2] One striking indication of affinity is that the stipulations of the

1. An excellent example of the so-called suzerainty treaty is the "Treaty Between Mursilis and Duppi-Tessub of Amurru," in *ANET*, 203–20.

2. Discussion was stimulated by the works of George E. Mendenhall, e.g., his article "Covenant," *IDB* 1:714–23. See my observations in *Approaches to the Bible: The Best of Bible Review*, ed. Harvey Minkoff, 2 vols. (Washington, D.C.: Biblical Archaeology Society, 1994–95), "Mendenhall Disavows Paternity of Gottwald's Marxist Theory," 2:114–19.

Mosaic covenant, according to the book of Deuteronomy, are sanctioned by the blessing and the curse. In a homiletical prologue to the Deuteronomic legislation (chapters 12–50) Moses invokes these divine sanctions.

> See, I am setting before you today a blessing and a curse: the blessing, if you obey the commandments of the LORD [Yahweh] your God that I am commanding you today; and the curse, if you do not obey the commandments of the LORD [Yahweh] your God, but turn from the way that I am commanding you today, to follow other gods that you have not known.
>
> —Deut. 11:26-28

Some have gone so far as to say that Moses became familiar with the international treaty form when he was serving in the pharaoh's court in Egypt. But this is unlikely. Some elements of the form, to be sure, are present in the Sinai story in Exodus 19–24, 32–34, but one has to stretch considerably to make the treaty form fit. Also, it is doubtful whether fugitives in the Sinai desert would have been influenced by an international treaty form. It is possible that the treaty form influenced Israelite tradition at the time of the occupation of Canaan, when Israelite tribes were bound together in a tribal confederacy, for several of the elements are found in Joshua's covenant ceremony at Shechem (Joshua 24). More likely, the treaty form was influential during the monarchy, especially in Deuteronomic circles, when other versions (Assyrian) of the ancient treaty form were known.

Whatever its significance for understanding Israel's social life and institutions, the suzerainty treaty form has a heuristic value in that it helps us to discover a pattern of symbolism that we might have missed otherwise. After a long review of scholarly discussion, E. W. Nicholson concludes that "covenant" is "a *metaphor* drawn from the world of treaties rather than an institution which formed the principle of cohesion among the twelve tribes of earliest Israel."[3] It is the task of biblical theology to understand this metaphorical world.

Covenant Blessings and Curses

The major elements of the treaty form are present in the book of Deuteronomy.[4] The opening part (chapters 1–4, 5–11) reviews the history of the relations between Yahweh and Israel, stressing the beneficent deeds that God has performed on behalf of the people, primarily the deliverance from Egyptian bondage. The central part of the book (chapters 12–26) contains the stipulations binding on the vassal or servant. Israel is not to "know," that is, to enter into relation with, any other god, but is to "love" wholeheartedly, that is, to be devoted to, Yahweh alone. Moreover, Israel is to conduct their social life according to the agreement made at Sinai, and that means to pursue justice and to recognize the rights of every

3. E. W. Nicholson, *God and His People* (Oxford: Clarendon, 1986), 82.

4. Moshe Weinfeld believes that the book of Deuteronomy displays the structure of the suzerainty treaties of the first millennium (Assyrian, Sefire); see *Deuteronomy and the Deuteronomic School* (Oxford: Clarendon, 1972); also his article "Covenant," *Encyclopaedia Judaica*, ed. Geoffrey Wigoder et al. (New York: Macmillan, 1971), 5:1019.

member of the community, including the resident alien. Finally, the last section (chapters 27–30), beginning with the curses in chapter 27, sets forth the sanctions of the covenant: the blessing of God for faithfulness, and the "curses of the covenant" for betrayal. Strikingly, the climactic passage in chapter 30 uses language similar to the ancient treaty form. The Mosaic speaker calls on "heaven and earth" to supervise the covenant between God and people to see whether the people are faithful, and he invokes the sanctions of the blessing and the curse.

> I call heaven and earth to witness against you today that I have set before you life and death, blessings and curses. Choose life so that you and your descendants may live, loving the LORD [Yahweh] your God, obeying him, and holding fast to him; for that means life to you and length of days, so that you may live in the land that the LORD [Yahweh] swore to give to your ancestors, to Abraham, to Isaac, and to Jacob.
>
> —Deut. 30:19-20

In Deuteronomy the promises to the ancestors, repeatedly mentioned (e.g., Deut. 1:8), have a different ring than in the Priestly version of the covenant with Abraham, Isaac, and Jacob.[5] Possession of the land and increase on it are not guaranteed by an "everlasting covenant," which endows them with perpetual validity; rather, the promises are qualified by the conditional "if" of the Mosaic covenant, found classically in the Eagles' Wings passage, "If you obey my voice and keep my covenant . . ." (Exod. 19:4-6). This conditional note sounds out loud and clear at the climax of Moses' sermons, as it did in the prologue (Deut. 11:26-28, quoted above):

> If you obey the commandments of the LORD [Yahweh] your God . . . then you shall live and become numerous, and the LORD [Yahweh] your God will bless you in the land that you are entering to possess. But if your heart turns away and you do not hear . . . I declare to you today that you shall perish; you shall not live long in the land that you are crossing the Jordan to enter and possess.
>
> —Deut. 30:16-18

There seems to be a hint of exile from the homeland here, a policy introduced by Assyrian conquerors in the eighth century B.C. In religious terms, God may bring judgment on unfaithful people by not allowing them to live long in the promised land. The claim on the land is a gift, not an irrevocable promise as in the Abrahamic "everlasting covenant." Life in the land is conditioned by the people's behavior. As we shall see, this conditional covenant is consonant with the preaching of the eighth-century prophet Hosea, and reached its consummate expression in the message of the great seventh-century prophet, Jeremiah.

The Command to Love God

One theme of Deuteronomic preaching deserves special consideration: the love of God. To "choose life," Moses is represented as saying, is to "love Yahweh," to "obey" Yahweh's commandments, to "hold fast" to Yahweh (Deut. 30:20, cited

5. See above, chapter 12.

above). Life is not mere extension of days or enjoyment on the good land (though those benefits are included); at the deepest level to live is to love God, to be centered in God.

The theme of love of God is stated in the form of a commandment in the so-called Shema (after the initial verb, "hear"). In rabbinical opinion, this affirmation—recited even today in Jewish homes and synagogues—is the heart of the whole Torah.

> Hear, O Israel! The LORD [YHWH] is our God, the LORD [YHWH] alone. You shall love the LORD [YHWH] your God with all your heart and with all your soul and with all your might.
>
> —Deut. 6:4-5 (NJPSV)

In this translation the word "alone" (instead of the familiar rendering "one") appropriately indicates that Yahweh is to be the sole center of one's devotion. In the realm of faith there is no place for a divided loyalty; rather, one must love God with the whole being—heart, soul (self), vital strength.[6] This is the practical or "existential" monotheism of Israel's faith, to be distinguished from theoretical or philosophical monotheism.

But why are the people commanded to love God? Can real love be commanded? In the Decalogue children are commanded not to love their parents but to honor and respect them (Deut. 5:16). It would be appropriate to hear the command to "fear" (be reverent before) the holy God, as in Ps. 46:10, "Be still and know that I am God," or, I would translate, "Be quiet and acknowledge that I am God." But can the love of God be commanded? Real love is a spontaneous, joyful giving of the heart to another.

The difficulty of the command is lessened somewhat by several considerations. First, some scholars understand "love" in the context of ancient treaties between an overlord and vassal, the so-called suzerainty treaties of the second and first millennia.[7] To take one striking example, the Assyrian king Esarhaddon is quoted as commanding his vassals to "love" his successor Ashurbanipal: "You will love as yourselves Ashurbanipal."[8] In the context of a treaty (covenant) between God and Israel, it is appropriate for the overlord to command the vassal (servant) to exhibit a love that is manifest in loyalty and obedience (see Deut. 11:1 and elsewhere).

Second, in Deuteronomy the Shema does not stand by itself as a stentorian command, but belongs in the context of God's prior love for the people. In the very next chapter, Deuteronomy 7, the people are reminded that Yahweh did not choose them because they were more numerous or powerful than other nations. Rather,

---

6. The Hebrew word *nephesh* should be translated not "soul," if that implies a body-soul dichotomy (as in Greek philosophy and much popular thinking), but "being" (see Gen. 2:7, NRSV) or "self" (cf. Ps. 103:1).

7. See, for instance, W. L. Moran, "The Ancient Near Eastern Background of the Love of God in Deuteronomy," *CBQ* 25 (1963) 77–87.

8. Quoted and discussed by Nicholson, *God and His People*, 61.

> It was because the LORD [Yahweh] loved you and kept the oath that he swore to your
> ancestors, that the LORD [Yahweh] has brought you out with a mighty hand, and
> redeemed you from the house of slavery, from the hand of Pharaoh king of Egypt.
>
> —Deut. 7:8

Behind the commandment, then, is the demonstration of the prior love and grace
of God.

> Know therefore that the LORD [Yahweh] your God is God, the faithful God who
> maintains covenant loyalty [*ḥesed*] with those who love him and keep his com-
> mandments, to a thousand generations.
>
> —Deut. 7:9

Finally, the commandment to love God may be understood as the beginning of an
ever-deepening relationship. This is the case in some marriages. The marriage
begins as a legal contract, a commandment to love and honor one another, but
within the contractual relationship the partners may find love that becomes deeper
and fuller as the years go by. So the love of God, within the covenant, may be a spiritual progress or, in John Wesley's terms, love that is going on toward perfection.

Response to God's Beneficent Deeds

We have seen that the suzerainty treaty form begins with a recitation of the overlord's beneficent deeds that the vassal is called to remember with gratitude and
faithfulness. First comes the story, then the obligation. At first glance, it would
seem that the preaching of Deuteronomy departs from this sequence of story and
commandment, for it begins with the people's sojourn at Sinai where, through the
covenant mediator, they received "the statutes and ordinances." By contrast, the
Old Epic tradition found in the book of Exodus begins with the exodus story
(chapters 1–18) and moves into the giving of the "law" at Sinai (chapters 19–24,
32–34). Yet this apparent difference between Exodus and Deuteronomy is not
real. Throughout Moses' preaching, the "saving experience" (i.e., the deliverance
from Egyptian bondage) is the presupposition of the "commanding experience"
(the giving of the law). The God who enters into covenant with the people and
makes demands on them is their liberator, as stated in the preface to the Ten
Commandments (Deut. 5:6) and echoed throughout Moses' sermons (Deut. 4:37;
6:22-23; etc.).

> Yahweh has taken you and brought you out of the iron-smelter, out of Egypt, to
> become a people of his very own possession, as you are now.
>
> —Exod. 4:20 (BWA)

Moreover, this act of deliverance belongs to the previous story of the ancestors, as can be seen from the so-called little historical credo, which gives the
substance of the Pentateuch (Torah) in a nutshell (Deut. 6:21-24; 26:5-9).[9]

---

9. Gerhard von Rad once maintained that "the little historical credo" constitutes the thematic
nucleus out of which the epic tradition evolved; see his memorable essay, "The Form-Critical

Furthermore, it belongs to the context of the story of God's "going before" the people in their ongoing journey, when God "carried them"—"just as one carries a child, all the way that you traveled until you reached this place" (Deut. 1:30-33). Moses exclaims:

> O Lord [Yahweh] GOD, you have only begun to show your servant your greatness and your might; what god in heaven or on earth can perform deeds and mighty acts like yours!
>
> —Deut. 3:24

Liberation for Service

Some interpreters find in the exodus story the basis for "liberation theology," which has been influential in Latin America, South Korea, the African American community, and elsewhere.[10] Moses' demand before the pharaoh, "Let my people go," is understood to mean that God is on the side of the poor and oppressed everywhere and that God acts to overthrow structures or regimes that hold people in bondage.[11] Indeed, the exodus story evinces "a preferential option for the poor."[12]

There can be no doubt that the God of the Bible demands justice, as evident from the summary of prophetic preaching in the book of Micah (6:1-8). In some respects this passage resembles "the covenant lawsuit" considered previously.

• Summons to Trial (6:1-2): The passage begins with a summons: Yahweh has a "controversy" (rib) with the people, and "the mountains" and "the hills" are to hear the case.[13]

• The Question before the Court (6:3-5): The aggrieved covenant party, Yahweh, asks who is to blame for a breakdown of relations, in view of Yahweh's actions in liberating the people from slavery, providing the leaders Moses, Aaron, and Miriam, and guiding them to the threshold of the promised land.

• The Judgment of the Court (6:6-8): Standing before the Judge, the people ask how they are to give a fitting response to "the mighty acts [literally 'righteous deeds'] of the LORD." The illustrations escalate into wild exaggeration: thousands

Problem of the Hexateuch," in *The Problem of the Hexateuch and Other Essays*, trans. E. W. Trueman Dicken (New York: McGraw-Hill, 1966), 1–78, summarized in his commentary *Genesis*, trans. John H. Marks, OTL (rev. ed.; Philadelphia: Westminster, 1972).

10. For liberation theology see J. Severino Croatto, *Exodus: A Hermeneutic of Freedom*, trans. Salvator Attanassio (Maryknoll, N.Y.: Orbis, 1981). For South Korea an important movement is *Minjung Theology*, or "people's theology." See Kwong-son So, *The Korean Minjung in Christ* (Hong Kong: CTC-CCA, 1992). For the African American community see James Cone, *God of the Oppressed* (New York: Seabury, 1975).

11. One of the best summaries and defenses of liberation theology is Robert McAfee Brown, *Theology in a New Key: Responding to Liberation Themes* (Philadelphia: Westminster, 1978).

12. A theme of Latin American theology, discussed in *The Ecumenist* 3, no. 3 (July–Sept. 1996) 54.

13. Some compare the suzerainty treaty form (discussed above), in which heavens, mountains, etc., are involved.

of sacrificial animals? rivers of oil? the extreme of child sacrifice? The judgment of the court is given in language that reflects the preaching of eighth-century prophets (Amos, Hosea, Isaiah):

> He has told you, O mortal, what is good;
> and what does the Lord require of you
> but to do justice, and to love kindness,
> and to walk humbly with your God?
> —Mic. 6:8

Liberation theologians, however, have sometimes given a one-sided interpretation, especially when exodus is treated as a separate theme, apart from the story of the Sinai revelation. It is clear from the exodus story that the purpose of God's liberating activity is to free people from the bondage of state slaves so that they may enter a new form of service—that is, to be "vassals" (servants) of the Great King, to invoke the suzerainty treaty form once again. At the burning bush Moses is sent to Pharaoh to liberate the people from Pharaoh's yoke of slavery so that they may "serve" (worship) God at Mount Sinai (Exod. 3:12). Their freedom is not self-determination, "the absence of restraint or necessity," to cite a modern dictionary definition. As Jon Levenson remarks appropriately, "Israel's freedom lies in their subjugation [*sub iugo*, 'under the yoke']"—the Mishnah calls this "the yoke of the Kingdom of Heaven."[14]

God's liberation is not complete until a band of slaves, delivered from oppressive bondage, is formed into a covenant community that is governed by God's torah, the basis of peace, order, and welfare. Freedom by itself can lead to license and chaos; order by itself can extinguish freedom. It is significant, then, that exodus and Sinai belong together, certainly in the final shaping of the tradition if not from the very first, at the original source of the whole tradition. God's liberating work began in rescuing slaves from the misery and suffering of imperial bondage; it was completed in shaping those slaves into a community regulated by "statutes and ordinances." Israel's real freedom was not freedom *from* but freedom *for*.

Divine Sovereignty and Human Freedom

The Mosaic covenant, as elaborated in Deuteronomic preaching, deals with the mystery—in the language of Emil Fackenheim, "the dialectical contradiction"—of divine sovereignty and human freedom, sometimes called "the paradox of grace."[15] In the covenant relationship, God remains sovereign. God's holiness is power—the power that brought the universe into being, the power that holds the stars in their courses, the power that shapes history. Therefore, the Sinai covenant, though a bilateral relationship between God and people, is not a parity covenant, between

---

14. Jon D. Levenson, "Exodus and Liberation," in *The Hebrew Bible, the Old Testament, and Historical Criticism* (Louisville: Westminster/John Knox, 1993), 148. This essay, in my judgment, is a probing—if somewhat one-sided—criticism of some of the weaknesses of liberation theology.

15. On the dialectical contradictions of Scripture, see above, chapter 9.

equals. Nonetheless, God's power as Lord of the covenant does not destroy human freedom but addresses it. If God's commitment to Israel involves choice, the same is true of the people. God puts them in a situation of choice, calling for active participation. A classic instance of Mosaic covenant theology is given in Joshua 24. There we read that Joshua, having told "all the people" the story of how God had liberated them from bondage and led them into the land, put to them the challenge: "Choose today whom you will serve" (Josh. 24:15).

The paradox of divine sovereignty and human responsibility is beautifully portrayed in the scene of Israel at the base of Mount Sinai, ablaze with the fire that symbolizes God's appearance in the human world. The mountain shakes with the power of God's holy presence—"earthquake, wind, and fire"—and the people stand back in fear. You would think that the display of the power of the holy God would paralyze, if not crush, any response of human freedom. Yet paradoxically, God's power does not overwhelm but calls to action, to responsibility.[16] This is evident from the magnificent Eagles' Wings passage that stands at the beginning of the Sinai narrative in the Old Epic tradition. Moses, the covenant mediator, is addressed:

> Thus you shall say to the house of Jacob,
>   and tell the Israelites:
> You have seen what I did to the Egyptians,
>   and how I bore you on eagles' wings
>   and brought you to myself.
> Now therefore, if you obey my voice
>   and keep my covenant,
> you shall be my treasured possession among all peoples,
>   for all the earth belongs to me;
> and you shall be for me a kingdom of priests,
>   and a holy nation.
> These are the words that you shall speak to the Israelites.
> —Exod. 19:3-4 (BWA)

Also, in this Eagles' Wings passage we encounter the paradox (dialectical contradiction) of the universal and the particular. All the earth belongs to Yahweh (cf. Ps. 24:1), but Israel is to belong to Yahweh in a special sense—"my treasured possession among all the peoples." As God's people, Israel will be "a kingdom of priests"—a curious expression that seems to refer to a unique priestly role that Israel will perform in the world.

Moreover, Israel is to be "a holy nation." Holiness refers to something separated from the profane world as belonging to the holy God. Here the usage of the term "nation" (goy) must reflect a time after David when Israel became a territorial state. As we have seen earlier, nationhood does not fully and essentially describe Israel's identity and role as a people ('am)—"the people of God."[17]

16. See the discussion of the making of the covenant (Exod. 24:1-11) in chapter 11 above.
17. Above, chapter 9.

The sequel of the invitation to be the people of God is a covenant service, held at the base of Mount Sinai. In this service, during which Moses officiates as the covenant mediator, the people pledge loyalty to their liberating God: "All that the LORD [Yahweh] has spoken, we will do, and we will be obedient" (Exod. 24:7). The covenantal service has influenced the Christian Eucharist, which echoes the theme of "the blood of the covenant" (Mark 14:14 and parallels).

Coexistence with God

The most daring theological implication of the Sinai covenant, as portrayed in the book of Exodus and echoed in the book of Deuteronomy, is that this people, Israel, is called into a life of coexistence with God, or as Abraham Joshua Heschel put it, a life of "partnership with God."[18] The Sinai covenant is based on the initiative of God, who invites the people into the relationship. Israel is not a slave but a free people: invited to be a partner with God and to assume full responsibility. To be sure, the covenant offers the people God's protection and the blessings of life. For it rests on the superior power of the covenant maker, on God's *hesed* or covenant loyalty and strong help for the weaker party. At one point the Deuteronomic preaching seems to echo the passage in Exod. 34:6-7 about the proclamation of the name (character) of Yahweh:[19]

> Know therefore that Yahweh your God is God, the faithful God who maintains
> covenant loyalty [*hesed*] with those who love him and keep his commandments, to
> a thousand generations, and who repays in their own person those who reject him.
> —Deut. 7:9 (BWA)

Moreover, if the relationship is to continue, it will be primarily because of the constancy of God's loyalty, for the people, according to a passage that sounds a note similar to Ezekiel 20, have been rebellious against Yahweh from the day they came out of Egypt until the present (Deut. 9:7, 24). Human freedom cannot destroy the sovereignty of God, who remains free to be gracious unto whom God wills (Exod. 33:19b).

A Conditional Covenant

One aspect of the Mosaic covenant seems to set it off sharply from the Abrahamic covenant: the former is conditional, the latter unconditional. According to the old story in Genesis 15, as we have seen earlier, Abraham was in a deep sleep when the covenant promise of land was given unconditionally; he was a passive recipient of the covenant promises. According to the Priestly version in Genesis 17 no laws were prescribed, but circumcision was given as a sign of membership in the covenant community.[20] By contrast, in the Mosaic covenant the covenant rela-

---

18. See my essay, "Coexistence with God: Heschel's Exposition of Biblical Theology," in *Abraham Joshua Heschel: Exploring His Life and Thought,* ed. John C. Merkle (New York: Collier Macmillan, 1985), 47–65.

19. On the proclamation of God's name, see above, chapter 7.

20. See the discussion above, chapter 12.

tionship is contingent on the people's behavior, whether they say yes or no to God in their daily living. The conditional "if" of the Eagles' Wings passage ("If you obey my voice and keep my covenant," Exod. 19:5), which resounds throughout Moses' preaching (e.g., 4:25-26; 5:29), is underscored with the sanction of blessing and curse: the blessing if the commandments are obeyed, and the curse if they are disobeyed (11:26-28). The people are called to decide whether to be the people of God by showing their loyalty to God in action, that is, by fulfilling those obligations that befit the relationship.

Freedom, then, has both possibilities and dangers, and this is what the Mosaic covenant recognizes. Freedom can be fulfilling if it is freedom in faithful covenant relationship to God, practicing the justice and mercy that befit a people whom God has delivered from oppression. Or freedom can be chaotic if it is the freedom that betrays the covenant relationship, by forgetting the story of God's beneficent deeds and consequently perpetrating violence or pursuing the idols of this world. In short, freedom can yield blessing, or freedom can bring a curse. Human beings who stand before the holy God, as at the assembly at Sinai, face these fateful alternatives. Mosaic preaching calls them to turn from false loyalties and to return to covenant loyalty, that is, to repent—a theme characteristic of prophets like Hosea and Jeremiah, as we shall see. The preaching is an urgent appeal: "Hear, O Israel," as in the Shema (Deut. 6:4-5).

The precarious dimension of human freedom, expressed in the conditional "if," is highlighted in a climactic passage found in Moses' third farewell address (Deut. 29:1—30:20). Moses has rehearsed the story of Yahweh's liberating deeds, preeminently the event of the deliverance from Egyptian bondage; and he has summarized the covenant law found in the Decalogue and the case law based on it. As he looks to the horizon of the future, when the people enter into the land and settle down, he envisions two possibilities: the blessing and the curse.

> See, I have set before you today life and prosperity, death and adversity. If you obey the commandments of the LORD [Yahweh] your God that I am commanding you today, by loving the LORD [Yahweh] your God, walking in his ways, and observing his commandments, decrees, and ordinances, then you shall live and become numerous, and the LORD [Yahweh] your God will bless you in the land that you are entering to possess.

—Deut. 30.15 16

Thus Israel can choose "life," but alternatively can choose "death"—terms that are understood not in a biological sense but as healthy, wholesome relations within the covenant.

> But if your heart turns away and you do not hear, but are led astray to bow down to other gods and serve them, I declare to you today that you shall perish; you shall not live long in the land that you are crossing the Jordan to enter and possess. I call heaven and earth to witness against you today that I have set before you life and death, blessings and curses. Choose life so that you and your descendants may live, loving the LORD [Yahweh] your God, obeying him, and holding fast to him; for

> that means life to you and length of days, so that you may live in the land that the
> LORD [Yahweh] swore to give to your ancestors, to Abraham, to Isaac, and to
> Jacob.
>
> —Deut. 30:17-20

Thus one can speak of the blessing of the Torah, as in Psalm 1; or one can speak
of "the curse of the law," as does Paul in Gal. 3:10.

Relationship between the Abrahamic and Mosaic Covenants

It is not sufficient to draw a theological contrast between the Abrahamic unconditional covenant and the Mosaic conditional covenant. While these two covenants
may be juxtaposed for the sake of comparison, they are not mutually exclusive, at
least in the perspective of Deuteronomic theology.

To understand this, we must consider the importance of God's promise of land
to the people, a promise that is grounded on and guaranteed by the covenant made
with Abraham (Genesis 15). Readers of Deuteronomy will be struck by the number of times that reference is made to the ancestors of Israel. This theme is appropriate, of course, for the story line of the preaching brings the people from Horeb
(Sinai), through the wilderness, to the very edge of the land. The people, it is
emphasized, are to go in and take possession of their inheritance, because it is the
land that "the God of [the] ancestors" (Deut. 1:11) "promised on oath" (8:1) or
"swore on oath" (of the covenant) to Israel's ancestors. God has given other peoples their lands, for instance, Edom, Moab, and Ammon (Deuteronomy 2), but has
assigned this particular land to Israel.

As we have seen, the Abrahamic covenant, according to Priestly understanding, guarantees the land to the people as an "everlasting possession" or "a holding
in perpetuity" (Gen. 17:8). An everlasting covenant entails, in this view, an everlasting possession. When Deuteronomic theologians linked the unconditional
Abrahamic promise to the conditional Mosaic covenant, however, the effect was
to relativize the land promise, that is, to make the possession contingent on the
behavior of the people on the land. *If* the people are unfaithful to the covenant, the
result will be that God will bring judgment on them, scattering them among the
nations, where they will worship worthless idols (Deut. 4:25-29). The meaning of
hardship is that Yahweh "disciplines" the people, just as a parent disciplines a child
(Deut. 8:5), so that, one would hope, they will come to their senses, seek Yahweh
their God, and return to the covenant relationship. This view is summarized in an
important passage that has in view the possibility of exile and return:

> When you have had children and children's children, and become complacent in
> the land, if you act corruptly by making an idol in the form of anything, thus doing
> what is evil in the sight of the LORD [Yahweh] your God, and provoking him to
> anger, I call heaven and earth to witness against you today that you will soon
> utterly perish from the land that you are crossing the Jordan to occupy; you will not
> live long on it, but will be utterly destroyed.
>
> —Deut. 4:25-26

Disaster, however, will provide an opportunity for a change of heart and for a new relationship.

> The LORD [Yahweh] will scatter you among the peoples; only a few of you will be left among the nations where the LORD [Yahweh] will lead you. There you will serve other gods made by human hands, objects of wood and stone that neither see, nor hear, nor eat, nor smell. From there you will seek the LORD [Yahweh] your God, and you will find him if you search after him with all your heart and soul. In your distress, when all these things have happened to you in time to come, you will return to the LORD [Yahweh] your God and heed him.
>
> —Deut. 4:27-30

Here we see how the Deuteronomic interpreters struggle with the paradox of grace. God is the Faithful One who, in the long run, does not go back on the word of promise. When Israel returns, like a prodigal son, God will be ready to receive the people and to establish them in their land.

> Because the LORD [Yahweh] your God is a merciful God, he will neither abandon you nor destroy you; he will not forget the covenant with your ancestors that he swore to them.
>
> —Deut. 4:31

Hope for the future, in this view, rests not in the people's military or economic power (8:11-18), for they are relatively weak, or on their righteousness (9:4-5), for they have been rebellious as long as Yahweh has known them; rather, the holy God acts in freedom—indeed in love—to maintain the covenant loyalty (*hesed*) sworn by oath to the ancestors (7:12-13). In mercy God will "confirm" or "establish" the everlasting covenant with Abraham—surely a paradox, for this covenant was "established" or "made firm" in the time of the ancestors!

Two Covenants That Supplement One Another
After this discussion, the difference and relation between the two covenants—the Abrahamic and the Mosaic—should be clearer. On the one hand, the ancestral covenant guarantees God's promise of land and numerical increase. This covenant is sworn by divine oath, that is, it is unconditionally grounded in God's holy will. It is made not with the people but with their ancestral representatives: Abraham and Sarah, and the rest. This covenant also gives the assurance that in the future "the God of the ancestors" will be the God of the people, being with them as their God. This covenant cannot be annulled in the last analysis, because it is based on God's faithfulness.

On the other hand, the Mosaic covenant is made with the people as a whole. According to the Old Epic in Exodus 19–24, the whole people were assembled at the base of Mount Sinai and Moses acted as their spokesman. When Moses announced the commandments of the covenant, the people answered unanimously: "All the words that Yahweh has spoken we will do." God and people are partners, bound to each other in covenant solidarity.[21] Moses is the mediator of the covenant, the one who represents God to the people and the people before God.

Furthermore, the Mosaic covenant deals with the laws that are to shape the lifestyle of the people. While the Abrahamic covenant dealt with land and increase, the Mosaic covenant deals with the way the people are to live on the land. It is a covenant of law, setting forth the covenant stipulations by which they are to live—or perish—on the land sworn by covenant oath to the ancestors. Perhaps this distinction between the people and their ancestors is drawn in a passage that serves to introduce the Deuteronomic version of the Ten Commandments:

> The LORD [Yahweh] our God made a covenant with us at Horeb. Not with our ancestors did the LORD [Yahweh] make this covenant, but with us, who are all of us here alive today.
>
> —Deut. 5:2-3

The covenant with the ancestors was a different covenant, one that promised land and increase. The covenant at Sinai, however, was a covenant that called the people to obedience to God's laws on the land. All generations of the people, including the present living one, are imagined to be participants in the assembly at the base of Mount Sinai. In worship, the past becomes present with solemn and saving power.

---

21. See the discussion of the covenant-making ceremony in Exod. 24:3-8 in chapter 17 above.

19. Covenant and Law

As we have seen, the Abrahamic covenant is a promissory covenant, one that guarantees the promise of land and posterity, whereas the Mosaic covenant is primarily a covenant of obligation. The giving of commandments by Yahweh, who graciously delivered the people from Egyptian bondage and took the initiative to enter into covenant with them, is fundamental to this theological perspective. Indeed, in this view covenant and law can be identified as one and the same thing. This is clear from a passage in Moses' sermon (Deut. 4:11-14; cf. 1 Kgs. 8:21), where he holds before the people's imagination the image of the sacred mountain, "blazing up to the very heavens, shrouded in dark clouds." At that time, when God spoke to Moses "out of the fire":

> He declared to you his covenant, which he charged you to observe, that is, the ten commandments.
>
> —Deut. 4:13

Here it is clear that covenant is inseparable from law. To keep the covenant is to observe God's statutes and ordinances in the land into which the people are moving.

Furthermore, this passage indicates that the laws, preeminently the Ten Commandments, are the substance of divine revelation. The Deuteronomic interpreter takes pains to emphasize that God's revelation was not visual but auditory: "You heard the sound of words but saw no form; there was only a voice" (4:12, 15). Human beings cannot "see" God (Exod. 33:20) but they are called to "hear." The voice does not communicate a conception of God or a future promise, but "words" that specify what God requires of the people. Obeying God's commandments is the token of a relationship with God that defines Israel as a separate community, "a people holy to God" (Deut. 7:6). Holiness is manifest in the actions of everyday life that distinguish Israel from other peoples.

The Handwriting of God

It is significant that here the "words" that God spoke are specified: the ten "words" (Decalogue) now found with slight modifications in two recensions: Exod. 20:1-17 and Deut. 5:6-21. Law is the essential content of God's revelation. This is underscored with a bold anthropomorphism: "the tablets of stone, written with the finger of God" (Exod. 31:18).

This point is also made in the Old Epic tradition of the sealing of the covenant in a ceremony at the base of the sacred mountain (Exod. 24:3-8). We read that Moses announced to the people "all the words [*debarim*] of Yahweh," referring to the ten commandments of Exod. 20:1-17, "and all the ordinances" (*mishpatim*), referring to the case laws or "ordinances" found in Exodus 21–23 (the so-called Covenant Code). The juxtaposition of "words" and "ordinances" must be the result

155

of editorial harmonization, for in the next act of the covenant ceremony the people respond, "All the words [*debarim*] that Yahweh has spoken we will do" (24:3). Moses then proceeds to write "the words [*debarim*] of Yahweh" in a book (24:4). Finally, after the blood ceremony that unites the two covenanting partners, Moses concludes by saying: "See the blood of the covenant that Yahweh has made with you in accordance with all these words [*debarim*]." The Decalogue (ten words) is clearly the basis of the Mosaic covenant; the *mishpatim* (case laws) found in the Covenant Code are supplementary.

In some churches today, for example, the United Methodist, the rite of Holy Communion includes the reading of the Decalogue and the use of the language "blood of the covenant" to describe the new covenant made through the sacrificial blood of Jesus Christ (Matt. 26:28; 1 Cor. 11:25). According to the Gospel of Matthew the new covenant (some would say "the second covenant") was modeled after the first, for it too was promulgated on a mountain and included the giving of a new law (Sermon on the Mount, Matthew 5–8) by a new Moses who came not to abrogate the Torah but to fulfill it. Christians need to get over a negative attitude toward torah (law, teaching) that has been influenced by Paul's interpretation, or possibly our misinterpretation of his polemical writing (e.g., Galatians).[1]

Thus the core of Israel's legal tradition is the Decalogue, around which other interpretive laws (ordinances) have gathered in the history of the tradition, as can be seen in Exodus 20–23. Around this core is also gathered priestly legislation, found especially in Exodus 25–31 and the book of Leviticus. From an original nucleus the law expanded as the core law was interpreted in ever new situations: the agricultural situation of Canaan, the complexities of the monarchy, the postexilic community, and so on. To take a secular analogy: it is something like life in the United States, where the American Constitution provides a fundamental legal core around which have gathered case laws, or a body of applications of the fundamental law. New situations call for the reinterpretation of the Constitution without changing its fundamental character.

The Ark of the Covenant

In Deuteronomic tradition the stress on the Decalogue is further evidenced in the statement that Moses put the tablets containing the Decalogue in the ark, "and there they are as Yahweh commanded me" (Deut. 10:5; cf. 2 Kgs. 8:9). The view of the ark as a repository for sacred objects may well be very ancient.

Another pentateuchal tradition, however, views the ark somewhat differently: it is the throne-seat on which Yahweh is invisibly enthroned, and it "goes before" the people during their wars and wanderings. The Song of the Ark, one of the oldest pieces of poetry in the Hebrew Bible, reflects this view. When the ark advanced at the head of the people, Moses exclaimed:

---

1. See the pointed, and appropriate, remarks of the Jewish theologian, Jon D. Levenson, *Sinai and Zion* (Minneapolis: Winston, 1985), 1–2.

> *Arise, O LORD [Yahweh], let your enemies be scattered,*
> *and your foes flee before you!*
>
> —Num. 10:35

When the ark came to rest at the end of the day's march, Moses would summon Yahweh to return to be with the myriads of Israel.

> Return, O LORD [Yahweh] of the ten thousand thousands of Israel!
>
> —Num. 10:36

One of David's great accomplishments, according to the story in the books of Samuel, was to bring the ancient palladium into the temple, where it was enshrined in the Holy of Holies. This event is memorialized in Psalm 24, which depicts Yahweh, the King of glory, being escorted in procession, presumably enthroned invisibly on the ark, through the gates of the city of Jerusalem.

> *Lift up your heads, O gates!*
>   *and be lifted up, O ancient doors!*
>   *that the King of glory may come in.*
> *Who is the King of glory?*
>   *The LORD [Yahweh], strong and mighty,*
>   *the LORD [Yahweh], mighty in battle.*
>
> —Ps. 24:7-8

In Psalm 132 the ancient Song of the Ark is reinterpreted in the light of God's triumphant march to the new "resting place" in the temple of Jerusalem.

These two views—the ark as Yahweh's throne-seat and as the repository for the two tablets of stone—are combined in the Solomonic prayer in 1 Kgs. 8:6-12, a Deuteronomistic passage. In the Deuteronomistic view, the two traditions are compatible, for the giving of the law, like the ark itself, is a sign of the presence of Yahweh among the people.[2]

The Ten Words

At first, the Ten Commandments were probably short, crisp commands or "ten words" (Decalogue) that amounted to two brief Hebrew words, as in *lo' tirtsah*, "You shall not murder"; *lo' tin'aph*, "You shall not commit adultery"; *lo' tignob*, "You shall not steal." In some cases the brief "word" was expanded with interpretive comments to provide explanation or motivation. A good example is the commandment to keep the Sabbath holy.[3]

In the Exodus version (20:8-11), on the one hand, the interpretive comment says that this commandment harks back to the Sabbath "hidden" in God's creation (Gen. 2:2-3). This accords with the overall movement from creation to Sinai in Priestly tradition, where the Sabbath, observed by God at creation, is the "sign" of the everlasting covenant.[4] In the Deuteronomic version (5:12-15), on the other

---

2. On the meaning of the ark in Priestly tradition, see above, chapter 13.
3. See further in this chapter.
4. See above, chapter 10.

hand, the commandment to observe a day of rest from work is connected with the saving event of the exodus: "Remember that you were a slave in the land of Egypt" (Deut. 5:15). This accords with Deuteronomy's emphasis on the inseparable relation between "the saving experience" and "the commanding experience," exodus and Sinai.[5] Thus in each covenant perspective—the Abrahamic (Priestly) and the Mosaic—we find a different explanation and motivation for keeping the commandments.

In this connection it is worth noting that in Priestly legislation the prescription for Sabbath rest is extended to the Jubilee, the fiftieth year that comes at the end of seven sabbatical cycles (7 x 7). On this year the land is to lie fallow, and humans and animals are to be at rest. In addition, there is to be a change in human relationships: slaves are to be set free, debts forgiven, and the overuse of the land corrected (see Lev. 25:8-17, 23-25; 27:16-25). Rosemary Radford Ruether suggests that this vision of "periodic redemption and restoration of right relation" has important ethical and ecological implications: "Modern revolutionary thinkers would have done better if they had taken the Jubilee, rather than the millennium and the Kingdom of God, as their models of historical change."[6]

Statutes and Ordinances

Looking over the "statutes and ordinances" found in the Decalogue and in the Covenant Code (Exodus 20–23, paralleled in Deuteronomy 5, 12–26), the first thing to observe is that this is covenant law, that is, law that applies to the people Israel, not to the nations generally. In keeping this law, Israel becomes "a people holy to Yahweh your God" (Deut. 7:6), that is, separated from the nations and their ways.

A major question for biblical ethics is whether, or to what degree, these covenant laws apply also to the state or to other societies. Of course, if the covenant community and the state were coextensive, the matter would be much simpler. But in a pluralistic society, and especially one that draws a separation between church and state, the question of applicability is often difficult.

Consider this question by examining the Decalogue more closely. The Decalogue falls into two general parts: the first having to do with relations to God, and the second with relations to the neighbor in the community. It is appropriate that in later rabbinical summary, the covenant law was reduced to two commands: one theological, to love God wholeheartedly; and the other social, to love the neighbor just as one loves or respects one's self (Mark 12:30-31).

The two parts would be relatively equal if, as in Jewish tradition, the opening sentence ("I am Yahweh your God who brought you out of . . . the house of slav-

5. See above, chapter 18.

6. Rosemary Radford Ruether, "Ecofeminism and the Spiritual Roots of Environmentalism," Harvard Divinity School Lecture, Oct. 1, 1992; see also her *Gaia & God: An Ecofeminist Theology of Earth Healing* (San Francisco: HarperSanFrancisco, 1992).

ery") is treated as the First Commandment, rather than a theological preface to the whole. Some interpreters (Roman Catholic, Lutheran) count the commandment about sole worship of Yahweh and the prohibition of graven images as one (Exod. 20:3-6; Deut. 5:6-10), and divide Exod. 20:17 (Deut. 5:21) into two commandments, thus making ten. Others (Anglican, Greek, Reformed) more defensibly count two commandments dealing with false worship: against worship of other gods and against image worship or idolatry. But apart from differences in numbering, it is clear that the first section (preface and first four commandments) has to do with Israel's relation to Yahweh, the God of the people. This is covenant law in the strict sense, pertaining primarily to Israel as a religious community.

First Part of the Decalogue
The First Commandment stipulates that members of this community must have a single religious loyalty: to the God, known by the cultic name Yahweh, who delivered them from Egyptian bondage. Other gods there may be, but they have no claim on this people. This corresponds to the exclusive (jealous) demand of the suzerainty covenant: vassals were not allowed to recognize (know) any other lord.[7] This is a kind of "existential monotheism," as we have seen.[8] Israelite poets pictured other gods as being members of the heavenly council, over which Yahweh presided.[9]

The Second Commandment expresses the official position of the cultic community, though there may have been exceptions in popular practice, as evidenced by Jeroboam's installation of calves to represent the god(s) who brought the people out of Egypt (1 Kgs. 12:26-30)—an echo of the incident of the worship of the golden calf at Sinai (Exodus 32). Israel is not to represent Yahweh in the form of a visual image of anything in creation: heaven above, earth below, subterranean realm. (This puts a restraint on visual art, lest one attempt to portray God.) Deuteronomy emphasizes this by saying that no "form" was seen when Yahweh spoke out of the fire, and that therefore no likeness, whether "male or female," or any animal, bird, or creeping thing on earth, is permissible (Deut. 4:15-18). This aniconic worship of Yahweh set Israel apart from other religions in which natural powers were personified or deities were represented in animal or human form. For Israel the only exception to this view, which reached its supreme expression in the poems of Second Isaiah (e.g., Isa. 40:18, 25), is that human beings are made "in the image of God," that is, to represent God's rule on earth.[10]

Also, Yahweh's name is not to be taken in vain or "used wrongly" (NRSV), that is, it cannot be manipulated for human purposes, as in magic (or some kinds of prayer), or—so the prophets would say—to endorse the pursuits of wealthy and powerful people or the political interests of a nation. The God whom Israel

7. On the suzerainty treaty (covenant) form, see above, chapter 18.
8. See above, chapter 17.
9. See previous discussion of "Yahweh and the Gods," above, chapter 8.
10. See above, chapter 11.

worships is not subject to human control and cannot be managed for one's personal or social advantage.

Finally, one day—the Sabbath—is separated from others as a segment of time belonging to God, the Creator (so in Exod. 20:11) and Redeemer (so Deut. 5:15). Keeping this day holy, by resting from work and usual daily activities, prevents the secularization that fills the times with only personal meaning (e.g., a birthday) or national significance (Fourth of July, Veterans' Day), excluding the dimension of the sacred. When the Sabbath is observed as holy, symbolized by the lighting of a Sabbath candle in a Jewish home, all the days are hallowed with reverence for God.

The Fourth Commandment of the Decalogue refers, of course, to "the seventh day" of the Jewish calendar (Friday sunset to Saturday sunset; cf. Gen. 1:5, 8, 13, etc.). Christians began to celebrate the day of resurrection, which according to the Gospels occurred "on the first day of the week, when the sabbath was over" (Matt. 28:1; cf. Luke 24:1), and eventually considered it to be the "Sabbath." This "discontinuity" with the Hebrew Bible persists to the present day, except in some circles, for example, the Seventh Day Adventists, who consider our Saturday as a day of rest and gladness, based on God's "separation" of the Sabbath at creation.[11] Whenever the day is celebrated, it is an expression, in worship and behavior, of God's sovereignty over the times of our life and reverence of the Creator who has created the world and all that is in it.

Second Part of the Decalogue
The remaining six laws of the Decalogue also have to do primarily with Israel as a covenant community, although ethical reflection may show that they are also relevant to human society generally. Respect for parents, prohibition against murder, against adultery, against theft, against perjury in a court of law: without these laws violence would reduce society to chaos.

Some of these laws protect the extended family, the basic institution of Israelite society. Respect for parents insures family solidarity and generational continuity, and sex within marriage protects family cohesion and the transmission of inheritance and tradition. It is noteworthy that the law against coveting, the only one dealing with a motive that may lead to action, is expanded in both the Exodus and Deuteronomy forms of the Decalogue, by indicating a potential invasion of the neighbor's property: his wife belongs to him, along with house, field, slaves, animals, and so on. Notice that in Deuteronomy 5 the neighbor's wife is mentioned first, then the house, whereas in Exodus 20 it is the neighbor's house that comes first. In either case, the wife is included with property belonging to the neighbor.

These laws that reflect their own time must be read with discrimination today, especially in the Christian community, where people sense both continuity and discontinuity. In my judgment, ethicists should discuss the basic laws apart from

11. On the significance of the Sabbath in Priestly perspective, see above, chapter 10.

the expansions and should propose explanations or motivations that interpret the meaning of covenant for our time. It is noteworthy that in the Sermon on the Mount Jesus provided a more radical interpretation of the law against killing by going behind the act to the motive (Matt. 5:21-26), as was done in the Mosaic law against coveting.

The command "You shall not kill" stands by itself in the Decalogue, without any explanation or motivation. Explanations and motivations should be added in discussions of biblical ethics. In antiquity, the explanation would have been added that life is a sacred gift from God and must be treated with reverence, for human beings are made in the image of God (see the Noachic covenant),[12] though exceptions were made as in the case of capital punishment (Gen. 9:6a) or legitimate war. In our time, qualifications of the commandment will have to be restated in the light of the New Testament and in the context of our different social situation. The "just war," if there be such, surely cannot allow the indiscriminate killing of civilian population, as in the case of Hiroshima and Nagasaki. That the planned murder of innocent victims in the Holocaust is prohibited under this law is self-evident. To take another illustration, some will argue that the abortion of a fetus in the womb comes under the prohibition of the absolute law, though exceptions may be made under certain circumstances: rape, incest, death of the mother. To make a potentially long discussion short, biblical ethics must work out new formulations of how the absolute law applies in modern circumstances.

Absolute and Conditional Law

Another thing that should be noticed about Israelite law is that it falls into two general types: absolute or apodictic law and conditional or case law. On the one hand, absolute law is set forth unconditionally, as in the Ten Commandments: You shall not kill. No conditions are allowed, no mitigating circumstances considered, as in the tersely formulated laws found in Exod. 22:18-20. The absolute laws (statutes)—and this goes especially for the Ten Commandments—set forth the basic policy, one might say the "constitution," of the covenant community.

The "ordinances" (mishpatim), on the other hand, adjudicate cases based on particular circumstances in the light of the basic policy law. For instance, it is not enough to hear the command "You shall not kill"; was the act premeditated or unintended (Exod. 21:12-14)? These "case" (casuistic) laws are usually formulated in a conditional style: "If . . . then . . ." (as in the Covenant Code of Exod. 20:22—23:32 and parallels in Deuteronomy 12–16). It is the task of judges to adjudicate difficult cases that are brought before them, though with due humility before God and in the recognition that in the final analysis "the judgment is God's."

> Give the members of your community a fair hearing, and judge rightly between one person and another, whether citizen or resident alien. You must not be

---

12. Discussed above, chapter 11.

partial in judging: hear out the small and the great alike; for the judgment is God's.

—Deut. 1:16-17

When Israelite law is compared with other legislation of the ancient Near East (e.g., the Code of Hammurabi or the Assyrian law codes), one senses that a spirit of humanitarianism breathes through it, with the result that there is less severity in punishment and a greater striving for justice for all classes of society.[13] This is especially evident in exhortations of the book of Deuteronomy: "Remember that you were a slave in the land of Egypt" (Deut. 5:15). The God who liberated a people from bondage is the vindicator of all who need the defense of the law: the orphan and widow, the poor and oppressed, the resident alien (sojourner) who lacks the full status of membership in the community. The book of Psalms provides many examples of oppressed persons who, in a time of humiliation and helplessness, cry out to Yahweh for help, confident that they will have a hearing before the Judge of the whole earth.

Notice too that the casuistic interpretations of the basic covenant law, found in the Covenant Code and its Deuteronomic parallels, reflect an attempt to understand the demands of the covenant in a new social situation, the agricultural economy of the land of Canaan. Thus we read about cases of an ox goring a person, of setting fire to a field or vineyard, of buying or selling a slave, and so on. No longer were the people on the move in the wilderness; they were settled in an agricultural society, which had its special circumstances. We can look back on this as a time of transition, when the covenant policy law was adapted to new situations. It is still true that the task of interpreters is to face anew the question of what God requires of a people when they face a new situation, such as the technological global economy of the late twentieth century. There is truth in the poet's words:

> *New occasions teach new duties,*
> *time makes ancient good uncouth.*[14]

Name Theology

One feature of Deuteronomic theology calls for special attention. Israel is enjoined to worship Yahweh at the central sanctuary, the one chosen by Yahweh (Deut. 12:1-31). This divine requirement became the basis for a great religious reform in 621 B.C. (2 Kings 22–23), when the temple of Jerusalem was held to be the divinely chosen sanctuary for sacrificial worship rather than local sanctuaries that were exposed to popular religion. On the eve of entrance into the land of the promise, Moses says to the people:

13. See Paul Hanson, "Conflict in Ancient Israel and Its Resolution," in *Understanding the Word: Essays in Honor of Bernhard W. Anderson*, ed. James T. Butler et al., JSOTSup 37 (Sheffield: JSOT Press, 1985), 185–205.

14. James Russell Lowell (1819–1891): "Under the Willows."

> You shall seek the place that the LORD [Yahweh] your God will choose out of all your tribes as his habitation to put his name there. You shall go there, bringing there your burnt offerings and your sacrifices, your tithes and your donations, your votive gifts, your freewill offerings, and the firstlings of your herds and flocks. And you shall eat there in the presence of the LORD [Yahweh] your God, you and your households together, rejoicing in all the undertakings in which the LORD [Yahweh] your God has blessed you.
>
> —Deut. 12:5-7

The new thing here is the Deuteronomic theology of the divine name. God chooses one shrine in the land of Israel "to put his name there, for his habitation" (Deut. 12:5), or as stated a bit later:

> The place [sanctuary] that Yahweh your God chooses to cause his name to dwell there.
>
> —Deut. 12:12 (BWA)

The verb translated "dwell" (*shakan*) is the same one used in Priestly theology for the "dwelling of God" in the sanctuary or tabernacle, for example, "Let them make me a sanctuary that I may dwell in their midst" (Exod. 25:8).[15] While Priestly theology affirms that God's "glory" fills the sanctuary, as evidence of God's presence, the Deuteronomic interpreter says that it is God's name that dwells there. The name, as we have seen, signifies the personal identity of Yahweh.[16] Here is another way of dealing with the paradox (dialectical contradiction) of the transcendence and immanence of God. God does not dwell in a temple built by human hands; rather, God's true dwelling place is in the heavenly temple. But God's name—or alter ego—dwells in the temple. It is there that people call on the name of the Lord and God is "enthroned on the praises of Israel" (Ps. 22:3).[17]

Solomon's Prayer of Dedication
It is instructive to study the account of Solomon's dedication of the temple (1 Kgs. 8:1-66), where these two views of God's presence, the Priestly and the Deuteronomistic, are brought together. When the ark, here regarded as a repository for the tablets of law (v. 9), was put in the innermost sanctuary, the Holy of Holies, "the glory of Yahweh" filled the temple (v. 11) as evidence of God's indwelling presence. This is supported by a quotation from an old poem found, according to the Greek Bible (Septuagint), in the Book of Jashar (cf. Josh. 10:13):

> *The LORD [Yahweh] has said that he would dwell [shakan] in thick darkness.*
> *I have built you an exalted house, a place [makon] for you to dwell in forever.*
>
> —1 Kgs. 8:12-13

15. See above, chapter 13.
16. See above, chapter 6.
17. See my study guide, *Out of the Depths: The Psalms Speak for Us Today* (Philadelphia: Westminster, 1983; rev. ed. forthcoming, 2000), especially chapter 2, "Enthroned on the Praises of Israel."

When Solomon gives his "Deuteronomistic" prayer, however, he declares that he built Yahweh a house (temple) so that Yahweh's name "might be there" (v. 16). Indeed, at one point in the prayer the view of God "dwelling" in an earthly temple is challenged:

> But will God indeed dwell [*yashab*] on the earth? Even heaven and the highest heaven cannot contain you, much less this house that I have built! Regard your servant's prayer and his plea, O LORD [Yahweh] my God, heeding the cry and the prayer that your servant prays to you today; that your eyes may be open night and day toward this house, the place of which you said, "My name shall be there," that you may heed the prayer that your servant prays toward this place. Hear the plea of your servant and of your people Israel when they pray toward this place; O hear in heaven your dwelling place; heed and forgive.
>
> —1 Kgs. 8:27-30

Hallowing the Name

One gets the impression that here a Deuteronomistic interpreter has difficulty with the Priestly view that God "dwells" in the temple. Certainly God does not reside (*yashab*) in the temple, as a human being lives in a house. Language has to be strained to express the paradox of God's transcendence and immanence, of God's distance and nearness (cf. Jer. 23:23-24). The Deuteronomistic interpreter states the paradox by saying that God, who dwells beyond the earthly sphere (in heaven), chooses to place the divine name on the temple and, in that sense, to be present in the midst of the worshiping people.

20. HISTORY VIEWED IN DEUTERONOMISTIC PERSPECTIVE

Just as the Priestly perspective is dominant in the final form of the Torah, so the canonical unit known as the Former Prophets is governed by the theology of the Mosaic covenant, set forth preeminently in the book of Deuteronomy. Indeed, the book of Deuteronomy has a pivotal position in the canon. On the one hand, it is the conclusion of the Pentateuch, where it has affinities with parts of Old Epic tradition (especially northern or Elohist epic); on the other hand, it provides the theological preface to the Former Prophets (Joshua through 2 Kings), a historical work that extends from the time of Israel's occupation of Canaan to the exile. When these two works, the Pentateuch and the Former Prophets, are linked together, the result is a huge story or macrohistory that begins with creation and traces the story of Israel to the tragedy of the fall of the nation in 587 B.C. and its immediate sequel.

The Deuteronomistic History

This historical work is often called the Deuteronomistic history, because it is governed by the theological perspective set forth in the book of Deuteronomy. The core of the book of Deuteronomy was probably the Torah scroll that, according to the account in 2 Kings 22–23, was found in the temple in about 621 B.C. When validated by the prophetess Huldah, this "book of the covenant" became the basis of the great reform of King Josiah reported near the end of the books of Kings.

The Deuteronomistic history, with the book of Deuteronomy as an introduction, runs into some 280 pages of Scripture (counting in the NRSV)—that is almost one-quarter of the Old Testament. Proportionately, it is as extensive as the Johannine corpus in the New Testament. In addition, one of the major prophetic books—the book of Jeremiah—in its final form comes from the hand of Deuteronomistic editors. This quantitative analysis gives some idea of the influence of the Deuteronomistic school of theology.[1]

In its final form the Deuteronomistic history was composed in the period of the exile, for the last event reported is the release of King Jehoiachin from imprisonment in 561 B.C. (2 Kgs. 25:27ff.). This history does not refer to the rise of Cyrus of Persia or his conquest of Babylon (539 B.C.) and the return of Jews to Palestine to restore their community, matters that are dealt with in another historical work, that of the Chronicler (Ezra, Nehemiah, 1–2 Chronicles), to which we will turn our attention later. Some scholars maintain that this history was com-

---

1. The adjective "Deuteronomic" refers to the book of Deuteronomy, or better the original core of the book; "Deuteronomistic" refers to the work of editors influenced by the Deuteronomic theological perspective.

posed in two editions: a first edition dating from Josiah's reign, before the king was killed at Megiddo in 609 B.C. while attempting to intercept Egyptian armies (2 Kgs. 23:28-30); and a second updated edition after Josiah's death and the exile of the people.[2]

The Rise and Fall of Israel

The question that Deuteronomistic historians raise, as they survey Israel's history from the occupation of Canaan to the end of the monarchy, is: Why was Israel's covenant history a history of failure? We can ascertain their answer to this existential question in two ways: (1) by considering how they use their sources (for instance, the Elijah narratives), that is, the way these materials function in the total narrative context; and (2) by considering their composition of key passages that serve as interpretive links. Among the latter are:

> A. *Highlighted divine addresses*
>   to Joshua (Josh. 1:1-9)
>   to Samuel (1 Sam. 8:7-9)
>   to David (2 Sam. 7:5-17)
>   to Solomon (1 Kgs. 9:1-9)
>
> B. *Climactic speeches or prayers equivalent to speeches*
>   by Joshua (Josh. 23)
>   by Samuel (1 Sam. 12)
>   by David (2 Sam. 7:18-29)
>   by Solomon (1 Kgs. 8:12-53)
>
> C. *Interpretive summaries*
>   epitomes of the cycles of apostasy and return
>   in the period of the judges (Judg. 2:6—3:6)
>   epitome of the Northern Kingdom's history
>   of failure (2 Kgs. 17:7-23)

In these passages we find the key to the message of Deuteronomistic historians presented in the situation of the exile when an uprooted people sought to understand their historical tragedy and to rediscover their roots.

A History of Failure

Humanly speaking, this whole history was a history of failure. No sooner did Joshua die (end of the Mosaic period) than the people lapsed into cycles of apostasy and return, at the end of which was the great mistake: demanding a king to "judge" them "like the nations" (1 Samuel 8).

For a time the people enjoyed political solidarity under the united kingdom of David (a unity that Josiah hoped could be restored). But after the death of

---

2. See the Introduction to the Books of Kings, *New Oxford Annotated Bible* (New York: Oxford Univ. Press, 1991) and comment on 2 Kgs. 23:28-30.

Solomon, a king who was truly "like the nations," the united monarchy broke up, and north and south went their independent ways until the Assyrians conquered the northern kingdom of Ephraim and carried many people into exile. This catastrophe, however, did not occur because of the superior political power of Assyria; it happened because the people misused their God-given covenant freedom. The people forgot their God-story, the story of how Yahweh their God liberated them from oppression in Egypt, and they turned from Yahweh's covenant to walk in the customs of other nations. This interpretation was given by preexilic prophets like Hosea and Jeremiah, as we shall see, and helps to explain why these historical books are regarded as "Former Prophets."

The Deuteronomistic history teaches that Yahweh was "slow to anger." In forbearance Yahweh warned the people "by every prophet and every seer, saying, 'Turn from your evil ways and keep my commandments and my statutes, in accordance with all the law that I commanded your ancestors and that I sent to you by my servants the prophets'" (2 Kgs. 17:13). To illustrate this divine appeal through prophets from time to time, the editors insert the once independent traditions concerning Elijah and Elisha (1 Kgs. 17—2 Kgs. 10). Here the Deuteronomistic historians sound the theme of "repentance," which was stated in the Deuteronomic preface (Deut. 4:29-31). Yet the people would not listen or change. They despised the covenant made with their ancestors, they forsook all the commandments God granted them, and they brought on themselves the curses of the covenant: the fall of the nation and exile from the land.[3] They failed in their covenant responsibility; "therefore the LORD [Yahweh] was very angry with Israel and removed them out of his sight; none was left but the tribe of Judah only" (2 Kgs. 17:18, RSV).

According to this history, the Southern Kingdom was given a chance to profit from the lesson of their compatriots to the north: but they too decided falsely, and brought on themselves the curses of the covenant. That seems to be the judgment of the prophetess Huldah as summarized in 2 Kgs. 22:16-17.

What would have happened had the people repented? Surely the historian knew that, in terms of pragmatic politics (*Realpolitik*), the Assyrians were following their own political ambitions and could not have cared less about the spiritual health of Ephraim, or later Judah. This history is written in retrospect—after the fact of the destruction wrought by the Assyrian war machine. The Israelite historian attempts to understand the events not in terms of world politics but in terms of Israel's covenant with God. The people had failed, and the consequence fell on them terribly. God was "angry with Israel" (see 2 Kings 17).

The Lesson of History
Here is a history that speaks powerfully to people who have the freedom to shape their destiny, at least in some degree. Why wait until it is too late, when catastrophe falls pitifully and ominously? The alternatives of life and death, of blessing and curse, are set before a people. Why follow national policies that are suicidal,

---

3. On the blessing and curse of the covenant, see above, chapter 18.

policies that will not bring the blessing of peace but the curse of violence and war-fare? The question is still relevant in our time of economic imbalances and alarm about the future of Earth. Crisis is a time of opportunity; the future is open, not fatalistically predetermined. Therefore, choose life, not death! The message of Deuteronomistic historians echoes in the preaching of great prophets like Hosea and Jeremiah, as we shall see.

Moses and David

Over the Deuteronomistic history falls the long shadow of Moses, as evidenced by the Deuteronomic preface (Deut. 1:6—4:40) and the climactic chapters of 2 Kings 22–23, where good king Josiah carries out a reform on the basis of the Mosaic torah found in the temple. Deuteronomistic historians introduce another major theme, however: Yahweh's "everlasting covenant" (berît 'olam) with David—a covenantal perspective that will occupy our attention in the next section (II.C, chapters 23–26). As in a Bach fugue, these two themes are woven together con-trapuntally throughout the exposition of the history of the monarchy.

The account of the dedication of the temple, found in 1 Kings 8, provides an excellent illustration of the interweaving of covenantal perspectives. The specific references to exile (8:46-51) indicate that this account is addressed to conditions of a time much later than Solomon's, when Assyria and Babylonia actually exe-cuted the policy of exiling captive peoples.

At the beginning the account gives primacy to the Mosaic covenant. The his-torian recalls the bringing of the ark of the covenant to Jerusalem and placing it in "the inner sanctuary of the temple, in the most holy place underneath the wings of the cherubim" (1 Kgs. 8:6). The ark, we are told, signifies the covenant that Yahweh made with Moses at Horeb, that is, Sinai (v. 9). The view of the ark as a repository for the Decalogue is, as we have seen, a Deuteronomic variation from Priestly tradition.

Solomon's long-winded prayer introduces the Davidic covenant perspective. In the first part (vv. 12–21)—the king's blessing of the people—the king says that Yahweh chose David as leader and also chose David's city to be the central sanc-tuary, where the ark was located and where God's name was present.

In Solomon's intercessory prayer (vv. 22–40), the king says that these promises have already been fulfilled. Significantly, an "if" is added, showing the influence of the conditional Mosaic covenant: God promises that a Davidic ruler will sit on the throne of Jerusalem "if only your children look to their way, to walk before me" (v. 25). This conditional "if" is picked up in a later passage (vv. 41–53) reflecting the situation of exile, which may be an expansion of the prayer. The "Mosaic if" begins with the people's freedom to break the covenant relationship: "If they sin against you—for there is no one who does not sin." The prayer continues by saying that, though the people will suffer the consequence of divine judgment (captivity and exile), they have the freedom to repent and return.

Yet if they come to their senses in the land to which they have been taken captive, and repent, . . . saying, "We have sinned and have done wrong, we have acted wickedly."

The prayer reaches its climax with an appeal to God's freedom, the freedom of divine grace and forgiveness:

Then hear in heaven your dwelling place their prayer and their plea, maintain their cause and forgive your people who have sinned against you. . . . For you have sep-arated them from among all the peoples of the earth, to be your heritage, just as you promised through Moses, your servant, when you brought our ancestors out of Egypt, O Lord [Yahweh] GOD.

—1 Kgs. 8:46-53

Apparently the Deuteronomistic historian senses no conflict between these two covenants, for God's promises have several aspects: the land that was given to the ancestors, the increase of the people on the land if they are faithful to the covenant, and the promises of grace to David, namely, temple and dynastic suc-cession. In this view, the people of God need not only a land upon which to fulfill their vocation but a leader upon whose shoulder rests the authority of government (cf. Isa. 9:6-7). Thus the two covenants belong together in the total picture.[4]

The Interrelation of the Two Covenants

In summary, the historian's view of the time from Israel's occupation of the land to the fall of the nation is based on the interrelation of these covenants. On the one hand, this is a history of failure. The people were given a glorious opportunity, but they missed it. They were not faithful to the covenant and suffered the conse-quences: loss of the gift of the land. The Southern Kingdom, Judah, also partici-pated in that history of failure. After two deportations of Judeans into exile, there was an attempt to restore some sort of stable social life in the land. But the gover-nor, Gedaliah, who was sympathetic toward the prophet Jeremiah, was murdered; and there was a further dispersion into Egypt, which included the prophet Jere-miah. Thus the reformation, which Josiah carried out on the basis of the Mosaic Torah, proved to be a failure.

Yet to the Southern Kingdom of Judah something special was given: the promises of grace to David. Hence the historian seems to hint that, while the peo-ple (northern and southern) had failed, God was not through. In spite of all polit-ical and religious failures, God would not go back on the promises of grace to David. So even though it was the worst of times, there was a hint—grounded in the Davidic covenant—that God may hold the future open in unexpected ways.

It is surely not accidental, then, that the Deuteronomistic history ends with the announcement of the release of Jehoiachin, a Davidic king, from prison, though

4. Jon Levenson argues forcefully that the two covenants do not stand in irreconcilable oppo-sition to each other, as some scholars maintain, but are compatible theologically. See his *Sinai and Zion* (Minneapolis: Winston, 1985), part 3, especially "Moses and David," 209–17.

kept under house arrest. It is a small sign, an ambiguous sign that nationalists could easily misunderstand. But in the perspective of God's covenant, especially the "everlasting covenant" with David, the future is not closed. Human beings may fail with amazing consistency, but Yahweh is the faithful God, who shows unexpected and undeserved loyalty (*ḥesed*) to the people and finally does not abandon his "heritage."

21. GOD AND WAR

Before turning to prophecy in the Mosaic tradition (Hosea and Jeremiah), a major theme of the Deuteronomistic history demands attention: God's involvement in war. The book of Joshua begins by assuring the new leader that Yahweh has given the people the land of Canaan and that, if he is obedient to "this book of the law" (Deuteronomy), no one will be able to stand against the invaders. Yahweh is quoted as saying:

> I hereby command you: Be strong and courageous; do not be frightened or dismayed, for the LORD [Yahweh] your God is with you wherever you go.
>
> —Josh. 1:9

In previous ages, God's participation in war was not as problematic as it has come to be in our time. In the seventeenth century, for instance, Oliver Cromwell's soldiers went into battle singing psalms (though the same songs could have been sung on the other side). The problem of God and war has assumed gigantic proportions in the twentieth century, which has witnessed two world wars and numerous, relatively smaller conflagrations. The United States entered the First World War with the religious passion of "making the world safe for democracy." The Second World War was more problematic, though theologians like Reinhold Niebuhr helped many people to see that an all-out fight against the evil Nazi regime was justifiable. As late as the Gulf War (1992) there were attempts to revive the ancient notion of the "just war."

Most people hate war, especially when it is forced on them, and cannot understand why in Scripture God is portrayed as speaking and acting in militaristic ways. Many are tempted to ignore or, like Marcion, to discard the Old Testament because the wrathful God of ancient Israel, in alleged contrast to the New Testament God of love, is celebrated as "the Lord of hosts" (or "armies"):

> *The LORD [Yahweh], strong and mighty,*
> *The LORD [Yahweh], mighty in battle.*
> —Ps. 24:8

With a mixture of laughter and seriousness modern readers say, quoting the Sunday School teacher trying to interpret to the class the book of Joshua, "That was before God became a Christian."

The problem is hardly solved by playing the New Testament against the Old. The church, in its wiser moments, has rightly insisted that the Old Testament is an essential part of the canon. Nevertheless, the church cannot have the Old Testament without facing the problem of its military language. In an earlier discussion, when considering the scriptural use of patriarchal language and imagery, I observed that God "condescends" to speak to us in human language, with its sociological limitations. If this is true of the use of "patriarchal" speech, it is also true in regard to "military" language. God speaks to us, as it were, at our human

171

level, though this divine accommodation does not provide a theological justification for either patriarchal society or the practice of war.[1]

The Lord of Hosts (Armies)

The proper place to begin reflection on this subject is with the recognition that war was taken for granted in the ancient world, especially in Canaan, which was a land bridge between Mesopotamia and Egypt, across which armies marched again and again. War was so much a part of ordinary life that biblical writers take note of exceptions, when "the land enjoyed rest" for a brief time (e.g., Judg. 3:11). For people living in the storm center of international politics, war was necessary for survival. In Israel's case it was natural to assume that the people's enemies were also Yahweh's enemies (Judg. 5:31) and that God was fighting actively for his people. "The Book of the Wars of Yahweh," an early poetic collection that has not survived (see Num. 21:14-15), seems to have celebrated the military victories of Israel during the occupation of Canaan.

Interestingly, the Israelite story, found in the prefatory ancestral history (Genesis 12–50), is not told in military terms. The narrators portray the people of Abraham, Isaac, and Jacob moving peacefully on the fringes of Canaanite society, negotiating with the native inhabitants on friendly terms. To be sure, the promises to Abraham include the assurance of possession of the land of Canaan (Gen. 15:18-19), but in the ancestral period, according to the book of Genesis, there are no military engagements with the Canaanites. The one exception to this peaceable picture is found in Genesis 14, a singular chapter that tells about the defeat of a coalition of four eastern kings by Abraham's small forces. This story, in the judgment of many scholars, was added to the basic fund of ancestral narratives from a special source. Its Melchizedek theme is picked up in Ps. 110:4, which in highly symbolic language portrays the exalted role of the anointed one (messiah), the priest-king of Jerusalem, in God's cosmic administration.[2]

In the book of Exodus, where the story of the people has its decisive beginning, military language becomes more dominant. The people go out of the land of Egypt "prepared for battle" (Exod. 13:18). As they approach the land of Canaan via the King's Highway in Transjordan, they engage in battle when negotiations for peaceful passage fail (Numbers 10, 11, 13, 14, 20, 21). The assumption of the continuing story is that, as Moses said to his father-in-law Jethro (Hobab), "Yahweh has promised good to Israel" by giving them "a land flowing with milk and honey" (Num. 10:29-30; cf. Exod. 3:7-8); nevertheless, they have to be ready to seize the gift by military force, if necessary.

1. See the discussion above, chapter 8.
2. See the later discussion of royal theology, chapter 23.

Holy War

In the exodus story, which the Deuteronomistic historians recapitulate, Yahweh is portrayed as a warrior. This is the case in the ancient Song of the Sea, probably from the twelfth century B.C.

> Yahweh is a warrior,
> Yahweh is his name.
> —Exod. 15:3 (BWA)

The warfare in which the Divine Warrior engages, however, contrasts with the kind of warfare in which the nations participated, with large numbers of forces or advanced military equipment.[3] Indeed, in the wars of Yahweh, faith in God's power is primary, not confidence in human strength or weaponry. In the story of the victory at the sea, Moses is represented as saying to the people:

> Do not be afraid, stand firm, and see the deliverance that the LORD [Yahweh] will accomplish for you today; for the Egyptians whom you see today you shall never see again. The LORD [Yahweh] will fight for you, and you have only to keep still.
> —Exod. 14:13

Yahweh needs only a small band of devotees, as in the case of Gideon's battle (Judg. 7:1-8). In such guerrilla warfare surprise maneuvers, scare tactics, ritual performance, or the presence of the ark are effective, as in the case of the battle for Jericho (Joshua 6) or Ai (Joshua 8). It is noteworthy that women took military action, as in the case of the prophetess Deborah (see the Song of Deborah, Judges 5), to say nothing of the subversive deed of Jael (Judg. 5:24-27). But whatever contributions the human warriors made, in the last analysis victory was given "not by your sword or by your bow" (Josh. 24:12).

A strong case has been made that faith in Yahweh, who performs miracles of deliverance, led Israel to reject the military policy of violence, introduced in the time of David, that relied on a modernized army and sophisticated weaponry such as chariots and horses.[4] The tension between "the way of the nations" and "the way of Yahweh" is reflected in one strand of tradition in the books of Samuel, where Samuel warns the elders of Israel against installing a king "like the nations," for the king will introduce radical social changes, including conscription of young men as charioteers or infantrymen, introduction of modern implements of war, appointment of a military class of people, and so on (1 Sam. 8:11-18). Modern views of war find no support in this understanding of war.

Some argue that the Old Testament, when interpreted theologically, indicates that God takes part in the sinful realities of human history in order to carry out a

---

3. See Gerhard von Rad, *Holy War in Ancient Israel*, trans. Marva Dawn (Grand Rapids: Eerdmans, 1991), especially the introduction by Ben C. Ollenburger, 1–33; also the important study by Patrick D. Miller, *The Divine Warrior in Early Israel*, HSM 5 (Cambridge: Harvard Univ. Press, 1973).

4. See Millard C. Lind, *Yahweh Is a Warrior* (Scottdale, Penn.: Herald, 1980).

saving purpose that embraces all nations and will ultimately result in world peace.[5] If Old Testament texts, especially in the prophets (e.g., Isa. 10:5-19; Jer. 1:11-19), are taken seriously it is probably impossible to avoid the affirmation that God is behind and within the warfare of human history, at least some wars that are intended to overthrow pharaonic structures of power and to bring justice for the oppressed. The powerful do not usually surrender power without the exertion of force of some kind, as Martin Luther King, Jr. once reminded us. In any case, the experience of the liberating action of Yahweh, who comes to the aid of the weak and oppressed, belongs to all levels of Israelite tradition. God is the champion of those who are victimized by power and acts to "put down the mighty and exalt those of low degree," as affirmed in Mary's Magnificat (Luke 1:46-55).

Faith and Ideology

There is a problem here, however. It is proper to say, as liberation theologians emphasize, that God is concerned about and champions the poor and oppressed everywhere. At the same time, God seems to have a special concern for the oppressed people Israel and, as asserted in the moving passage Exod. 3:7-8, intervenes to give them justice: a land, a future, a place in the sun. This theological portrayal we are given in the book of Judges: as the supreme Judge (Hebrew *shophet*) God acts to champion the justice of the people Israel when they are oppressed in times of crisis. It is also the presupposition of many of the Psalms: the people cry out to God in the confidence that God will hear their cry and act to deliver them.

The justice of God usually eludes human comprehension, as in the case of Abraham on the eve of the holocaust of Sodom and Gomorrah (Gen. 18:22-33). Yet it is not justifiable, in my reading of the biblical texts, to say that God's universal role as "Judge of the whole earth" (Gen. 18:25b) conflicts with God's actions to obtain justice for Israel. Rolf Knierim pushes this tension to the extreme of rejecting the notion of God's choice (election) of Israel. The special relationship between God and Israel, he says, "must be regarded as a witness to a particularistic view of God and history, which is not commensurate with a universalist view of history, and certainly not with a view of God's presence in history universally."[6] This view, however, fails to do justice to the relationship between the universal and the particular, a dialectical contradiction that we have found to be inherent in Israel's experience of the presence of God in history.[7]

---

5. See Peter Craigie, *The Problem of War in the Old Testament* (Grand Rapids: Eerdmans, 1978).

6. Rolf P. Knierim, *The Task of Old Testament Theology: Substance, Method, and Cases* (Grand Rapids: Eerdmans, 1995), 171–75, 450–52; quotation, 173. He writes that this view is "the most serious theologized perversion of the notion of God and, thus, the most serious among all possible and actual similarly sinful theologized ideologies" (452). See the penetrating review of this work by Jon Levenson, *RelSRev* 24, no. 1 (1998) 39–42.

7. See Emil Fackenheim, *God's Presence in History* (New York: New York Univ. Press, 1970), discussed above, chapter 9.

The Lot of the Native Peoples

Nevertheless, one cannot escape that conclusion that there is an ineradicable "ideological taint" in the telling of the Israelite story about how God fights for the people Israel and gives them the land of Canaan, which came to be known as "the promised land."[8] One aspect of the Deuteronomic portrayal that is especially troublesome in the modern world is the fate of the indigenous peoples.[9] At the burning bush Moses was assured that God would deliver the Israelites from bondage in Egypt and bring them "to a good and broad land, a land flowing with milk and honey" (Exod. 3:8). This promise would be realized, however, by dispossessing the native peoples: "the Canaanites, the Hittites, the Amorites, the Perizzites, the Hivites, and the Jebusites." From a sociological point of view, holy war—the kind of war waged before the Davidic monarchy—was an ideology in the sense that it justified the cause of the people and legitimated their occupation of the land.

It is too easy to dismiss these natives as ancient peoples who flourished for a while in a remote corner of the world and disappeared from the historical scene, though some of them—like the Hittites—have been rediscovered by modern archaeologists, as we have seen in the case of the suzerainty treaty.[10] The lot of these forgotten peoples, however, demands attention in our time when native populations, who have lost their lands to invaders, are crying for justice.

The problem of the native peoples is exacerbated in the book of Deuteronomy, where Moses is represented as telling the people that the land is God's gift and that they are to take it by force from the native inhabitants, "seven nations mightier and more numerous than you." In strong language the Israelite invaders are told to "make no covenant with them and show them no mercy"; rather, the Israelites must "break down their altars, smash their pillars, hew down their sacred poles, and burn their idols with fire" (Deut. 7:1-6).

To be sure, some strong reasons for this negative attitude toward Canaanite culture are given. For one thing, the Mosaic sermon warns that the Israelites may be "ensnared" by aspects of native culture (Deut. 7:25). Also, they are told that God is dispossessing the native peoples not because of Israel's "righteousness" but because of "the wickedness of these nations" (9:4). Nevertheless, it is easy to see how native peoples of the United States, Canada, Australia, the Hawaiian Islands, or elsewhere, who feel the hurt of loss of land and destruction of their culture, would be turned off by this aspect of Deuteronomic preaching. Moses' exhortation could be used as a justification for taking land and destroying native culture, as has happened repeatedly ever since Columbus's discovery of the New World. Indeed,

---

8. See the earlier discussion of the promises to Abraham, specifically the promise of land, chapter 12.

9. Some of this discussion is extracted from my essay "Standing on God's Promises," in *Biblical Theology: Problems and Perspectives: In Honor of J. Christiaan Beker*, ed. Steven J. Kraftchick et al. (Nashville: Abingdon, 1995), 145–54.

10. See above, chapter 18.

we remember too well chapters of American history in which the biblical motif of "the promised land" was appropriated at the expense of Native Americans.

The Gift of Good Land

The title essay of a collection of essays by Wendell Berry dealing with ecological and agricultural matters, "The Gift of Good Land," may provide some help in facing this difficult problem.[11] The main interest in Berry's essay is to develop a biblical basis for ecological responsibility. He proposes turning to the book of Deuteronomy, rather than the story of the Garden of Eden, in which Adam and Eve are placed in the garden to take care of it. "The giving of the Promised Land to the Israelites," he writes, "is more serviceable than the story of the giving of the Garden of Eden, because the Promised Land is a divine gift to a fallen people." That makes the gift "more problematical" and the receiving of the gift "more conditional and more difficult."[12]

In speaking of a "fallen people," Berry is using traditional Christian language. What he means, I believe, is that any people—not just ancient Israel—receives God's gifts in a situation where self-interest and human pride tarnish them. In sociological language, the gift has an "ideological taint" that justifies and supports the social group. The theme of God's gift of land to a people, Berry goes on to say, "sounds like the sort of rationalization that invariably accompanies nationalistic aggression and theft"; and he draws attention to "the similarities to the westward movement of the American frontier." Berry argues, however, that whereas the movement into the American frontier produced an ethic of greed and violence, the Israelite conquest of Canaan from the very first was informed by an ethic of responsibility based on the view that the land is God's undeserved gift. To quote again: "The difficulty but also the wonder of the story of the Promised Land is that, there, the primordial and still continuing dark story of human rapaciousness began to be accompanied by a vein of light which, however improbably and uncertainly, still accompanies us."[13]

Several points deserve attention. First, the story of the promise to Israel's ancestors pertains to a people of the past, ancient Israel. It is "historically conditioned," referring to Israel at a particular time long ago. It should not be construed as a divine mandate for other peoples in other times and historical situations to engage in territorial expansion or cultural domination at the expense of native populations.

Moreover, the story is about an ancient people who, like every people and nation from time immemorial, has been inescapably involved in the "dark history"

11. Wendell Berry, *The Gift of Good Land* (San Francisco: North Point, 1981), 167–281. For an introduction to this contemporary writer, see "Toward a Healthy Community: An Interview with Wendell Berry," *Christian Century* 114, no. 28 (1997) 912–16. Writes the interviewer: "Berry has a passionate love for the land [of the local community] and a concern that people live in responsible relationship with the land and with one another."

12. Ibid., 169.

13. Ibid., 170.

of struggle for power and for land, the strife in parts of the former Yugoslavia being a recent example. Hence the formulation of God's promise to ancient Israel has an ideological coloration. Just as the promises of grace to David provided the justification for the Davidic throne (Psalm 78), as we shall see, so the promise of land to Abraham and his descendants provided a theological rationale for the conquest of Canaan.

In the perspective of the community of faith, however, God works through the sufferings, dislocations, and tragedy of human history (including the tragedy of Israel when the nation fell and many people were carried into exile) to achieve a purpose that will ultimately benefit all peoples. The promise to Abraham and Sarah also included the assurance that in God's purpose Israel's role would benefit "all the families of the earth" (Gen. 12:3; cf. Isa. 49:6). Perhaps native people, who have been overrun by invaders, may say in retrospect that some good came of it after all and that, in the words of Joseph, "Even though you intended to do harm to me, God intended it for good" (Gen. 50:20). Such positive statements are more easily made by the oppressor than by the oppressed, as an African American student once observed in this connection.

Finally, in later Jewish tradition God's promise of land was broadened to mean "earth, world" (Hebrew 'erets can mean either "earth" or "land") under the influence of the universal implications of "all the families of the earth" (Gen. 12:3). In this larger sense, which transcends the limitations of national territory or political ideology, Paul declared that the promises to Israel's ancestors have been endorsed by God's revelation in Jesus Christ, including the promise that Abraham would inherit "the world" (Rom. 4:13).[14]

The Metaphor of the Divine Warrior

Given Israel's fierce struggle for survival and for living space, it was inevitable that the people prayed and trusted that Yahweh would be on their side in the struggle for possession of the land of Canaan. Yet faith in Yahweh, the Divine Warrior, cannot be reduced to ideology, for at least two reasons.

First, Yahweh was not always the supporter of the people Israel whether right or wrong; on the contrary, Yahweh acted to discipline the people for their covenant failures. The Deuteronomistic historians stress this critical theology of war. According to the epitome in Judg. 2:6—3:6, which interprets the whole period of the early judges (rulers) of Israel, Yahweh allowed alien nations to oppress Israel for a time, in order to "test" the people—"to know whether Israel would obey the commandments of Yahweh, which he commanded their ancestors by Moses" (Judg. 3:4). Similarly, the fall of the Northern Kingdom in 722 B.C. at the hand of the Assyrian Empire is interpreted as the discipline of Yahweh for their rejection of the commandments of the covenant (2 Kgs. 17:18). This teaching is hardly what the defenders of the political establishment want to hear.

14. See the discussion above, chapter 12.

In this respect, the Deuteronomistic historians are consistent with the preaching of the great prophets. These prophets—like Amos, Isaiah, Micah, Jeremiah—oppose the popular prophets who preach a message that people want to hear in wartime, proclaiming "peace, peace, when there is no peace." They perceive that God's real enemies are not out there somewhere in the international sphere but are God's own people.

> *Therefore says the Sovereign, the* LORD *[Yahweh] of hosts, the Mighty One of Israel:*
> *Ah, I will pour out my wrath on my enemies,*
>   *and avenge myself on my foes!*
> *I will turn my hand against you;*
>   *I will smelt away your dross as with lye*
>   *and remove all your alloy.*
>
> —Isa. 1:24-25

Yahweh is raising a "foe from the north" to bring judgment on the land of Israel (Jeremiah); the Assyrian dictator is "the rod of Yahweh's anger" (Isa. 10:5-14), who would perform the "strange work" of divine judgment on Mount Zion (Isa. 28:21).

Second, from the very first the language about the Divine Warrior tends to move away from actual history into a world of imagination. This can be seen from the account of the conquest of Canaan given by the Deuteronomistic historian in the book of Joshua. The account is clearly glorified, as in the case of the story of the fall of Jericho. Indeed, the problematic evidence of archaeology leads many scholars to wonder whether there was a "conquest" at all; they see evidence of a slow process of infiltration and occupation of the land by means of treaty, intermarriage, and negotiation.[15] Perhaps that is an extreme judgment, but it is clear that the present form of the story invites the reader into a symbolic world, where the Divine Warrior calls for radical faith.

Moreover, from the very first there is a disposition to understand God's activity in mythical terms. This is evident in the Song of the Sea (Exod. 15:1-8). Here Yahweh's enemies are Pharaoh's armies, who are thrown into the sea, a divine deliverance celebrated in the earlier Song of Miriam (Exod. 15:19-20). Yet the poem is redolent of Canaanite imagery from the myth of Baal's triumph over his adversaries (Sea, River) and his building of a temple in which to celebrate his triumphant kingship.[16] When the Song of the Sea is compared with later Israelite poetry (e.g., Ps. 74:12-17; 114; Isa. 51:9-11), it is apparent that God's enemies are not in a narrow sense flesh and blood but powers of chaos that threaten to challenge the Creator's sovereignty or to eclipse order with disorder.

The movement from history to symbolism that transcends the literal world of

---

15. For a brief summary, see my discussion of the invasion of Canaan, *Understanding the Old Testament* (4th ed.; Englewood Cliffs, N.J.: Prentice-Hall, 1986), 137–40; abridged paperback ed. (Englewood Cliffs, N.J.: Prentice-Hall, 1997), 110–28.

16. See Frank M. Cross, "The Song of the Sea and Canaanite Myth," in *Canaanite Myth and Hebrew Epic: Essays in the History of the Religion of Israel* (Cambridge: Harvard Univ. Press, 1973), 112–44.

politics reaches its climax in apocalyptic, as we will see in due course. There was a time when the Divine Warrior, performing a "strange work" (Isa. 28:21), moved against the people Israel in judgment and in mercy; ultimately, however, God will be triumphant over all mythical enemies that victimize people, whether in Israel or the nations at large. Toward that eschatological victory of the Divine Warrior an apocalyptic writer points in a passage that linguistically echoes the ancient Baal myth:

> On that day the LORD [Yahweh] with his cruel and great and strong sword will punish Leviathan the fleeing serpent, Leviathan the twisting serpent, and he will kill the dragon that is in the sea.[17]
>
> —Isa. 27:1

The New Testament is in line with this apocalyptic vision of the end-time triumph of the Divine Warrior. Indeed, Jesus is portrayed not as an ordinary warrior who fights with a sword but as a warrior, equipped with nonmilitary weapons, who goes out to engage in warfare against all the hosts of evil, symbolized by Satan's kingdom (dominion). A hymn that Christians used to sing highlights the ancient metaphor of the Divine Warrior marching forth to claim the ultimate victory over the forces of evil.

> *The Son of God goes forth to war,*
> *a kingly crown to gain,*
> *His blood-red banner streams afar:*
> *Who follows in His train?*
> *Who best can drink his cup of woe,*
> *triumphant over pain,*
> *Who patient bears his cross below,*
> *he follows in His train.*[18]

This hymn once appeared in practically all hymn books, but has been dropped in recent revisions (e.g., United Methodist, Presbyterian, Chalice), presumably because of the prominent use of a military metaphor. This quiet censorship falls in the category of what the poet Kathleen Norris calls "the war on metaphor."[19] When one studies the words of the hymn carefully, however, one will discover that it is anything but militaristic; moreover, it is openly inclusive ("A noble army, men and boys, The matron and the maid"). It would be better, in my estimation, to retain the hymn in our hymnody, but use it with a poet's appreciation of the metaphorical language.

---

17. See my essay, "The Slaying of the Fleeing, Twisting Serpent: Isaiah 27:1 in Context," in *Uncovering Ancient Stones: Essays in Memory of H. Neil Richardson*, ed. Lewis M. Hopfe (Winona Lake, Ind.: Eisenbrauns, 1994), 3–15.

18. By Reginald Heber, 1827; quoted from an older version of *The Hymnbook of Presbyterian and Reformed Churches* (1955).

19. Kathleen Norris, "The War on Metaphor," in *The Cloister Walk* (New York: Riverhead, 1996), 154–58, in which connection she specifically discusses modern revision of hymnals and liturgy. I am grateful to my wife, Monique, for this reference.

Summary

In summary, the issue of God and war is a complex subject in the Christian Bible, both Old and New Testaments.

- Military language was inescapable in ancient Israel, especially because of its geographical location astride the path of marching armies.
- The "wars" of Yahweh were limited engagements, using guerrilla tactics, not the warfare of nations employing large armies and advanced military equipment.
- The Divine Warrior did not always come to the support of Israel, but—according to the prophets—used a foreign army to perform the "strange work" of divine judgment on a sinful people.
- As prophecy moved to apocalyptic, military language was used symbolically to portray God's aggression against, and triumph over, the powers of evil that victimize people and threaten God's creation.
- The New Testament is profoundly influenced by the apocalyptic vista of the struggle between the dominion of God and the dominion of evil (or "the evil one," as in the Lord's Prayer, Matt. 6:13). In this symbolic world, Jesus is the Divine Warrior who marches to war and wins the victory that liberates people from all forms of bondage and powers of darkness.

22. Prophecy in the Mosaic Tradition

We have seen previously (chapter 16) that the Priestly view of history, with which the Abrahamic covenant of Genesis 17 is associated, provides the basic perspective of the Priestly prophet Ezekiel. Now we shall see that the Mosaic covenant is the platform of the great northern prophet, Hosea, as it is also of the great southern prophet, Jeremiah. Indeed, there are striking affinities between Hosea and Jeremiah. Hosea, who preceded Jeremiah by at least a century, was active in the Northern Kingdom of Ephraim (Israel), a few years before its fall in 722 B.C. under the impact of Assyrian invasion; and Jeremiah was active in the Southern Kingdom, just before its collapse under the massive might of Babylonian invasion in and around the year 587 B.C. It was the task of these prophets, in their respective times, to interpret the meaning of these tragic events. They did so in terms of the Mosaic covenant made at Sinai as portrayed classically in the book of Exodus.

Eighth-Century Prophets

Some have argued that the symbol of Israel's covenant with Yahweh was a "theological innovation" of eighth-century prophets, who used it in their preaching to counter the notion that God is on the side of Israel and that therefore no evil could befall the Israelite state.[1] Eighth-century prophets certainly emphasized the covenant relationship, as we shall see, but they were dependent on a received tradition of the Mosaic covenant at Sinai.

A century earlier, about the middle of the ninth century, the great prophet Elijah appeared, seen through the mists of legend. In a dramatic ceremony on Mount Carmel, he called on the people to pledge their exclusive loyalty to Yahweh, rather than compromising theologically with the Canaanite god of storm and fertility, Baal (1 Kings 18). Returning to "the mountain of God" (Sinai, Horeb), where he experienced a theophany in a cave comparable to one granted to Moses (cf. Exodus 33), Elijah protested that the Israelites had "forsaken [Yahweh's] covenant" (1 Kgs. 19:10) and had left him virtually alone as a devotee of the Mosaic faith.[2]

Moreover, at the beginning of the monarchy, according to narratives found in the books of Samuel, there appeared a prophet in the Mosaic tradition, Samuel, who warned of the dangers of monarchy and called for allegiance to Yahweh as king (1 Samuel 8, 12). Before the founding of the monarchy, a great covenant ceremony was held at Shechem, when Joshua challenged the people to serve Yahweh,

---

1. The view, reminiscent of that of Julius Wellhausen in the nineteenth century, has been espoused by E. W. Nicholson, *God and His People* (Oxford: Clarendon, 1986), chap. 10.

2. See above, chapter 5.

their liberating God, with wholehearted and sincere loyalty: "Choose whom you will serve!" (Josh. 24:15).

You Only Have I Known!

In the eighth century, then, the theme of the covenant was not new; the innovation was how the prophets gave a new twist to the Mosaic covenant as they interpreted the historical experiences of Israel at a time when Assyrian imperialism was sweeping over the ancient world.[3]

Amos, the first of the eighth-century prophets, does not explicitly refer to the Sinai covenant, but it is apparently presupposed in an oracle directed "against" the people of Israel.

> Hear this word that the Lord [Yahweh] has spoken against you, O people of Israel, against the whole family that I brought up out of the land of Egypt:
>> *You only have I known*
>> *of all the families of the earth;*
>> *therefore I will punish you*
>> *for all your iniquities.*
>> —Amos 3:1-2

The verb "know" is a covenant verb, as we have found earlier; it refers to the personal knowing that involves relationship and commitment.[4] Here the surprising twist is that God's knowing Israel (in covenant relationship) does not mean support and approval, but on the contrary, judgment and punishment. Amos does not go so far as to say that Yahweh has completely rejected Israel. To be sure, in a play on words (*qayits*="summer fruit"/*qets*="end"), he portrays Yahweh announcing ominously that "the end has come on my people Israel" (8:2), that is, the calamitous end of Israel as a kingdom (cf. 5:1-3; 9:8). But in Amos's view, the punishment for breach of covenant is not a punishment unto death, but rather a terrible doom that leaves, at best, only a pitiful "remnant of grace" (3:2; 5:15b). He is so interested in administering a homiletical shock to those "at ease in Zion," who "feel secure on Mount Samaria" (6:1), that he does not concern himself with what lies beyond the tragedy of faithless Israel. He is more concerned to emphasize that a faithful relationship with God is not displayed in the performance of pious rituals but in obeying God's commandments, preeminently the call for justice in the community.

> *Take away from me the noise of your songs,*
> *I will not listen to the melody of your harps,*
> *But let justice roll down like waters,*
> *and righteousness like an everflowing stream.*
> —Amos 5:23-24

---

3. See the acclaimed (prize-winning!) essay by Philip J. King, "The Great Eighth Century," *BR* 5 (August 1989) 22–33, 44.

4. See above, chapter 9.

Steadfast Love, Not Sacrifice

With Hosea it is the same, yet the accent is different. Like Amos (Amos 3:1), he turns to the story that portrays Yahweh's relationship to Israel and Israel's relationship to God. The story reaches back to the great root experiences that marked the beginning of the divine-human relationship.

- I am Yahweh your God from the land of Egypt (12:9).
- By a prophet [Moses] Yahweh brought Israel up from Egypt (12:13).
- I have been Yahweh your God ever since the land of Egypt (13:4).
- When Israel was a child I loved him, and out of Egypt I called my son (11:1).

The language of covenant—"your God," "my people"—resounds throughout the prophet's message. It was at Sinai that Yahweh made a covenant, entering into special relationship with Israel and expecting the people to be faithful in their obligations. Yet at the very threshold of the covenant land, if that is the meaning of the allusion to the place Adam (cf. Josh. 3:16), Israel's history of covenant failure began.

> But at Adam they transgressed the covenant;
>   there they dealt faithlessly with me.
>
> —Hos. 6:7

To be in covenant with God is to "know" God, that is, to know God relationally like a husband and wife (cf. Gen. 4:1); but Israel's corporate life, in the realms of religion and politics, displayed betrayal of God's covenant demands, a lack of "knowledge of God."

> Set the trumpet to your lips!
>   One like a vulture is over the house of
>   the LORD [Yahweh],
> because they have broken my covenant,
> and transgressed my law.
>
> —Hos. 8:1

He complains that Israel's covenant devotion (ḥesed) is transient, like morning dew that quickly vanishes; therefore God's "words" (oracles), spoken by the prophets, have a cutting edge that hurts, even kills.

> For I desire steadfast love [ḥesed], and not sacrifice,
>   the knowledge of God rather than burnt offerings.
>
> —Hos. 6:6

On two occasions, according to the Gospel of Matthew, Jesus asked his critics to go and learn what this text means (Matt. 9:13; 12:27).

"Love That Will Not Let Go"

In one respect Hosea goes further than Amos: the Mosaic covenant, in his view, means not just punishment but also the possible rejection of Israel. God has entered into the covenant relationship freely and, if the people are unfaithful, God can freely annul it. That seems to be the ominous meaning of the naming of one of the prophet's children.

> Then the LORD [Yahweh] said: "Name him Lo-ammi [i.e., 'not my people']; for you are not my people and I am not your God."
>
> —Hos. 1:9

Unlike the Abrahamic covenant, which Hosea does not mention, the Mosaic covenant holds no guarantee for Israel's future welfare. The present crisis is a time for the people to shape up and change their ways (repent), lest divine judgment bring about an annulment of the relation between God and people.

Yet paradoxically the prophet holds out hope for the future, a hope that is based not on Israel's behavior but on the incredible grace of God, whose covenant faithfulness is greater and deeper than the strict terms set by the covenant. This is the message of the marvelous poem (Hos. 11:1-9) in which the prophet shifts from the husband-wife metaphor (chapters 1–3) to the parent-child image to portray God's loving, nurturing care for the people. The prophet portrays a struggle that goes on within the heart of God, so to speak. Should the Parent discipline this people as severely as they deserve? Should the Parent give up on and reject a child that persists in rebellious ways? Strictly speaking, the covenant could be terminated by God's complete rejection of Israel, if the people fail in the relationship. But God's commitment is based on love, like that of a parent only far greater, love that finally cannot stand to let the people go. In the last analysis this is what it means for God to be "the Holy One in your midst."[5]

> *How can I give you up, Ephraim?*
> *How can I hand you over, O Israel?*
>
> . . .
>
> *My heart recoils within me;*
>   *my compassion grows warm and tender.*
> *I will not execute my fierce anger;*
>   *I will not again destroy Ephraim;*
> *for I am God and no mortal,*
>   *the Holy One in your midst,*
>   *and I will not come in wrath.*
>
> —Hos. 11:8-9

Walter Brueggemann describes this as "a radical recharacterization of holiness":

> The holiness of Yahweh is drawn into the covenant categories of Israel's faith, so that the Holy One is the related One. . . . By linking "Holy One" to the term "of Israel," Israel's testimony asserts that this completely separated One is the charac-

---

5. See Walther Eichrodt, "'The Holy One in Your Midst': The Theology of Hosea" (trans. Lloyd Gaston), *Int* 15 (1961) 259–73.

teristically related One. Yahweh's holiness, in this formulation, is in and with and for Israel.[6]

Because of this holy love, beyond the time of the broken covenant God will make a new covenant. In the end time the people will respond as in the (honeymoon) "days of her youth, as at the time when she came out of the land of Egypt" (Hos. 2:15). Then God will show pity on those who deserve no pity:

> and I will say to Lo-ammi,
> "You are my people";
> and he shall say, "You are my God."
> —Hos. 2:23

Jeremiah, a Prophet Like Moses

The "Mosaic" themes of covenant making, covenant breaking, and covenant renewal are interpreted in Jeremiah's preaching with even greater power. In its present form the book of Jeremiah comes to us from Deuteronomistic editors who, as we have seen, edited the history that extends from Joshua through the monarchy to its final demise in the seventh century, the time of Jeremiah and Ezekiel. It is often difficult, if not impossible, to separate the words and deeds of Jeremiah from their Deuteronomistic interpretation (as in Jeremiah's temple sermon, chapter 7). The problem is complicated by the fact that Jeremiah may have supported, at least initially, the reform of King Josiah, which was based on the book of the torah of Moses—the core of the book of Deuteronomy (see 2 Kings 22–23).

The Deuteronomistic interpreters apparently regarded Jeremiah as a prophet like Moses.

> By a prophet the LORD [Yahweh] brought Israel up from Egypt,
> and by a prophet he was guarded.
> —Hos. 12:13

This theme is set forth in an important passage in the book of Deuteronomy (18:15-22) where Moses tells the people that God will guide them into their new life on the land:

The LORD [Yahweh] your God will raise up for you a prophet like me from among your own people; you shall heed such a prophet.

> —Deut. 18:15

The passage goes on to say that, just as Moses acted as covenant mediator between God and people at Sinai, so God will raise up "a prophet like you" who will speak for God to the people. Yahweh is quoted as saying: "I will put my words in the mouth of the prophet, who shall speak to them everything that I command" (v. 18).

This passage seems to mean that Moses will be followed by a series of prophets "like Moses," who will call the people to repent, prophets like Samuel, Elijah, and

6. Walter Brueggemann, *Theology of the Old Testament* (Minneapolis: Fortress Press, 1997), 289.

Hosea. In any case, that was the view of Deuteronomistic interpreters who have given us the book of Jeremiah: they understood Jeremiah to be one of those prophets in the Mosaic succession whom God raised up from time to time to warn the people and persuade them to return to covenant fidelity with God (cf. 2 Kgs. 17:13-15). It is noteworthy that in the New Testament this prophecy of the coming Mosaic prophet is applied to Jesus, whom God "raised up" from the dead (Acts 3:22-23; cf. 7:35-37).

A Covenant Mediator

The view of Jeremiah as a prophet like Moses was rooted in Jeremiah's own message. This is immediately evident in the account of Jeremiah's call at the beginning of the book (Jer. 1:4-10), which resembles the story of Moses' call and commission in the book of Exodus (Exodus 3 and 4). Like Jeremiah (1:6), Moses also protested his inadequacy for the task, specifically that he was no speaker (Exod. 3:11; 4:10). Both received the divine assurance that God would be with them, enabling them to meet opposition (Exod. 3:12; Jer. 1:8). Moreover, God's promise to Jeremiah, "I have put my words in your mouth" (Jer. 1:9), is a clear echo of what is said regarding the prophet like Moses in the book of Deuteronomy ("I will put my words in the mouth of the prophet," Deut. 18:18).

The role of the covenant mediator, according to the portrayal of Moses given in the Torah, was twofold: (1) to speak God's words to the people; and (2) to represent the people before God, for example, in intercessory prayer. The major aspects of Jeremiah's message and ministry qualify him as a prophet in the Mosaic tradition. He is commissioned to speak God's words (Jer. 1:9); and, being sensitively identified with the people, he was qualified (like Samuel before him) to "stand before" Yahweh and plead for the people (cf. Jer. 15:1).

Remembering and Forgetting the Story

Several themes of Moses' preaching, as summarized in the book of Deuteronomy, ring out in Jeremiah's message. First, Jeremiah appeals to the people's story that rehearses the saving deeds of God manifest in the deliverance from Egypt, the guidance through the wilderness, and the inheritance of the land. The trouble is— and here Jeremiah agrees with Hosea (cf. Hos. 13:4-8)—that when Israelites came into the land they forgot the story, which portrays God's liberating deeds and their responding commitment to Yahweh. What is more, they turned to another story to find the meaning of life, namely, the Canaanite story of the loves and wars of Baal and his consort.

In a "covenant lawsuit," found in Jer. 2:4-8, the Divine Suzerain calls the vassal or "servant" to task.[7] Notice the literary form of the passage.

---

7. Compare the summary of the suzerain's beneficent deeds in the suzerainty covenant (treaty) form; above, chapter 18.

Summons to Court. The poet depicts Yahweh, the aggrieved party, summoning the people to a trial:

> Listen to the word of the LORD [Yahweh], people of Jacob, all you families of Israel. These are the words of the LORD:
>> *What fault did your forefathers find in me,*
>>> *that they went so far astray from me,*
>> *pursuing worthless idols and becoming worthless like them;*
>> *that they did not ask, "Where is the LORD*
>>> *who brought us up from Egypt*
>> *and led us through the wilderness,*
>>> *through a barren and broken country,*
>>> *a country parched and forbidding."*
>>>> —Jer. 2:4-6 (REB)

Indictment. The questioning moves into indictment: Yahweh brought the people "into a plentiful land, to eat its fruits and its good things"; but when they entered, they "defiled my land" with their false lifestyle. They were misled into this covenant betrayal by priests, interpreters of the law, rulers, and prophets.

>> *The priests no longer asked, "Where is the LORD*
>>> *[Yahweh]?"*
>> *Those who handled the law had no real*
>>> *knowledge of me,*
>> *the shepherds of the people rebelled against me;*
>>> *the prophets prophesied in the name of Baal*
>>> *and followed gods who were powerless to help.*
>>>> —Jer. 2:8 (REB)

The Judge's Verdict. Finally Yahweh places a charge before the court: "my people" have done something for which there is no precedent or parallel—they have exchanged their "glory" (their God) for no-gods. Yahweh appeals to the members of the heavenly court:

>> *Be aghast at this, you heavens,*
>>> *shudder in utter horror, says the LORD [Yahweh].*
>> *My people have committed two sins:*
>>> *they have rejected me,*
>> *a source of living water,*
>>> *and they have hewn out for themselves cisterns,*
>>> *cracked cisterns which hold no water.*
>>>> —Jer. 2:12-13 (REB)

In these terms Jeremiah addresses the people of God who have a special story to tell. To forget that story, or to turn to another story, is disastrous, for the story is the basis of knowledge of God and of the community's identity.

Stipulations of the Covenant

We now turn to a second theme of Jeremiah's preaching. Closely connected with the basic experience, God's deliverance from Egyptian bondage, is the other crucial experience: the giving of the law that signifies the covenant relationship. Exodus and Sinai, the two "root experiences," are inseparable. When Jeremiah declares (2:8) that the "interpreters of the law" did not "know" God (the knowing of relationship), he stands in agreement with Hosea. That northern prophet also announced Yahweh's covenant lawsuit, which cited the commandments of the Decalogue:

> Hear the word of the LORD [Yahweh],
>   O people of Israel;
>   for the LORD [Yahweh] has an indictment[8]
>   against the inhabitants of the land.
> There is no [covenant] faithfulness or loyalty [hesed],
>   and no knowledge of God in the land.
> Swearing, lying, and murder,
>   and stealing and adultery break out;
>   bloodshed follows bloodshed.
> Therefore the land mourns,
>   and all who live in it languish;
> together with the wild animals
>   and the birds of the air,
>   even the fish of the sea are perishing.
>   —Hos. 4:1-3

Here is a splendid example of what literary critics call "pathetic fallacy": nature mourns for the lost welfare of the covenant. But this is more than a poetic device. Both Hosea and Jeremiah have a profound poetic awareness of the interrelationship of the people and the land on which they live.[9] Human behavior can "pollute" God's land (Jer. 2:7b), even as the whole creation may share the creative birth pangs of a new age (see Rom. 8:22-23). The modern split between nature and history, which is largely responsible for the ecological crisis, is challenged in texts like these. Human beings must live in responsible relation to the land, not as masters over it who can do as they please.

Turning Around

Finally, Jeremiah—true to Mosaic tradition—calls for decision, that is, turning away from false loyalties and returning to the fidelity of the covenant relationship. Jeremiah sees the people at a turning point, where everything depends on how the people respond. It is a crisis of life or death, blessing or curse.

---

8. The Hebrew term *rib*, translated "indictment," is the term for a legal controversy or lawsuit.
9. I am told by a ministerial friend (David Andrews) that early Puritan preachers used to preach that covenant obedience affected the agriculture of the land.

One of the key verbs in the prophet's vocabulary is the verb *shub*, a verb of turning. In a negative sense the verbal noun means turning away, apostasy; in a positive sense the verb means a turning to, a return—that is, repentance. Emphasizing the conditional "if" of the Mosaic covenant, Jeremiah seems to say that the promise to Abraham, that nations would be blessed by him (Gen. 12:1-3), depends on the people's repentance.

> *If you return, O Israel, says the LORD [Yahweh],*
>   *if you return to me,*
> *if you remove your abominations from my presence,*
>   *and do not waver,*
> *and if you swear, "As the LORD [Yahweh] lives!"*
>   *in truth, in justice, and in uprightness,*
> *then nations shall be blessed by him,*
>   *and by him they shall boast.*
>
> —Jer. 4:1-2

To Jeremiah, the present is a time of urgency: a time for soul searching, for measuring the "values" (idols) that people serve. That is why the prophet reminds the people of their root experiences: so that they may know the identity of their saving God and their identity as a people called by God. Also, that is why the prophet portrays an ominous future when a "foe from the north" will come upon them: so that they may awake from their dream world and "know" the God who is at work, seeking justice and peace. Jeremiah is puzzled—and he suggests that God is puzzled—about the people's misuse of their freedom, their stubborn refusal to sense the crisis and repent (turn around).

> *When people fall, do they not get up again?*
> *If they go astray, do they not turn back?*
> *Why then has this people turned away*
>   *in perpetual backsliding [turning away]?*
> *They have held fast to deceit,*
>   *they have refused to return.*
>
> —Jer. 8:4-5

He likens them to a horse "plunging headlong into battle" (Jer. 8:6). Even the birds know the times of their migration, but "my people do not know the ordinance of Yahweh" (8:7).

Could the people repent? Could a people set in its ways change its lifestyle? That is a relevant question even today, when people are locked into an economy that concentrates wealth at the top and victimizes the increasing number at the bottom, or a lifestyle that pollutes the natural environment and threatens the continuation of life on Earth. In passionate, hard-hitting language Jeremiah sought to awaken the people to the seriousness of their predicament. But Jeremiah was no easy optimist. He sensed that the people were in bondage to their lifestyle and could not change—like a person who is addicted to a drug. Only the most severe shock treatment could shake them out of their habits and make liberation possible.

In contrast to popular prophets, who preached soothing words, his task was to preach the judgment of God, through which God mercifully makes possible a new beginning.

Threat of the Return of Chaos

True to the Mosaic covenant heritage, Jeremiah regards it as his prophetic task to warn the people and to spell out "the curses" of the covenant, that is, the unavoidable consequences of the people's behavior. At one point he portrays the awful possibility that God would not just abrogate the covenant with Israel but would bring a terrible judgment on the world, like that of the great flood, when the earth was on the verge of returning to precreation chaos (*tohu wabohu;* cf. Gen. 1:2).

> I looked on the earth, and lo, it was waste and void;
>   and to the heavens, and they had no light.
> I looked on the mountains, and lo, they were quaking,
>   and all the hills moved to and fro.
> I looked, and lo, there was no one at all,
>   and all the birds of the air had fled.
> I looked, and lo, the fruitful land was a desert,
>   and all its cities were laid in ruins
> before the LORD [Yahweh], before his fierce anger.
>   —Jer. 4:23-26

Poetry like this, which universalizes the threat of God's impending judgment, anticipates the later style of prophecy known as apocalyptic, which sees God's relationship with Israel in the context of the ominous threat of powers of chaos to God's whole creation.[10]

In the perspective of Mosaic covenant theology, God takes a risk in making a covenant commitment to a people. It is human freedom that makes the present precarious and that threatens the Israelite community, and ultimately the world as a whole, with chaos. In Lutheran and Calvinistic terms, the problem is the bondage of the will.

Beyond Tragedy

Yet even in this covenantal view, which throws great weight on human responsibility, God does not lose control—not completely. The prospect of catastrophe is God's way of alerting people, through prophetic messengers, to the true seriousness of the crisis. The sufferings of history are God's shock treatment, intended to bring people to their senses. Beyond tragedy, so Jeremiah insisted, God will make a new beginning, a new covenant.

This hope burned so fiercely in Jeremiah's heart that, while the Babylonian army was pounding at the gates of Jerusalem, he bought a parcel of land and had

---

10. See later, chapter 35.

the deed legally notarized. What a powerful symbol: a man in prison, in a city about to fall, who makes an investment for the future! The issue is not the future value of real estate on the market but, in the worst of times, hope in the God who gives people a future.

According to the famous passage about "the new covenant" (Jer. 31:31-33), there must be a radical change in human nature before the weakness of the Mosaic covenant can be overcome. God's law must be written on the heart, not just on law books; and the knowledge of God must be so inward that no longer will it be necessary to teach one another, saying "Know the Lord." As a covenant partner, Israel remains free to respond to God's initiative, but paradoxically God "promises to make possible the very response which he inexorably demands."[11] Above all, God's forgiveness would ultimately heal the wounds of the people and inaugurate a lasting relationship, indeed, an everlasting covenant.

> This is the covenant that I will make with the house of Israel after those days, says the LORD [Yahweh]; I will put my law within them, and I will write it on their hearts; and I will be their God, and they shall be my people.
>
> —Jer. 31:33

The Christian community affirms that this new beginning in history was initiated through God's grace and forgiveness in Jesus Christ. As we well know, distinctive Christian writings proclaiming that the new age had dawned were eventually designated according to Jeremiah's prophecy of the new covenant.

Jeremiah's Temple Sermon

At one point in his ministry, Jeremiah delivered a sermon that got him into trouble. The "temple sermon" is summarized in Jer. 7:1-5, and his arrest immediately following the sermon and the near loss of his life is reported in Jeremiah 26. Since we are on the verge of turning to the royal covenant theology associated with David, it is appropriate to consider this sermon as a transition from Mosaic to Davidic theology. For it is a forceful attack on the false confidence that was generated by one aspect of Davidic theology.

In this sermon, as reported by Deuteronomistic interpreters,[12] Jeremiah lashes out against false confidence in the temple. The people were saying that the temple of Jerusalem guaranteed that Yahweh was in their midst, making them safe and secure from all alarm. They were glibly chanting the theological cliché, "The temple of Yahweh, the temple of Yahweh, the temple of Yahweh," supposing that God's presence with them gave them freedom to live as they pleased. Jeremiah attacks this temple theology by saying that worshipers had converted the temple

---

11. Nicholson, *God and His People*, 216.

12. Although the sermon in its present form shows the heavy influence of Deuteronomistic language, its substance undoubtedly goes back to Jeremiah.

into "a cave of robbers" where thieves take refuge to count their spoil—words that were quoted by Jesus at the time of his "cleansing of the temple" (Matt. 21:13).

A true Mosaic prophet, Jeremiah adds the conditional "if" of the Mosaic covenant: "If you truly amend your ways . . . [and that means obeying the Ten Commandments that are cited in part, vv. 5–6], then I [Yahweh] will dwell with you in this place, in the land that I gave of old to your ancestors forever and ever" (7:5-7). As things are now, said the prophet, this house is not a holy place that will stand forever, but will suffer the fate of the ancient shrine of the confederacy at Shiloh (which was destroyed during Israel's war with the Philistines). No wonder that Jeremiah was arrested and charged with apostasy! During his trial (Jeremiah 26) he was saved from execution only because some remembered that the prophet Micah had spoken similar words about the destruction of Jerusalem a century earlier.

So interpreted, the Mosaic covenant did not make for popular preaching. The reactions are portrayed in various narratives collected in the last part of the book of Jeremiah. In one of these, we find Jeremiah in conflict with the prophet Hananiah, who apparently preached on the platform of Davidic covenant theology, promising that the temple treasures would be returned and that God would stand by his promises of grace to the Davidic king (Jeremiah 28). To understand this prophetic conflict, we turn to the "everlasting covenant" with David that in various ways interacted with the conditional covenant with Moses.

PART II
CONTINUED

C. THE DAVIDIC COVENANT

"I [Yahweh] have made a covenant with my chosen,
I have taken oath to David, my servant:
I will establish your line in perpetuity,
I will make your throne stable for generations
to come."

PSALMS 89:3-4 (BWA)

23. THE PROMISES
OF GRACE TO DAVID

So far we have considered two major covenant perspectives found in the Old Testament: one associated with Abraham, and one with Moses. On the one hand, the Abrahamic covenant, we have seen, is unilateral in the sense that it expresses God's absolute commitment to a people, unconditioned by their behavior. This covenant, grounded in *sola gratia*, assures that the people will have a land and that they will increase on the land. It is a covenant of promise.

The Mosaic covenant, on the other hand, is more bilateral, for God and people are partners, having made a contractual agreement with each other. A heavy responsibility falls on the people, for they are called on to decide to serve their liberating God and to live in accordance with covenant obligations—God's commandments. If—and the conditional is important—if they prove unfaithful, deciding to live in a way that betrays the covenant relationship, they will suffer severe consequences—indeed, the whole thing could be called off. While the Abrahamic covenant is a covenant of promise of land and increase, the Mosaic covenant has to do with the behavior of the people on the land. It is a covenant of law, under the sanctions of blessing and curse.

The contrast between these two covenants is obvious, as it was to Paul, who draws a contrast between the Abrahamic covenant of promise and the Sinaitic covenant of obligation, which puts people under the blessing or the curse (see Gal. 5:6-14).

A Royal Covenant

We turn now to another way of symbolizing God's relation to the people and to the world: the royal covenant associated with David and with Zion. "Zion" is the ancient name for the southeastern ridge of the hill on which the city of Jerusalem was founded (mountain climbers will regard "mountain" as an extravagant translation). According to 2 Sam. 5:6-10 David's warriors took "the stronghold of Zion" from the pre-Israelite citizens (Jebusites) and David made it his capital, "the city of David." The temple was later built immediately to the north of this area, and because this shrine was regarded as God's chosen dwelling place (Ps. 132:13), it came to be known also as "the city of God" (Pss. 46:4-5; 87:3).[1] I have previously observed that Jon Levenson, in *Sinai and Zion*, regards Zion as one of the two symbolic mountains that dominate the Scriptures of ancient Israel.[2]

---

1. See Karen Armstrong, *Jerusalem: One City, Three Faiths* (New York: Knopf, 1996), for an early history of Jerusalem.

2. John D. Levenson, *Sinai and Zion* (Minneapolis: Winston, 1985). On the mountain symbolism, see above, chapter 17.

A Symbolic Vista

Like the Abrahamic and Mosaic covenants, this one too has its own symbolic vista or imaginative construal. Here the key elements in the pattern of symbolization are monarch and temple.

These two institutions, so basic to the cultures of the ancient Near East, were alien to Israel's "root experiences" of exodus and Sinai. Indeed, the Davidic covenant perspective was a "new theology," not easily absorbed into Israelite tradition. Conservatives who stood in the Mosaic tradition, like the prophet Samuel, opposed the new theology. In 1 Samuel 8, Samuel is portrayed as warning the people of the dangers of having a king "like the nations": this innovation would entail the loss of civil liberties enjoyed during the tribal confederacy. Further, the ideology of sacred kingship, known throughout the ancient Near East, would be a theological challenge, for it threatened the rejection of Yahweh as king, that is, the repudiation of Israel's theocracy.

Moreover, conservatives opposed the policy of building a temple (house) for Yahweh such as the great gods of the ancient world had. In 2 Samuel 7 the prophet Nathan is portrayed as opposing, at least initially, David's plan to build a house for Yahweh. In a dream, so the story goes, Nathan was told to say to David:

> Are you the one to build me a house to dwell in? I have not dwelt in a house from the day I brought the Israelites up out of Egypt to this day. I have been moving from place to place with a tent as my dwelling.
>
> —2 Sam. 7:5-6 (NIV)

The task of David's theologians was to adapt these two institutions that originally were alien to Israelite experience—dynastic kingship and sacramental temple—to Israel's faith so that they could become symbols for expressing the relationship between God and people, indeed, between God and the world. Their success is evidenced in the fact that David escorted the ark, the Mosaic symbol of Yahweh's presence in the midst of the people, into Jerusalem (see the processional ritual in Ps. 24:7-10). In the book of Psalms, the temple is regarded as the place where Yahweh "tabernacles" or "tents" in the midst of the people:

> *How lovely is your dwelling place [tabernacle],*
> *O Lord [Yahweh] of hosts!*
> *My soul longs, indeed it faints*
>   *for the courts of the Lord [Yahweh];*
> *my heart and my flesh sing for joy*
>   *to the living God.*
>
> —Ps. 84:1-2

Moreover, the king was regarded as God's special agent or "messiah" (1 Sam. 24:6), anointed for the leadership of the people, and in this sense the prototype of the one who is to come, the ideal ruler. The term "anointed one" (Hebrew *mashiah*, Greek *christos*) refers to *function* as God's instrument, not to the divine nature of the officeholder. (Notice that the Persian king Cyrus is called Yahweh's "messiah," or anointed one, in Isa. 45:1, for he is the agent of God's purpose.)

Thus here we have a perspective that embraces urban symbolism (Zion, the city) and royal symbolism (the king, "Yahweh's anointed one"). Of course this covenant perspective or "trajectory" had a profound influence on the New Testament portrayal of the Messiah, God's chosen agent to introduce God's dominion on earth, starting at Jerusalem (Zion).

Ideology and Faith

Before proceeding further, we must pause to consider a major question that hangs especially over the Davidic covenant. This covenantal perspective appears to be an "ideology," a sociological term that refers to a body of ideas and practices intended to justify or sanction a sociopolitical program.[3]

Some interpreters maintain that the Davidic covenant is essentially ideological. It was formulated to uphold and legitimate the power of the Davidic state, specifically to keep a single dynasty in office and to quell revolutionary movements. As such, it emphasized order at the expense of freedom. The Davidic covenant, according to some scholars, was a kind of "fall from grace." The period of grace, it is said, was the time of the tribal confederacy when the Mosaic covenant insured freedom and an egalitarian way of life. In the time of David, and especially Solomon, however, the ancient political ideology, derived from pre-Davidic (Jebusite) Jerusalem and the larger Mediterranean world (Syria, Egypt, Mesopotamia), "was superimposed upon the Yahwist tradition and remained there forever, though radically transformed in the New Testament tradition."[4]

There is a large element of truth in this sociological approach. Psalm 78—to take one witness to Davidic theology—is a document that seeks to justify the new social reality of the Davidic monarchy. Here a psalmist addresses the people, perhaps on the occasion of a public festival, in the manner of a wisdom teacher who looks back over Israel's history and traces its meaning. This bard perceives two threads interwoven in the story of Israel: the bright thread of Yahweh's marvelous deeds, and the dark thread of Israel's faithlessness ("Israel" in this case refers to Ephraim, the Northern Kingdom). Yahweh made a covenant (a reference to the Mosaic covenant) and gave the covenant commandments. Northern Israel, however,

> *did not keep God's covenant,*
> *but refused to walk according to his law.*
> *They forgot what he had done,*
> *and the miracles that he had shown them.*
> —Ps. 78:10-11

3. See the ideological dimension of the promise of land, above, chapter 21.
4. This has been emphasized in the writings of George E. Mendenhall, e.g., "The Monarchy," *Int* 29 (1975) 155–70; quotation from p. 168. This sociological view was also advocated by Walter Brueggemann, "Trajectories in Old Testament Literature and the Sociology of Ancient Israel," *JBL* 98 (1979) 161–85.

Divine grace and patience abounded, but the people's sin increased more and more.

Finally Yahweh could take it no longer. Says the psalmist, Yahweh "forsook his dwelling [the old tent of meeting] among the people" and delivered his "glory" (an allusion to the ark) into captivity. Resolved to make a new beginning, Yahweh "awoke as from sleep," and "put his adversaries to rout" (vv. 65–66). The recital of the story of northern covenant failure reaches a climax in the new beginning that God made in southern Israel, that is, the kingdom of Judah.

> He [Yahweh] rejected the tent of Joseph,
>   he did not choose the tribe of Ephraim;
> but he chose the tribe of Judah,
>   Mount Zion, which he loves.
>   —Ps. 78:67

The rejection of northern Israel and the choice of Judah is evidenced in two divine actions: first, Yahweh "established his sanctuary on Mount Zion" with spacious dimensions of creation: "like the high heavens" of the cosmos, "like the earth" that the Creator established firmly (v. 69); second, Yahweh designated David as "his servant," taking him from the sheepfolds and making him the shepherd (ruler) of the people (vv. 67–72). God's choice of Zion, God's choice of David: these are the twin pillars on which the Zion "ideology/theology" rests.

Psalm 78 draws our attention to a major problem in the community of faith: the temptation to present a theological justification of a sociopolitical program. We can find plenty of illustrations of the ideological dimension of faith in the history of Christianity—or of any religion, for that matter. Religion becomes an ideology when it is used to support and justify a national way of life or when God is portrayed as being "on our side" in the social struggle or even in war.[5] In modern times, religion became an ideology when the Bible was used to support sociological realities, such as the institution of slavery, patriarchal society, or capitalistic economy.

It must not be supposed, however, that the Davidic covenant was unique in having an "ideological taint." Other construals of God's covenant with the people are not immune from ideological coloration. In the final form of the Pentateuch, the Abrahamic covenant is closely connected with the Priestly (Zadokite) establishment of the Jerusalem temple. The Priestly presentation justifies and legitimates the authority and standing of the priests, particularly those who can trace their lineage back through Zadok to Aaron and Moses. Moreover, the Mosaic covenant, as expressed for instance in the book of Joshua, is closely connected with warfare to possess the land of Canaan. In this "Mosaic" view, Yahweh, the Divine Warrior, is the champion of Israel's political cause and justifies their taking the land from the native population.

A sociological approach to the Bible raises a fundamental question for people in the community of faith today, which treasures the Old Testament as sacred

---

5. During the 1996 presidential election campaign one group ran television commercials entitled "God is on Our Side."

Scripture: The burning issue is the relation between faith and ideology, or stated differently, between the Bible as "Word of God" and "human words" in which God's revelation is communicated. This issue should be faced squarely in any exposition of biblical theology.

In facing this theological question, we should not be surprised to find that Scripture bears the imprint of the sociological situation in which the relationship between God and people was expressed. As we have seen previously, God condescends to speak in the limitations of human language, and that includes the limitations of the sociological situation in which language functions.[6] This, however, is only the starting point, from which the theologian proceeds to consider the symbolic power of biblical language. Specifically, the theological task is to consider how the various covenants, despite their sociological coloration, symbolize the relationship between God and people in such a way as to transcend and survive the original social situations in which they arose.[7]

In a pathbreaking essay on this subject, Patrick D. Miller proposes three criteria for distinguishing faith from ideology.[8] First, faith is open to the voice of self-criticism, as expressed preeminently in the preaching of the great prophets. The king's position as Yahweh's anointed does not exempt him from searching criticism, as in the case of King David (see 2 Sam. 12:7: "You are the man!"). Political power must be exercised "under God," as Americans acknowledge in their Pledge of Allegiance.

Second, faith looks beyond the narrow interests of the social group to other peoples who live beyond the political boundary and are included in God's concern. We shall see that this ecumenical horizon belongs peculiarly to Davidic theology, which envisions "the city of God" as the world center to which the nations will ultimately come to find peace and well-being (Isa. 2:2-4).

Third, faith hears a moral demand for justice that is not confined to Israel's society but is worldwide. God's justice, being rooted and grounded in the cosmic order, is a universal moral demand. This too is a major accent of Davidic/Zion theology, as we shall see later when turning to the prophecy of Isaiah.

Cosmological Symbolism

Psalm 78, quoted above, concludes by saying that Yahweh "chose Mount Zion" as his sanctuary and that Yahweh "chose David to be his servant." We noticed earlier that the Mosaic pattern of covenant symbolism, found especially in the book of Deuteronomy, is analogous to, and probably influenced by, the suzerainty treaty form current outside of Israel. Also, the interpreters of the Davidic covenant have

6. On God's "accommodation," see above, chapter 8.

7. This question I explored in an address to the Catholic Biblical Association, "Biblical Theology and Sociological Interpretation," *TToday* 42 (1985) 292–306.

8. Patrick D. Miller, "Faith and Ideology in the Old Testament," in *Magnalia Dei: The Mighty Acts of God: Essays on the Bible and Archaeology in Memory of G. Ernest Wright*, ed. F. M. Cross et al. (Garden City, N.Y.: Doubleday, 1976), 464–79.

been influenced by, and indeed borrowed from, a symbolic vista known outside Israel. For in the ancient world monarch and temple belonged to a pattern of cosmological symbolism. In ancient Egypt, for example, this symbolism expressed the integration of society into the cosmic order and made possible a stable social order that remained essentially unchanged through several dynasties. The pharaonic structure, it was believed, belonged to the harmony of the cosmic order of creation.

In his monumental study of *Order and History*, the political philosopher Eric Voegelin maintains that the exodus from Egypt was not just a political event but a revolutionary departure from the "cosmological symbolization" of Egyptian culture and an entry into a new symbolic dimension in which an individual, typified by Moses, became the channel of the revelation of the transcendent God. Like some liberation theologians, but for different philosophical reasons, Voegelin maintains that under David (and especially under Solomon), who adopted the way of thinking prevalent in the ancient Near East, Israel fell back into a pharaonic outlook.[9]

The influence of the cosmological symbolism of the ancient Near East is apparent even in the architecture of Solomon's palace/temple complex as described in the account of Samuel/Kings. The whole plan, including temple and palace, expresses an architectural style that was influenced by the culture of Canaan and the ancient Near East. Like other ancient temples excavated by archaeologists, it had a tripartite structure (1 Kgs. 6:2-6): an entrance portico (*'ulam*), a main hall (*hekal*), and an inner sanctuary (*debir*) or "Holy of Holies" (v. 16).[10] It is significant that the temple-palace complex was constructed by a Phoenician (Canaanite) architect, Hiram of Tyre (1 Kgs. 5:1-11; 1 Chron. 14:1-2).

The historian goes into some detail about the temple and palace complex, giving measurements of height, width, and elevation. When one stands back and looks at the whole Solomonic building program, several distinctive features stand out.[11] First, as elsewhere in the ancient world, the king was a temple builder (2 Samuel 7). Only the king had the financial resources for such an expensive project; and only the king could raise the labor force and skilled workers. Aspiring to be a king "like the nations" (cf. Saul, 1 Sam. 8:5), Israel's first dynastic king, David, was a temple builder, though the plan was executed by his son and successor in the dynasty.

---

9. Eric Voegelin, *Order and History*, vol. 1: *Israel and Revelation* (Baton Rouge: Louisiana State Univ. Press, 1956); discussed above, chapter 2. See the previous discussion of liberation theologians such as George E. Mendenhall, Norman A. Gottwald, and Walter Brueggemann in chapter 18.

10. See the architectural sketch in NIV, p. 481; also my *Understanding the Old Testament* (4th ed.; Englewood Cliffs, N.J.: Prentice-Hall, 1986), 238–39; abridged paperback ed. (1997), 214–15. For archaeological parallels see William G. Dever, *Archaeology and Biblical Research* (Seattle: University of Washington Press, 1990), 110–17.

11. Here I am influenced by Niek Poulssen, *König und Tempel im Glaubenszeugnis des Alten Testaments*, SBM 3 (Stuttgart: Katholisches Bibelwerk, 1967), whose view is summarized in my review, *CBQ* 31 (1969) 450–52.

Second, the temple, located adjacent to the palace, was part of a unified layout. The building complex showed the inseparable relation between king and temple, monarchy and cult. Indeed, the temple built by Solomon was actually a royal shrine, on royal property, having royal support. The king had jurisdiction over the temple (it may even be called "the king's sanctuary"; cf. Amos 7:13) and sometimes officiated at temple services (cf. 1 Kings 8). The relation between temple and king is even clearer in the presentation of the Chronicler, in which the historian, omitting the whole exodus story, hastens to tell about David's plans to build a temple (1 Chronicles 13–17) and devotes seven chapters to its construction (2 Chronicles 1–7).[12] Pilgrimages to this central shrine were actually expressions of national allegiance (cf. Psalm 137).

Finally, both temple and monarch belonged to a symbolic whole that included heaven and earth, the celestial and the terrestrial. The earthly temple was God's "palace" or "dwelling place," where God (or God's name) was present (1 Kgs. 9:3), corresponding symbolically to the heavenly palace where God is enthroned as king.

The Temple in Cosmic Symbolism

In an important study entitled *Zion, the City of the Great King* (echoing a phrase from Ps. 48:1), Ben Ollenburger presents a comprehensive and illuminating discussion of Zion theology.[13] He shows that the theme of Yahweh as cosmic king was fundamental in the worship services of the temple of Jerusalem.

Let us consider the major features of Zion theology. In this symbolic vista, the earthly temple was regarded as a model of the heavenly temple, on the premise of the correspondence between the macrocosm and the microcosm, the celestial and the terrestrial. In a Priestly passage in the Pentateuch we find a hint that the Jerusalem sanctuary (the tabernacle) was constructed according to a heavenly model or "pattern" shown to Moses on the mountaintop (Exod. 25:9, a theme echoed in Heb. 8:5), just as Babylonian temples were thought to be miniature replicas of heavenly prototypes. Indeed, the Chronicler's history (1 Chron. 28:11-19) claims that David designed the temple according to a "model" or "plan" (*tabnith*), the same word as in Exod. 25:9, which rabbis later understood to be a heavenly prototype.[14] Furthermore, the sanctuary was imagined to be at the "center" (navel) of the earth, the meeting place of heaven, earth, and underworld (see fig. 6).[15] The temple hill was even likened to Mount Zaphon in the far north, the

12. The Chronicler's work is treated subsequently, chapter 25.

13. Ben C. Ollenburger, *Zion, the City of the Great King: A Theological Symbol of the Jerusalem Cult*, JSOTSup 41 (Sheffield: Sheffield Academic Press, 1987).

14. See Samuel Terrien, "Presence in the Temple," Chapter 4, in *The Elusive Presence* (San Francisco: Harper & Row, 1978); an earlier, basic study is Ronald E. Clements, *God and Temple: The Idea of the Divine Presence in Ancient Israel* (Oxford: Blackwell, 1965).

15. See Mircea Eliade, "The Symbolism of the Center," in *Cosmos and History: The Myth of the Eternal Return* (New York: Harper and Bros., 1959), 12–17. See also my discussion of "The Songs of Zion," in *Out of the Depths* (Philadelphia: Westminster, 1983; rev. ed. forthcoming, 2000).

mythical Canaanite Mount Olympus where El, the high god, presided over the heavenly council of gods.

> *Great is the* LORD *[Yahweh], and most worthy of praise,*
> *in the city of our God, his holy mountain.*
> *It is beautiful in its loftiness,*
> *the joy of the whole earth.*
> *Like the utmost heights of Zaphon is Mount Zion,*
> *the city of the great King.*
>
> —Ps. 48:1-3 (NIV)

This cosmic symbolism is implicit in the account of the prophet Isaiah's call (Isaiah 6). Standing in the earthly temple of Jerusalem, the prophet found himself transported into the heavenly temple, where Yahweh is enthroned as cosmic king. The drama that was enacted in the earthly temple (the choral anthem, the burning incense on the altar, the acclamation of Yahweh as king) also was going on in the heavenly temple.

Owing to the correspondence between the heavenly and the earthly, one could say in religious symbolism that God, who is enthroned in the cosmic temple, is also present (or "dwells") in the earthly temple. In this double sense the words of Habakkuk are often used even today as a call to worship:

> *The* LORD *[Yahweh] is in his holy temple;*
> *let all the earth keep silence before him!*
>
> —Hab. 2:20

In this manner poets express one of the dialectical contradictions inherent in the experience of God's historical presence: transcendence and immanence, distance and nearness. The cosmic symbolism makes it possible to affirm that the earthly temple is God's dwelling place, where the holy God is truly present to worshipers. As we read in Psalm 46, Zion is "the holy habitation of the Most High"; God is "in the midst of her" (i.e., Zion, the city of God), giving present security and ultimate peace. Hence the repeated antiphon at the end of two stanzas (possibly at the end of all three originally):

> *The* LORD *[Yahweh] of hosts is with us;*
> *the God of Jacob is our refuge.*
>
> —Ps. 46:7, 11

The Cosmic Significance of the King

Just as the temple was the place where God is present on earth, so the ruler (king or queen) was regarded as the channel through whom cosmic blessing and righteousness flow into society.[16] The monarch enjoyed ex officio a unique relation to

---

16. Ollenburger, in *Zion*, argues that the symbols of Davidic throne and Jerusalem temple belong to separate traditions. It is true that the symbols can be treated separately as in royal psalms (e.g., Psalms 18, 73) or in Zion psalms (Psalms 46, 48); but in some psalms the two symbols belong together (e.g., Psalms 78, 84, 132).

FIGURE 6. *Correspondence of Heavenly and Earthly Spheres: Macrocosm and Microcosm**

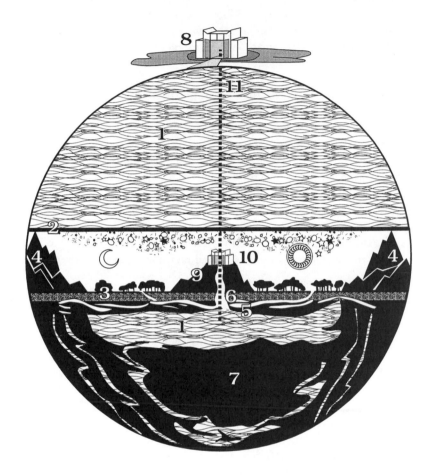

(1) Waters above and below Earth; (2) The firmament; (3) Surface of Earth; (4) Mountain-pillars supporting the Firmament; (5) The Fountains of the Great Deep (cf. Gen. 7:11); (6) The Navel (center) of the Earth; (7) Sheol (the Underworld); (8) The Celestial Temple (Heavenly Zion); (9) Earthly Mount Zion; (10) The Earthly Temple (miniature replica of cosmic temple); (11) *Axis Mundi* (imaginary line through symmetrically arranged parts of the cosmos).

*A view like this is presupposed in Hebrews 8:1-7 and Revelation 21:1-5.

God: he was regarded as the son of God, and in some ancient Near Eastern texts was described as "the image of God," that is, the one consecrated to be God's representative on earth. Indeed, in one biblical psalm the king is addressed as "god," if we follow the received Hebrew text (Ps. 45:6). This psalm is an ode for a royal wedding, when extravagant praise would be expected.[17]

The image of the king as "son of God" is found in Psalm 2, a psalm frequently quoted in the New Testament. Perhaps this was originally a coronation poem portraying the king as one installed as God's vice-regent in Zion, God's chosen sanctuary. Yahweh declares, "I have set my king on Zion, my holy hill," and gives him a protocol that certifies: "You are my son; today [this day of coronation] I have begotten you" (Ps. 2:6, 7). In this theological perspective, Isaiah looked forward to the advent of a Davidic king who would carry the throne name Immanuel, "God with us" (Isa. 7:14), and would sit on the Davidic throne to rule with justice as God's representative (Isa. 9:2-7).

In this way of thinking, the institutions of temple and monarchy are cosmological symbols that usher us into the spacious dimension of the cosmic order. The primary axis is vertical, the relation between heaven and earth, the cosmic order in relation to the social order, in contrast to the horizontal plane of history that, as in the Abrahamic or Mosaic covenants, moves from promise toward fulfillment. In adopting this pattern of symbolization, Israel has, so to speak, "entered the cosmos." Creation theology is a fundamental dimension of this perspective, as we shall see.

Reinterpretation of Cosmological Symbolism

During the monarchy, then, Israel adopted the symbolism of throne and temple to express God's relation to the people and through them to the world of nations. In Davidic theology this symbolism is reinterpreted by being linked with Israel's adoption of the institution of monarchy under David and Solomon. Davidic theologians affirmed that it was in remembered historical time, not in the mythical realm beyond history, that Yahweh chose and established the institutions of monarchy and temple. The institution of kingship did not have a primordial origin, as in the Sumerian King List, which states that in primeval times "kingship was lowered from heaven";[18] rather, it had a historical beginning in Israel when, as recorded in books of history (Samuel, Kings), Yahweh chose David to be the shepherd of the people. Moreover, the temple mount was not always a sacred place, the mythical center of the cosmos where creation began (as in Egyptian texts); rather, in a specific historical time God chose Zion, and chose the shrine that David proposed to build, as the divine dwelling place in the midst of the people.

17. On the symbolism of kingship see especially Ollenburger, *Zion.* He maintains that various texts differentiate the symbolism of Zion from Yahweh's commitment to the Davidic king.
18. See *ANET,* 265–66.

The most radical change, however, was that Israelite interpreters placed the symbolism of throne and temple in the context of God's special covenant with David. Like the Abrahamic covenant, this one is also called an "everlasting covenant" (*berît 'olam*), which guarantees the unbroken continuity of the Davidic line. There is good reason to believe that this royal theology was not a "theological reconstruction" made in a late period (the exile), when the Davidic monarchy was idealized, but rather "reflects the actual history of the Davidic period."[19] In an ancient poem, David's "last words," David is quoted as saying:

> Is not my house like this with God?
> For he has made with me an everlasting covenant,
> ordered in all things and secure.
> Will he not cause to prosper
> all my help and my desire?
> —2 Sam. 23:5

Closely related to this text is the oracle of the prophet Nathan, in which Yahweh makes a solemn oath of commitment to David and his house (2 Sam. 7:11b-17). The story goes that David proposed to build a "house" (temple) for Yahweh, only to be told that Yahweh would build him a "house" (dynasty) that would endure. Further, even though particular kings committed offenses in office, God would not withdraw covenant loyalty (*hesed*). This unilateral covenant is quite similar to the Abrahamic covenant; indeed, it has been suggested that David may have become acquainted with this southern type of covenant theology at Hebron, where he reigned before making Jerusalem his capital.[20] Be that as it may, the Davidic covenant, like the Abrahamic, is based on grace alone, not on human behavior.

Nathan's oracle contains the two essential elements or royal covenant symbolism: the unbroken continuity of the Davidic dynasty and of the temple as God's dwelling place in the midst of the people. The oracle stipulates that Yahweh will make a "house" (dynasty) for David.

> I will raise up after you your offspring, who will issue from your body, and I will stabilize his kingdom. He shall build a "house" for my name, and I will establish his royal dynasty in perpetuity [*'ad 'olam*].   (BWA)

Moreover, a special relationship will exist between God and the Davidic ruler.

> I will be father to him, and he will be son to me. When he does wrong, I will chasten him with the rod of human punishment, and with the stripes of human justice, but my loyalty [*hesed*] I will not withdraw from him, as I did in the case of Saul,

---

19. This is argued by Antti Laato, "Second Samuel 7 and Ancient Near Eastern Royal Ideology," *CBQ* 59 (1997) 244–69, on the basis of the persistence of similar promises to Assyrian kings of "an eternal dynasty."

20. Ronald E. Clements, *Abraham and David: Genesis 15 and Its Meaning for Israelite Tradition*, SBT 2/2 (Naperville, Ill.: Allenson, 1967).

whom I removed before you. Before me your house and your kingdom will stand secure in perpetuity ['ad 'olam];your throne will be established in perpetuity ['ad 'olam].

—2 Sam. 7:14-16 (BWA)

Notice especially that, according to Nathan's oracle, the Davidic ruler would enjoy a special relation to God: "son" in relation to "father." In the Mosaic covenant, the people Israel is regarded as God's son (Exod. 4:22-23; Hos. 11:1); here the anointed one is the son of God, as in Peter's confession at Caesarea Philippi according to the Matthean version (Matt. 16:16).

The Davidic and Mosaic Covenants

The Davidic covenant stands in theological tension with the Mosaic covenant. Whereas the Mosaic covenant stresses that Israel binds itself voluntarily to Yahweh, the suzerain, in response to beneficent deeds, the Davidic covenant stresses that Yahweh, by a solemn oath, is bound to David and his dynasty unconditionally and "forever."

In Israel, as elsewhere in the ancient Near East, the king is fundamentally responsible for securing "justice and righteousness." This is accomplished by the administration of law (cf. the famous Code of Hammurabi) and the use of royal edicts to release people from social burdens.[21] In difficult cases the king is the highest court of appeal, and ideally is the channel through whom the "righteousness" of the cosmic order flows into society (see Psalm 72). In Israel, however, the king is not the source of law, but is subject to the revealed torah, as stipulated in the law found in Deut. 17:14-20. The king is not "above the law," as shown dramatically in Nathan's parable (2 Sam. 12:1-14) with its pointed indictment, "You are the man!" In Israel, political power must be exercised under the judgment of God.

Moreover, there is a conditional element in the royal covenant, perhaps under the influence of the Mosaic covenant. Recall that in the Deuteronomistic history themes of the Mosaic and Davidic covenantal perspectives are worked together, with the result that the language of "if" is added to the royal covenant (e.g., 1 Kgs. 8:25).[22] If a king commits offenses in office, he is subject to punishment, as in the case of David's sin with Bathsheba (2 Samuel 11). But the endurance of the covenant, in this view, is not contingent on human freedom, which makes for social unrest in the present and the potential unleashing of powers of chaos in society. This covenant is the basis for social stability, which is rooted not in the authority of the king but in the cosmic rule of God mediated through the anointed one. At the end of the book of Judges a contrast is drawn between the time of the tribal confederacy, when freedom was sometimes carried to excess, and the order of the

---

21. See Moshe Weinfeld, *Social Justice in Ancient Israel and in the Ancient Near East* (Minneapolis: Fortress Press, 1995).
22. See above, chapter 18.

Davidic monarchy: "In those days there was no king in Israel; all the people did what was right in their own eyes" (Judg. 21:25).

The second element of Davidic covenant theology is also implied in this oracle, especially when read in its narrative context and supplemented with some of the psalms. In 2 Samuel 6, the chapter just before Nathan's oracle, David is described as escorting the ark into Jerusalem with great pomp and ceremony, dressed so scantily that his wife was incensed at his "playboy" antics. The ark was eventually placed in the Holy of Holies, the innermost shrine of the Jerusalem temple, built by David's son, Solomon. Regarded as the throne stool on which Yahweh is seated invisibly, the ark was the symbol of God's real presence in the temple.

Both of these aspects of Davidic theology—the promises of grace to David, and the temple as God's dwelling place—are celebrated in Psalm 132:

> The LORD [Yahweh] swore to David a sure oath
> from which he will not turn back:
> "One of the sons of your body
> I will set on your throne.
> If your sons keep my covenant
> and my decrees that I shall teach them,
> their sons also, forevermore,
> shall sit on your throne."
>
> —Ps. 132:11-12

Here the influence of the Mosaic covenant is apparent as evident in the conditional "if": the king is subject to God's law (cf. Deut. 17:18-20). This psalm also contains the second element of the Davidic covenant: the choice of Zion as God's dwelling place.

> For the LORD [Yahweh] has chosen Zion;
> he has desired it for his habitation:
> "This is my resting place forever;
> here I will reside, for I have desired it."
>
> —Ps. 132:13-14

Summary

In summary, the Davidic covenant, which has affinities with the Abrahamic covenant, represents a distinctive pattern of symbolizing the relationship between God and Israel and indeed between God and the world. It is a unilateral covenant, grounded solely in God's solemn oath, unconditioned by human behavior; therefore it assures stability, security, and hope for the future despite the contingencies of history.

Moreover, in this view the God who is enthroned in cosmic transcendence is "God with us," present in the midst of the people through the office of the anointed one and dwelling in their midst in the temple. At this point there is affinity with the Priestly theology of the tabernacling Presence.

Further, Davidic covenant theology, despite its ideological coloration, carries us into the spacious realm of creation theology. King and temple symbolize God's ordering of creation and God's will that the social order reflect the peace and righteousness of the cosmic order. The people learned to sing a "new song"—with the new notes of the kingdom of God that is to come on earth as it is in heaven.

Finally, in this covenant the primary symbols are throne and temple. The Davidic king rules ex officio as God's representative. In poetic language, the monarch is described as Yahweh's anointed, indeed, the "son of God" (Ps. 2:7) who is seated "at the right hand of God" (Psalm 110). Also, the temple of Zion is the *axis mundi*, the center, to which not only Israel but all peoples must come to find order, well-being, and peace. The ecumenical horizon of this covenant perspective is expressed in the well-known poem, found in both Isaiah (2:2-4) and Micah (4:1-4), that portrays the eschatological consummation when all nations will make a pilgrimage to the center, the elevated temple mountain of Zion, in order to hear the word of God that brings order, security, and peace.

24. THE COSMIC RULE
OF YAHWEH IN ZION

No covenantal perspective is more prominent in the Bible, both the Old Testament and the New, than the one associated with David. To be sure, it is not found explicitly in the Priestly Torah, though, as we have noted, there are affinities between the everlasting covenants made with Abraham and with David. Furthermore, the Davidic covenant is a subordinate theme in Deuteronomy and the Deuteronomistic history, which on the whole is governed by the Mosaic covenantal perspective. In other literature, however, the theology of the Davidic covenant provides the major perspective: the book of Psalms, the book of Isaiah, and the Chronicler's history. Each of these units of Scripture we shall consider in successive chapters.

Psalms: A Davidic Hymnbook

We have already found that the Davidic covenant is the subject of some of the psalms. Psalm 89, for instance, is a poetic celebration of the promises of grace to David given in Nathan's oracle (2 Sam. 7:4-17, echoed in Ps. 89:28-37), first in the major key of hymnic praise (vv. 1–27) and then in the minor key of lament (vv. 28–51) with its poignant question:

> Lord [Yahweh], where is your steadfast love [ḥesed] of old,
> which by your faithfulness you swore to David?
> —Ps. 89:49

Also we have touched on the storytelling Psalm 78, which reaches a climax in God's choice of David and of Zion, and Psalm 132, where the twin themes of Davidic king and Jerusalem temple are treated side by side. Having looked at a few trees, however, we now must stand back and look at the forest as a whole: the Psalms as a book.

The book of Psalms as a completed whole is attributed to David, "the sweet singer of Israel" (2 Sam. 23:1, as some translate). David is specifically associated with some psalms whose superscriptions relate the psalm to a particular event in David's career. For instance, Psalm 51 is associated with David's "sin with Bathsheba" (2 Samuel 11). The Hebrew expression *ledawid*, found at the head of a number of psalms, may mean "dedicated to David" or "belonging to a Davidic collection" (e.g., Psalm 11). The composition, singing, and collection of some psalms can undoubtedly be traced back to the man who was reputed to be a favorite singer of songs. However, the attribution of the book of Psalms to David does not mean that he was the author of the whole collection. Rather, Davidic "authorship" must be understood theologically. David symbolizes the king who represents the people as they come before God in worship.

Also, the structure or arrangement of the book of Psalms is significant theologically. The preface to the Psalter consists of two psalms, one a psalm in praise of God's torah or "instruction" (Psalm 1), and the other a royal psalm, dealing with the installation of Yahweh's "anointed" (messiah) on the holy hill of Zion (Psalm 2). Since both of these psalms stand outside the first Davidic collection, which comprises Psalms 3–41, and unlike other psalms in this collection they have no headings ascribing them to David, we may safely assume that they were located here by an editor for the purpose of sounding major themes of worship: rejoicing in the torah and the hope for a messianic king to rule in Zion. Mixed in with hymns, laments, and thanksgivings are a number of royal psalms that highlight the imagery of kingship (e.g., Psalms 45, 110, 118).[1]

The Theological Center of the Book of Psalms

Just as the organization of a modern hymnal may indicate its overall theological flavor, so the canonical shape of the book of Psalms may contribute to our theological understanding of the book as a whole. Gerald H. Wilson has suggested an interesting way to understand the present shape of the book of Psalms.[2] He notes that the Psalter opens with a psalm of the Davidic covenant (Psalm 2), that there is a royal psalm at the end of book II (Psalm 72), also that there is another royal psalm at the end of book III (Psalm 89), though this one, as we have seen, shifts from praise to lament about the failure of the promises of grace to David. Looking at books I–III, Wilson suggests that the placement of these psalms is intended to display the failure of the Davidic covenant and the need for a larger theological view. The problem is resolved, he maintains, in book IV, which he calls "the editorial center of the final form of the Hebrew Psalter," especially the psalms of God's dominion clustered in Psalms 93, 95–99. In these psalms, sovereignty is lifted from the human level (trust in kings and princes) to the cosmic level (trust in the God who is cosmic king and creator).

This is an attractive, even tempting, hypothesis. It enables us to see that the book of Psalms was not just thrown together but was composed in its final form to make a theological statement. The hypothesis is challenged, however, by the structure of the book of Psalms itself, for Psalm 132, which comes after the psalms of Yahweh's enthronement, presents a restatement of the tenets of the Davidic covenant: election of the Davidic king and choice of the temple of Zion. The truth is that Israelite interpreters never regarded the Davidic covenant as superseded, but held on to the promises of grace to David, though lifting them above the level of prosaic historical reality. It is noteworthy that Augustine in his great work, *The City of God* (book 17), devoted great attention to Psalm 89.

---

1. See my classification of the psalms in *Out of the Depths* (rev. ed.; Philadelphia: Westminster, 1983; rev. ed. forthcoming, 2000), especially the outline in appendix A.

2. Gerald H. Wilson, *The Editing of the Hebrew Psalter*, Society of Biblical Literature Dissertation Series 76 (Atlanta: Scholars Press, 1985).

The Cosmic Dominion of God

Despite its vulnerability, this hypothesis has the merit of drawing attention to a central teaching of the Psalms as an edited hymnbook. While the Mosaic covenant emphasizes the dimension of Israel's history, the Davidic covenant is deeply rooted in mythopoetic symbolism. Davidic covenant theology explodes beyond the limitations of Israel's sacred history and Israel's covenant community by announcing that the God whom Israel worships is not Israel's God in a narrow, possessive, or exclusive sense, but the God who is creator of heaven and earth and the sovereign of all nations. This is an ecumenical theological perspective.

Located at the center of the Psalter, the psalms of Yahweh's dominion sound forth the central message of the whole book: the sovereign rule (kingdom) of God. Today the word "kingdom" sounds foreign, especially in the United States, which has had no experience with monarchy, and for some the language is too heavily laden with masculine imagery. Is there another word in English that conveys the interrelated meanings of (a) the power of a sovereign (b) who rules over a territory and (c) is accorded allegiance by subjects? "Rule" stresses the sovereign's control, but lacks the spatial dimension. "Realm" conveys the spatial dimension but lacks the emphasis on sovereignty. "Regime" suggests a system of management but lacks a personal dimension of loyalty. The "monarchy" or "empire" of God sounds forced and is too political. For the sake of being honest with Scripture the word "kingdom" should be retained, as in most modern translations (NRSV, REB, NIV, NJB). If we shift terminology to soften the emphasis on divine sovereignty, perhaps the best word is "dominion of God."[3]

In the psalms of Yahweh's dominion, then, the horizon expands from the praise of "our God"—the God revealed in Israel's historical experience—to an ecumenical vision of God's worldwide sovereignty, which is not bounded by politics or geography.

To be sure, these psalms do not lose contact with the plane of history, even Israel's history. There are occasional references to episodes of Israel's story, such as the years of testing in the wilderness (Ps. 95:8-10), the leadership of Moses, Aaron, and Samuel (99:6-7), or the choosing of a heritage (land) for Israel (47:3-4; cf. 98:2-3). By and large, however, the primary axis of these psalms is the vertical relation of heaven and earth, not the horizontal one of the fulfillment of God's promise in history. "The real center of action, in the Covenant of David," remarks J. C. Rylaarsdam, "lies in the primordial, the cosmic, and the pre-temporal world that antedates the world of human contingency."[4] These Davidic psalms, he goes on to

---

3. Proposed in *The New Testament and Psalms: An Inclusive Version*, ed. Victor Gold et al. (New York: Oxford Univ. Press, 1995), as in the Lord's Prayer: "Your dominion come." On the larger question of how divine sovereignty is exercised, see my essay, "The Kingdom, the Power, and the Glory: The Sovereignty of God in the Bible," *TToday* 53 (1996) 5–14.

4. J. C. Rylaarsdam, "Jewish-Christian Relationship: The Two Covenants and the Dilemmas of Christology," *JES* 9, no. 2 (1972) 249–70, quotation 261. Reprinted in *Grace upon Grace: Essays in Honor of Lester J. Kuyper*, ed. James I. Cook (Grand Rapids: Eerdmans, 1975), 70–84, quotation 78. In this essay Rylaarsdam compares the Mosaic and Davidic covenants.

say, move in a mythical dimension: they "sing about the triumph of God as Creator by recalling his establishment of order (*zedek*), by the overcoming of chaos and anarchy in struggles that lie in that mythical past." Therefore the social order—especially the Davidic dominion—is securely founded.

> Yahweh's Kingship, and the Davidic kingship as well, rests on a series of decrees which are eternal and unchangeable: the world is established, it will not be moved. Yahweh is King forever; mightier than the breakers of the many waters [i.e., the forces of chaos]. He decrees the place of the nations in the scheme of things; and by that same immutable decree David is his first-born. He [David] has set his right hand over the sea and the rivers [cf. Ps. 89:25], a token which coordinates his rule with that of Yahweh himself.

He concludes this summary by saying that Davidic theology soars above the contingencies and changes of human history.

> The focus is on the Alpha of the beginning; and the psalms repeatedly appeal to this *me az* [from time of old], this primordial *illo tempore* [those ancient times], as the rock of assurance amid the instabilities of time and history.[5]

Israel's Theology of Divine Kingship

Several things deserve attention in this summary of Davidic theology. First, these psalms move in the spacious horizon of creation—not just creation in the primordial past (as in Genesis 1), but the whole creation that is radically dependent on the Creator for its order and permanence. The earth belongs to Yahweh who made it, founding it securely on the waters of chaos (Ps. 29:10). Creation is not just an event of the remote past but also includes the present cosmic order that the Creator sustains against continuing disruptions of the powers of chaos. In this creation theology, the whole *'erets* (earth), not narrowly *'erets yisra'el* (the land of Israel), belongs to the Lord (Yahweh) who made it, founding it on the waters of chaos (Ps. 24:1). Hence worship becomes ecumenical. All peoples are invited to join Israel in worshiping the God who is creator and king.

> For he [*Yahweh*] spoke and it came to be;
> he commanded, and it stood firm.
> —Ps. 33:9

Moreover, the invitation to praise God is extended to the whole realm of nature: heaven and earth, the sea and fields, the trees and the forest. Here we do not find the dichotomy between "history" and "nature" that has contributed to the present ecological crisis. God's dominion embraces the great whole.[6]

Creation versus Chaos

Second, these psalms celebrate Yahweh's dominion by recalling divine triumphs that occurred in the primordial era, "those ancient times." The language moves

---

5. Ibid.
6. See Rosemary Radford Ruether, *Gaia & God: An Ecofeminist Theology of Earth Healing* (San Francisco: HarperSanFrancisco, 1993), chap. 11.

beyond historical recital, found for instance in the storytelling Psalms 105 and 106, into the imaginative realm of mythical exploits of creation. Yahweh is portrayed as the Divine Warrior who came, comes, and will come to overcome the powers of chaos symbolized by the sea, the rivers, the floods. An ancient Israelite hymn displays strong influence of Canaanite poetry:

> Yahweh sits enthroned over the flood,
> Yahweh sits enthroned as king forever!
> —Ps. 29:10 (BWA)

The same language occurs in one of the hymns of Yahweh's dominion (93:3-4), where the poet portrays "the floods," "many waters," and "the sea" lifting up their stormy waves, as though seeking to challenge the sovereignty of Yahweh. But the tumult is in vain:

> More majestic than the thunders of mighty waters,
> more majestic than the waves of the sea,
> majestic on high is the LORD [Yahweh]!
> —Ps. 93:4

Establishment of Cosmic Order

Third, the result of these mythical victories in the primordial past is that Yahweh the creator has established right order or "righteousness." The cosmic King has issued a series of eternal decrees that shape and govern the future, including the establishment of the Davidic throne and the assignment of lands to Israel and other peoples (Pss. 93:5; 97:8). Therefore the dominion of Yahweh, the Creator and cosmic King, is to be proclaimed among all nations:

> Say among the nations, "The LORD [Yahweh] is king!
> The world is firmly established;
> it shall never be moved.
> He will judge the peoples with equity."
> —Ps. 96:10

To be sure, there are flare-ups of disorder, when it seems that God has lost control. Israelite poets, however, are confident that Yahweh is sovereign, even though that sovereignty may be hidden at present or seemingly threatened by powers of chaos, evident in attacks of foreign enemies, disruption of fertility, or social breakdown. Confident that God is fully in control, poets looked to the future in the expectation that God would come to judge (rule) the earth with righteousness and truth (Ps. 96:10-13). Thus God's dominion provides "the rock of assurance amid the instabilities of time and history" (Rylaarsdam). The worship of "the King, all glorious above," resounds in Christian worship services even today, as in our hymn, "O, Worship the King."

> The earth with its store of wonders untold,
> Almighty, thy power hath founded of old;

> *hath established it fast by a changeless decree,*
> *and round it hath cast, like a mantle, the sea.*

Current Battles against the Powers of Chaos

Finally, the founding of the Davidic kingdom is seen to be part of the cosmic order that God has established. As the "son of God," or in some ancient Near Eastern texts "the image of God," the earthly ruler is God's representative through whom the cosmic order is mediated to earthly society, so that there may be justice and peace (Psalm 72). The king's battles against his enemies are seen in the perspective of God's warfare against the powers of chaos:

> *I will set his hand on the sea*
> *and his right hand on the rivers.*
> —Ps. 89:25

Although the Israelite king is not considered divine or an incarnation of God, in some sense his task is to make the dominion of God a reality in human society. Through the king, the social order is related harmoniously to the cosmic order.

In one respect, New Testament portrayals of the coming of God's dominion are similar to this worldview. Jesus' battles against Satan's dominion, as portrayed in the Synoptic Gospels (especially Mark), are part of God's ongoing warfare against the powers of evil in order that there may be a "new creation." In apocalyptic visions, which we will consider later, faithful people are called to take part in the struggle against evil and, as in the conclusion to the Lord's Prayer, to pray that God will deliver persons from "the evil one."[7]

The Enthronement of God

It is appropriate that the songs of God's dominion belong in a hymnbook, for it is in worship that people are invited to leave the ordinary world, with its illusory values and misleading ways, and to enter imaginatively into God's world, where God is "enthroned on the praises of Israel" (Ps. 22:3).[8] Perhaps it is in imagination that we discern the real world that belongs to God and, as we sing in one of our hymns, affirm "That though the wrong seems oft so strong, God is the Ruler yet."[9]

The psalms of Yahweh's kingship (Psalms 47, 93, 94–99) reflect a cultic festival, perhaps analogous to the New Year's festivals celebrated in surrounding countries such as Babylonia. On that occasion, as the great Scandinavian scholar Sigmund Mowinckel proposed, the dominion of Yahweh was not just expressed hymnically; it was celebrated in a ritual drama of Yahweh's ascension to the divine

---

7. See the discussion of "The Dominion of God versus the Dominion of Evil," below, Chapter 33.

8. See the insightful study by Walter Brueggemann, *Abiding Astonishment: Psalms, Modernity, and the Making of History* (Louisville: Westminster/John Knox, 1991).

9. "This Is My Father's World," by Maltbie D. Babcock (1858–1901).

throne.[10] The ritual included a reenactment of David's bringing the ark to Jerusalem (Ps. 132:6-10; cf. 2 Samuel 6), the triumphal procession through the gates of the city (Ps. 24:7-10), and the placement of the ark in the Holy of Holies of the temple, where Yahweh "sits enthroned upon the cherubim" (99:1).

Psalm 47 is an excellent witness to this view. Here the theme of Yahweh's ascension is announced: God (Yahweh) has "gone up" (ascended) amid shouts of acclamation and with the sound of the shofar (trumpet):

> *God has gone up with a shout,*
> *The Lord [Yahweh] with the sound of a trumpet.*
> *Sing praises to God, sing praises;*
> *sing praises to our King, sing praises.*
> —Ps. 47:5-6

Since, however, the earthly temple was regarded as the counterpart of the heavenly, on the principle of the relationship between the macrocosm and the microcosm, the drama symbolized Yahweh's ascension to the heavenly throne.[11] Thus "the great king" (47:2) not only reigns in Zion, where anthems of praise are sung, but over the whole earth.

> *God is king over the nations;*
> *God sits on his holy throne.*
> *The princes of the peoples gather*
> *as the people of the God of Abraham.*
> *For the shields [rulers] of the earth belong to God;*
> *he is highly exalted.*
> —Ps. 47:8-9

The throne ascension, analogous to the coronation of an earthly monarch, was accompanied by trumpet fanfare, shouts of acclaim, and songs of joy. Emissaries from foreign nations ("the princes of the peoples," 47:9) were apparently included in this ecumenical celebration.

The Lord Is King!

The keynote in these psalms is the cultic exclamation, *YHWH malak* (93:1; 96:10; 97:1; 99:1), which may be translated "The LORD [Yahweh] has become king" (so REB), a translation that refers to an event that has happened. Alternatively, the cultic cry may be rendered "The LORD is king" (so NJPSV; NRSV; cf. NJB) or "the LORD reigns" (NIV), a translation that indicates Yahweh's eternal kingship.

The first-mentioned translation, while grammatically justifiable, is questionable if it implies regaining a kingship that has been lost. Unlike Baal in the

10. Sigmund Mowinckel's view is set forth in *The Psalms in Israel's Worship*, trans. D. R. Ap-Thomas, 2 vols. (Nashville: Abingdon, 1962), summarized in my *Out of the Depths*, "The Festival of Zion," Chapter 6. The whole subject is discussed helpfully by Ben C. Ollenburger, *Zion, City of the Great King*, JSOTSup 41 (Sheffield: JSOT Press, 1987), 33.

11. On the macrocosm in relation to the microcosm, see above, chapter 23.

Canaanite religion, Yahweh is not involved in "the myth of the eternal return"[12]—a dying-rising god who is subject to the powers of death and darkness. Some suggest that the language is existential, referring to the confession that God has been dethroned in human life and needs to be reenthroned; but this is rather forced. In all probability the exclamation refers to God's eternal kingship: Yahweh is king forever! God was king "from of old" (Ps. 93:2), God is acclaimed as king now (47:7), and God will come as king to judge the earth (98:9). All the tenses—past, present, and future—must be employed to praise the God who was, who is, and who is to come.

In this language the biblical poets express the faith that human security is grounded in the rule of God who is transcendent—beyond the historical realm where powers of chaos are at work. From our human point of view, the disorder and suffering in the world seem to challenge the sovereignty of God. But above the waters of chaos—so faith affirms poetically—God sits enthroned as the eternal King, holding the cosmos in being and maintaining the order of cosmic law. It is the eternity of God, who remains God even though the earth be destroyed, that inspires a poet to affirm in a well-known Zion psalm:

> *God is our refuge and strength,*
>   *a very present help in trouble.*
> *Therefore we will not fear, though the earth should change,*
>   *though the mountains shake in the heart of the sea;*
> *though its waters roar and foam,*
>   *though the mountains tremble with its tumult.*
>   —Ps. 46:1-3

God's Dominion as Future Horizon

God's dominion has a future horizon; for God's kingdom has *not* come on earth as it is in heaven. People still experience the threat of chaos, the shaking of earth's foundations, the sinister powers of death and darkness. In faith's imagination, however, the King, whose throne is securely established from of old, will come.

> *Let the sea roar, and all that fills it;*
>   *the world and those who live in it.*
> *Let the floods clap their hands;*
>   *let the hills sing together for joy*
> *at the presence of the* LORD *[Yahweh], for he is coming*
>   *to judge the earth.*
> *He will judge the world with righteousness,*
>   *and the peoples with equity.*
>   —Ps. 98:7-9; cf. 96:10-13

The Christmas carol, "Joy to the World, the Lord Is Come," echoes the jubilant notes of this psalm (see Ps. 98:4-9).

---

12. See Mircea Eliade, *Cosmos and History: The Myth of the Eternal Return* (New York: Harper and Bros., 1959).

These psalms, as we have noticed, may reflect a cultic festival that was celebrated in the Jerusalem temple during the period of the monarchy. If so, in the final
form of the Psalter the poetic language bursts beyond the limitations of the cult
and becomes an expression of praise for all times and all peoples. Imagination portrays the eschatological coronation of God!

This imaginative portrayal is found in the magnificent passage, Isa. 52:5-7,
where language transcends historical reality. The poet gives a concrete picture,
such as people of the time probably experienced. The countryside beyond the
walls of Jerusalem is desolated by war; the people are huddled in the city, anxiously
wondering how the battle goes with those fighting against hopeless odds; the sen-
tinels are on the ramparts of the city gate, scanning the surrounding territory for
any sign of activity. Suddenly in the distance the watchmen spy a single runner, a
herald who approaches to announce that the war is over, that peace is at hand, that
a new day is breaking. In Hebrew the word of the herald of good news is described
in four participles (translated "who . . ."):

> *How beautiful upon the mountains*
> *are the feet of the messenger:*
> *who announces shalom,*
> *who proclaims tidings of good,*
> *who publishes victory [salvation],*
> *who says to Zion: Your God reigns!*
> —Isa. 52:7 (BWA)

Here too the herald's exclamation may be translated, "Your God has become king"
(REB), although more likely the poet refers to the imminent display of God's royal
rule that is everlasting: past, present, and future. It is noteworthy, however, that in
this passage the poet envisions the triumphant return of God to Zion (52:8). The
Divine Warrior has "bared his holy arm before the eyes of all the nations" (52:10),
with the result that God's people in the ruined places of Jerusalem experience
deliverance, and "all the ends of the earth shall see the salvation of our God."

The theological overtones of this language of God's dominion, specifically
God's coming to the temple of Zion with saving power, are picked up in the New
Testament.[13] The Gospel of Mark begins with the announcement of the imminent
coming of God's kingdom:

> Now after John was arrested Jesus came to Galilee, proclaiming the good news of
> God, and saying, "The time is fulfilled, and the kingdom of God has come near;
> repent, and believe in the good news."
> —Mark 1:14-15

13. See below, chapter 35.

25. History Viewed
in Davidic Perspective

We turn now to a major presentation of the Israelite story: the Chronicler's history, especially 1 and 2 Chronicles. This important theological writing has unfortunately been out of bounds for most modern biblical readers. Earlier generations, however, who read the Bible from cover to cover, were influenced by this portion of Scripture. We are told that John Newton's famous song, "Amazing Grace," was influenced by 1 Chron. 17:16. According to this passage David "sat before Yahweh" and said: "Who am I, O Lord God, . . . that you have brought me thus far?" ("'Tis grace that brought me safe thus far.") Also, in some churches the offertory prayer is used: "All things come from you, O God, and of your own have we given you" (1 Chron. 29:14b).

The Chronicler's History

The Chronicler's history includes the books of 1 and 2 Chronicles (the last two books of the Hebrew Bible) and, in the judgment of many scholars, also the books of Ezra and Nehemiah. Even if the two historical works belong together, which is a debatable point, there are important differences between them. One obvious theological difference is that the books of Chronicles stress the Davidic covenant, with its twin institutions of monarchy and temple, while saying little about the Mosaic tradition; whereas the books of Ezra and Nehemiah stress the Mosaic covenant and minimize the importance of Davidic theology. There is good reason, then, to consider the Chronicler's work as a separate theological statement.

In connection with our study of the Mosaic pattern of symbolization we turned to another historical work, the so-called Deuteronomistic history. We found that Deuteronomistic historians attempted to understand Israel's history of failure, culminating in the fall of the nation and the exile of the people, in the light of the covenant perspective associated with Moses. These historians also attached great importance to the royal covenant associated with David, but that covenant was subordinated to the primary Mosaic covenant. The Chronicler's history reverses the priority, placing primary emphasis on God's promises of grace to David. To be sure, the Mosaic Torah, here called "the book of Moses" (2 Chron. 25:4; 35:12), in its halakic or "legal" sense is invoked, as we shall see; but the key to understanding Israel's history, according to these theologians, is Yahweh's covenant promises of grace to David. Indeed, some have argued that Chronicles "was written to vindicate the definitiveness of David's covenant over Sinai."[1]

---

1. Robert North, S. J., "The Chronicler," in *New Jerome Biblical Commentary*, ed. Raymond E. Brown et al. (Englewood Cliffs, N.J.: Prentice-Hall, 1990), 364.

It is striking that Chronicles was written in a time when monarchy had ceased in Israel and when builders of the Second Temple looked back to the glory of the First Temple, the one built by Solomon. This "historical" work, composed after the time of Ezra and Nehemiah (probably ca. 400 to 300 B.C.), relies primarily on the source of Samuel/Kings, although it also refers to unknown sources. The story is retold, however, in such a way as to give an imaginative construal in the perspective of Davidic theology. The Chronicler's work soars beyond the concrete history, with which modern historians attempt to deal, into a symbolic vista perceived by religious imagination.

A Theological Revision of History
As in the case of the Deuteronomistic history, we may ascertain the theological perspective of the Chronicler in two ways. First, let us examine the way sources are used. Unfortunately, most of the sources referred to are no longer extant, if indeed they ever existed. It would be a great day for archaeology if one of them should turn up, for instance, "the records of the prophet Nathan" (1 Chron. 29:29) or "the story of the prophet Iddo" (2 Chron. 13:22). Fortunately, one of the Chronicler's sources is readily available, namely, Samuel–Kings (specifically 1 Samuel 32 to 2 Kings 25). The Chronicler's perspective is indicated by how he uses this source, sometimes quoting verbatim, sometimes condensing, sometimes omitting, sometimes changing to accord with special interests.

The scope of this work extends from creation (Adam) to the fall of the nation and the exile of the people. The first part, from creation to David, is spanned by genealogies (1 Chronicles 1–9; cf. Matthew's genealogy, which begins with David and leads to Jesus). Amazingly the historian skips over the period of the ancestors (Genesis 12–50) and the root experiences of exodus and Sinai (Exodus–Numbers), and the period of the tribal confederacy (Joshua, Judges) and comes immediately to the decisive beginning in Israel's history: the covenant with David and the building of the temple. In this regard the Chronicler is comparable to the prophet Isaiah of Jerusalem, who likewise ignores Israel's sacred history, even exodus and Sinai, and focuses on the Davidic king and the temple of Zion (see below, chapter 26).

Theology Set Forth in Key Addresses
The second way to ascertain the Chronicler's perspective is to study key addresses that are introduced at transitional points in the narrative. Illustrative of these is the account of the warfare between Abijah (sometimes spelled Abijam), son of Rehoboam, who was Solomon's son and successor, and Jeroboam, king of northern Israel (2 Chronicles 13). Readers are carried back to the time of the breakup of the united kingdom (922 B.C.) and the split into Northern and Southern Kingdoms, each claiming to worship Yahweh, the God of Israel. The Deuteronomistic historian says precious little about King Abijah (1 Kgs. 15:1-2), but the Chronicler gives an extended account of his war with Jeroboam I, founder of the Northern Kingdom. The account includes Abijah's speech on a mountain in the

hill country of Ephraim, as the two armies confronted one another (2 Chron. 13:3-12). In this dramatic setting the speech makes these points:

- Yahweh, God of Israel, gave the kingship over Israel forever to David and his sons by "a covenant of salt"—a covenant that lasts, because salt is a preservative (v. 5).[2]
- You northerners suppose that you can withstand "the kingdom of Yahweh in the hands of the sons of David" because of your military might and the religious innovations of Jeroboam (v. 8). These included setting up calf images of Yahweh, installing a separate priesthood, and gathering the people for worship at northern sanctuaries (cf. 1 Kings 12).
- But this strategy will not work. Yahweh is "our God whom we have not forsaken." The evidence that we worship God in truth is that we have the proper priesthood, the proper worship, and the proper sanctuary (the Jerusalem temple; v. 10).
- So, "God is with us," leading us in battle. In opposing us, you are really fighting against Yahweh, the God of our ancestors, and you cannot succeed (v. 12).

This is clearly not an unbiased account of a war between northern and southern Israel (is there ever an unbiased military account?); rather, it is an ideological claim, that is, an attempt to justify the Southern Kingdom of Judah and the religion of the Jerusalem temple. Who is on the Lord's side? The question was raised not just in a contest between armies but in the division within the people of God into north and south, Ephraim and Judah. The people of Judah, according to this view, were confident that God was with them and that, because of their faithfulness, they were on the winning side.

This ideological account, of course, has many historical parallels: people who are confident that God is on their side in a political struggle, warriors who invoke God to help them win battles, or clergy who claim that they are properly ordained and stand in the true succession. It is even reported that during time-outs some professional football players pray that God will help their side to attain victory. Here we come up against the whole question of faith and ideology, which as we have noticed previously, attends all covenant theologies.[3]

The Chronicler's Major Theological Convictions

Davidic theology, however, cannot be reduced to pure ideology, as we shall see when considering the message of the prophet Isaiah (chapter 26). This is evident from two major convictions expressed in the Chronicler's history.

Obligation to the Revealed Law of God

The first conviction is based on Mosaic tradition: the people and their leaders are subject primarily to the law of God, not to human regulations. In previous discus-

---

2. The "everlasting covenant" with David we have considered above, chapter 23.
3. See above, chapters 21 (promise of land) and 23 (legitimation of Davidic rule).

sions we have noticed that *torah,* which means "teaching," has two dimensions: story (haggadah) and commandment (halakah). The specific obligations of the covenant were set forth within the whole story of God's actions on behalf of Israel. In the Chronicler's history, however, the emphasis falls heavily on the commandments written in the Mosaic torah:

> According to all that is written in the law of the LORD [Yahweh] that he commanded Israel. —1 Chron. 16:40

> Keep the law of the LORD [Yahweh] your God. . . . Observe the statutes and the ordinances that the LORD [Yahweh] commanded Moses for Israel.
> —1 Chron. 22:12-13

> According to the commandment of Moses for the sabbaths, etc. —2 Chron. 8:13

> Keep the law and the commandment. —2 Chron. 14:4

> To offer burnt offerings to the LORD [Yahweh], as it is written in the law of Moses.
> —2 Chron. 23:18

> According to what is written in the law, in the book of Moses. —2 Chron. 25:4

> Priests and Levites "took their accustomed posts according to the law of Moses the man of God." —2 Chron. 30:16

> Burnt offerings . . . as it is written in the law of the LORD [Yahweh]."
> —2 Chron. 31:3

Strangely, in none of these cases is there mention of the exodus or the guidance in the wilderness. It has been observed that if we had only the Chronicler's history we would never know that there was an exodus out of Egypt.[4]

In Chronicles the Torah, understood in its halakic sense, is undoubtedly identified with the whole Pentateuch, not just the book of Deuteronomy, as in Josiah's reform. The Pentateuch, in substantially its final form, was the Torah of Moses that Ezra brought back to Judah from Babylonian exile and that became the constitutional basis of the restored community (see Nehemiah 9). The book of Psalms, as we have seen, begins with the announcement that those persons are blessed (happy) who meditate on the torah "day and night," making it the basis of their life and thought (Psalm 1).

Yahweh's Covenant with David

The second conviction, which is much more dominant in Abijah's speech, is that Yahweh has "chosen" David to be ruler and has chosen the Jerusalem temple, including its priesthood. Accordingly, the Chronicler jumps into Israel's history (as presented in the Deuteronomic "source") at the point of David's rise to power (1 Chronicles 9–15). All at once we are told about David bringing the ark to

---

4. C. Mangan, *1–2 Chronicles, Ezra, Nehemiah,* OTM 13 (Wilmington, Del.: Michael Glazier 1982), 16.

Jerusalem, accompanied by the singing of psalms (1 Chronicles 16). Then follows immediately Nathan's oracle of dynastic promise to David, which was taken over from 2 Samuel 7 with few changes (2 Chronicles 17). Unsavory episodes, such as the Bathsheba affair, are passed over in order to give attention to David's plans for the construction of the temple and the organization of its liturgical and musical service (1 Chronicles 22–29).

In this connection David's address in 1 Chronicles 22 deserves attention. Here David gives a speech to Solomon, in which he charges him with the task of building a temple and assures him of prosperity if in his wisdom he observes "the statutes and the ordinances that the Lord [Yahweh] commanded Moses for Israel" (22:7-16). In succeeding chapters David organizes the priests and Levites and assigns them their duties (chapter 23), as well as the Aaronic priests descended through Zadok (chapter 24), the musicians (chapter 25), other functionaries (chapter 26), and finally those dealing with civil and military affairs (chapter 27). Above all, David submits to Solomon the plan (*tabnith*) of the temple (28:11-12, 18-19), just as Moses, in Priestly tradition, constructed the tabernacle and its furnishings according to the pattern (*tabnith*) that Yahweh showed him on the mountaintop (Exod. 25:9). Seen in the perspective of Davidic covenant theology, David appears as a figure even greater than Moses!

Temple and King

Written late in the biblical period, the Chronicler's history is an impressive witness to the power of the Davidic covenant symbolism to survive, despite the end of the monarchy and the destruction of Solomon's Temple. The twin convictions of the Davidic covenant are stressed in David's speech to the assembled officials of Jerusalem (1 Chronicles 28). Here David recalls that Yahweh chose the temple as a resting place for the ark and "the footstool of Yahweh's throne" (v. 2); that Yahweh chose him to be "king over Israel forever" (v. 4); and that Solomon, commissioned to carry out David's plan, would "sit upon the throne of the kingdom of the LORD [Yahweh] over Israel" (v. 5). Here the institutions of throne and temple are brought closely together in the imaginative vista of the Chronicler. Indeed, the cosmic dominion of God seems to be manifest in the earthly kingdom of David.

This is an amazing portrayal of David, which far exceeds historical reality. In a time when there was no king on the Davidic throne, the king is portrayed as one who rules as God's representative, indeed who sits on the earthly throne of *God's* kingdom. The Chronicler's lively imagination has produced a view of history that has messianic overtones. As Gerhard von Rad remarks,[5] the Davidic king is portrayed with such a *doxa* (glory) that the reader is prompted to ask with John the Baptist: "Are you the one who is to come, or shall we expect another?"

---

5. Gerhard von Rad, "The Historical Work of the Chronicler," in *Theology of the Old Testament*, trans. D. M. G. Stalker, 2 vols. (New York: Harper & Row, 1962–65), 1:347-54.

The Chronicler's history provides a point of transition to our next major subject, "Trials of Faith and Horizons of Hope." This history work was composed during the period of the Second Temple, the so-called postexilic period, when the complex phenomenon known as Judaism was emerging. It was a time of suffering and dislocation, yet also a time of "waiting for God" in hope of the coming of God's dominion on earth as it is in heaven. Before turning to this subject, however, let us pause to consider the great prophet who stands in the circle of Davidic/Zion theology: Isaiah of Jerusalem.

26. PROPHECY IN
THE ZION TRADITION

Like the Abrahamic and Mosaic covenantal perspectives discussed previously, the Davidic covenant also had a profound influence on prophecy, as evident from the message of the eighth-century prophet, Isaiah of Jerusalem. As pointed out earlier, it is significant that each of the three major covenant perspectives has its chief prophetic spokesman: Ezekiel speaks out of the Priestly tradition; Jeremiah is a "prophet like Moses"; and Isaiah of Jerusalem stands in the tradition of Davidic or Zion theology.

The Seminal Message of Isaiah

It is not easy to separate out the distinctive message of Isaiah from the book that bears his name. After a century or so of intensive study, many scholars agree that the book falls into three major parts divided roughly into First Isaiah (chapters 1–39), Second Isaiah (chapters 40–55), and Third Isaiah (chapters 56–66). This oversimplified analysis indicates that the book of Isaiah has undergone a long and complex history of traditions, from the time when the eighth-century prophet "bound up" his "teaching" in a scroll among his disciples (8:16) to the final shaping of the book in its present canonical form, probably in the early period of the Second Temple (ca. 520–515). Later we shall look at the book as a whole, when considering the movement from prophecy to apocalyptic (chapter 33).

In order to ascertain the seminal message of the eighth-century prophet, Isaiah of Jerusalem, we shall restrict our attention to the first part of the book (chapters 1–39) and, within that compass, especially to chapters 1–12 and 28–33. Some of the oracles against the nations (chapters 12–23) reflect Isaiah's preaching. But chapters 24–27, the so-called Apocalypse of Isaiah, and chapters 34–35, the Little Apocalypse, come from the period of Third Isaiah, when prophecy was becoming apocalyptic in tone. Chapters 36–39, paralleled for the most part in 2 Kgs. 18:13—20:19, serve as a bridge from the first part of the book, predominantly a message of divine judgment, to the second (beginning at Isa. 40:1), which gives a message of hope and consolation.

The King, the Lord of Hosts

One of the first things that strikes the reader who turns to so-called First Isaiah is that this prophet, unlike Hosea and Jeremiah, does not appeal to the exodus/Sinai root experiences, at least not explicitly. To be sure, there is a passing reference to what Yahweh "did in Egypt" (10:26) and a poetic depiction of a highway from Assyria analogous to one Israel used in the exodus from Egypt (11:16). But these references, if they reflect the prophet's message (which some doubt), are exceptions that prove the rule. The Mosaic covenant tradition has not made a significant impact on the message of this eighth-century prophet.

While the preaching of the prophets Hosea and Jeremiah moves primarily on the horizontal plane of Israel's history, the message of Isaiah is oriented in the vertical axis of heaven and earth, the eternal and the temporal, macrocosm and microcosm. Isaiah's message soars above Israel's sacred story (exodus, Sinai covenant, sojourn in the wilderness, occupation of the land) into the symbolic world of Yahweh's cosmic rule, which we explored in a preceding chapter (chapter 24). As Isaiah perceived in his vision in the temple, Yahweh is the King par excellence, who is seated on a celestial throne, "high and lifted up," that is, transcendently (Isa. 6:1). In response, the prophet exclaimed:

> Woe is me! I am lost, for I am a man of unclean lips, and I live among a people of unclean lips; yet my eyes have seen the King, the LORD [Yahweh] of hosts.
>
> —Isa. 6:5

In this theological perspective, Yahweh is the eternal King, before whose transcendent majesty no human power can claim ultimate sovereignty, no social or economic order can escape criticism, no cultural or national values can boast ultimacy. The prophet envisages God's appearance on the horizon of the future to judge all the proud symbols of human achievement, including economic wealth, military fortifications, and commercial exploitation of the seas.

> *For the LORD [Yahweh] of hosts has a day*
> *against all that is proud and lofty,*
> *against all that is lifted up and high;*
> *against all the cedars of Lebanon,*
> *lofty and lifted up;*
> *and against all the oaks of Bashan;*
> *against all the high mountains,*
> *and against all the lofty hills;*
> *against every high tower,*
> *and against every fortified wall;*
> *against all the ships of Tarshish,*
> *and against all the beautiful craft.*
> *The haughtiness of people shall be humbled,*
> *and the pride of everyone shall be brought low,*
> *and the LORD [Yahweh] alone will be exalted on that day.*
>
> —Isa. 2:12-17

In this powerful poetry Isaiah develops a theme sounded in the psalms that celebrate Yahweh's enthronement as king (Psalms 47, 93, 95–99). The nations of the earth and the whole realm of nature are summoned to praise the cosmic king,

> *for he is coming to judge the earth.*
> *He will judge the world with righteousness,*
> *and the peoples with his truth.*
>
> —Ps. 96:13

The Holy One of Israel

The keynote of Isaiah's message is that Yahweh, the Holy One, who is enthroned in cosmic majesty, dwells in the midst of the people, and in this sense is "God with us." The first Isaianic collection (chapters 1–12) is appropriately rounded off with a song that strikes this fundamental theme.

> *Sing praises to the* LORD *[Yahweh], for he has done gloriously;*
>   *let this be known in all the earth.*
> *Shout aloud and sing for joy, O royal Zion,*
>   *for great in your midst is the Holy One of Israel.*
> —Isa. 12:5-6

The sense of the holy resounds in the account of the prophet's inaugural vision in the temple, where a celestial choir sings an anthem of praise:

> *Holy, holy, holy is the* LORD *[Yahweh] of hosts;*
>   *the whole earth is full of his glory.*
> —Isa. 6:3

The anthem sounds a note of universalism: it is not just the temple of Jerusalem (tabernacle) that is filled with the glory of God (as in Priestly tradition), but "the whole earth is full of God's glory," even as the heavens display the glory of the Creator (cf. Ps. 19:1).

The prophet uses the divine epithet repeatedly: *qadosh yisra'el*, "the Holy One of Israel" (1:4b, 10:20; 12:6; etc.).[1] The epithet does not refer in a broad sense to the *mysterium tremendum*, the divine mystery beyond all human experience and conceptuality, to recall Rudolf Otto's classical study, *The Idea of the Holy*;[2] rather, the term designates the holy God who has turned toward a people and who in prayer may be addressed by a personal name (YHWH). The formula signifies close relationship between God and people—not in the possessive sense sometimes implied in popular religion ("My God," "Our God") but in the sense that God is inescapably involved in Israel's life story as critic and savior. In this double sense, "God is with us" (Immanuel)—in judgment and in grace.

As expressed in Isaiah's message, the experience of the holy evinces dialectical contradictions or theological paradoxes. One paradox, mentioned above, is that of the universal and the particular: the God whom Israel worships is not the Holy One of Israel in a narrow sense but is actually God of the whole earth and the entire cosmos. Another is the paradox of transcendence and immanence: the God who is "high and lifted up" in cosmic splendor is inescapably present "in your midst," "the Beyond in the Midst" (Bonhoeffer). To recall a line from a wonderful poem in the book of Hosea (Hos. 11:1-9), Yahweh is "God, not a human, the Holy One in your midst" (v. 9b).

---

1. See my essay, "The Holy One of Israel," in *Justice and the Holy: Essays in Honor of Walter Harrelson*, ed. Douglas A. Knight and Peter J. Paris (Atlanta: Scholars Press, 1989), 3–19.

2. Trans. John W. Harvey (2d. ed.; New York: Oxford University Press, 1950); see above, chapter 5.

Cosmic Order and Social Order

In Isaiah, however, this sense of Yahweh's holy presence in the midst of the people is expressed in a different pattern of symbolism than in the case of Hosea or other prophets in the Mosaic tradition. Isaiah's preaching is informed by the twin images of temple and kingship. It is through these sacral institutions that the cosmic "righteousness" of God is mediated to society and the holy God is present in the midst of the people.

At first glance, the symbolic vista of Isaiah has striking affinities with the mythical symbolism of the ancient Near East. In the ancient world the cosmic kingship of the high god was manifest in society through the sacral institutions of temple and kingship. In ancient Egypt, for instance, as Eric Voegelin has shown,[3] "cosmological symbolization" expressed the integration of society into the cosmic order and made possible a static social order that remained essentially unchanged through several dynasties. In this Egyptian view, the pharaonic social structure reflected the harmony of cosmic order.

Some interpreters, especially those associated with Solomon's court, may have held a similar view of the monarchy. Psalm 72, whose superscription associates the poem with Solomon, speaks of the ideal king as one who mediates cosmic "righteousness" (or right order) to society, with the result that the king is the upholder of justice for the helpless and the source of blessing and prosperity. Indeed, the king, revered as the son of God, was crowned with a kind of supernatural halo, as suggested in the lofty language of Psalm 72:

> May he live while the sun endures,
>   and as long as the moon, throughout all generations,
> May he be like the rain that falls on the mown grass,
>   like showers that water the earth.
>   —Ps. 72:5-6

Indeed, in a wedding ode, the king is addressed as "god," if we follow the received Hebrew text (Ps. 45:6), and therefore is invested with sovereign power. In short, Yahweh's rule as cosmic King in the heavenly temple is manifest sacramentally through the reign of the Davidic king (God's "son") and in the Jerusalem temple (God's "dwelling place" or tabernacle). Isaiah speaks in the name of "the LORD [Yahweh] of hosts who dwells on Mount Zion" (Isa. 8:18).

Isaiah's Reinterpretation of Cosmological Imagery

While this view is similar to the cosmological symbolism of the ancient Near East, there is a vast difference, owing to the holiness of God, which, as in Isaiah's temple experience, establishes a gulf between the divine and the human, between God's cosmic kingship and earthly dominion. Before the transcendent majesty of

---

3. See the discussion of Eric Voegelin's *Israel and Revelation* above, chapter 2.

the Holy One of Israel, the whole social order is "relativized." As E. W. Nicholson says in his study of God's covenant with Israel:

> The presupposition of such a relativizing of the social order was a radical differentiation between the divine and the human world, between God and his creation, so that the human world is not viewed as simply continuous with the divine: the divine-human continuum is split apart, so that the human world even can be viewed as being at loggerheads with its creator. In short, the transcendence of God over the human world is emphasized.[4]

Stated differently, the institutions of temple and monarchy are divested of their divine authority and ultimacy (desacralized) and are seen in relation to a social entity that holds power in society (relativized).

In Isaiah's message the images of king and temple belong to the "everlasting covenant" with David. In this context the metaphors have a different ring than in the cosmological symbolism of the ancient Near East. Since Yahweh is the Holy One, the transcendent Ruler and Creator, what is required is not the integration of society into a changeless cosmic order but, rather, the change of the social order so that it conforms to the will of the cosmic King. Isaiah senses a conflict between the kingdom of God and the kingdoms of this world: the two are "at loggerheads" (Nicholson). The prophet looks forward to a time when the conflict will be resolved and God's kingdom will come on earth as it is in heaven. In this sense, this theological perspective is "soteriological," to use a Christian theological term, that is, it is concerned with salvation (wholeness, welfare, peace).

Hence the proper response to Yahweh's utter holiness is humility and penitence (the fear of the Lord). Humility before God's transcendent majesty, expressed in Isaiah's temple vision, will occur in the social world on the Day of Yahweh's appearance. The encounter with the holy God on that day will be dreadful because, in contrast to the proud and the mighty on earth, God demands and executes justice.

> *People are bowed down, everyone is brought low,*
> *and the eyes of the haughty are humbled.*
> *But the LORD [Yahweh] of hosts is exalted by justice,*
> *and the Holy God shows himself holy by righteousness.*
> —Isa. 5:15-16

God's Demand for Social Justice

Yahweh's demand for social justice resounds through the prophet's preaching found within the first booklet, chaps. 1–12. In a powerful poem found in the preface to this collection (1:10-26), the prophet declares that God is not interested in the people's temple sacrifices and will not even listen to their prayers, for "your

---

4. Nicholson, *God and His People* (Oxford: Clarendon, 1986), 207. Here Nicholson seems to be talking about the Mosaic covenant, but the observation is more pertinent in regard to the Davidic covenant, which lies beyond his study.

hands are full of blood" (1:15). Those who misuse power to oppress the weak and defenseless need more than ritual cleansing.

> *Wash yourselves; make yourselves clean;*
> *remove the evil of your doings*
> *from before my eyes;*
> *cease to do evil,*
>   *learn to do good;*
>   *seek justice,*
> *rescue the oppressed,*
>   *defend the orphan,*
>   *plead for the widow.*
>
> —Isa. 1:16-17

The theme of justice is stated powerfully in the "song of the vineyard" (Isa. 5:1-7), in which the prophet portrays God's disappointment with "my people." A farmer planted a vineyard and lavished attention on it, expecting a good harvest of grapes. But the vineyard yielded wild grapes, prompting the owner to plan to tear it down. The threat to command the clouds to pour no rain on the fruitless vineyard (v. 6) indicates the meaning of the metaphor. Yahweh is the farmer who had planted a vineyard (the house of Israel, the people of Judah), expecting it to yield a good harvest. But alas, to God's great disappointment, "his pleasant planting" failed, as the poet indicates by a play on words that is hard to reproduce in English translation: God looked for *mishpat* (justice) but found *mispah* (bloodshed), for *tsedaqah* (righteousness) but heard *tse'aqah* (a cry of distress) (v. 7). The paronomasia, or play on words, may be sensed in English word pairs such as "justice/violence," "righteousness/rottenness."

To summarize, in Isaiah's portrayals of God's coming to judge the earth, the once sacred institutions of temple and kingship retain their symbolic value: the city of Jerusalem with its temple, and the monarch who sits on the throne of David. When reinterpreted in the Davidic covenant, however, they are invested with a different meaning than in the cosmological symbolism of the ancient Near East. They give poetic expression to the dominion of the holy God, who transcends all earthly institutions and who is nevertheless present "in the midst of the people" in judgment and mercy.

God's Strange Work

When God "comes to judge the earth," the two institutions of Mount Zion—the Jerusalem temple and the Davidic monarchy—will not escape the impact of the divine epiphany.

First, Zion, the city of God, will stand secure, not because of military fortifications but because it is God's chosen dwelling place. According to Isaiah, however, God is about to do something surprising in the eyes of those who suppose that God's coming will vindicate the people's interests and support their way of life. On Mount Zion—the place that God has chosen as the sign of God's dwelling in the midst of Israel—God will perform a "strange work" (Isa. 28:21)—strange because God seems to be abandoning the city of God and leaving it to be destroyed by invaders. Isaiah gives the central tenet of Davidic theology a new twist, saying that "God is with us" means, at least in part, that the judgment of God is inescapable. The agency of divine judgment, according to Isaiah, will be the Assyrian monarch; he is "the rod of Yahweh's anger," as portrayed in a powerful poem (10:5-19). Of course, the Assyrian dictator does not see things this way; he thinks that his successful feats result from his military power and political strategy. That is how all great military leaders (Julius Caesar, Alexander the Great, Napoleon, etc.) view their conquests. But, asks the prophet, "shall the ax vaunt itself over the one who wields it?" (10:15). Even the chosen military agent cannot escape the sovereignty of God's judgment. When God has finished the *opus alienum*, the "decree of destruction," on Mount Zion, the Assyrian agent will be cast aside and judged for his arrogant boasting.

By means of this strange work, the city of Zion will be purified, as fire removes dross and impurity, and it will become, as it was in the beginning, "the faithful city," a city of righteousness (Isa. 1:21-26). A "remnant," purified by suffering, will turn to God in troubled times, trusting the overruling sovereignty of the God, who brings down the high and mighty and elevates those of low degree (a theme later developed in Mary's psalm, the Magnificat: Luke 1:46-55). Beyond tragedy, Isaiah declared, Zion will emerge in resplendent glory as the center to which all nations would ultimately make a pilgrimage in order that they may find peace and security by hearing God's teaching (Isa. 2:2-4).

Isaiah's theme of the vindication of Zion is a major current that runs through the whole book of Isaiah. Zion imagery was used extensively in the apocalyptic reinterpretation of Isaiah's message, as we shall see in due course.[5]

The One Who Is to Come

Isaiah also used royal imagery in his portrayal of the future consummation. Not only will there be a New Jerusalem—a City of God purified in the fire of divine judgment—but also a righteous leader will appear to shepherd the people. Faithless kings may sit on the throne of David in the present age, but the time is coming when a faithful "son of God" will sit on the Davidic throne, ruling in justice and righteousness. This monarch will be the agent of God's dominion, through whom the righteous order of God's creation will be realized in the social order. In contrast to other kings, whose reigns are transient, his rule will be endless.

> *His authority shall grow continually,*
> *and there shall be endless peace*
> *for the throne of David and his kingdom.*
> *He will establish and uphold it*

---

5. See later discussion, chapter 32.

> *with justice and with righteousness*
> *from this time onward and forevermore.*

—Isa. 9:7

This exquisite poem (Isa. 9:2-7) concludes with the ringing announcement: "The zeal of the LORD [Yahweh] of hosts will do this" (cf. 2 Kgs. 19:31), indicating that the coming of this ruler will not occur in the ordinary course of pragmatic politics but will be accomplished in God's determination. In that day, the throne name Immanuel (God with us) will have a positive meaning, as indicated by the lofty names of the future Davidic king:

> *Wonderful Counselor, Mighty God,*
> *Everlasting Father, Prince of Peace.*

—Isa. 9:6

The Jewish translation (NJPSV, v. 5) gives quite a different reading; the coming king will have a long name, full of meaning:

> *The Mighty God is planning grace;*
> *The Eternal Father, a peaceable ruler.*

The Basis of Security

Here, then, is a pattern of symbolism that grounds human security in the transcendent, majestic sovereignty of the holy God—not in the changes and fortunes of human history. It imposes on rulers and people the sovereign demand of justice, with consequent divine judgment on the powerful who shirk their responsibility; but it enables people to relax in the confidence that God is creator and the ruler of history. Indeed, according to Isaiah this is what faith means: to be firm in trust of God, who executes righteousness, and not to be shaken, not to be moved. Such faith is the foundation stone that God lays in Zion, the city of God:

> *Thus says the Lord [Yahweh] GOD,*
> *See, I am laying in Zion a foundation stone,*
> *a tested stone,*
> *a precious cornerstone, a sure foundation:*
> *"One who trusts will not panic."*

—Isa. 28:16

Those who trust, that is, who place their faith in God rather than in human achievements, will enjoy deep security, even in difficult times. This theme of "walking humbly with God" in faith (cf. Mic. 6:8) is expressed exquisitely in a passage that has come to be a favorite for many.

> *For thus said the Lord [Yahweh] GOD, the Holy One of Israel:*
> *In returning and rest you shall be saved;*
> *in quietness and in trust shall be your strength.*

—Isa. 30:15

The basis for true security, said the prophet, lies in a "return to God"—in quiet, relaxed confidence in God's sovereignty, not in the feverish attempt to gain security through military preparation (cf. Ps. 46:8-10).

Excursus: Immanuel, God with Us

Isaiah's appeal for "the humble walk with God," however, is based on God's promises of grace to David and God's choice of Zion as God's dwelling place in the midst of the people. This is evident from Isaiah's treatment of the theme Immanuel (God with us). The theme deserves special treatment in view of its importance in the Christian community.

The Immanuel prophecy is found in a booklet (Isa. 7:1—8:15) contained in the first section of Isaiah. In the present arrangement of the book of Isaiah, it is connected immediately with the report of Isaiah's call (chapter 6).

The passage reflects a concrete historical situation in the life of the people, and especially the royal court. A few years after Isaiah's public ministry began, encircling forces of small nations—Ephraim and Syria to the north (2 Kgs. 16:5-9) and Edom and Philistia to the south (2 Chron. 28:17-18)—attempted to force the kingdom of Judah into a military coalition for the purpose of stopping Assyrian aggression into the west. At that time, King Ahaz, a descendant of David, was on the throne of Judah and was bewildered about what foreign policy he should pursue.

The dramatic account of Isaiah's encounter with King Ahaz in the tense political crisis is portrayed in a little passage in the prophet's memoirs (Isa. 7:1-17). Holding his little son Shear-yashub ("a remnant shall return") by the hand, Isaiah met the king as he was inspecting the water supply of the city. They met in the vicinity of the Upper Pool near the Virgin's Spring (Spring of Gihon) on the eastern border of the city, from which a gently sloping aqueduct—"the waters of Shiloah that flow gently" (8:6)—carried water outside the city walls around the curve of the hill of Ophel southward to the Lower Pool. The spring supplied the city with water, especially precious during a military siege.

The Prophetic Word

The passage falls into two parts: the prophetic word (7:1-9) and the prophetic sign (7:10-17). Christian readers are apt to concentrate on the second part (the sign), raising such questions as: Who is this wonder child? Who is his mother? What is the manner of the child's birth? How did the Hebrew word 'almah, which refers only to a young woman of marriageable age, come to be taken as a prophecy of the Virgin Birth (Matt. 1:23; cf. Luke 1:27)?[6] These questions have their proper place. It is important, however, to concentrate on the *relationship* between the two parts of the account: prophetic word and prophetic sign. In the Old Testament a futuristic sign, introduced by the formula "this shall be a sign unto you," is given to confirm a word of God already spoken. The word precedes

---

6. There is a special word in Hebrew for "virgin" (*bethulah*), though it is not used here.

the sign; the sign confirms the word by giving it visibility and actuality—to those who perceive in faith.

The prophetic word was spoken into a situation of great political tension and anxiety. "The heart of the king and the people," so we read, "trembled as the trees of the forest tremble in the wind" (Isa. 7:2). Ahaz, a weak Davidic king, was no match for the crisis. His throne was at stake, for the allies wanted to get rid of him and put a non-Davidic prince, "the son of Tabeel," on the throne of Judah (7:6). Moreover, the crisis had a spiritual dimension: would God go back on the promises of grace made to David (see the lament in Ps. 89:38-51)? The king, suffering a failure of nerve, was thinking of sending to Assyria for help, though at the expense of making Judah a vassal state of the empire. (In the end, this is what the faithless king did, according to 2 Kings 16.)

Isaiah, however, saw the political crisis in the larger perspective of faith in the God who sits enthroned as eternal King, before whom all the events of human history take place (cf. Ps. 33:13-17). Indeed, the prophet addressed the king in language that reflects the practice of holy war, with the prebattle "oracle of salvation." As in other cases, this oracle began with the admonition "fear not" (Isa. 7:4; cf. Exod. 14:13; Josh. 1:9) and continued with a summons to have faith in Yahweh of hosts, the Divine Warrior. In this perspective, it was foolish to fear small nations such as Syria and Ephraim, whose political power was already exhausted, like a burned-out torch. The "oracle of salvation," which contains a play on words, cannot be adequately translated into English:

> 'im lo' ta'aminu   If your faith is not firm,
> ki lo' te'amenu   you will not stand firm.

This may be paraphrased: "If your faith in Yahweh the King is not sure, your Davidic throne will not be secure." In other words, abandon human *alliance* and put your *affiance* in Yahweh, for no conspiracy of nations can prevail against God, who has chosen the Davidic king to be his son and Zion to be his holy hill (see Ps. 2:4-9). Isaiah's call for humble faith is akin to the great psalm concerning the city of God, which echoes with the refrain "Yahweh of hosts is with us," and which reaches a climax in the oracle addressed to the militaristic nations to cease frenzied military action and know the God who makes wars to cease.

> *Let be then: Learn that I am God,*
> *high over the nations, high above the earth.*
> —Ps. 46:10 (NEB)

Or as the Jewish translation (NJPSV, v. 11) reads:

> *Desist! Realize that I am God!*
> *I dominate the nations;*
> *I dominate the earth.*

Isaiah's counsel to relax ("let be") and walk humbly with God had a certain political wisdom. At the level of pragmatic politics, the prophet offered the king a helping hand by trying to prevent him from engaging in a suicidal foreign policy. He urged the king to avoid panic and to take a realistic view, for the attacking kings were weak incumbents who had almost exhausted their resources. There are times in politics, to echo the words of an American president, when "the only thing to fear is fear itself." Isaiah's word was not a call to political inaction but to a coolheaded realism in the immediate emergency.

Isaiah, however, was more than a pragmatic politician, for his oracle of salvation was based on his vision of divine transcendence. Despite their pretensions and anxieties, human beings do not carry the burden of the world, Atlaslike, on their frail shoulders. The dominion belongs to God, who is free to open up unexpected possibilities even when people find themselves in what seems to be a no-exit situation. Faith in God's overruling sovereignty, then, liberates people from misplaced faith in human efforts to plan, shape, and control the future.

Thus the prophet put before king and people a question that is both realistic and radical. What is the basis of ultimate trust? Do people look to the gently flowing waters of Shiloah, which symbolize the silent and invisible power of God's dominion? Or do they turn to the mighty waters of the Euphrates, which represent the imposing pride and power of empire? Isaiah calls for faith that transfers commitment from what is human and transient to what is absolute and eternal: the transcendent God, Yahweh the cosmic King. Those who walk humbly with God, the prophet declares, can face the crises of life unafraid and can live toward God's future—not in the anxiety of military preparedness but

> —not in the anxiety of military preparedness but "in quietness and confidence" (Isa. 30:15, quoted above). This call to relaxed faith in God's overruling sovereignty is also expressed in a well-known line from Ps. 46; even though the nations are in an uproar of war and violence, "Be still, and know that I am God." (vs. 10; see above, p. 231). The same note is echoed in one of our hymns, set to the beautiful music of Jean Sibilius' *Finlandia*:
>
> > *Be still, my soul: Your God will undertake*
> > *To guide the future, as in ages past.*
> > *Your hope, your confidence let nothing shake;*
> > *All now mysterious shall be bright at last.*
> > *Be still, my soul: the waves and winds still know,*
> > *The Christ who ruled them while he dwelt below.*
> > (words by Katherina von Schlagel, 1752)

The Prophetic Sign

The prophetic word that Yahweh would uphold the Davidic throne was accompanied by a sign: in due course a Davidic heir to the throne would be born and would carry the lofty throne name Immanuel, signifying that "God is with us."

The holiness of God, however, transforms the meaning of Immanuel, so that it does not connote the comforting assurance of popular religion. In a bold reversal of the view that the Divine Warrior fights for Israel against its enemies, this prophet declares that God's "enemies" are God's own people.

It is not easy to live in the presence of the holy God "who dwells on Mount Zion." For on the "holy hill" Yahweh is performing a strange work (Isa. 10:12; 28:22),[7] a work of judgment that is intended to purify the city of God so that it may be "the faithful city, the city of righteousness." The baby Immanuel will grow up in a time of devastation (7:15-17), but judgment is not God's last word; it is only the prelude to a new beginning. A purified remnant of the people will look to the future when Immanuel will reign on the Davidic throne (9:2-7). God's holiness, according to this prophet, is the manifestation of divine judgment tempered with divine mercy. God's judgment is inescapable, yet God's mercy gives hope for the future. This is the significance of the sign of Immanuel, which was transposed into a new key in the New Testament.[8]

"The City of the Great King"

In summary: the preceding discussion has shown that Davidic covenantal theology was "generated" by events in the historical experience of Israel. Both temple and throne were involved in Israel's attempt to find a place in the sun and to find security in the political struggles of the ancient Near East. Israel adopted a king "like the nations" to find security in the embattled corridor of Canaan, where peoples were vying for control. And Israel built a temple "like the nations" in order to worship God in the majestic architectural style of their neighbors.

These two realities—throne and temple—were, however, viewed in mythical perspective. They belong to a metaphorical world as well as the real historical world. That symbolism continued, indeed was reasserted more emphatically, when the Davidic monarchy came to an end and the temple of Jerusalem was destroyed. No longer did these institutions serve, at least in part, an ideological purpose, but were metaphors in a pattern of symbolization.

The Davidic king became a symbol and prototype of the one who was to come in order to introduce a new age of peace and justice. The Davidic symbolism finds powerful expression in the poem in Isa. 9:2-7 and in a Christmas carol that echoes Isaiah's prophecy, based on a fifteenth-century German folk song and harmonized by Michael Praetorius (1609):

> Lo, how a Rose e'er blooming,
> from tender stem hath sprung!
> Of Jesse's lineage coming
> As men of old have sung.
> It came, a flow'ret bright,
> Amid the cold of winter,
> When half spent was the night.

---

7. On the *opus alienum*, see above, chapter 6.

8. See further my study, "God with Us—In Judgment and in Mercy: The Editorial Structure of Isaiah 5–10 (11)," in *Canon, Theology, and Old Testament Interpretation: Essays in Honor of Brevard S. Childs*, ed. Gene M. Tucker, David L. Petersen, and Robert R. Wilson (Philadelphia: Fortress Press, 1988), 230–45.

The temple, established on Mount Zion, became a symbol of God's presence in the world, as in the powerful poem Ps. 46:4-7. The temple symbolizes Zion, the city of God, which represents God's dominion on the earth, as in Augustine's great work, *The City of God*. The symbolism of Zion is also used in John Newton's hymn (1779):

> *Glorious things of thee are spoken,*
> *Zion, City of our God,*
> *God whose word cannot be broken,*
> *formed it for his own abode.*

Today Jews say prayers at the Western Wall, an architectural remnant of the ancient temple; and Christians visit the Holy City and its sacred places. These people, if they read Scripture with poetic imagination, move beyond the prose of history into a metaphorical world where David's throne and the Jerusalem temple are powerful symbols of God's dominion in the cosmos and human history.

PART III
TRIALS OF FAITH
AND HORIZONS OF HOPE

All this has come upon us,
yet we have not forgotten you,
or been false to your covenant.

. . .

Because of you we are being killed all day long,
and accounted as sheep for the slaughter.

PSALM 44:17, 22

27. THE CRISIS
OF COVENANTAL THEOLOGIES

We have found that three covenantal perspectives govern much of the literature of the Old Testament: the Priestly, the Mosaic, and the royal. In major bodies of Scripture each of these is associated with an outstanding figure: the promissory covenant with Abraham and Sarah; the covenant of law with Moses, Miriam, and Aaron; and the covenant of dynastic leadership with David. It is too simple to think of these covenants as belonging exclusively to a particular period or "dispensation." To be sure, in the Bible they follow one another in historical sequence: the Abrahamic covenant was instituted in the ancestral period; the Mosaic covenant in the time of the exodus and the Sinai sojourn; and the Davidic covenant at the beginning of the united monarchy. Whenever and however each of these patterns of symbolization arose, we should think of them as running alongside of each other during most of the biblical period, like the trajectories of three jet planes whose jet streams parallel each other in the course of flight.

In the Old Testament, then, we find a theological pluralism. The situation is similar to the New Testament, where we find different christological perspectives: the apocalyptic perspective of Mark, the salvation history view of Luke–Acts, the Logos christology of the Johannine literature, or the Pauline theology of divine grace. Just as there is christological pluralism in the New Testament, so there is theological diversity in the Old Testament.

The Interrelationship of the Covenants

In the Old Testament, pluralism does not arise out of intellectual differences or partisan strife, as is often the case in modern societies; rather, it is rooted in the fundamental experience of the holy God in the midst of the people. Each of these covenant perspectives nuances the God-human relationship in a different way, with a distinctive symbolic vista. Hence all of them are necessary to express God's relation to Israel, human beings, and the world. If one of them were lacking, the richness of biblical theology would be diminished. Each covenant has its place in the economy of God's saving purpose.

Also, these covenantal perspectives—as we have seen again and again—give expression to certain polarities (Fackenheim: "dialectical contradictions") that are inherent in the experience of the presence of the Holy One in the midst of the people. For instance, in the Abrahamic covenant, we find the polarity of the universal and the particular. The God whose sovereignty is universal chooses to enter into relationship with a particular people, the descendants of Abraham and Sarah. The Mosaic covenant evinces the polarity of divine sovereignty and human freedom. The God who is the Sole Power, who is praised as God Almighty (El Shaddai, Gen. 17:1), calls human beings to responsible freedom. And the Davidic

239

covenant deals with the paradox of divine transcendence and divine immanence. The God who is transcendent or "far off" is also immanent or "near," that is, sacramentally present in the temple and graciously manifest in the rule of the Davidic king.

Further, it is wrong to segregate the covenants from each other, on the supposition that they are independent or even antithetical. Some theologians want to separate the Mosaic covenant from the Davidic covenant, on the supposition that the latter is a "fall from grace," or in sociological terms, a lapse into ideology.[1] It may be difficult for *us* to integrate these covenants; but those who have given us the Scriptures in their final form apparently perceived no fundamental incompatibility. The covenants are interrelated, and interact with each other, adding richness and depth to the scriptural presentation.[2]

Combination of Abrahamic with Mosaic Covenant

To recall one example, the Torah in its final Priestly version emphasizes the everlasting covenant made with Abraham, but in tandem with this covenant goes the Mosaic covenant, as evidenced by the insertion of the book of Deuteronomy into the Torah story just before the death of Moses. In this canonical context, the Mosaic covenant is included within the Abrahamic covenant: it is, one might say, an extension or elaboration of the obligations of the people who are embraced within the Abrahamic covenant. Before Israel was a people, before they decided to accept the covenant obligations at Sinai, they were already embraced within God's covenant of grace. Accordingly, the Priestly narrator says, on the eve of the exodus, that "God heard their groaning, and God remembered his covenant with Abraham, with Isaac, and with Jacob" (Exod. 2:14). In Exod. 6:2-8 the Priestly writer interprets the deliverance from Egypt as a fulfillment of the promise of the Abrahamic covenant. Hence this covenantal sequence shows the prevenience of God's grace. God takes the initiative to be involved with the people even before the people seek God in their distress.

Combination of Mosaic with Davidic Covenant

We have also found that two covenants are combined in the Deuteronomistic history. It is on the basis of the Mosaic covenant that the historian explains Israel's history of failure, resulting in the fall of the nation in 587 B.C. Through a series of prophets, in this view, God appealed to the people to exercise their freedom responsibly and to be faithful to the covenant obligations (2 Kgs. 17:13-14). They refused to listen to prophets "like Moses," however, and they suffered the consequences. In this theological perspective, the tragedy was all their fault: the curses of the covenant fell on them.

---

1. See works by George Mendenhall, Norman Gottwald, and Walter Brueggemann mentioned in chapter 18 above.

2. See Jon D. Levenson, "The Davidic Covenant and Its Modern Interpreters," *CBQ* 41 (1979) 205–19.

Yet running through this history of tragedy, like a bright thread, is the Davidic covenant of leadership—an everlasting covenant that stresses God's absolute commitment to the line of David. In his "Deuteronomistic prayer," on the occasion of the dedication of the temple, Solomon begins by invoking the Davidic covenant:

> O LORD [Yahweh], God of Israel, there is no God like you in heaven above or on earth beneath, keeping covenant and steadfast love [*hesed*] for your servants who walk before you with all their heart. . . . Therefore, O LORD [Yahweh], God of Israel, keep for your servant my father David that which you promised him, saying, "There shall never fail you a successor before me to sit on the throne of Israel, if only your children look to their way, to walk before me as you have walked before me."
>
> —1 Kgs. 8:23-35

Solomon concludes the prayer (like many prayers it was actually a speech to God) by appealing to the Mosaic tradition:

> Let your eyes be open to the plea of your servant, and to the plea of your people Israel, listening to them whenever they call to you. For you have separated them from among all the peoples of the earth, to be your heritage, just as you promised through Moses, your servant, when you brought our ancestors out of Egypt, O Lord [Yahweh] GOD.
>
> —1 Kgs. 8:52-53

When this history ends, with a picture of a Davidic king receiving hospitality in the court of the Babylonian emperor, there is a hint that, despite the failure of the people as explained by the Mosaic covenant, God will not finally go back on the promises of the everlasting covenant with David.

Combination of Davidic with Mosaic Covenant
The interaction of covenant perspectives is also evident in the case of royal theology. God's unconditional covenant with David is qualified by the conditional "if" of the Mosaic covenant, so that if kings misuse the powers of their office, thereby ignoring God's "decrees," they will be punished (2 Sam. 7:14).

> *If your sons keep my covenant*
> *and my decrees that I shall teach them,*
> *their sons also, forevermore,*
> *shall sit on your throne.*
> —Ps. 132:12

Further, we have found that the Chronicler's history, which bypasses exodus and Sinai and comes immediately to God's election of David and of the Jerusalem temple, throws great emphasis on the halakic or statutory side of "the torah of Moses."[3]

---

3. See the previous discussion, chapter 25.

Relation of Davidic to Abrahamic Covenant

There are affinities and differences between the Davidic and Abrahamic (Priestly) covenants. For one thing, both are regarded as covenants in perpetuity (everlasting covenants) because they are grounded not on the character or behavior of the covenant recipient but on the freedom and grace of God. The theological interrelationship of these covenants is evident, for instance, in a passage in Ezekiel that combines the future "everlasting covenant" with David with the promises to the ancestors and to God's tabernacling presence in the midst of the people.

> They shall live in the land that I gave to my servant Jacob, in which your ancestors lived; they and their children and their children's children shall live there forever; and my servant David shall be their prince forever. I will make a covenant of peace with them; it shall be an everlasting covenant with them; and I will bless them and multiply them, and will set my sanctuary among them forevermore. My dwelling place shall be with them; and I will be their God, and they shall be my people.
> —Ezek. 37:25-27; cf. 16:60

A purpose of the Davidic covenant, as can be seen from this passage, is to establish a line of kings, the Davidic dynasty, while the Priestly covenant legitimates "an everlasting priesthood" (Exod. 40:15; Num. 25:13), that is, the priestly succession of the line of Aaron (Exod. 40:15).

Suffering as a Theological Problem

Thus Israel's historians interpreted the story of the people by referring to the covenants associated with Abraham, Moses, and David. But even when combined or interrelated, these covenantal perspectives proved to be inadequate to understand the suffering of the people, which reached its height in the fall of Jerusalem in the sixth century B.C.

An illustration of the problem is the case of good King Josiah, whose reign the Deuteronomistic historian treats favorably in 2 Kings 22–23. In 621 B.C. he carried out a great religious reform based on a "book of the law" (probably the substance of Deuteronomy) that was found in the temple during renovations. Josiah wanted to strengthen the nation religiously and perhaps restore the Davidic empire. But he was the victim of a tragic event. In 609 B.C. Pharaoh Necho, king of Egypt, marched his army northward to support Assyrian allies, who were threatened by the rise of Babylonia. Josiah tried to intercept Necho at the pass of Megiddo, but lost his life in the battle (1 Kgs. 23:28-30).

The military accident seemed to defy explanation. After all, Josiah was a great, reforming Davidic king, supported by the promises of grace to David. He did everything in his power to restore the country to the demands of the Mosaic covenant, which was the religious purpose of the great reform of 621 B.C. The prophet Jeremiah, who was critical of royal misuse of power, had a good word to say about Josiah. Mourning the death of Josiah, Jeremiah said that the reigning king, Jehoiakim, should have emulated his father.

Are you a king
  because you compete in cedar?
Did not your father eat and drink
  and do justice and righteousness?
  Then it was well with him.
He judged the cause of the poor and needy;
  then it was well.
Is not this to know me?
  says the LORD *[Yahweh].*
  —Jer. 22:15-16

The final tumultuous decades of the Southern Kingdom of Judah forced on Israel's interpreters the question of why bad things happen to good people, to recall the title of a well-known book.[4] Good King Josiah was dead and the people were in mourning. The nation was crumbling and hope for the future was eclipsed. The fall of Jerusalem was not only a national tragedy but a personal tragedy for many innocent individuals, from the king to the ordinary citizen. It was a crisis for any covenant theology that affirmed that the holy God was present in the midst of the people. The sufferings of the time not only strained covenant theologies but led inevitably to the question of theodicy, "the justice of God." As we have seen, Ezekiel had to cope with the question of God's fairness (Ezek. 18:25-29; 33:17-20); and the question of God's justice, raised by Abraham on the eve of the holocaust of Sodom and Gomorrah (Gen. 18:23-22), hovers over the whole scriptural tradition.

Is God with Us?
Thus the problem of suffering—some would call it the problem of evil—precipitated a crisis in covenant theology. The major covenantal patterns of symbolization, we have seen, give expression to Israel's sense of the holy: "the Holy One in your midst." Yet this basic testimony to God's presence in Israel's midst was put to a severe test in the period of intense suffering and social dislocation that began with the fall of Jerusalem in 587 B.C. This tragic event cut incisively into all of Israel's covenantal perspectives, intensifying the question that was raised by murmuring people in the wilderness: "Is Yahweh present with us or not?" (Exod. 17:7).

Much of the literature of the Old Testament, at least in its final form, bears the impress of this historical tragedy. The Priestly Torah, which stresses the Abrahamic covenant, was given its final form during the exile and, with Deuteronomy added, was substantially the book of Moses that became the constitutional basis of the restored community under the leadership of Ezra and Nehemiah. Also the Deuteronomistic history was addressed to people who had experienced the shattering events of the destruction of Jerusalem and the exile of important elements of the population. Prophets like Jeremiah and Ezekiel were

---

4. Rabbi Harold S. Kushner, *When Bad Things Happen to Good People* (New York: Schocken, 1981).

called to interpret these events, and even the book of Isaiah, in its final form, reflects the suffering entailed by the loss of temple and homeland. Just as the exodus was the crucial event of Israel's past, so the events of the fall of Jerusalem and the destruction of the temple of Zion were impressed deeply on the memory of the people. The catastrophe marks a division in the Old Testament between "preexilic" and "postexilic."

When the Face of God Is Hidden

The mournful poems found in the book of Lamentations poignantly express the sorrow over the destruction of the city. The poet raises a dirge:

> *How lonely sits the city*
> > *that once was full of people!*
> *How like a widow she has become,*
> > *she that was great among the nations!*
> *She that was a princess among the provinces,*
> > *has become a vassal.*
> > > —Lam. 1:1

The city of Zion is in shock:

> *Look and see*
> *if there is any sorrow like my sorrow,*
> > *which was brought upon me,*
> *which the* LORD *[Yahweh] inflicted*
> > *on the day of his fierce anger.*
> > > —Lam. 1:12

Yet in spite of suffering that seemed to eclipse the sovereignty of God, these mourners stubbornly trusted in God's faithfulness. Running through the doleful poems in the book of Lamentations is an unshakable confidence in God's "mercies" or ḥesed (faithfulness). The popular evangelical hymn, "Great Is Thy Faithfulness," is based on one of the laments of the book of Lamentations:

> *The steadfast love of the* LORD *[Yahweh] never ceases,*
> > *his mercies never come to an end;*
> *they are new every morning;*
> > *great is your faithfulness.*
> > > —Lam. 3:22-23

Moreover, the book of Psalms, which in its final form comes from the period of the Second Temple (rebuilt ca. 520–515 B.C.), reflects the historical tragedy. Two-fifths of all the psalms are laments—poems in which persons of faith cry to God *de profundis*, out of the depths of distress: "My God, why hast thou forsaken me?" (Ps. 22:1, KJV) or "O Lord, how long wilt thou hide thy face from me?" (13:1, KJV).[5] These laments, like those of Lamentations, come from the time when the

---

5. For the theology of lament, see my study guide, *Out of the Depths* (Philadelphia: Westminster, 1983; rev. ed. forthcoming, 2000), Chapter 3, "The Trials of Faith."

"face" (presence) of God is hidden or, to echo the title of a book by the great Jewish philosopher Martin Buber, the time of "the eclipse of God."

Failure of Covenant Theology

It is striking that some psalms show how a particular covenant perspective becomes the basis for lament. Psalm 89 is a good example. Earlier, when dealing with Davidic covenant theology, we noticed that the first part of this psalm (vv. 1–37) is a song of praise to God for the promises of grace to David.[6] Echoing Nathan's oracle to David in 2 Samuel 7, the poet declares that God has made an absolute commitment and will not go back on it, even though particular kings in the Davidic line may fail in office. Confidence in God's faithfulness (*hesed*) prompts the poet to look beyond the insecurities of history to the cosmic realm where God is enthroned as ruler. The social order, according to the poet, is grounded in the cosmic order, in God's righteousness.

> *Righteousness and justice are the foundation of your throne;*
> *steadfast love and faithfulness go before you.*
>
> —Ps. 89:14

The second part of the psalm, however, is a poignant lament, raised during some political catastrophe, that calls into question God's dominion manifest on earth through the rule of the Davidic king:

> *How long, O LORD [Yahweh]? Will you hide yourself forever?*
>
> . . .
>
> *Lord [Yahweh], where is your steadfast love [hesed] of old,*
> *which by your faithfulness you swore to David?*
>
> —Ps. 89:46, 49

Also the Mosaic covenant provides the basis for the powerful lament of Psalm 44. The poet recalls "the faith of our ancestors" (as we do in a hymn by that title)—the wonderful stories that parents told about God's saving acts in the past. But just look at the present distress of God's people! The poet complains that "you have rejected us and abased us . . . you made us turn back from the foe . . . you have made us like sheep for slaughter . . . you have made us the taunt of our neighbors" (vv. 9–13). The murmuring continues:

> *All this has come upon us,*
> *yet we have not forgotten you,*
> *or been false to your covenant*
>
> . . .
>
> *Because of you we are being killed all day long,*
> *and accounted as sheep for the slaughter. . . .*

6. See above, chapter 23.

> *Rouse yourself! Why do you sleep, O Lord [Yahweh]?*
> *Awake! Do not cast us off forever!*
> *Why do you hide your face?*
> *Why do you forget our affliction and oppression?*
> —Ps. 44:17-24

Here faith in the God of the covenant is strained, almost to the breaking point. Experiences of suffering seem to indicate that God does not pay attention, as though God were "asleep" and must be "awakened." In his great book *The Prophets*, Rabbi Abraham Joshua Heschel quotes some of the poignant verses from Psalm 44 on the opening page, where he dedicates his study to the victims who perished in the Holocaust.[7]

Is Suffering Deserved Punishment?

The theological crisis expressed in these laments called into question the fundamental premise of covenant theology, whether Abrahamic, Mosaic, or Davidic, namely, that suffering is deserved punishment for sin or failure. This is the dominant interpretation of suffering in the Old Testament. Jesus was once tested on this question, as bystanders recalled the collapse of a tower that killed several people (Luke 13:4-5). Did that accident show "that they were worse offenders than all the others living in Jerusalem?" Jesus refused to be drawn into the question of why innocent people suffer, but his answer, "I tell you, no!" refutes any explanation based on the simple doctrine of retribution—that suffering is punishment for sin.

All the prophets, whatever their view of God's covenant with the people, agreed on one point: the sufferings of the present age are traceable to a defect in Israel's will, to a misuse of freedom, to covenant infidelity. Isaiah said that Yahweh, like a parent, had nurtured children who proved to be rebellious (Isa. 1:2-3); suffering would be purgative, refining Israel's character:

> *I will turn my hand against you;*
> *I will smelt away your dross as with lye*
> *and remove all your alloy.*
> *And I will restore your judges as at the first,*
> *and your counselors as at the beginning.*
> *Afterward you shall be called the city of righteousness,*
> *the faithful city.*
> —Isa. 1:25-26

Jeremiah told the people that the impending judgment of God was not an inexorable fate but the consequence of the people's false lifestyle: "Your ways and your doings have brought this upon you. This is your doom; how bitter it is!" (Jer. 4:18). In this perspective, suffering was a kind of shock treatment, intended to awaken people to the crisis so that they might change their lifestyle (i.e., repent). Ezekiel turned the people's complaint about God's unfairness back on themselves:

7. Abraham J. Heschel, *The Prophets* (New York: Harper & Row, 1962).

it is your ways that are unjust, he said; the responsibility is yours (Ezek. 18:25-29).

> Cast away from you all the transgressions that you have committed against me, and
> get yourselves a new heart and a new spirit! Why will you die, O house of Israel?
>
> —Ezek. 18:31

This covenantal interpretation of suffering is good as far as it goes. Actions do have consequences—a point that wisdom teachers also were driving home, as we shall see. The truth of this view is sometimes evident in family life, where one may perceive, perhaps with the help of pastoral counseling, that the sins of parents are visited on their children. This truth may also be evident in social life, where people experience the backlash of nature because of a careless materialism that ignores "the cry of the environment,"[8] or reap the social consequences of a policy that turns a deaf ear to the cries of the poor. The question is, however, how far can one go with the explanation that suffering is deserved punishment for human failure? We will face this question later, when dealing with wisdom literature, especially the book of Job.

How Long, O Lord?

This question, typical of psalms of lament (e.g., Psalm 13) was raised in various ways by interpreters who sensed that a great avalanche was about to sweep over the land and destroy the Holy City and its people. It was raised incisively by the prophet Habakkuk, around the time of the battle of Carchemish in 605 B.C., when the Babylonians asserted their claim to world power. This prophet, a contemporary of Jeremiah and Ezekiel, shared the theological convictions of the previous prophets of judgment: that Israel's sufferings were deserved punishment for sin. Standing on that theological platform, however, he dares to expostulate with God. His dialogue with God begins with a cry of lament (cf. Psalm 13):

> O LORD [*Yahweh*], *how long shall I cry for help,*
>   *and you will not listen?*
> *Or cry to you "Violence!"*
>   *and you will not save?*
> *Why do you make me see wrongdoing*
>   *and look at trouble?*
> *Destruction and violence are before me;*
>   *strife and contention arise.*
>
> —Hab. 1:2-3

It is bad enough to see "violence" within the community of Israel, where those who wield power oppress the weak. But the prophet also sees violence magnified to a colossal world scale, as evident in the Babylonian armies that sweep over the world, scoffing at every fortress in their way and boasting of their military power.

In this question-and-answer dialogue, Habakkuk learns that God is doing a surprising thing, for—believe it or not—God has "ordained" this world power for

---

8. See P. Joranson and K. Butigan, eds., *The Cry of the Environment and the Rebuilding of Christian Creation Tradition* (Santa Fe: Bear and Co., 1984).

judgment. That, of course, is what previous prophets had been saying, like Isaiah, who described the Assyrian Empire as "the rod of Yahweh's anger" with which God was performing the "strange work" of judgment on Zion. Habakkuk agrees—in part. Yes, Israel is culpable, but the punishment does not fit the crime. The situation has apparently gotten out of God's control; for the invading force is like a chaotic flood that overflows the banks of God's purpose and obliterates all relative moral distinctions.

> *Your eyes are too pure to behold evil,*
> *and you cannot look on wrongdoing;*
> *why do you look on the treacherous,*
> *and are silent when the wicked swallow*
> *those more righteous than they?*
> —Hab. 1:13

On his watchtower of faith Habakkuk receives an answer to his prayer: Wait! What God is doing now is not clear; the present is a time when God's "face" is hidden. But in God's good time everything will become clear. "If [the vision] seems to tarry, wait for it"; in the meantime "the righteous live by faith" (Hab. 2:4b)—faith that holds on to God even when times are troubled and the light of God's purpose is eclipsed (2:3-4).

Waiting for God

Habakkuk's dialogue with God did not answer the questions. Indeed, the answer, "wait patiently for the Lord and liberation will come in due time," only strengthens the force of his initial question: "How long, O Lord?"—a question with which apocalyptic prophets had to deal, as we shall see. But Habakkuk's prophecy provides a good introduction to literature of the postexilic period, when the inadequacy of the covenant explanation of suffering as deserved punishment for sin was tried in the balance and found wanting. In the community of faith, people learned to wait patiently for God, like watchmen who watch for the morning.

> *I wait for the* LORD *[Yahweh], my soul waits,*
> *and in his word I hope;*
> *my soul waits for the Lord [Yahweh]*
> *more than those who watch for the morning,*
> *more than those who watch for the morning.*
> —Ps. 130:5-6

Waiting for God is faith that turns to the horizon of the future in the expectation that God will conquer evil powers and introduce God's dominion on earth. In the fast pace of the human race, runners—even athletic youth—may fall exhausted,

But those who wait for the LORD [Yahweh] shall renew their strength,
   they shall mount up with wings like eagles,
they shall run and not be weary,
   they shall walk and not faint.
                    —Isa. 40:31

In the following pages, we shall explore this theme of "waiting for God" in two kinds of Scripture: torah that blends with wisdom, and prophecy that moves into apocalyptic. Both of these literary types deal with the "mystery" or "secret" of the dominion of God. But each represents a different approach to the mystery that, if known, would enable us to perceive how things hang together and the meaning of the struggles of human history. Wisdom explores the divine mystery "from below," that is, from the angle of human experience. By contrast, apocalyptic purports to deal with the matter "from above," that is, in the perspective of the "revelation" (apocalypse) given to a prophetic seer.

PART III
CONTINUED

A. FROM TORAH TO WISDOM

The teaching of the LORD is perfect,
  renewing life;
The decrees of the LORD are enduring,
  making the simple wise;
The precepts of the LORD are just,
  rejoicing the heart;
The instruction of the Lord is lucid,
  making the eyes light up.
The fear of the Lord is pure,
  abiding forever;
The judgments of the Lord are true,
  righteous altogether,
More desirable than gold,
  than much fine gold;
sweeter than honey,
  than drippings of the comb.

PSALM 19:7-10 (NJPSV, vv. 8-11)

28. Rejoicing in the Torah

We have found that the exile, and everything associated with it, was a time when faith was put to the test. In the time of the eclipse of God, how do the people of God live? How do they retain a sense of orderly community when powers of chaos threaten to pull them apart? How do they find a way into the future when the purpose of God is not clear in the present? What holds this people together, enabling them to survive and giving them a sense of identity and vocation? These were existential questions for the remnant refined in the crucible of suffering.

God's Teaching

One answer to such questions is given in Torah observance. In a time of change and uncertainty, when the foundations are shaking, the people are not left to grope in an uncharted wilderness. For in the Torah God has given guidance on the way that they should walk (*halak*, "walk, go"). Indeed, the Hebrew word *torah*, as noted previously, means "guidance, instruction," and is so rendered in the NJPSV (e.g., in the torah psalms 1; 19:7-13; 119).

> *Happy is the man who has not followed the*
> *counsel of the wicked,*
> *or taken the path of sinners,*
> *or joined the company of the insolent;*
> *rather, the teaching of the Lord is his delight,*
> *and he studies that teaching day and night.*
> —Ps. 1:1 (NJPSV)

In the Mosaic covenant tradition, as we have seen, torah cannot be reduced to law. Torah bears witness to the root experiences: "the saving experience" and "the commanding experience" (Fackenheim). In one sense, torah is story. It is narrative or haggadah. The people tell an old, old story, "the story of our life."[1] But in another sense, torah is commandment or halakah. At Sinai the people say, "All that Yahweh has spoken we will do and we will be obedient" (Exod. 24:7). The relation of these two, haggadah and halakah, is inseparably close, like Siamese twins.

In this comprehensive sense the Torah became the basis of the people's life in the restored community of Judaism under the leadership of Ezra and Nehemiah (ca. 400 B.C.). Ezra's reading of "the book of the torah of Moses," according to Nehemiah 8, must have been based on the Pentateuch approximately in its final form, later known as "the five books of Moses" or, in rabbinical terms, "the five-fifths of the Torah."

---

1. This echoes the title of a chapter in a book by H. Richard Niebuhr, *The Meaning of Revelation* (New York: Macmillan, 1941), chap. 2.

Torah Piety

Several things happened in the course of the transmission of the Torah. First, torah was written down; it became "Scripture." In the initial covenant ceremony described in Exod. 24:1-11, Moses "told the people the words of the Lord [Yahweh]" (v. 3), and then proceeded to write them down (v. 4) in "the book of the covenant." Writing down the torah gave it greater permanence, especially when the text was scrupulously guarded and meticulously copied. Above all, a written text calls for creative interpretation, as can be seen from the story in Nehemiah 8, where the reading of the Torah was accompanied by oral interpretation for the purpose of giving "the sense, so that the people understood the reading" (Neh. 8:8). In the New Testament, Jesus is portrayed as reading from Jewish Scripture (the book of Isaiah) and giving an interpretation (Luke 4:16-22).

It was the torah of Moses in written form that prompted the great reformation of Josiah, based on the book of torah found in the temple (which we have considered earlier). The written torah was eventually extended to include the whole Mosaic torah, referred to as "the book of Moses" in the Chronicler's history (e.g., 2 Chron. 25:4). In the modern period, this gave rise to controversial discussions of "the Mosaic authorship of the Pentateuch." However, the issue is not authorship in the modern sense but authority of a tradition endorsed with the name and inspiration of Moses.

Second, there was a definite shift of emphasis to the halakic or statutory dimension of torah. We see this already in the book of Deuteronomy, where "covenant" is identified with commandments (Deut. 4:11-14) and where the ark of the covenant is regarded as a box containing the Decalogue.[2] Also we have seen this shift in the Chronicler's history, which, bypassing the story of the exodus, emphasizes the halakic side of the Mosaic torah.[3]

Many Christians are "turned off" by the great emphasis on "law" or "commandment" in the Old Testament. Perhaps they are influenced by Paul, who many think took a negative attitude toward "the law" (see his discussion in Rom. 5:12-21).[4] They are probably influenced even more by the individualism of modern American culture and the middle-class understanding of freedom as "the absence of restraint or necessity." So viewed, torah is a heavy burden, a suffocating "legalism." This popular view, however, contrasts with the torah piety represented in the book of Psalms, where people take delight in God's commandments and declare that God's torah "rejoices the heart," as stated in Ps. 19:8. One of the festivals of Judaism is *Simhat ha-torah,* "Rejoicing in the Torah."

The reason for this rejoicing is that, owing to the revelation of God's will in the Torah, people do not have to live in a situation of moral relativism, making ethical decisions only on the basis of personal taste or cultural values. According to the torah psalms (Psalms 1, 19, 119), the divine will that orders human life brings

2. See above, chapter 19.
3. See above, chapter 26.
4. On Paul's treatment of "the Law," see J. C. Beker, *Paul the Apostle* (Philadelphia: Fortress Press, 1980).

peace, health, and wholeness. To discern God's will, however, takes diligent study, long meditation, and patient prayer within the community of faith. Above all, the written torah must be read in the light of subsequent tradition, which helps to interpret the meaning so that people may understand. In the Jewish community the Mosaic Torah is read through the lens of the Talmud and rabbinical commentary; in the Christian church it is read through the lens of the New Testament and Christian tradition.

The Wise and the Foolish

The book of Psalms, often described as the hymnbook of the Second Temple, opens with two prefatory psalms that set the tone of the whole work.[5] Psalm 1 is a beatitude on those who study the Torah constantly ("day and night"); and Psalm 2 portrays the coronation of the anointed one ("God's son") on the holy hill of Zion. These introductory psalms reflect the Mosaic and Davidic covenant traditions, showing that, in the view of the compilers of the hymnbook, these two covenants belong together in Israel's praise of God.

The assumption of Psalm 1 is that the revelation of God's will is given in the Torah in written form, and therefore can be read and studied. The poem draws a distinction between persons who delight in God's Torah and who seek God's guidance on the one hand, and, on the other, the "wicked" or "ungodly" who ignore God's teaching, supposing that they can get along well enough on their own. Here the issue is not separating people into "good guys" and "bad guys." Rather a distinction is drawn between those who humbly seek to live by God's revealed will and those who, like the "fool" of Psalm 14 (Psalm 53 is almost identical), live by a practical atheism that prompts them to think that they can live as they please and get away with it.

> Fools say in their hearts, "There is no God."
> They are corrupt, they do abominable deeds;
> there is none who does good.
> The LORD [Yahweh] looks down from heaven on
>   humankind
> to see if there are any who are wise,
> who seek after God.
>
> —Ps. 14:1-2

Psalm 1 may be compared with the similar poem in Jer. 17:5-8 that is structured according to the sanctions of curse and blessing of the Mosaic covenant. On the one hand, a curse falls on those who "trust in mere mortals," "whose hearts turn away from Yahweh"; on the other, blessing is on those who put their trust in Yahweh. This poet also invokes the image of a tree planted by a flowing stream.

5. See above, chapter 24.

> *They shall be like a tree planted by water,*
>   *sending out its roots by the stream.*
> *It shall not fear when heat comes,*
>   *and its leaves shall stay green;*
> *in the year of drought it is not anxious,*
>   *and it does not cease to bear fruit.*
>   —Jer. 17:8

Elsewhere in the book of Psalms a line is drawn between two types of people, variously called the righteous and the wicked, the proud and the humble, the wise and the foolish. As we have noticed in connection with Psalm 1, the distinction is not based on intelligence or social standing or, in the first instance, on conduct, but rather on humble trust in and reliance on God. Lest human beings, who are all too prone to judge (cf. Matt. 7:1), draw the dividing line between the righteous and the unrighteous on the basis of their standards or prejudices, the poem ends with the declaration that the judgment finally belongs to God, who "knows the way of the righteous" (Ps. 1:6).

God's Discipline

The Torah, then, is God's gift, which gives life and light; therefore the proper response is to praise God for the Torah. Psalm 119, an acrostic or alphabetical psalm[6]—the longest psalm in the Psalter—is a sustained meditation on the Torah as God's wonderful gift. Those who have the patience and persistence to read this long psalm through from beginning to end will notice that the poet gives expression to experiences of suffering and hostility, and raises the cry, typical of laments, "how long must your servant endure" (119:84).

> *My soul [being] languishes for your salvation;*
>   *I hope in your word.*
> *My eyes fail with watching for your promise;*
>   *I ask, "When will you comfort me?"*
>   —Ps. 119:81-82

In general, suffering is regarded as God's way of "humbling" devout persons so that they may be brought back to the right path (vv. 67, 75). Suffering, when endured in faith, is God's discipline or teaching; therefore, one should wait in hope through the long midnight of the soul for the fulfillment of God's promise (v. 148). This teaching about God's corrective discipline is in line with Deuteronomic preaching.

> Remember the long way that the LORD [Yahweh] your God has led you these forty years in the wilderness, in order to humble you, testing you to know what was in your heart, whether or not you would keep his commandments. He humbled you by letting you hunger, then by feeding you with manna, with which neither you

---

6. Each eight-line stanza begins with a successive letter of the Hebrew alphabet. See the arrangement in NIV.

nor your ancestors were acquainted, in order to make you understand that one does not live by bread alone, but by every word that comes from the mouth of the LORD [Yahweh].

—Deut. 8:2-3

Torah as a Source of Wisdom

Above all, the Torah is a source of wisdom. Therefore devout persons can gain more understanding than their teachers (a comforting thought!) and senior persons with long experience.

> O how I love Your teaching!
>   It is my study all day long.
> Your commandments make me wiser than my enemies;
>   they always stand by me.
> I have gained more insight than all my teachers,
>   for Your decrees are my study.
> I have gained more understanding than my elders,
>   for I observe Your precepts.
> —Ps. 119:97-100 (NJPSV)

This quotation shows the very close relation between torah and wisdom. The relation between torah observance and wisdom is one of the central themes of Deuteronomic preaching:

You must observe [the statutes and ordinances] diligently, for this will show your wisdom and discernment to the peoples, who, when they hear all these statutes, will say, "Surely this great nation is a wise and discerning people!"

—Deut. 4:6

Torah and wisdom were increasingly mentioned in the same breath. They are closely associated in a wisdom book of the Old Testament, Ecclesiastes (or Qohelet),[7] and are virtually identified in the Wisdom of Ben Sira (or Sirach), a wisdom writing—quite like the book of Proverbs—found in the larger (Greek) Old Testament.[8] At one point the sage summarizes his discussion of wisdom:

> All this is the book of the covenant of the Most High God,
>   the law that Moses commanded us
>   as an inheritance for the congregation of Jacob.
> —Sir. 24:23

Therefore, wisdom comes from meditating on the Torah:

---

7. Steven Bishop suggests that Qohelet attempts to link wisdom and torah in such a way that torah supersedes wisdom.

8. In Protestant tradition this book (written ca. 180 B.C.) belongs to the Apocrypha; in the Roman Catholic canon it is regarded as "deuterocanonical," that is, secondary in the sense that it was added to the canon later than primary canonical books.

Reflect on the statutes of the Lord,
and meditate at all times on his
commandments.
It is he who will give insight to your mind,
and your desire for wisdom will be granted.
—Sir. 6:37

It is significant that the Psalter, which begins by praising God's torah, also includes a number of psalms that are usually classified as wisdom psalms (37, 49, 112, etc.). Torah observance enables one to find the good life, which is the goal of wisdom.

The Well-Ordered Life

The well-ordered or "centered" life, which one may achieve through meditation on and observance of the Torah, corresponds to the cosmic order that the Creator has ordained. This is the teaching of Psalm 19, taken as a whole.

The psalm comprises two distinct pieces. The first part (vv. 1–6) appears to be an old hymn in praise of El, the ancient Semitic name of the high God, creator of heaven and earth. The poet affirms that the phenomena of the heavens, especially the sun, are constantly proclaiming the glory of the Deity in a great anthem of praise, inaudible to human ears. This theme is picked up in the great hymn of Joseph Addison (1672–1719) based on Haydn's *The Creation*, a hymn that reflects— to the dismay of some—the Enlightenment confidence in the power of reason to perceive God's ways.

What tho' in solemn silence all,
  Move round the dark terrestrial ball?
What tho' nor real voice nor sound
  Amid their radiant orbs be found?
In reason's ear they all rejoice,
  and utter forth a glorious voice,
For ever singing, as they shine,
  "The hand that made us is divine."[9]

In Psalm 19, which reflects the sun symbolism of the ancient Near East (see Akhenaton's hymn to the Aton, the sun disk), the celestial bodies praise their Creator by functioning harmoniously in an ordered whole. Some knowledge of God is available to human wisdom through contemplation of the works of creation (cf. Rom. 1:19-20), though not knowledge of God's will and purpose for human life.

9. Properly "reason's ear" should connote reason that is informed by faith. It is too bad that, because of Enlightenment rationalism, this hymn is dropped from some hymnbooks, when other hymns, reflecting modern philosophical presuppositions, are included (e.g., the revision of "Sing Praise to God who Reigns Above" to "Sing Praise to God our Highest Good" in the *New Century Hymnal* [Cleveland: Pilgrim, 1995], hymn #6). The view of God as our Supreme Value is quite different from the view of divine transcendence expressed in the unrevised version.

That saving knowledge, according to the second part of the poem (vv. 7–14), is given in the wonderful revelation of God's will to the people of God. The poet testifies that in the Torah God has broken through the silences of the cosmos so that people no longer need to stumble in darkness. Sometimes these two parts of the psalm are regarded as separate pieces (Ps. 19A, vv. 1–6; 19B, vv. 7–14), but they belong together, certainly in the final form of the poem. For the order of life resulting from observance of the Torah corresponds to the order of creation based on God's ordering of the whole—also a teaching of Israel's sages, as we shall see. The hymn of Isaac Watts (1674–1748) expresses this correspondence:

> *The heavens declare thy glory, Lord;*
> *In every star thy wisdom shines;*
> *But when our eyes behold thy Word,*
> *We read thy Name in fairer lines.*

29. THE WAY OF WISDOM

Much of the literature of the Old Testament concentrates on Israel's peculiar experiences of the presence of God, centering in the exodus and Sinai, and in Zion and the Davidic king. The key term is "covenant," that is, God's relationship to the people, and the people's relationship to God, summed up in the formula, "I will be your God and you will be my people." As we have seen, the relationship between the holy God and the people Israel is nuanced in several major patterns of covenant symbolization.

Prophet, Priest, and Sage

The wisdom literature, such as the books of Proverbs, Ecclesiastes, and Job, however, scarcely mention the characteristic themes of Israel's faith: the choice of Israel, the covenant at Sinai, the coming of the Day of Yahweh, the temple as the place of the divine presence, the messianic king to come. Old Testament theologians have had difficulty relating Israel's wisdom literature to the "mainstream" of Israel's theological traditions. Some have gone so far as to say that wisdom is an alien tradition that lies outside the realm of Old Testament theology.

Part of the problem is the difficulty of defining what is the "mainstream." We should probably think of several streams running more or less parallel with one another, and at times touching each other. From at least the period of the monarchy, sages had an important role as interpreters of the will and way of God. In one of Jeremiah's confessions, in connection with plots against his life, it is said that "teaching of the law [*torah*] by the priest will not be lost, nor will counsel [*etsah*] from the wise, nor the word [*dabar*] from the prophets" (Jer. 18:18). This oblique reference indicates that the sage had standing in the Israelite community along with priests and prophets. The task of the sage was to give God's "counsel" (*'etsah*), just as the priest interpreted God's torah (Jer. 2:8) and the prophet proclaimed God's "word" (Jer. 1:9).

Moreover, we have seen that God's torah was the source of wisdom. The interpreters of the torah could claim "we are wise, for we have the torah of Yahweh" (Jer. 8:8); but Jeremiah insisted that the conflict between their torah and the prophetic word of Yahweh resulted from a "lying pen," that is, willful misinterpretation. The implication of these passages from Jeremiah is that ideally, when there was no human distortion, priestly torah, prophetic word, and the sage's wisdom were authoritative for the community, since all proceed from God.

Wisdom in the Royal Court

Wisdom has influenced all of Israel's covenantal traditions, but it is especially compatible with royal (Davidic) covenant theology. It is significant that Solomon was regarded as the sponsor of Israel's wisdom movement and, indeed, the composer of some wisdom sayings. In 1 Kgs. 4:29-34, the historian claims that Solomon wrote many proverbs and songs, and that his wisdom surpassed all the sages of the Orient. According to one rabbinical opinion, Solomon wrote Canticles (Song of Songs), with its portrayal of erotic love, in his youth; Proverbs, with its stress on practical problems, in his middle age; and Ecclesiastes, with its melancholy pessimism, in his old age. Making due allowance for exaggeration and the snowballing of tradition, there is no reason to doubt that Solomon took an active interest in the cultivation of wisdom in Israel. If the priest functioned in the temple, and the prophet in the vicinity of holy places, then the sages were at home primarily in the royal court.

That being the case, it is not surprising to find in the book of Proverbs many allusions to the rule of kings and princes. Indeed, the social order depends on the superior wisdom of the king, just as the cosmic order reflects inscrutable divine wisdom.

> *It is the glory of God to conceal things,*
> *but the glory of kings is to search things out.*
> *Like the heavens for height, like the earth for depth,*
> *so the mind of kings is unsearchable.*
> —Prov. 25:2-3

Hence it is imperative to "fear the LORD [Yahweh] and the king" (Prov. 24:21).

Wisdom and Social Stability

One thing that strikes the reader of the book of Proverbs is that its wisdom sayings display concern for the stability of the social order. "By justice a king gives stability to the land" (Prov. 29:4); and by defending the poor with equity his throne is long enduring (29:14). Familial values, transmitted through the teaching of mothers and fathers, are to be cherished (e.g., 23:22, 25), and this means the proper discipline of children (23:13-14). The righteous should be concerned for the rights of the poor (29:7), but both "rich and poor meet together," for "the LORD [Yahweh] is the maker of them all" (22:2). One should know the proper way to act in the presence of rulers and other superiors (25:6-7); one should not attempt to get wealth hastily, realizing that it is evanescent anyway (28:20, 22). Those who want to be successful should avoid overindulgence (23:20-21), be faithful to "the wife of your youth" (5:20), work hard on the land (28:19), and shun laziness (6:6-11), drunkenness (23:20-21), or unwise business ventures (6:1-5). In a well-ordered and stable society, people should act in a manner befitting their station: rulers should display justice toward their subjects; citizens should show proper respect for princes; servants and masters should show the proper attitude toward one another; children should respect their parents and preserve the family heritage. In all situations the virtues of prudence, self-control, and modesty are appropriate. The counsel given in the Wisdom of Ben Sira (in the Apocrypha), the longest of Israel's wisdom books, runs along similar lines.

These wisdom sayings lack the cutting edge of a prophet like Isaiah, who was critical of kings and all who exercise power, and who sensed a conflict between the cosmic dominion of God and the mundane order. The book of Proverbs gives the impression of social conservatism, based on a concern for law and order. Even the beautiful conclusion of the book, which praises the virtues of "the good wife" who is "a crown to her husband" (cf. 12:4), assumes the patriarchal structure of ancient Israelite society (31:10-31).

> *She opens her mouth with wisdom,*
> *and the teaching of kindness is on her tongue.*
> *She looks well to the ways of her household,*
> *and does not eat the bread of idleness.*
> *Her children rise up and call her happy;*
> *her husband too, and he praises her:*
> *"Many women have done excellently,*
> *but you surpass them all."*
> —Prov. 31:26-29

Even yet, some argue that family stability requires a subordination of the wife to the husband, although this relationship—ideally at least—presupposes mutual respect and love (cf. Eph. 5:21-33).

Theological Concerns of Wisdom Literature

Yet Proverbs, and related wisdom literature, also expresses important theological concerns.[1] Roland Murphy, who has presented one of the best treatments of the theology of wisdom literature, maintains that the wisdom perspective, which turns to the realm of daily experience, belongs in the context of Israel's worship of God as creator and redeemer. To be sure, "the covenant relationship to the Lord does not figure directly in the wisdom experience; it is bracketed, but not erased."[2]

Let us consider briefly some of the theological dimensions of Israel's wisdom.

The Fear of the Lord

The proper place to begin is with the fundamental premise of Israel's sages, expressed in the recurring proverb:

> *The fear of the LORD [Yahweh] is the beginning of wisdom,*
> *and the knowledge of the Holy One is insight.*
> —Prov. 9:10 (cf. 1:7; 15:33)

In a poem found at the beginning of the Wisdom of Ben Sira, the fear of the Lord is extolled as "fullness of wisdom, . . . the crown of wisdom, . . . the root of wisdom" (Sir. 1:11-30).

---

1. See, among others, Ronald E. Clements, *Wisdom in Theology* (Grand Rapids: Eerdmans, 1992); idem, *Wisdom for a Changing World: Wisdom in Old Testament Theology* (Berkeley: Bibal, 1990).

2. Roland Murphy, *The Tree of Life*, Anchor Bible Reference Library (New York: Doubleday, 1990), 124. See his discussion of "Wisdom Literature and Theology," Chapter 8.

"Fear" may not be the best translation of the Hebrew expression, for in current usage the primary dictionary meaning of "fear" is "emotional agitation in the face of danger." What is meant here is the secondary dictionary meaning: "extreme reverence and awe, as toward a supreme power." Here again we come to the "ground bass" of the holiness of God, discussed at the beginning of this study (part I). Reverential awe is the attitude that a person should display before God, the Holy One, who is beyond the grasp of unaided human wisdom. Such an attitude is the inescapable response to God's judgments, but it is also the appropriate response to God's grace and forgiveness.

> But there is forgiveness with you [Yahweh]
>   so that you may be revered [feared].
>   —Ps. 130:4

In the proverb that the fear of the Lord is the beginning of wisdom, as Gerhard von Rad observes,[3] we have in a nutshell Israel's epistemology or theory of knowledge. Knowledge does not lead to faith, but faith is the prerequisite for understanding. The opposite of wisdom is not ignorance but foolishness. The fool gropes in confusion and stumbles because of failure at the starting point of faith.

> The fear of the LORD [Yahweh] is the beginning of knowledge;
>   fools despise wisdom and instruction.
>   —Prov. 1:7

This is the criterion for distinguishing between the wise and the foolish, the righteous and the wicked, the good and the bad. It should be added that this wisdom is not regarded as a human accomplishment or a sign of superior intelligence, but as a gift of God that, paradoxically, must be sought.

This faith is not "belief," if that means assent to a body of doctrine, but is trust in Yahweh, the Holy One, who is known in Israel's tradition and worshiped in Israel's cult (Exod. 6:2-9; 34:6-8). Doubtless, the use of the tetragrammaton (sacred name, YHWH) does not have any "intrinsic importance," as Roland Murphy reminds us.[4] In using the sacred name, Israel's sages do not attempt to bring wisdom literature into the context of Israel's covenantal history. Here the oft-used expression "fear of the Lord" means reverence of God in a wider sense, reflecting the intention of going beyond the limitations of Israel's experience, as in the so-called Elohistic Psalter (Psalms 42–83), which strongly prefers to use "God" (Elohim) rather than "the Lord" (Yahweh). In wisdom literature the sage reflects on everyday human experience, and is not limited to meditating on the Torah "day and night" (Psalm 1).

The sages' constant emphasis on "the fear of the Lord" prevents Israel's wisdom sayings from becoming pragmatic "secular" advice, in the modern sense, like

---

3. See Gerhard von Rad's excellent book, *Wisdom in Israel*, trans. James D. Martin (Nashville: Abingdon, 1972), 65–73.

4. Murphy, *Tree of Life*, 126.

Benjamin Franklin's aphorisms. The appeal for trust in God and reverence before God's holiness suffuses Israel's wisdom with a religious fervor.

> Trust in the LORD *[Yahweh]* with all your heart,
>   and do not rely on your own insight.
> In all your ways acknowledge him,
>   and he will make straight your paths.
>   —Prov. 3:5-6

People have understandably turned to the book of Proverbs down through the ages, finding in it the language to express a faith that sustains them in everyday life.

Living in Harmony with the Divine Order
Again, Israel's sages sought to discover the divine order that is built into the very nature of things and with which human life must be in harmony if one is to enjoy well-being and success.

At first glance, this view seems to agree with the Deuteronomic theme of the two ways: the way of the righteous that leads to life, and that of the wicked that leads to death (Deut. 30:15-20). Also we read in Proverbs:

> But the path of the righteous is like the light of dawn,
>   which shines brighter and brighter until full day.
> The way of the wicked is like deep darkness;
>   they do not know what they stumble over.
>   —Prov. 4:18 (cf. 12:28)

In the case of Deuteronomy, however, the source of wisdom is the Torah: obedience to covenant law yields prosperity and success, disobedience brings hardship and disaster. The Deuteronomic interpreter, like the prophet Hosea (Hos. 4:1-4, 6; 6:6), is talking about a covenantal "knowledge of God" rooted in the exodus and Sinai tradition. In Israel's wisdom, however, "the blessing and the curse" (Prov. 3:33-35) are based on a broader foundation than Israel's sacred story. Israel's sages speak about an encounter with reality in everyday life. God has constituted the world in such a way that those who are in harmony with the structure of reality find success and happiness, and those who flout the divine order experience disillusionment and ultimate disaster.

Hence Israel's sages perceive that actions have consequences: that is the way life is.

> Whoever digs a pit will fall into it,
>   and a stone will come back on the one who
>   starts it rolling.
>   —Prov. 26:27

This action-consequence syndrome, however, is not an impersonal "law" that operates apart from God; rather, God is the one who has established the moral order and who supervises it so that an individual reaps the fruits of action. These fruits are not just the consequences of one's action but in a profound sense the reward of God.

> *If your enemies are hungry, give them bread to eat;*
> *and if they are thirsty, give them water to drink;*
> *for you will heap coals of fire on their heads,*
> *and the LORD [Yahweh] will reward you.*
> —Prov. 25:21-22 (cf. Rom. 12:20)

Social Order and Cosmic Order

In our previous study we have found that Davidic covenant theology broke beyond the limitations of Israel's sacred history and moved into the vast context of heaven and earth, the cosmic and the mundane. It is significant that Psalm 89, a psalm of the Davidic covenant, contains a hymnic passage in which Yahweh is praised in the heavenly council (see 89:5-7) for his power as creator, demonstrated in the crushing of the powers of chaos and the establishment of the order of creation.

> *O LORD [Yahweh] God of hosts,*
> *who is as mighty as you, O LORD [Yahweh]?*
> *Your faithfulness surrounds you.*
> *You rule the raging of the sea;*
> *when its waves rise, you still them.*
> *You crushed Rahab[5] like a carcass;*
> *you scattered your enemies with your mighty arm.*
> *The heavens are yours, the earth also is yours;*
> *the world and all that is in it—*
> *you have founded them.*
> —Ps. 89:8-12a

Wisdom theology is akin to royal theology in that it too belongs in a vertical heaven-earth dimension.[6] In a broad sense "wisdom theology is creation theology," as the Old Testament theologian Walther Zimmerli asserts.[7] Wisdom deals with the cosmic or created order, on which the human social order is founded.[8]

This view of the correspondence between the created order and the social order was undoubtedly influenced by Egyptian wisdom. It is noteworthy that the exhortations found in Prov. 22:17—24:22 (book III), which resemble the teaching of Egyptian sages, are apparently modeled after the Egyptian wisdom writing called "The Instruction of Amen-em-ope."[9] Moreover, in ancient Egypt *maat*, which roughly may be translated as "truth" or "justice," was regarded as the cosmic foundation on which pharaonic society was established, thereby guaranteeing

---

5. Rahab and Leviathan were names of the mythical sea monster, symbol of the powers of chaos and disorder.

6. On this dimension of Davidic theology, see above, chapter 13.

7. Walther Zimmerli, "The Place and the Limit of Wisdom in the Framework of the Old Testament Theology," in *Studies in Ancient Israelite Wisdom*, ed. James Crenshaw (New York: KTAV, 1976), 314–26. See p. 316.

8. See further chapter 30 below.

9. *ANET*, 421–25. See R. N. Whybray, *The Book of Proverbs*, CBC (Cambridge: Cambridge Univ. Press, 1972), 126–41.

social stability and harmony. Similarly in Psalm 89, a psalm of the Davidic covenant, the psalmist states that God's cosmic throne is founded on "righteousness and justice" (v. 14). Accordingly, the Davidic throne, which corresponds to the cosmic order, is secure:

> For our shield [king] belongs to the LORD [Yahweh],
> our king to the Holy One of Israel.
>
> —Ps. 89:18

In this ancient Near Eastern way of thinking, God's power as creator is evidenced not just by creation "in the beginning," as in Genesis 1, but also in the divine maintenance of "right order" in the cosmic and mundane spheres in the face of the powers of chaos (Rahab, Leviathan, Sea), which in human society are manifest as enemy invasion, infertility of the land, or social confusion. H. H. Schmid goes so far as to say that this ancient Near Eastern view provides "the broad horizon of biblical theology," both in the Old Testament and in the New.[10] This view has been endorsed by E. W. Nicholson, who maintains, however, that there was an "inner-Israelite controversy" between ancient creation theology and the covenant faith. In this "history of two increasingly conflicting world-views, the preaching of [Israel's] prophets may be said to have marked the beginning of the triumph of the one over the other."[11] Stated differently, the conflict was not between Israel and the religions of the environment but was one within the community of faith itself.

The Mystery of God's Wisdom

Finally, the sages of Israel recognized that the search for wisdom "from below," that is, from the human situation, even when grounded in religious faith, leads into mystery. The knowledge of "the Holy One" (Prov. 9:10) leads to the boundary of human thought and imagination where one must confess in awe and wonder that "God's thoughts are not our thoughts" and that "God's ways are not our ways" (cf. Isa. 55:8-9). Gerhard von Rad calls attention to the fact that wisdom sayings often break out into hymnic praise before the marvelous display of the mystery and majesty of God's creation.[12]

This sense of the mystery of divine wisdom was apparently not dominant in Israel's early wisdom tradition. Wisdom, at least in most circles, was very practical. It provided guidance on such matters as proper court etiquette, prudence in business affairs, avoidance of ensnaring sexual relations, and so on. Further, wisdom was important in politics. We are told that the counsel of Ahithophel, David's advisor, was "as if one consulted the word of God" (2 Sam. 16:23). Also, in the period of David wise women were consulted in political crises (2 Sam. 14:1-21; 20:14-22). Sages investigated both nature and human nature to ascertain the

10. See H. H. Schmid, "Creation, Righteousness, and Salvation" (trans. Bernhard W. Anderson and Dan G. Johnson), in *Creation in the Old Testament*, ed. B. W. Anderson, IRT 6 (Minneapolis: Fortress Press, 1984), 102–17.

11. E. W. Nicholson, *God and His People* (Oxford: Clarendon, 1986), 209; cf. pp. 204–5.

12. Von Rad, *Wisdom in Israel*, 162.

behavior that accords with "the way things are" or, in theological terms, the order of creation. This is evident, for instance, in the numerical proverb:

> *Three things are beyond me;*
> *Four I cannot fathom:*
> *How an eagle makes its way over the sky;*
> *How a snake makes its way over a rock;*
> *How a ship makes its way through the high seas;*
> *How a man has his way with a maiden.*
> —Prov. 30:18-19 (NJPSV)

Generally speaking, however, the sage was regarded as a kind of seer who could see behind the particulars of daily experience to the "secret" of things. He or she could see in the behavior of creatures, like the ant (Prov. 6:6-11) or the hawk (Job 39:26-30), wisdom lessons. There was considerable optimism, at least in the circles represented by the book of Proverbs, about the quest for divine wisdom. The God-fearing sage has the capacity to search out the meaning of experience, to know the two ways (cf. Psalm 1) and to walk in the right path.

> *A scoffer seeks wisdom in vain,*
> *but knowledge is easy for one who*
> *understands.*
> —Prov. 14:6

In some wisdom circles, however, there was considerable skepticism about the human ability to penetrate the mystery of God's plan. God's wisdom is hidden in the creation and is inaccessible to human beings. As stated in the beautiful poem in Job 28, which seems to be a separate piece in the book, miners can dig deep into the earth in search of precious stones, but they search in vain for the wisdom that is with God.

> *God understands the way to it,*
> *and he knows its place.*
> —Job 28:23

Thus when a sage starts with "the fear of Yahweh" or "the knowledge of the Holy One," he or she eventually stands in the presence of God's unfathomable holiness—beyond anything we can think or imagine. After marveling at God's power as creator, evident in the wonders of nature and the victory over the mythical powers of chaos (Sea, Rahab, the fleeing serpent), Job exclaims:

> *These are but the outskirts of [God's] ways;*
> *and how small a whisper do we hear of him!*
> *But the thunder of his power who can understand?*
> —Job 26:14

30. Wisdom in God's Creation

In the previous study we have seen that, in a broad sense, wisdom theology is creation theology. The social order is secure, free from the threats of chaos, when it is in harmony with God's ordering of creation. It is not surprising, then, to find in the book of Proverbs, among exhortations to seek wisdom, a testimony to God's primordial creation:

> *The LORD [Yahweh] by wisdom founded the earth;*
> *by understanding he established the heavens;*
> *by his knowledge the deeps broke open,*
> *and the clouds drop down the dew.*
>
> —Prov. 3:19-20

Wisdom Tabernacles in Israel

In the Wisdom of Ben Sira (Sirach), a wisdom work outside the Hebrew Bible but included in the Greek Bible (Septuagint), sages connect cosmic wisdom with Israel's sacred story. In the beginning Wisdom, like everything else, was created by God's commanding word and therefore has universal sway over all humankind.

> *I came forth from the mouth of the Most High,*
> *and covered the earth like a mist.*
> *I dwelt in the highest heavens,*
> *and my throne was in a pillar of cloud.*
> *Alone I compassed the vault of heaven*
> *and traversed the depths of the abyss.*
> *Over waves of the sea, over all the earth,*
> *and over every people and nation I have held sway.*
>
> —Sir. 24:3-6

God searched among all people for a "resting place" where Wisdom might tabernacle ("make her tent"; cf. John 1:14) and found it in Israel, which has the Torah, and particularly in the temple of Zion.

> *In the holy tent I ministered before him,*
> *and so I was established in Zion.*
> *Thus in the beloved city he gave me a resting place,*
> *and in Jerusalem was my domain.*
> *I took root in an honored people,*
> *in the portion of the Lord, his heritage.*
>
> —Sir. 24:10-12

By contrast, the book of Proverbs makes no reference to Israel's sacred story: the ancestors of Israel, the exodus from Egypt, God's covenants with the people, and so forth. The perspective is universal, ecumenical, and cosmic, like that of the creation psalm, 104, which also lacks any reference to Israel's covenantal history and, indeed, displays affinities with the Egyptian "Hymn to the Aton." In the manner of ancient sages, the Israelite psalmist catalogues the various creatures of God's creation and at the climax exclaims:

> O LORD, *how manifold are your works!*
> *In wisdom you have made them all;*
> *the earth is full of your creatures.*
>
> —Ps. 104:24

In this psalm creation is not just a mythical event of the past when God brought order out of chaos (104:5-9); rather, it is a continuing creation in which God maintains the regularities on which all life, animal and human, depends (104:27-30).

The Personification of Wisdom

Since the creation displays divine wisdom, sages began to reflect on the place of wisdom in God's creation. In their view, wisdom is not just a human capacity or human achievement; rather, "the play of wisdom" represents God's presence in the world.[1] The question is: what is the relation between God and Wisdom? Is Wisdom an agent of God? an aspect or quality of God? identical with God? This huge "metaphysical" question reappeared in different terms in Christian theological debates about whether the Son of God is "of like being" or "of the same being" in relation to God.

We may begin to tackle this question by recognizing that in Israel's wisdom tradition Wisdom is sometimes personified, that is, portrayed as having "personality." In other words, Wisdom is not an abstraction but is a person, indeed a feminine person ("she").

Wisdom as a Prophetess
In some passages Wisdom is portrayed as a woman who performs the role of a prophetess, or spokesperson for God. She stands in the marketplace or at the city gate, appealing to people to heed her instruction and amend their ways (Prov. 1:20-33; 8:1-21). Not only does the prophetess plead for repentance, or change of lifestyle, but also she announces judgment—the inevitable consequence of their "turning away."

> *Because they hated knowledge*
> *and did not choose the fear of the LORD [Yahweh],*
> *would have none of my counsel,*
> *and despised all my reproof,*
> *therefore they shall eat the fruit of their way*
> *and be sated with their own devices.*

---

1. Samuel Terrien, "The Play of Wisdom," Chapter 4, in *The Elusive Presence* (San Francisco: Harper & Row, 1978), especially 351–61.

> *For waywardness kills the simple,*
>   *and the complacency of fools destroys them;*
> *but those who listen to me will be secure*
>   *and will live at ease, without dread of disaster.*
>   —Prov. 1:29-33

Opposed to Woman Wisdom is Lady Folly (sometimes translated "Stranger Woman," "Foolish Woman") who, like a harlot, seduces people to follow her foolish ways (Prov. 2:16-19; 9:13-18). Individuals find themselves having to choose between these two women, one the embodiment of wisdom, the other of foolishness. Divine blessing is bestowed on those who decide for Woman Wisdom; divine judgment, in the form of consequences of decision, comes on those who yield to the allurements of Lady Folly. Unfortunately, the portrayal of women at this point is based on old stereotypes of the relation between males and females. As Kathleen O'Connor wisely remarks:

> Both Wisdom Woman and Stranger Woman are male creations that project onto women all that is good and bad in human nature. As stereotypes they harm women by failing to represent them as human beings, and they also misrepresent men by portraying them as helpless victims of preying females.[2]

Lady Folly disappears after the first nine chapters of the book of Proverbs.

Wisdom's Role in Creation

The personification of Wisdom in the context of God's creation occurs in three major passages. (1) Outside the Hebrew Bible (Apocrypha) in the magnificent poem in praise of Wisdom, Sirach 24 (ca. 180 B.C.), considered above. (2) Also outside the Hebrew Bible, in the Wisdom of Solomon (chapters 7–9), produced in the circle of Hellenistic Judaism, probably in the latter part of the first century B.C. (3) In the Hebrew Bible itself the personification of Wisdom is portrayed in the wonderful poem found in Prov. 8:22-31.

The last poem is one of the most important passages theologically in the Bible. In the chapter as a whole (Proverbs 8), Wisdom is presented as a prophetess who appeals to people to follow her ways and find health and wholeness. Enclosed within this poem is a remarkable passage (vv. 22–31) in which Wisdom's role is traced back to the time when God created heaven and earth. Wisdom was with God in the beginning, assisting God in creation.

This passage has its own literary integrity. It begins (8:22-23) with a thematic announcement of Wisdom's primordial status:

> *The LORD [Yahweh] created me at the beginning of his work,*
>   *the first of his acts of long ago.*

---

2. Kathleen M. O'Connor, "Wisdom Literature and Experience of the Divine," in *Biblical Theology: Problems and Perspectives*, ed. S. J. Kraftchick et al. (Nashville: Abingdon, 1995), 183–95; quotation, p. 188.

> *Ages ago I was set up,*
> > *at the first, before the beginning of the earth.*

In the next lines (8:24-26) the preexistence of Wisdom is elaborated in a series of negations introduced by "not yet" or "before":

> *Before the mountains had been shaped,*
> > *before the hills, I was given birth;*[3]
> *before he made the earth with its fields,*
> > *or the first of the dust of the world.*
> > > (BWA)

The poem then moves to a series of positive assertions, introduced by "when":

> *When he established the heavens, I was there,*
> > *when he drew a circle on the face of the deep,*
> *when he made firm the skies above,*
> > *when he established the fountains of the deep,*
> *when he assigned to the sea its limit,*
> > *so that the waters might not transgress his command,*
> *when he marked out the foundations of the earth,*

The poem reaches its climax and conclusion with the assertion that Wisdom was present and, in some sense, took part in God's creative work (8:30-31). The "then" of v. 30 introduces the conclusion (apodosis) of the negative and positive assertions.

> *then I was beside him, like a master worker,*
> *and I was daily his delight,*
> > *rejoicing before him always,*
> *rejoicing in his inhabited world,*
> > *and delighting in the human race.*

In each of these parts of the poem, the personification of Wisdom is stressed in a sequence of verbs: "I was set up [established]," "I was brought forth," "I was there," "I was beside him." Interestingly, in the latter part of v. 25 a maternal verb describes God as "giving birth" to Wisdom: "before the hills, I was given birth" (v. 25b, NIV).

Wisdom's role in God's creation would be clearer if we knew for sure what the rare Hebrew word *amon* means in v. 30. Does it mean "darling child" (cf. REB)? "craftsman at his side" (NIV)? "with Him as a confidant" (NJPSV)? "like a master worker" (NRSV)? Depending on which translation one follows, one is given a picture of Wisdom playing before the Creator like a little child, an artisan or craftsperson who collaborates with God, or a "confidant" who shares with God the secret of creation. The Greek Old Testament (Septuagint) lends some weight to the figure of an artisan. In any case, Wisdom is superior to anything else in God's

---

3. This maternal verb is translated "brought forth" in NRSV, in NIV "was given birth."

creation, since she was preexistent, present with God in the beginning, the first of God's creative works.[4]

The Relation of Wisdom to God

The big theological questions in this passage have to do with the relation of Wisdom to God. First, keeping in mind that the passage is part of a larger discourse in which Wisdom is portrayed as a prophetess (Proverbs 8), one may ask whether this language goes beyond poetic personification. Here Wisdom is associated with the Creator: separate from God, present with God in the beginning, and a participant in the work of creation. Roland Murphy thinks that something more than personification is involved:

> Wisdom is somehow identified with the Lord; she is the revelation of God, not merely the self-revelation of creation. She is the divine summons issued in and through creation, sounding through the vast realm of the created world, and heard on the level of human experience.[5]

Kathleen O'Connor goes further, proposing that Wisdom is virtually identical with God. "She is a separate being that partakes of the reality that she symbolizes, so that ultimately she is indistinguishable from the Creator."[6]

This personification of Wisdom, highly poetic and imaginative, suggests a very close association with God, nearly amounting to identification. But it is difficult to escape the interpretation that Wisdom is, in some sense, subordinate to God.[7]

However one resolves this problem, the portrayal of Wisdom in close, intimate association with God is a step in the direction of later christological thinking. The prologue to the Gospel of John affirms that in the beginning the Word (Logos) was "with God" and was the agent through whom all things were made (John 1:1-3; cf. Col. 1:15-20). The one big difference is that the poem in Proverbs 8 does not state that Wisdom was "God" (divine), as in John 1:1b. Rather, she was given birth by God and was the first of God's creative works.

Wisdom as Feminine

The second question has to do with the feminine identity of Wisdom. This cannot be dismissed on the linguistic grounds that in Hebrew the word for wisdom (*hokmah*) is feminine, as it is also in Greek (*sophia*); for, remember, the context of this passage is the portrayal of Wisdom as a woman, a prophetess.

---

4. See further Leo G. Perdue, *Wisdom and Creation: The Theology of Wisdom Literature* (Nashville: Abingdon, 1994).

5. Roland Murphy, *The Tree of Life*, Anchor Bible Reference Library (New York: Doubleday, 1990), 138.

6. O'Connor, "Wisdom Literature," 188.

7. O'Connor (ibid., 192) admits that Proverbs 8, which "appears to subordinate [Wisdom] to God," is "the chief problem" for her proposal.

If Wisdom is female, and if Wisdom is associated with God, this has tremendous theological implications. Some years ago a "Re-imagining Conference" was held in Minnesota, at which some interpreters held up Sophia (Greek) as a goddess, that is, the representative of the feminine dimension of deity. To speak of Wisdom as "goddess" goes too far; for it is stated that Wisdom was with God in the beginning and was God's agent, but Wisdom is never explicitly identified as "God." As we have seen earlier, Israelite interpreters rejected the god-goddess relationship in a pantheon.[8] Theologically speaking, the holy God is beyond sexuality.

The portrayal of Wisdom in Proverbs 8, however, represents a major break with the dominantly masculine metaphors of Israel's covenantal traditions. This shift is consistent with, if not demanded by, creation theology in the Old Testament. If humanity, male and female, is made in the image of God, then both masculine and feminine metaphors are necessary to "image" (imagine) God.[9]

Moreover, wisdom literature attempts to deal with one of the major paradoxes (dialectical contradictions) inherent in the experience of the holy God in the world: God's transcendence and God's immanence. As creator, God is not only prior to and beyond the creation but also active within it, upholding and maintaining it. We have found that this paradox is dealt with in various ways in Israel's covenant traditions, notably in the Davidic theology of Immanuel, "God with us."[10] In Hellenistic circles, out of which the Wisdom of Solomon came, God's immanence in the universe is portrayed as female wisdom:

> For wisdom is more mobile than any motion;
> because of her pureness she pervades and penetrates all things.
> For she is a breath of the power of God,
> and a pure emanation of the glory of the Almighty;
> therefore nothing defiled gains entrance into her.
> For she is a reflection of eternal light,
> a spotless mirror of the working of God,
> and an image of his goodness.
> Although she is but one, she can do all things,
> and while remaining in herself, she renews all things;
> in every generation she passes into holy souls
> and makes them friends of God, and prophets.
> —Wis. 7:24-27

In this view, Wisdom, as the "emanation of the glory of the Almighty," pervades the whole cosmos. There can be no sharp separation between the celestial and terrestrial, the cosmic and the mundane, God and the world, for God as creator is present and active in the whole. Divine revelation, then, is not confined to

---

8. See above, chapter 8.

9. See Elizabeth Johnson, *She Who Is: The Mystery of God in Feminist Theological Discourse* (New York: Crossroad, 1994), chaps. 2, 5.

10. See above, chapter 26.

God's speaking to the people, Israel; rather, God—the same God known and worshiped in Israel—may be encountered in the ordinary world, as one is overwhelmed with awe at the mystery and marvel of human life or the beauty that flames in flower or star.[11]

This cosmic view of Wisdom, which goes beyond the perspectives of Israel's covenants, is being explored anew in our time of ecological crisis. According to Rosemary Radford Ruether, the "sacramental tradition," which perceives God's immanence in the universe, "provides the basis for an 'I-Thou' relation to nature, an experience of being close to God in the majesty and beauty of the creation." "This sacramental view," she points out, "complements the covenantal tradition," which demands social justice. Here is a perspective, cosmic and universal in scope, that calls for responsible care of the natural environment.[12]

11. See Kathleen O'Connor's excellent discussion of "Some Theological Currents of the Wisdom Literature," namely, "Revelation in Ordinary Life," "Openness to Humanity," and "The Ungraspable Deity" ("Wisdom Literature," 185–87).

12. Rosemary Radford Ruether, *Gaia & God: An Ecofeminist Theology of Earth Healing* (San Francisco: HarperSanFrancisco, 1993).

31. The Justice of God

Israel's sages displayed two attitudes toward the quest for wisdom. According to some, wisdom—when based on the fear (awe) of Yahweh—is not limited to instruction on the right course of action; it can also provide some understanding of the divine order of things. Even though a great gulf is fixed between the holy God and the human world, the chasm is bridged by God, who gives faithful persons the power of discernment. Other sages, however, insisted that Wisdom (capitalized) eludes human grasp completely. Wisdom is the supreme prerogative of the Holy One, the Creator, whose ways are impenetrable. Divine Wisdom is beyond the human ken.

Skepticism and Faith

In some wisdom circles the inaccessibility of God's wisdom led to skepticism about the power of human reason. This is evident in a passage that comes from an appendix to the book of Proverbs, which may be regarded as a sage's dispute within himself,[1] or with someone else, about the search for wisdom. Note the movement of the poem (Prov. 30:2-9, NJPSV).

Failure of Human Wisdom (30:2-3). The sage feels weary, even drained of human resources, after a search that has led nowhere.

> *I am brutish, less than a man;*
> *I lack common sense.*
> *I have not learned wisdom,*
> *nor do I possess knowledge of the Holy One.*

The Elusive God (30:4). A series of ironic questions call for the answer "God," but the Creator is inaccessible and eludes human knowledge.

> *Who has ascended heaven and come down?*
> *Who has gathered up the wind in the hollow of his hand?*
> *Who has wrapped the waters in his garment?*
> *Who has established all the extremities of the earth?*
> *What is his name or his son's name, if you know it?*

God's Revelation (30:5-6). Discordantly another voice interrupts, saying that it is unnecessary, indeed wrong, to engage in a struggle to know God rationally, for God has revealed divine wisdom, presumably in the Torah ("every word of God is pure"), and shields those who have faith (cf. Eccl. 12:9-14).

---

1. Compare the ancient Egyptian tale of the dispute with one's soul (self) over suicide in *ANET*, 405–7.

> *Every word of God is pure,*
> *A shield to those who take refuge in Him.*
> *Do not add to His words,*
> *Lest He indict you and you be proved a liar.*

Accepting the Limitations of Human Wisdom (30:7-9). At this point the sage seems to be in agreement with the final editors of the book of Ecclesiastes: "The sum of the matter, when all is said and done: Revere God and observe His commandments" (Eccl. 12:13, NJPSV). God has given enough light by which to live, so one should live modestly—free from illusions and with sufficient income to enjoy a good life.

> *Two things I ask of you; do not deny them to me before I die:*
> *Keep lies and false words far from me;*
> *Give me neither poverty nor riches,*
> *But provide me with my daily bread,*
> *Lest, being sated, I renounce, saying,*
> *"Who is the LORD?"*

In some respects this wisdom discourse displays affinities with the dialogue of the book of Job, though in the latter case the dialogue moves eventually from a conversation on the human level, between friends, to a word from God.

> *Where were you when I laid the earth's foundations?*
> *Speak if you have understanding.*
> *Do you know who fixed its dimensions*
> *Or who measured it with a line?*
> *Onto what were its bases sunk?*
> *Who set its cornerstone*
> *When the morning stars sang together*
> *And all the divine beings shouted for joy?*
> —Job 38:4-7 (NJPSV)

This questioning echoes that of the skeptical sage discussed above (cf. Prov. 30:4), with this major difference: in Job's case, it is God who puts the questions that rebuke the presumptions of human wisdom.

Job and the Issue of Theodicy

Unlike the dispute of the sage found in the appendix to the book of Proverbs, the reader of the book of Job is told plainly why God is a problem. It is because of undeserved human suffering. Why do the righteous suffer in a world created and ruled by the God of justice and mercy? Here we run straight into the problem of theodicy, the justice of God.

In the history of Western philosophy many discussions of theodicy attempt to understand the justice of God within the rational categories of the human world. In philosophical ontology (philosophy of being), God is the Supreme Being, the summit of an ascending order that reaches from animal, to human, to divine being.

As the image of God, human being is said to be "consubstantial" (of the same nature) with God, that is divine, and therefore is capable of grasping the "mind of God."[2] Israel's reflective sages, however, set forth another approach to theodicy. In their view God is not the highest Being but the Creator—the God who is transcendent to, outside, and beyond the whole order of being. God's thoughts are not our thoughts, nor are God's ways our ways; therefore the problem of theodicy reaches beyond the capacity of human reason.

Dissonance in the Book of Job
The question of theodicy is sharpened by the literary composition of the book of Job. It is structured so as to create a dissonance between the narrative sections, found at the beginning (prologue) and end (epilogue), and the poetry that has been inserted between. The old Job narrative, which the author has appropriated, sets forth the simplistic view that faithfulness to God is rewarded with health, happiness, and prosperity; the central poetic sections, however, debate the validity of this doctrine and find it to be woefully inadequate.

> Prose Prologue (1:1—2:13)
> Poetry
>   Lament (chap. 3)
>   Dialogue with friends (chaps. 4–27)
>   Poem on Wisdom (chap. 28)
>   Job's Final Defense (chaps. 29–31)
>   Voice from the Whirlwind:[3]
>   First speech (chaps. 38–39)
>   and Job's submission (40:1-5)
>   Second speech (40:6—41:34)
>   and Job's repentance (42:1-6)
> Prose Epilogue (42:7-17)

When one considers the book as a whole, as a literary unity, the discordance of these two views sounds out loud and clear.

Israel's sages recognized that, just as wise parents discipline their growing children, so God disciplines persons for their welfare.

> My child, do not despise the LORD's [Yahweh's] discipline,
>   or be weary of his reproof,
> for the LORD [Yahweh] reproves the one he loves,
>   as a father the son in whom he delights.
>   —Prov. 3:11-12

2. In *Israel and Revelation* (discussed above, chapter 2), Eric Voegelin advocates this consubstantiality, or continuity between the human and the divine (e.g., pp. 467, 515), but this lofty view of human being can hardly be justified by Old Testament texts, including the *imago Dei* of Gen. 1:26-28.

3. This outline omits chapters 32 through 37, the speeches of Elihu. Since Elihu is not listed among Job's conversationalists (3:11-13), it is generally assumed that this section was added by the final editor of the book.

This teaching, picked up in the Epistle to the Hebrews (Heb. 12:7), is found repeatedly in Scripture. The prophet Isaiah preached this interpretation: suffering refines and purifies, strengthening metal by removing dross (Isa. 1:25).

For Job, however, the difficulty with this teaching was that, in his case, the punishment exceeded any wrong that he may have done. Though not a paragon of human perfection, Job was "blameless," that is, a man of moral rectitude, one who was in right relation with God and with humans (cf. Abraham, Gen. 17:1-2). With increasing passion, he stood on the ground of his own integrity, despite the attempts of his friends to explain his suffering in terms of human wisdom. Indeed, the argument with the friends proved to be a dispute with God about the apparent injustice of God's ways. He dared to confront God with the absurdity of his situation: a God-fearing, innocent man who is punished by God in a manner that exceeds any meaningful discipline.

God as the Problem

For Job, God was not an intellectual problem, as for many modern people who are tempted by atheism. Rather, Job was obsessed with God who, like Francis Thompson's "Hound of Heaven," was pursuing him inescapably. At one point, Job echoes the words of a psalmist who is amazed that the Creator is concerned about small, transient human beings (Ps. 8:3-4), but Job's words have a different ring:

> *What is man, that You make much of him,*
> *That You fix Your attention upon him?*
> *You inspect him every morning,*
> *Examine him every minute.*
> *Will you not look away from me for a while,*
> *Let me be, till I swallow my spittle?*
> —Job 7:17-19 (NJPSV)

Job's problem was with God—not with some evil powers at work in the world. God's creation is fundamentally good, despite the human experience of poverty, illness, strife, violence. "He does not look for the discordant note in the world," Gerhard von Rad remarks; "it is with God that something is wrong."[4] So he pursued his quest for God with great passion, finding no help at all in the "wisdom" of his friends, who knew the right things to say but espoused a theology that did not help a person who was in deep trouble. At one point Job, like Jeremiah, summoned God to a court trial in which his case could be argued fairly before God.

> *O, that I knew where I might find him,*
> *that I might come even to his dwelling!*
> *I would lay my case before him,*
> *and fill my mouth with arguments.*

---

4. Gerhard von Rad, *Wisdom in Israel*, trans. James D. Martin (Nashville: Abingdon, 1972), 305.

> *I would learn what he would answer me,*
> *and understand what he would say to me.*
> *Would he contend with me in the greatness of his power?*
> *No; but he would give heed to me.*
> *There an upright person could reason with him,*
> *and I should be acquitted forever by my judge.*
>
> —Job 23:3-7

Undeserved Suffering

In our study of the covenantal perspectives of the Old Testament we have found a remarkable agreement about the meaning of suffering: suffering is God's judgment on the people for their failure in covenant responsibility. To be sure, there are differences in theological accent. Sufferings in various forms represent the "curses" of the covenant for disobedience (Deuteronomy). Or suffering is the crucible in which God refines out the dross, so that the faithful remnant may be spared (Isaiah). Or suffering is the just punishment for offenses against the holy God (Ezekiel). Or suffering is God's discipline, God's teaching, so that a rebellious child may mature (Hosea, Jeremiah). In none of the covenantal perspectives is suffering, whether through a historical event or a natural occurrence, explained as an accident, a blow of fate, or an attack of demonic powers. The people are culpable. In the time of the fall of the nation, however, when the foundations of the Israelite community were shaken by seismic international events, this theological consensus was questioned. The usual prophetic interpretation of suffering was challenged forcefully in Habakkuk's dialogue with God (Hab. 1:1—2:5).[5] In the face of injustices on both the national and international scene, he raised the cry "How long?" heard in psalms of lament (e.g., Psalm 13):

> *O LORD [Yahweh], how long shall I cry for help,*
> *and you will not listen?*
> *Or cry to you "Violence!"*
> *and you will not save?*
>
> —Hab. 1:2

Walking in the valley of death's deep shadow (Ps. 23:4), people cried out—as they do today—to God for justice.

The issue of theodicy, or the justice of God, had a peculiar poignancy and intensity for Israel's interpreters.[6] For one thing, Israelite monotheism, which reached its full flowering in the poems of so-called Second Isaiah (Isaiah 40–55), permitted no explanation that could shift the problem to an offense against some deity other than Yahweh or to an unknown god. Theodicy was the supreme price

---

5. Discussed above, chapter 17.
6. See James L. Crenshaw, ed., *Theodicy in the Old Testament*, IRT 4 (Philadelphia: Fortress Press, 1983).

that had to be paid for a zealous belief in one God who, somehow, is in charge of all events, whether for good or ill (cf. Isa. 45:7). Moreover, Israelite monotheism did not allow for the view, expressed in some ancient myths, that evil is intrinsic to the creation and has to be overcome again and again if the divine order is to be maintained.[7] Israelite poets borrowed the mythical language of the Divine Warrior's battle against the powers of chaos (Sea, Floods, Rahab, Leviathan) but used it, especially in cultic contexts, to celebrate Yahweh's cosmic dominion over the gods and all historical powers. According to the creation story of Genesis 1, the creation is essentially good—"very good." It is creaturely freedom, manifest especially in human beings, that poses a threat to God's creation. Given the essential goodness of God's creation, why then do bad things happen to righteous people, like Job?

Expostulation with God

Job represents those persons of faith in the Old Testament period—some known, many nameless—who dared to expostulate with God. According to the dictionary, expostulation means "to reason with a person earnestly, objecting to his/her actions or intentions." In a vivid passage in Israel's ancestral traditions we are given a picture of Abraham expostulating with God on the eve of the holocaust of Sodom and Gomorrah and diplomatically pressing the question of theodicy: "will not the Judge of the whole earth do justice?" (Gen. 18:22-33 [BWA]). Moses, the great mediator of the covenant, dared to argue with God about the wisdom of judging a rebellious people too severely, reminding God of the promises of the covenant (Exod. 32:11-14). In one of his "confessions," written as the testimony of a suffering prophet, Jeremiah dared to initiate a lawsuit against God and charged:

> You have been to me like a spring that fails,
> Like waters that cannot be relied on.
> —Jer. 15:18 (NJPSV)

Further, as we have seen, Habakkuk, appalled by the terrible avalanche of Babylonian military power that was sweeping over the world, entered into a dispute with God, raising the question of how long God would allow injustice to run rampant.

People with this kind of faith do not endure absurdity submissively and patiently: they protest, they wrestle, they express an "agonistic" faith (from Greek *agonistes*, sports terminology referring to wrestling). It is instructive to compare biblical heroes of the faith with Greek tragic heroes, for instance, Job *agonistes* and

---

7. Jon Levenson, in *Creation and the Persistence of Evil: The Jewish Drama of Divine Omnipotence* (San Francisco: Harper & Row, 1988), maintains that at creation God did not overcome chaos completely but gained mastery over it and will not be triumphant until the consummation. See my response in "The Kingdom, the Power, and the Glory: The Sovereignty of God in the Bible," *TToday* 53, no. 1 (1996) 5–14, especially "God's Sovereignty as Creator," 6–9.

Oedipus *agonistes*.[8] In both Greek tragedy and the book of Job, persons have to cope with a given situation. But the Greek tragic heroes wrestle with the ambiguities of their fate without argument; they accept their lot grimly, as many people do today. By contrast, the people of Israel speak up and raise questions vehemently, that is, they expostulate with the Divine.[9]

These two styles of wrestling reflect two entirely different worldviews. In Greek culture, fate (*moira*) was the dominating power—greater than humans or gods. A tragic hero, like Oedipus, could assert himself in *hubris* (heroic pride, presumption) against Fate but could not escape *nemesis* (retribution), which levels all things to their proper place. In the worldview of the Old Testament, however, there is no notion of people being in the power of impersonal, implacable fate, such as we find in the lines of the poet William Ernest Henley ("Invictus"):

> *In the fell clutch of circumstance,*
> *I have not winced or cried aloud,*
> *And 'neath the bludgeonings of Fate,*
> *my head is bloody but unbowed.*

A completely different attitude toward life is found in ancient Israel. In the Bible, both evil and good are somehow embraced within the Creator's purpose, even though human wisdom cannot perceive how or why. Moreover, the God known and worshiped in Israel is not a capricious mischief maker or an arbitrary tyrant, but the God of *ḥesed*, of faithfulness.[10] In the conviction that God is faithful and trustworthy, far beyond anything we can think or imagine, people may boldly protest, wrestle, expostulate.

The Voice from the Whirlwind

Job did receive an answer from God, who spoke out of an awesome whirlwind. Job's questions were ignored, however; he was only reminded that God, not Job, puts the questions.

> *Who is this that darkens counsel by words without knowledge?*
> *Gird up your loins like a man,*
> *I will question you, and you shall declare to me.*
> —Job 38:2-3

What follows is a series of questions, in which Job was told that he does not have the wisdom to grasp the secret of God's creation.

The inattention to Job's existential questions may imply that it is foolish to suppose that God is concerned about our human problems; God has bigger busi-

---

8. See the illuminating comparison of the two types of piety by U. Milo Kaufmann, "Expostulation with the Divine: A Note on Contrasting Attitudes in Greek and Hebrew Piety," *Int* 18 (1964) 171–82.

9. See Leo G. Perdue, *Wisdom in Revolt: Metaphorical Theology in the Book of Job*, JSOTSup 112 (Sheffield: Almond Press, 1991).

10. See discussion of the characterization of Yahweh, chap. 7.

ness to attend to. More likely, the reader should understand that a great gulf is fixed between human wisdom and God's wisdom, and therefore God does not think as we think, or act as we do. In any case, Job finally stands before the *mysterium tremendum*, the sheer holiness of God, and repents for his presumption in trying to judge God by human standards. Strikingly, he seems to move beyond the limitations of human words into an ecstatic vision of God.

> *I had heard of you by the hearing of the ear,*
> *but now my eye sees you.*
> —Job 42:5

The poetry ends with a sacramental view of the creation, in which the works of the Creator display God's ineffable glory.

Since the prose folktale (prologue and epilogue) constitutes the literary frame of the poetic sections, and the book is to be read and interpreted as one composition, it is significant that in the end God commends Job for his "agonistic" faith that boldly seeks understanding. The friends, who proved to be poor "pastoral counselors" in a situation of suffering, were rebuked because they "have not spoken of me what is right, as my servant Job has" (42:7-8). Like Abraham, Job had survived the test and had demonstrated the "fear" or reverence of God (cf. Gen. 22:12) that is the beginning of wisdom.

The Hiddenness of God

The book of Ecclesiastes (called Qohelet in Hebrew)[11] takes the skeptical side of the dialogue about the quest for wisdom. There is only enough human wisdom to live prudently between the unalterable boundaries of life and death and even to find some joy in the midst of suffering. The writer advocates reverence before God (5:7; 7:18), but God's wisdom is inaccessible and God is hidden from human perception.

Like Job, Ecclesiastes stands squarely in the midst of the problem of human suffering. With prophetic boldness, Qohelet speaks out against the wickedness perpetrated in the seats of justice and the anguished cries of the oppressed in society (Eccl. 3:16—4:3). He is appalled by the long delays that occur before God metes out punishment to the wicked and by the numerous cases where there is no difference between the lot of the righteous and of the evildoers (8:10—9:3). He senses that the lament in the face of violence and oppression, "How long, O Lord," goes unanswered, at least within the lifetime of the people who cry out for a divine answer to the problem of injustice.

Hence Ecclesiastes is in radical disagreement with sages who support the view expressed in a wisdom psalm: "I have been young and now am old; yet I have not

---

11. Martin Luther translated Qohelet as "the Preacher," but this discourse is more like a rambling lecture than a sermon. The RSV appropriately translates as "the Teacher."

seen the righteous forsaken, or their children begging bread" (Ps. 37:25). This facile assurance is also voiced in the Wisdom of Ben Sira:

> Consider the generations of old and see:
>   has anyone trusted in the Lord and been disappointed?
> Or has anyone persevered in the fear of the Lord and been forsaken?
>   Or has anyone called upon him and been neglected?
> For the Lord is compassionate and merciful;
>   he forgives sins and saves in time of distress.
>   —Sir. 2:10-11

Against such unrealistic optimism the Teacher (Qohelet) protests vehemently. His mantra, stated at the beginning and reverberating to the end, is "Vanity of vanities, all is vanity." The use of the superlative idiom, "vanity of vanities," emphasizes the utter futility of human life. Early Skeptical Greek philosophy probably influenced this wisdom writing.[12]

Qohelet's discourse is a challenge to those who think that human wisdom can perceive the purpose of God in this world. From God's standpoint, everything may belong to a meaningful whole, but humans are denied this angle of vision. The natural world, from our point of view, is governed by a changeless cycle, in which the four elements of the universe—the earth, the sun, the wind, and the sea—endlessly repeat their movements. Caught in the monotonous cycle and the transience of the natural world, the melancholy sage has the courage to realize that human life is brief and powerless (Eccl. 1:2-11) and that, as Bertrand Russell puts it in powerful modern prose, "the slow, sure doom falls pitiless and dark."[13]

The Times of Our Lives

In the famous chapter on the "Times of Our Lives" (3:1-15), the sage observes that the times come one after another, each with its particular meaning, but no discernible purpose runs through them. Experience of time, or better, times (plural), is characteristic of human beings, but they cannot perceive how the times belong together in an ultimately meaningful whole.

> [God] has made everything suitable for its time; moreover, he has put a sense of past and future into their minds, yet they cannot find out what God has done from the beginning to the end.
>   —Eccl. 3:11

Viewing the world of human experience *sub specie aeternitalis* God can make sense of the whole, but from the standpoint of limited human wisdom everything is transient and adds ultimately up to "vanity." Human beings are like animals in that they must die, but are unlike animals in that they know that they must die. "Who knows

---

12. See the essay by Steven Bishop, "Is Qoheleth a Pyrrhonist?" presented to the Society of Biblical Literature (November 1996), in which he traces the influence of Greek Pyrrhonism.

13. Bertrand Russell, "A Free Man's Worship," in *Why I Am Not a Christian* (New York: Simon & Schuster, 1957), 104–16.

whether the human spirit goes upward and the spirit of animals goes downward to the earth?" (3:21).

In the same pessimistic—some would say realistic—vein, the Teacher is critical of work or creative skill because it reflects the competitive desire to outstrip fellow human beings (4:4), the passionate lust for wealth that brings no satisfaction (5:10—6:9), and the weak character of most people, who are easily overcome by temptations of the moment. The sage concedes that, despite human weaknesses, it is good to have companions and to enjoy marital bliss. Finally, in a famous passage on old age (11:7—12:8), he advises young people to remember their Creator in the days of their youth, to celebrate life and to revel in God-given happiness, before the shadows lengthen and old age begins to take its toll.

Taking Life Seriously

Today many people live by Qohelet's philosophy, even though they may never have read his book. Yet this sage did not advocate being like the fool in the Psalms (Ps. 14:1; 53:1) who says in his heart (mind) that there is no God and therefore you should live as you please. On the contrary, the Teacher took God more seriously than many of the pious or orthodox. He believed that human beings, God's noblest creatures, are capable of wisdom, though not the kind of wisdom that can grasp the secret or mystery of God's creation (Eccl. 6:10-13). God's purpose is hidden from our view; the holy God transcends our world. The sage maintained, however, that God wills that human beings experience joy during their allotted life span and that they take life seriously.

Obtaining a Wise Heart

It is instructive to compare wisdom literature like Job and Ecclesiastes, written from a standpoint of skepticism, with the great Psalm 90, written from the position of faith in God. In this consummate expression of trust in God the Creator, some of the notes of Israel's wisdom literature are heard. The poet is overwhelmed by the eternity of God, "our help in ages past, our hope for years to come," to borrow the language of a church hymn.

> *O Lord [Yahweh], You have been our refuge*
>   *in every generation.*
> *Before the mountains came into being,*
>   *before You brought forth the earth and the world,*
>   *from eternity to eternity You are God.*
>   —Ps. 90:1-2 (NJPSV)

The awareness of God, who transcends the times from beginning to end, overwhelms the poet with a melancholy awareness of the brevity and transience of human life, which is lived under the judgment (wrath) of God.

> *All our days pass away in Your wrath;*
>   *we spend our years like a sigh.*

The span of our life is seventy years,
or, given the strength, eighty years;
but the best of them are trouble and sorrow.
They pass by speedily, and we are in darkness.
—Ps. 90:9-10 (NJPSV)

Here human mortality is viewed not just as biological weakness but in some sense as the consequence of human sin (cf. Rom. 6:23). Life is lived toward death, which comes all too quickly, and toward the final judgment of God, from whose penetrating scrutiny there is no escape. The poet prays that awareness of the common human condition may lead us (the community of faith) to the wisdom based on the fear (reverence) of the Lord.

Teach us to count our days rightly,
that we may obtain a wise heart.
—Ps. 90:12 (NJPSV)

This psalm does not advocate "happiness," if that means a trouble-free life, but rather the "contentment" that comes from the knowledge that all of our days, despite their brevity and sorrow, are embraced within the faithfulness and compassion of God.

Satisfy us at daybreak with Your steadfast love [ḥesed]
that we may sing for joy all our days.
Give us joy for as long as You have afflicted us,
for the years we have suffered misfortune.
—Ps. 90:14-15 (NJPSV)

PART III
CONTINUED

B. FROM PROPHECY TO APOCALYPTIC

For I [Yahweh] am about to create new heavens
and a new earth;
the former things shall not be remembered
or come to mind.

ISAIAH 65:17

32. Prophecy in a New Idiom

We have seen that Israel's sages sought to discover the divine secret of creation only to realize finally that it is inaccessible to human wisdom. Another approach to the cosmic secret was set forth in prophecy, especially the new idiom of prophecy known as apocalyptic (from Greek *apokalypsis*, meaning "revelation"). In literature of this type, God reveals the divine secret, especially the secret of the coming of God's kingdom, to a seer or prophet who divulges it to the circle of the faithful. The movement is "from above"—from God to human beings—not "from below"—from the human world to God.

God's Plan for the Future

The view that God reveals the divine secret to a seer is deeply rooted in the history of prophecy. The classical prophets, beginning especially with Amos, did not want to be regarded as clairvoyants in the popular sense (Amos 7:12-16; cf. Jer. 23:25-32), like Samuel of old (1 Sam. 9:9). Despite such disclaimers, however, they were seers in a sophisticated sense who discerned God's plan for the future. The prophet Amos declared that the storm cloud taking shape on the international horizon signified the judgment of God on the social injustices of Israel's society.

> Surely the Lord GOD *[Adonai Yahweh] does nothing*
> *without revealing his secret*
> *to his servants the prophets.*
> *The lion has roared;*
> *who will not fear?*
> *The Lord* GOD *[Adonai Yahweh] has spoken;*
> *who can but prophesy?*
> —Amos 3:7-8

Some of Israel's prophets used the metaphor of the heavenly council to express the conviction that they were commissioned to declare God's plan for the future (see 1 Kgs. 22:19-23). In Isaiah's inaugural vision (Isa. 6:1-7) the microcosmic earthly temple was transformed into the macrocosmic heavenly temple, where the prophet stood in the presence of the cosmic King, who was enthroned "high and lifted up," and heard the divine decree that would shape the future. Jeremiah insisted that the trouble with the popular prophets, who preached what the people wanted to hear, was that they lacked the proper credentials.

> For who among them has stood in the council of
> the LORD *[Yahweh]*
> *to perceive and to hear his word,*
> *or who has given heed to his word and listened?*
> —Jer. 23:18 (RSV)

The great prophets of Israel, in various and diverse ways, announced the mystery or secret of the coming of God's kingdom on earth as it is in heaven. Their message of social justice was set within this eschatological context.

Apocalyptic Visionaries

The theme of the divine secret was taken up in the new style of prophecy called apocalyptic, which flourished in the postexilic period. These interpreters sought to understand the problem of evil, which, as we have seen previously, defied explanation in terms of Israel's covenant failure (sin). In their view, evil was evident in powers of chaos at work in human history and indeed in the whole creation. Aware that the spread of evil and violence was a threat to the sovereignty of God, and consequently to the meaning of human history, a seer announced a God-given answer to the lament, "How long?" As in the passage from Jeremiah cited above (Jer. 23:18), sometimes an apocalyptic seer used the metaphor of the heavenly council. The seer Daniel, for instance, envisioned himself standing in the heavenly council, in the presence of the cosmic Judge, and hearing in coded language a disclosure of the nearness of the time of God's triumph over the forces of evil (Dan. 7:13-18).

Gerhard von Rad drew attention to the close relation between apocalyptic "knowledge" (*gnosis*) and the wisdom of Israel's sages.[1] There are, admittedly, significant affinities between the two. Both share a universal perspective that reaches beyond the particular history of Israel into the cosmic panorama of creation. Moreover, the seer is a kind of sage. Daniel is portrayed as a sage whose knowledge, based on divine revelation, was superior to that of Babylonian diviners (Dan. 1:3ff.; 2:48). But the wisdom of the apocalyptic visionary has an entirely different basis than the wisdom we have studied. It is not the wisdom of a sage who reflects on daily experience; rather, it is knowledge of the mystery of the future that is revealed to a seer and communicated to an esoteric community. Jesus stood in line with this apocalyptic view when he said to his disciples, according to the Gospel of Mark,

> To you has been given the secret [Greek *mysterion*] of the kingdom of God, but for those outside, everything comes in parables.
>
> —Mark 4:11

From Classical Prophecy to Apocalyptic

The movement from classical prophecy to apocalyptic can be traced within the book of Isaiah, from its inception in the message of the eighth-century prophet to its final composition during the period of the Second Temple (rebuilt 520–515 B.C.). In the past there has been a general consensus that the book falls into

---

1. Gerhard von Rad, *Old Testament Theology*, trans. D. M. G. Stalker, 2 vols. (New York: Harper & Row, 1962–65), 2:301–7. He later qualified his earlier view that the origin of apocalyptic could be traced to wisdom rather than prophecy; see *Wisdom in Israel*, trans. James D. Martin (Nashville: Abingdon, 1972), 277.

three major parts: the message of Isaiah of Jerusalem (found within the compass of chapters 1–39), the message of so-called Second Isaiah during the exile (chapters 40–55), and the later writings found at the conclusion of the book, so-called Third Isaiah (chapters 55–66). What is the relation of these three parts to the book as a whole?

The Book of Isaiah as a Whole
Lately some scholars have proposed moving beyond the "three Isaiahs," a tripartite division that was supposedly an "assured gain" of so-called historical criticism, to a consideration of the book as a whole.[2] To use language introduced in another connection,[3] the proposed approach is synchronic rather than diachronic. Or as Edgar Conrad puts it: "It is possible to conceive of the book as a composite created from diverse materials at a particular point in time rather than a document evolving through time."[4]

There is much to be said for this holistic approach. The book of Isaiah was read as a whole in the Essenelike community at Qumran (founded in the second century B.C.) or in the early Christian community. Nevertheless, there are *theological* advantages that accrue from studying stages in the composition of the book. For instance, our appreciation of the message of so-called Second Isaiah (chapters 40–55) is enhanced by understanding the concrete historical situation out of which the poems came and to which they were addressed.[5] The text itself demands this; for instance, the poet hails Cyrus of Persia as Yahweh's "messiah" (anointed one), chosen to liberate peoples from bondage and oppression (Isa. 44:28; 45:1). Moreover, when this anonymous prophecy is interpreted in its historical context, the poet-prophet appears as a pastoral theologian, who addresses the sufferings and anxieties of a people shattered and dislocated by war and longing for a new beginning in their homeland.[6]

Viewed as a whole, the book of Isaiah bears witness to the transformation of prophecy into apocalyptic.[7] In his commentary on the first part of the book of

2. See Edgar W. Conrad, *Reading Isaiah* (Minneapolis: Fortress Press, 1991); Katheryn Pfisterer Darr, *Isaiah's Vision and the Family of God* (Louisville: Westminster/John Knox, 1994).

3. See the comparison of the approaches of Eichrodt and von Rad above, chapter 3.

4. Edgard W. Conrad, "Reading Isaiah and the Twelve as Prophetic Books," in *Writing and Reading the Scroll of Isaiah: Studies of an Interpretive Tradition*, ed. Craig C. Broyles and Craig A. Evans (Leiden: Brill, 1997), 1:3-18 (quotation, p. 4). See also idem, "The End of Prophecy and the Appearance of Angels/Messengers in the Book of the Twelve," *JSOT* 73 (1997) 65–79.

5. James Muilenburg's illuminating Introduction to and Exegesis of Isaiah 40–66, in *IB* 5:385–773, still claims attention.

6. It is noteworthy that Walter Brueggemann, who "brackets out" questions of "historicity" as beyond the pale of Old Testament theology (*Theology of the Old Testament* [Minneapolis: Fortress Press, 1997], 118–19), is nevertheless concerned to understand "the later Isaiah" (and other texts) in the context of the exile. "The historical rootage of these texts in exile is of enormous importance for the project of Old Testament theology" (278–79).

7. See Paul Hanson, *The Dawn of Apocalyptic: The Historical and Sociological Roots of Jewish Apocalyptic Eschatology* (rev. ed.; Philadelphia: Fortress Press, 1979).

Isaiah (Isaiah 1–39), Ronald E. Clements observes that "this development from prophecy to apocalyptic forms one of the most striking features in the literary growth of the book of Isaiah."[8] To appreciate the theological significance of this shift, it is appropriate to turn to the message of Second Isaiah, which is a "halfway house," as it has been called, in the transition from prophecy (First Isaiah) to apocalyptic (Third Isaiah).

Second Isaiah's Message

Second Isaiah's message (Isaiah 40–55) is grounded in the seminal message of the eighth-century prophet, Isaiah of Jerusalem, the major prophetic interpreter of royal covenant theology. We have seen that Isaiah's proclamation of the dominion of God, the cosmic King, centers in two symbolic institutions: the temple of Zion and the Davidic monarchy.[9] The poet-prophet, Second Isaiah, transposes this message into a new key in the time of Israel's exile in Babylonia. Like a pastoral theologian, he speaks to a dislocated, suffering people whose faith in God had been strained to the breaking point:

> *Why do you say, O Jacob,*
> *and speak, O Israel,*
> *"My way is hidden from the* LORD *[Yahweh],*
> *and my justice*[10] *is disregarded by my God?"*
> —Isa. 40:27

Again we hear the question about God's justice, voiced this time in the existential terms of a people uprooted from their homeland.

The author known as First Isaiah received his commission in the temple, where he was transported in a vision to the heavenly council and heard God's decree for the future (Isaiah 6). Significantly, Second Isaiah echoes this council metaphor in the first of his poems (Isa. 40:1-11). Addressing members of the heavenly council, Yahweh, the cosmic King, commands that a message of comfort be sent from heaven to earth.

> *Comfort, O comfort my people,*
> *says your God.*
> *Speak tenderly to Jerusalem,*
> *and cry to her*
> *that she has served her term,*
> *that her penalty is paid,*

---

8. Ronald E. Clements, *Isaiah 1–39*, New Century Bible Commentary (Grand Rapids: Eerdmans, 1981), 22. See also my essay, "The Apocalyptic Rendering of the Isaiah Tradition," in *The Social World of Formative Christianity and Judaism: Essays in Tribute to Howard C. Kee*, ed. Jacob Neusner et al. (Philadelphia: Fortress Press, 1988), 17–38.

9. On royal covenant theology, see above, chapter 23.

10. NRSV translates here "right"; the Hebrew word *mishpat* could better be translated "justice."

that she has received from the LORD's *[Yahweh's] hand*
double for all her sins.

—Isa. 40:1-2

The metaphor of the divine council is evident in that its members are addressed in plural Hebrew verbs ("comfort," "speak," "cry," "proclaim") and they respond in antiphonal voices (v. 3; cf. v. 6). Listening in on the deliberations of the heavenly council, the prophet feels that he is among those addressed: "Then I said, 'What shall I proclaim?'" (v. 6).

The substance of the "good news" that is to be carried from heaven to earth is that the time of the coming of God's dominion is near. For Israel, the people of God, this means that the sentence of punishment for their sins is over and that a new day is at hand. Comfortingly the people are told that God's covenant promises made of old are still valid. Human existence is transient, like the flowers of the field, but God's word of promise is permanently valid.

The grass withers, the flower fades;
but the word of our God will stand forever.

—Isa. 40:8

Despite Israel's lament (Isa. 40:27), God has not forgotten their "justice."

Marching to Zion

Consider how this poet treats the various covenant traditions discussed in our study. First, it is noteworthy that Second Isaiah does not refer to the conditional Mosaic covenant, and in this respect agrees with his mentor, Isaiah of Jerusalem, who also failed to do so.[11] In terms of the Mosaic covenant, the people of Israel have suffered their penalty, more than enough ("twofold") for their sins (40:2). Some other covenant language must be used to express the unconditional pardon and grace that God now offers.

Although Second Isaiah does not refer to the Sinaitic covenant, he does—unlike Isaiah of Jerusalem—employ the imagery of Israel's sacred history.[12] In glorious colors the poet portrays the people marching to Zion: the exodus or "going out" of captivity, the victory at the sea where God conquered the powers of chaos (mythically symbolized as Rahab, the chaos monster: 51:9-11), and the march on "the highway of God" through the wilderness (40:3) to the temple of Jerusalem, where God is acclaimed King (40:9-11). Zion, the city of God, hears a herald announcing good tidings:

How beautiful upon the mountains
are the feet of the messenger who announces peace,

11. See the discussion of Isaiah's prophecy, above chap. 25.

12. On this poet's use of historical imagery, mainly the exodus, see my essay, "Exodus Typology in Second Isaiah," in *Israel's Prophetic Heritage: Essays in Honor of James Muilenburg*, ed. B. W. Anderson and Walter Harrelson (New York: Harper & Row, 1962), 177–95.

> who brings good news,
>   who announces salvation,
>   who says to Zion, "Your God reigns."
> —Isa. 52:7

This heraldic announcement echoes the exciting proclamation heard in psalms that celebrate God's enthronement: "Yahweh is king!"[13]

The new exodus, Second Isaiah announces, will be like the former exodus from Egyptian bondage:

> Thus said the LORD [Yahweh],
>   Who made a road through the sea
> And a path through mighty waters,
> Who destroyed chariots and horses
>   And all the mighty host—
> They lay down to rise no more,
>   They were extinguished, quenched like
> a wick.
> —Isa. 43:16-17 (NJPSV)

But God is about to do a "new thing," which will be so wonderful that the former things pale in significance:

> Do not remember the former things,
>   or consider the things of old.
> I am about to do a new thing;
>   now it springs forth, do you not perceive it?
> —Isa. 43:18-19a

Here is faith that does not turn to the archaic past, longing for the good old days, but stands on tiptoe, facing the new age that God is about to introduce. Even now those new things, those acts of new creation, are evident, if one has the eyes of faith to perceive them.

The Promises of Grace to David

Turn now to the Davidic covenant, which was fundamental in the prophetic message of Isaiah of Jerusalem.[14] This covenant, with its promises of the security of Zion and the unbroken continuity of the Davidic dynasty, had foundered on the rocks of tragic historical reality, as evident from the poignant lament at the conclusion of Psalm 89 (vv. 38–51). In the time of Second Isaiah there was no longer a king on the throne of Jerusalem, and the city of Zion was in ruins. In accord with Zion theology, Second Isaiah announces a marvelous social transformation: Jerusalem and its temple will be rebuilt (44:26-28). Unlike the former Isaiah, however, he does not announce the coming of an anointed one (messiah) to sit on the throne of Jerusalem. Indeed, he calls a foreign ruler, Cyrus of Persia, God's

13. See the discussion of Psalms 47, 93–99 above, chapter 24.
14. See above, chapter 23.

anointed (messiah) because he will be the agent who will accomplish God's purpose (45:1-7).

In the message of Second Isaiah, the promises of grace to David are not neglected. Strikingly, the Davidic covenant is reaffirmed by shifting the promises of this "everlasting covenant" from the Davidic dynasty to the people. To the community[15] God says:

> *Incline your ear, and come to me;*
>   *listen, so that you may live.*
> *I will make with you [plural] an everlasting covenant,*
>   *my steadfast, sure love [hesed] for David.*
>
> —Isa. 55:3

The poet goes on to say that Israel, the people of God, will be instrumental in including other nations in the saving purpose of God, as promised in the Abrahamic covenant (cf. Gen. 12:1-2).

> *See, I made him [David] a witness to the peoples,*
>   *a leader and commander for the peoples.*
> *See, you shall call nations that you do not know,*
>   *and nations that do not know you shall run to you,*
> *because of the LORD [Yahweh] your God, the Holy One of Israel,*
>   *for he has glorified you.*
>
> —Isa. 55:4-5

The Suffering Servant

According to Second Isaiah, Israel has a special role in the saving purpose of God that embraces all nations. In this spacious theological context appears the theme of the suffering servant, which is completely absent in the prophecy of Isaiah of Jerusalem. This is not the place to enter at length into the much-discussed question of the identity of the servant, a question raised, according to a New Testament story, by an Ethiopian eunuch (Acts 8:26-39).[16] Suffice it to say that in the four servant poems we are given an interpretation of suffering that goes beyond anything found in Israel's covenant traditions.

Here suffering is not regarded as punishment for Israel's covenant failure (sin); rather the servant's suffering is vicariously borne for other peoples. The nations confess that "he was wounded for our transgressions, he was bruised for our iniquities" (Isa. 53:5; RSV). The servant's suffering is, in some sense, substitutionary, for "the Lord [Yahweh] has laid on him the iniquity of us all" (53:6). There is no sug-

15. All the Hebrew verbs are in the plural, showing that God addresses this promise of grace to the people. See Edgar Conrad, "The Community as King in Second Isaiah," in *Understanding the Word: Essays in Honor of Bernhard W. Anderson*, ed. James T. Butler et al., JSOTSup 37 (Sheffield: JSOT Press, 1985), 99–112.

16. The four servant poems are Isa. 42:1-4; 49:1-6; 50:4-9; 52:13—53:12. See my discussion in *Understanding the Old Testament* (4th ed.; Englewood Cliffs, N.J.: Prentice-Hall, 1986) 488–50; (abridged paperback ed.; Englewood Cliffs, N.J.: Prentice-Hall, 1997), 436–40.

gestion, however, that the servant suffers in order to satisfy divine wrath. From the first the poems of Second Isaiah assert that God's comforting word for Israel is based on divine grace and forgiveness.

At one point, the servant is compared to "a lamb led to the slaughter," which echoes language that the prophet Jeremiah used in one of his confessions (Isa. 53:7; cf. Jer. 11:19). Yet there is a profound difference. The servant suffers passively in silence: "he opened not his mouth" (Isa. 53:7; RSV), while Jeremiah—like Job—expostulated with God. The servant's suffering, however, is not just a historical fate that falls brutally on an innocent one, for it occurs in the will of God ("it was the will of the LORD [Yahweh] to bruise him," v. 10) and within the mystery of God's redemptive purpose. Accordingly, the suffering and humiliation of the servant are embraced within God's ultimate vindication and exaltation, the notes on which the poem begins (52:13-15) and ends (53:10-12).

The Everlasting Covenant with Noah

Since the Mosaic and Davidic covenants are theologically inadequate, Second Isaiah turns to the "everlasting covenant" with Noah after the flood to express the unconditional grace of God and the new beginning (or new creation) that is at hand.[17]

> *This is like the days of Noah to me:*
>   *Just as I swore that the waters of Noah*
>   *would never again go over the earth,*
> *so I have sworn that I will not be angry with you,*
>   *and will not rebuke you.*
> *For the mountains may depart*
>   *and the hills be removed,*
> *but my steadfast love [*hesed*] shall not depart from you,*
> *and my covenant of peace shall not be removed,*
>   *says the LORD [Yahweh], who has compassion on you.*
>   —Isa. 54:9-10

The everlasting covenant with Noah is theologically appropriate because, first, it was a covenant of grace, granted in spite of the fact that the inclination of the human heart continued to be evil (Gen. 8:21). Likewise, according to Second Isaiah, Yahweh's forgiveness is free and unconditioned by the behavior of the people. God's word of promise does not go forth in vain but accomplishes God's saving purpose.

> *For as the rain and the snow come down from heaven,*
>   *and do not return there until they have watered the earth,*
> *making it bring forth and sprout,*
>   *giving seed to the sower and bread to the eater,*

17. On the Noachic covenant see above, chapter 11.

> *so shall my word be that goes out from my mouth;*
> *it shall not return to me empty,*
> *but it shall accomplish that which I purpose,*
> *and succeed in the thing for which I sent it.*
> —Isa. 55:10-11

Second, reference to the Noachic covenant is appropriate because it is a covenant of creation, embracing humans, animals, and the earth itself. Second Isaiah brings out clearly the creation theology implicit in the royal covenant theology of Isaiah of Jerusalem.

In these poems, creation appears in several senses. For one thing, Yahweh is praised as the creator of the people, the one who formed them in the womb (Isa. 44:1-2, 24). Also, creation may refer to the new historical events that God brings about, the "new thing" that God does (43:18-19). However, the poet's emphasis falls especially on cosmic creation.

> *Lift up your eyes on high and see:*
> *Who created these?*
> *He who brings out their host and numbers them,*
> *calling them all by name;*
> *because he is great in strength,*
> *mighty in power,*
> *not one is missing.*
> —Isa. 40:26

In the message of Second Isaiah, the doctrine of creation undergirds everything that is proclaimed. Because Yahweh, the Holy One, is the creator of "the ends of the earth" and of the starry expanse, Yahweh is powerful to save Israel and redeem the world. No other deity can demonstrate the power to create the heaven and the earth and even to bring about a new creation.

> *Thus says the Lord [Yahweh],*
> *the Creator of the heavens,*
> *he who is God,*
> *who made the earth and fashioned it*
> *and by himself fixed it firmly,*
> *who created it not as a formless waste*
> *but as a place to be lived in:*
> *I am the Lord [Yahweh], and there is none other.*
> —Isa. 45:18 (REB)

Shift in Theological Emphasis

So far, standing in the "halfway house" of Second Isaiah, we have looked back to the seminal message of Isaiah of Jerusalem in the attempt to understand what theological shifts took place in the movement of prophecy toward apocalyptic. Now, from the same vantage point, let us look forward to the last chapters of the book and to the final apocalyptic rereading of the Isaiah tradition in the canonical book of Isaiah.

The next section of the book of Isaiah, so-called Third Isaiah (Isaiah 56–66), is not apocalyptic in the full-blown sense; it is sometimes designated as proto-apocalyptic, that is, prophecy that is beginning to turn into apocalyptic. Here we stand at the "dawn of apocalyptic," to cite the title of Paul Hanson's study of Third Isaiah.[18] In the final edition of the book of Isaiah, materials of more definitive apocalyptic character were added. These include "the little apocalypse" of Isaiah 24–27 and the twin chapters 34 and 35, which now serve as a transition to Second Isaiah.

It lies beyond our present purpose to trace the history of the composition of the book of Isaiah; rather, we are concerned with the theological shifts in emphasis as prophecy changed into apocalyptic or, one might say, as Second Isaiah led on to Third Isaiah.

A New Creation

First, in this transition there was a shift in emphasis from the history of the people Israel to the cosmic dimension, which includes heaven and earth and the whole course of human history from creation to consummation. On the one hand, Mosaic prophets like Hosea and Jeremiah concentrate primarily on the politics and economics of the mundane realm; and they perceive that world in the light of the sacred story that centers in exodus and Sinai. On the other hand, Isaiah of Jerusalem ushers us into the symbolic world of Zion, the city of God, which will endure eternally, despite all historical vicissitudes, because it is God's earthly dwelling place (see Psalms 46 and 48).

In apocalyptic imagination the concrete realities of history are transfigured with a transcendent meaning. Nations like Assyria or Babylonia are no longer agents of God for chastening the people Israel but are symbols of sinister powers at work in history, threatening the city of God and the divine plan for Israel and the nations. God's victory over these forces will be not only a vindication of Zion, and therefore of all the poor and helpless of the earth, but also a new creation in which there will be no more suffering and violence. This apocalyptic note sounds out in a beautiful poem in Third Isaiah:

> *For I am about to create new heavens*
> *and a new earth;*
> *the former things shall not be remembered*
> *or come to mind.*
> *But be glad and rejoice forever*
> *in what I am creating;*
> *for I am about to create Jerusalem as a joy,*
> *and its people as a delight.*

18. Hanson, *The Dawn of Apocalyptic.*

I will rejoice in Jerusalem,
    and delight in my people;
no more shall the sound of weeping be heard in it,
    or the cry of distress.

—Isa. 65:17-19

Comfort for the Afflicted

In the transition from prophecy to apocalyptic another shift in emphasis took place: from a call to repentance to a message of consolation. It is noteworthy that the poetry of Second Isaiah, which stands at the turning point of the book of Isaiah, begins with a word of comfort announced in the heavenly council by the cosmic King: "'Comfort, O comfort my people,' says your God" (Isa. 40:1).

In one of his studies of apocalyptic, Paul Hanson suggests that the difference between prophecy and apocalyptic may be expressed in terms of the metaphor of the heavenly council. "Prophetic eschatology is transformed into apocalyptic at the point where the task of translating the cosmic vision into the categories of mundane reality is abdicated."[19] In his temple vision, as we have seen, Isaiah of Jerusalem was called to carry a heavenly message to the people of Israel. He was commissioned to translate a vision of cosmic righteousness and order into human society, that is, to preach for social change so that the mundane realm might conform to the will of the cosmic King, whose heavenly throne is "founded on righteousness and justice" (Ps. 89:14).

Apocalyptic visionaries, however, did not consider "translation of the cosmic vision" to be their primary task. They received from the heavenly throne a message of comfort that had to do with the coming of God's kingdom on earth and the beginning of a new age. In answer to the lament, "How long?" they heard the answer, "not long." To be sure, they could sound the call to repentance in their own way. According to the Gospel of Mark, Jesus' preaching began with the call "repent, for the kingdom of God is at hand" (1:15). But apocalyptic visionaries placed the primary emphasis on offering a message of comfort to the afflicted in times of trial.

The reason for this "abdication" of the prophetic task of translating the heavenly vision into the realities of social life is to be found in a deeper and more radical perception of the problem of evil. As we have seen, in classical prophecy the sufferings of the times were explained by the people's failure or sin. The great prophets did not say that the people were victimized by demonic powers external to Israel's life. Rather, the problem—in their perception—lay within the people: their false way of life, their service of alien gods, their refusal to bring society into conformity with the righteousness of God's cosmic order. Apocalyptic writers, however, found this explanation of evil to be inadequate. It was not enough to call for repentance and to blame the people for their failure of responsibility. They perceived that Israel, and all peoples, were caught in the grip of monstrous historical

19. Paul Hanson, "Old Testament Apocalyptic Reexamined," *Int* 25 (1971) 454–79.

forces that challenged the sovereignty of God. Evil, in their view, is located not just "in here," in the heart, but out there, in colossal empires, oppressive structures of power, evil that sweeps like an avalanche over innocent people.

Overcoming the Powers of Chaos

Accordingly, apocalyptic writers revived the ancient myth of the battle of the Divine Warrior against the powers of chaos and the decisive victory that demonstrated God's power as King. This ancient myth influenced the pattern of the Song of the Sea (Exod. 15:1-18): (1) Yahweh's battle against adversaries, (2) Yahweh's triumph at the sea, and (3) Yahweh's enthronement as triumphant King in the sanctuary.[20] At one point Second Isaiah invoked the myth to portray Yahweh's power to create a people and give them a future. In this poetic view, the Divine Warrior's victory at the Reed Sea was not just a victory over flesh and blood (the army of Pharaoh) but a victory over the uncanny powers of evil, symbolized by the monster of chaos, Rahab. The poet addresses the "arm" of the Divine Warrior to achieve a similar victory in the future:

> *Awake, awake, put on strength,*
>   *O arm of the LORD [Yahweh]!*
> *Awake, as in days of old,*
>   *the generations of long ago!*
> *Was it not you [the "arm"] who cut Rahab in pieces,*
>   *who pierced the dragon?*
> *Was it not you who dried up the sea,*
>   *the waters of the great deep;*
> *who made the depths of the sea a way*
>   *for the redeemed to cross over?*
>   —Isa. 51:9-10

This imaginative poetry should not be construed to mean that God actually sleeps through times of suffering and tragedy and has to be "awakened" to action. Here the poet is drawing a correspondence between the event at the sea in the past and the new event of the "passing over" of liberated people into the promised land of the future.

In apocalyptic imagination the Divine Warrior's victory is not restricted to Israel's history but belongs to a universal drama, in which the kingdom of God opposes the powers of evil that afflict and crush people. These visionaries portray a New Jerusalem, a new age, indeed, a new creation. In this perspective, the coming of God's kingdom on earth will be the time of God's triumph—not only over human sin and failure but also over all the powers of evil that have tyrannized people and corrupted human history from time immemorial. Many people of the mod-

20. See above, chapter 18.

ern age, who feel helpless in the face of massive social forces or colossal evil, have come to a new appreciation of the apocalyptic myth.

The Ultimate Conquest of Evil

In the Isaiah Apocalypse (Isaiah 24–27) a passage portrays the final triumph of the Divine Warrior over the monster of evil, known as Tiamat in Babylonian tradition and Rahab/Lotan (Leviathan) in Canaanite mythology. The language is redolent of the Canaanite myth of Baal's conquest of his adversary, Lotan the "fleeing serpent":

> On that day the LORD [Yahweh] with his cruel sword,
> his mighty and powerful sword, will punish
> Leviathan that twisting sea serpent,
> that writhing serpent Leviathan,
> he will slay the monster of the deep.
>
> —Isa. 27:1 (REB)

God will ultimately "exorcise" history, vanquishing the powers of chaos that have lingered ever since creation.[21]

A line can easily be drawn from this apocalyptic passage to the portrayal of the consummation found in the Apocalypse of John (Revelation). According to that Christian visionary, at the time of the final triumph of the Divine Warrior, the powers of evil—symbolized mythically by "the great dragon, . . . that ancient serpent, who is called the Devil and Satan" (Rev. 12:9)—will be overcome. Moreover, "the sea"—the locus of the powers of chaos—will be no more (Rev. 21:1).

---

21. See further my essay, "The Conquest of the Fleeing, Twisting Serpent: Isaiah 27:1 in Context," in *Uncovering Ancient Stones: Essays in Memory of H. Neil Richardson,* ed. Lewis M. Hopfe (Winona Lake, Ind.: Eisenbrauns, 1994), 3–15.

33. THE DOMINION OF GOD VERSUS THE DOMINION OF EVIL

We have found that the justice of God is a burning issue in the Old Testament, especially in the literature reflecting the homelessness and struggles experienced in the aftermath of the fall of Jerusalem in 587 B.C. Some have even suggested that Job "symbolized exiled and restored Israel,"[1] though this is probably an overinterpretation. In any case, the question of theodicy did not arise out of a reflective monotheism that attempted to uphold the sole sovereignty of God; it arose out of the experience of suffering in a world where, in the perspective of faith, God is present and active.

Other religions and philosophies are not necessarily tantalized by this problem. In mainline Buddhism the problem does not arise since this religion does not affirm belief in God or God's creation. Buddhism shows a way, attractive to many people, to transcend suffering and turmoil, but it does not deal with theodicy. Another major world religion, Islam, emphasizes surrender to the sovereign will of God as set forth in the Koran and promises that the injustices of this life will be eclipsed in a glorious postmortem existence, a prospect that allegedly makes even suicide bombing, in the service of Allah, justifiable. One could go on. For the Judeo-Christian faith, however, theodicy is a poignant and inescapable issue because of the conviction that God, the Creator, is present and active in the world. This faith is summed up pregnantly in one prophetic word: Immanuel, God with us. Christianity received and intensified Israel's witness, expressed in various covenantal traditions, to the real presence of God in the world.

From Prophetic Word to Apocalyptic Vision

In our previous study we have seen that classical prophecy, in the face of the colossal violence and monstrous evil manifest in human history, moved into a new type of prophecy known as apocalyptic. The book of Isaiah in its final form displays an apocalyptic rendering of the Isaiah tradition.[2]

In the transition from prophecy to apocalyptic several things happened. First, the prophetic message moved from the plane of ordinary mundane affairs into a suprahistorical realm, where God's dominion clashes with the powers of evil. A seer announces the "secret" or "mystery" of God's kingdom, which is hidden from people involved in ordinary political or economic reality. Second, in dealing with

---

1. Kathleen O'Connor suggests this possibility in "Wisdom Literature and Experience of the Divine," in *Biblical Theology: Problems and Perspectives*, ed. Steven J. Kraftchick (Nashville: Abingdon, 1995), 185.

2. As shown in my essay, "The Apocalyptic Rendering of the Isaiah Tradition," in *The Social World of Formative Christianity and Judaism: Essays in Tribute to Howard C. Kee*, ed. Jacob Neusner et al. (Philadelphia: Fortress Press, 1988), 17–38.

the execution of God's plan the seer resorts to highly symbolic language that has to be decoded. Mythical language, such as the Divine Warrior's victory over the monster of chaos, is used to express the meaning of the historical drama. Finally, the perspective becomes universal, including not just the history of Israel but also the whole sweep of the times from creation to consummation. To be sure, Zion— the city where God is sacramentally present (Ps. 46:4-5)—remains central in the new scenario. Zion is to rejoice, for God will vindicate her and bring back her sons and daughters to their homeland. But Zion is the center of the world, the meeting place of heaven and earth, and hence all peoples and nations will make a pilgrim- age to Zion, the holy city, to find ultimate peace and security by listening to God's torah or teaching (Isa. 2:2-4). Poets envision a New Jerusalem, in which there will be no more violence or suffering (Isa. 65:17-25). The vision of "the new Jerusalem, coming down out of heaven from God," is also found in the Apocalypse (Revelation) of John, the last book of the New Testament (Revelation 2–4).

Generalizations are risky, but one way to explain the difference between the two styles of prophecy is to say that in classical prophecy the role of the prophet is to proclaim the *word* of God so that people may repent; in apocalyptic, the role of the seer is to portray a *vision* of God's future so that people may find comfort and hope. True, classical prophets speak about visions, usually for the purpose of setting forth their credentials to speak the word of God (Amos 7:7-9; 8:1-3; Jer. 1:1-12, 13-19). In apocalyptic, however, there is a shift to dreams and visions that, when explained by an interpreter, disclose God's plan for the future.[3] The first part of the book of Zechariah, for instance, contains eight mysterious visions; the book of Daniel also contains cryptic visions whose meaning is tantalizingly elusive.

The Day of Judgment
At the end of the Old Testament, according to the arrangement of the Christian Bible, are found thirteen small prophetic writings that, in general, treat the theme of the coming of God's day of judgment. This arrangement, which includes the book of Daniel, marks one of the important differences between the Christian Bible (Old Testament) and the Hebrew Bible, as noted earlier.[4] On the one hand, in the Hebrew Bible the Book of the Twelve is placed before the Writings (Kethubim), which includes the book of Daniel. On the other hand, in the Christian Bible, which is influenced by the Greek translation (Septuagint), these small prophetic books, along with the book of Daniel, are placed at the end of the Old Testament, just before the New Testament. Appropriately, the libretto of Handel's *Messiah*, after citing passages from the comforting message of Second Isaiah ("Comfort Ye," Isa. 40:1-3; "Every Valley Shall Be Exalted," 40:4; "And the Glory of the Lord," 40:5), dips into this prophetic collection:

3. See Susan Niditch, *The Symbolic Vision in Biblical Tradition*, HSM 30 (Atlanta: Scholars Press, 1983), who notes a shift in the pattern of the vision in the transition from prophecy to apoca- lyptic.
4. See above, chapter 1.

> *Yet once a little while, and I will shake*
> *the heavens and the earth.*
> —Hag. 2:6-7

> *But who may abide the Day of his coming?*
> —Mal. 3:2

> *And he shall purify the sons of Levi.*
> —Mal. 3:3 (KJV)

What binds these prophetic books together theologically is that they all deal with the coming *Dies Irae*, "the day of wrath," when God will judge the sins of the people of God and the evil that tyrannizes the world.

At first glance, the prophetic legend of Jonah seems to be an exception. But this short story also deals with the message of divine judgment that Jonah was commissioned to preach to Nineveh, the capital of the hated Assyrian Empire that had oppressed the Israelite people. (See the bitter enmity toward Assyria expressed in the book of Nahum.) What disturbed Jonah was the possibility that if the Ninevites repented in response to his preaching, God would relent in his judgment, for "there's a wideness in God's mercy," to quote the words of a hymn by Frederick W. Faber (1854). Citing the ancient tradition about the proclamation of Yahweh's "name" (Exod. 34:5-7), Jonah explains his anger and depression in a prayer:

> O LORD [Yahweh]! Is not this what I said while I was still in my own country? That is why I fled to Tarshish at the beginning; for I knew that you are a gracious God and merciful, slow to anger, and abounding in steadfast love [*ḥesed*], and ready to relent from punishing. And now, O LORD [Yahweh], please take my life from me, for it is better for me to die than to live.
> —Jonah 4:2-3

To pray for God's mercy on Nineveh was as unthinkable as it was for many Americans during the Gulf War to express God's concern for Iraq, the modern occupant of Assyrian territory.

Apocalyptic Views of God's Future Action

These prophetic writings, then, are eschatological in that they point to God's future action to vindicate Zion and, with her, all the poor and helpless of the earth. Some of this literature, however, moves beyond the prophetic eschatology, found for instance in Amos and Hosea, into definitely apocalyptic eschatology. This is true of the first of the group, the book of Daniel, which portrays in highly symbolic terms the coming of God's kingdom. In the arrangement of the Christian Bible, Daniel appropriately follows the book of Ezekiel, which specializes in cryptic symbolism, as evident especially in the apocalyptic description of the mysterious foe from the north: Gog from the land of Magog (Ezek. 38:1—39:29). Ezekiel aptly has been called "the father of apocalyptic."

Other books in this group of prophetic writings are also apocalyptic in tone. For instance, the book of Joel portrays the coming of God's day of judgment in the strange symbolism of an army of locusts that ravished the land. The book of Zechariah also belongs in the category of apocalyptic eschatology. Most scholars divide the book into two parts, Proto-Zechariah (chapters 1–8) and Deutero-Zechariah (chapters 9–14). Despite discontinuities between the two parts, however, there are also important continuities, such as the centrality of Zion, the divine purification of the community, and the universal scope of God's rule on earth.[5]

The second part of the book of Zechariah (Deutero-Zechariah), which is closely related to the ensuing prophecy of Malachi, ends with a portrayal of the final battle of history and the advent of God's kingdom. In imaginative language the visionary portrays the coming of the Divine Warrior to fight for Zion (14:1-5), cataclysmic upheavals of nature (vv. 6–7), Zion as the source of vitality (vv. 8–9), and the elevation of Zion as the rest of the earth is depressed to the level of the Arabah, the area south of the Dead Sea (vv. 10–11). Here we stand on the ground of full-blown apocalyptic.

These examples of Old Testament apocalyptic are only the tip of the iceberg, as it were. In the period from approximately 200 B.C. to A.D. 200 a vast apocalyptic literature appeared, such as 2 Esdras in the Apocrypha or the writings of the Qumran community on the shores of the Dead Sea. In this period of great historical insecurity and cultural change, Christianity erupted out of the heart of Judaism and was strongly influenced by apocalyptic prophecy, as we shall see.

Theological Themes of Apocalyptic

While apocalyptic literature is vast and diverse, and therefore not easily summarized, several theological themes are characteristic of the apocalyptic way of thinking.[6]

Violence in the Earth

Apocalyptic seers perceive that people—and the earth itself—are victims of violence. In the previous chapter we noticed that apocalyptic interpreters wrestle with the problem of evil at a different level—perhaps we should say at a more profound level—than prophets who believed that social change would come through repentance. The notion that evil is wrongdoing for which the people are responsible was weighed in the balance of suffering and found wanting. People are often not only the perpetrators of evil but also the victims of it. Evil manifests itself as an insidious, perhaps we should say "demonic," power in history, prompting

---

5. See Rex A. Mason, "The Relation of Zech 9–14 to Proto-Zechariah," *ZAW* 88 (1976) 227–39.

6. See further Klaus Koch, *The Rediscovery of Apocalyptic*, trans. Margaret Kohl (London: SCM, 1972), who discusses eight motifs generally found in apocalyptic literature.

"people of the lie" to masquerade as good and twisting good into evil.[7] It manifests itself typically as a colossal military power—an Assyria or a Babylonia—that sweeps inexorably over small peoples. It lurks in structures of power that crush the poor and helpless in society. In short, evil manifests itself as "violence"—the theme of Habakkuk's lament (Hab. 1:2) and the motive for the great flood (Gen. 6:11).

As we have seen, the question with which apocalyptic interpreters deal is not how the human heart can be changed (the question of repentance) but rather how essentially evil structures can be changed so that society may be healthy. In their estimation, history needs to be exorcised of the evil that holds terrible sway and even threatens the sovereignty of God.[8] For instance, in apocalyptic symbolism Babylon is not just the evil empire known to historians (see Isaiah 13) but is a code word for the sinister and oppressive power of evil that victimizes people, as in the apocalypse of Daniel (chapter 4) or the apocalypse of John (Revelation 18).

Dualism of the Two Ages

Apocalyptic interpreters are dualistic in their view of history. They perceive two dominions (kingdoms) struggling for ascendancy: the dominion of God and the dominion of evil. This is not a metaphysical dualism, rooted in ultimate reality or the depths of the Divine, for God's original creation was good, indeed "very good" (Gen. 1:31). Rather, this is a postcreation dualism rooted in creaturely rebellion against God—rebellion that is evident not only in human sin but also in cosmic revolt by celestial beings. The conflict between the God forces and the evil forces was eventually expressed in terms of the myth of Satan, a heavenly being who revolted against God and set up a rival kingdom into which human beings are seduced.

These two dominions—the kingdom of God and the kingdom of evil (Satan)—may also be described as two "ages" or "worlds," that is, times of history. The present "age," in the apocalyptic view, is under the dominion of evil (or, as in the Lord's Prayer, of "the evil one"), and it will be succeeded by the "new age," when evil is overcome and all things are made new. Apocalyptic interpreters speak of "this age" (*haʿolam hazzeh*) and "the age to come" (*haʿolam habbaʾ*).

God's Intervention

To people victimized by the powers of evil, apocalyptic visionaries announced that God is about to shake the evil empire to its foundations and liberate its victims. That is the only way that a new age of peace and justice can come: God must destroy the whole evil system. As said previously, social change will come not by changing the human heart but by changing the oppressive structures under which

---

7. See M. Scott Peck, *People of the Lie: The Hope for Healing Human Evil* (New York: Simon & Schuster, Touchstone Book, 1983).

8. See further my essay, "The Slaying of the Fleeing, Twisting Serpent: Isaiah 27:1 in Context," in *From Creation to New Creation*, OBT (Minneapolis: Fortress Press, 1994).

people live. In the apocalyptic view liberation will come not by education, social planning, or revolutionary activity, but by an impending catastrophe in which the earth will be reduced to a wasteland.

This view is expressed powerfully in a poem found in the Little Apocalypse of Isaiah:

> Behold,
> The LORD [Yahweh] will strip the earth bare,
> And lay it waste,
> And twist its surface,
> And scatter its inhabitants.

The poet goes on to say that the catastrophe will level all social differences:

> Layman and priest shall fare alike,
> Slave and master,
> Handmaid and mistress,
> Buyer and seller,
> Lender and borrower,
> Creditor and debtor.
> The earth shall be bare, bare;
> It shall be plundered, plundered;
> For it is the LORD [Yahweh] who spoke this word.
> —Isa. 24:1-3 (NJPSV)

In the following verses, the poet declares that this catastrophe will be the result of the people's lifestyle: they have broken the "everlasting covenant"—the Noachic covenant (Genesis 6–9), which rests on God's law of reverence for life, animal life and especially human life, which is made in the image of God (see Gen. 9:1-17).

> The earth is withered, sear;
> The world languishes, it is sear;
> Both sky and earth[9] languish.
> For the earth was defiled
> Under its inhabitants;
> Because they transgressed teachings,
> Violated laws,
> Broke the ancient [everlasting] covenant.
> That is why a curse consumes the earth,
> And its inhabitants pay the penalty;
> That is why earth's dwellers have dwindled,
> And but few men are left.
> —Isa. 24:4-6 (NJPSV)

Whether this vision will be realized in an "ecological backlash" because of the violent lifestyle and atmospheric pollution of human beings remains to be seen.

9. Alternate reading.

How long? Not long!

Again, apocalyptic visionaries announce that the time is near when God will come with power, shaking the foundations of the earth and making a new beginning, a new creation. In answer to the cry of lament, "O Lord, how long?" the answer is given: Not long! (Recall Martin Luther King, Jr.'s powerful preaching!) Oppressed people do not have to wait indefinitely, past the limit of endurance, for the kingdom of God is coming with power, it is "at hand" (cf. Mark 1:15).

The "mystery" or "secret" that apocalyptic visionaries announce to the faithful is the imminence of God's triumph; indeed some of them boldly announce God's timetable. This is the theme of the well-known story of Nebuchadnezzar's dream (Daniel 2). According to the story, Nebuchadnezzar, king of Babylonia, had a terrible dream that shook him up. He called his magicians, enchanters, and sorcerers and demanded an explanation, though making their task impossible by saying that they not only had to interpret the dream but tell him the dream too, otherwise "off with their heads." Daniel, however, had superior wisdom, for he prayed to the God of heaven and "the mystery" (Aramaic *raz*) was revealed to him in a night vision (Dan. 2:17-23).

The interpretation of Nebuchadnezzar's dream, announced by Daniel to the king, communicated the divine secret in symbolic language (Dan. 2:31-35). The king saw an image composed of materials in descending order of value (gold, silver, bronze, iron, clay mixed with iron), symbolizing four oppressive empires, each qualitatively inferior to the previous one. A stone, supernaturally quarried ("not by human hands"), struck the composite image, symbolizing the catastrophic power of God that destroys the old regimes. The stone became a great mountain that filled the whole earth, symbolizing the spread of the dominion of God from its base in Zion to include the whole world.

The Inevitability of God's Victory

Finally, in the apocalyptic perspective God's decisive triumph over all the powers of evil is certain. Sometimes this is expressed in terms of a sequence of kingdoms characterized by decreasing quality (Daniel 2) or by increasing evil (Daniel 7). So viewed, there is no "progress," to use a word in currency since the Enlightenment of the eighteenth century; rather, things will get worse and worse until the end time comes and God's dominion supervenes. The periodization of history as a succession of kingdoms demonstrates the inexorable movement of history toward the dominion of God, which will introduce a radical new beginning.

In the apocalyptic view, there is an inevitability about the triumph of God's kingdom, as though the outcome of the whole drama were known and determined in advance. This deterministic language should not be construed to mean that people need only fold their arms and wait, because everything is "cut and dried" in advance. Apocalyptic does not support a failure of nerve, or a pessimistic view of history, although this is hard to understand for those who suppose that history is under the control of human planning, science, or wisdom. On the contrary, the apocalyptic message urges people to stand firmly in faith, even when the odds are overwhelmingly against them and when they are called on to endure persecution and martyrdom. Apocalyptic literature calls people to "an ethic of fidelity."[10] It summons the faithful to strive actively toward the kingdom of God in the confidence that God is in control and will soon triumph over powers of evil, darkness, and death.

The Apocalypse of Daniel

This spirit of confidence is reflected in the apocalypse of Daniel, which was written at the time of the Maccabean revolution (ca. 168 B.C.) as a tract for revolutionaries. The conviction that history moves inevitably, and by prearranged plan, toward the coming of God's kingdom on earth fired the zeal of a small band of the faithful, enabling them to act in hope when, humanly speaking, everything was against them. "The people who are loyal to their God shall stand firm and take action" (Dan. 11:32). If God was for them, who could be against them (cf. Rom. 8:31-39).

A Vision in the Night

The vision in Daniel 7 deserves special attention. This chapter has been a happy hunting ground for modern interpreters who attempt to calculate the end of the world by reflecting on the identity of the fourth beast. Despite modern fantasies, the account of Daniel's vision is indeed very important, if for no other reason than that its apocalyptic imagery had a great influence on the New Testament vision of the coming of the Son of Man (e.g., Mark 13:24-27; 14:61-62).

The chapter opens with a night vision. The four winds (note the universal language) were stirring up the great sea, the abyss of chaos, in a manner reminiscent of the portrayal in the Genesis creation story (Gen. 1:2), where the Spirit or "wind" of God churned up the waters of chaos. Out of the sea arose four beasts, symbolizing the four world empires (probably Babylonia, Media, Persia, Greece). Each beast was more terrible than its predecessor, showing the deterioration of history, and the last beast was horrible beyond imagining: "terrifying and dreadful and exceedingly strong" (Dan. 7:7). This beast was different from its predecessors. It had "ten horns" and one of them had something like human eyes and "a mouth speaking arrogantly" (7:7-8). (A veiled allusion to a line of Syrian rulers following Alexander the Great [332 B.C.] and culminating in Antiochus IV, who arrogantly boasted divinity.)

Then the scene shifts from earth to heaven. The heavenly council is in session, the cosmic King is presiding. The NRSV arranges the description in poetic form:

> As I watched,
> thrones were set in place,
> and an Ancient One[11] took his throne,

10. Sibley Towner, *Daniel*, Interpretation (Richmond: John Knox, 1984).
11. Aramaic, "Ancient of Days."

> his clothing was white as snow,
>   and the hair of his head like pure wool;
> his throne was fiery flames,
>   and its wheels were burning fire.
> A stream of fire issued
>   and flowed out from his presence.
> A thousand thousands served him,
>   and ten thousand times ten thousand stood attending him.
> The court sat in judgment,
>   and the books were opened.
>   —Dan. 7:9-10

One Like a Son of Man

In the seer's vision, God pronounces judgment on the evil empires, especially the last. Then the seer beholds another figure, "one like a human being,"[12] who approaches the heavenly throne to hear the King's decree. To him is given an ever-lasting kingdom, in contrast to the earthly kingdoms that rule for a time and pass away.

> As I watched in the night visions,
> I saw one like a human being
>   coming with the clouds of heaven.
> And he came to the Ancient One,
>   and was presented before him.
> To him was given dominion
>   and glory and kingship,
> that all peoples, nations, and languages
>   should serve him.
> His dominion is an everlasting dominion
>   that shall not pass away,
> and his kingship is one
>   that shall never be destroyed.
>   —Dan. 7:13-14

In the vision, Daniel was puzzled about all of this, and turned to a court attendant standing nearby, asking for the meaning. The interpretive angel (7:16) explained that the tyranny represented by the succession of ferocious beasts will come to an end and that "the holy ones of the Most High" will be given an everlasting dominion.

Several things should be noticed. First, in this vision the figure—"one like a human being"—does not come from the abyss below, the locus of the powers of chaos, but comes from above, transcendently, with the clouds of heaven. Also, this figure does not have a beastly visage (symbolizing fierce violence) but a friendly face, "one like a human being." Probably the meaning is not "the human one" (as in the *Inclusive Language Lectionary*) but "the angelic one" or "heavenly being," since

---

12. Aramaic *bar 'enash*, literally "son of a man." Here "son" refers to a member of a group, in this case, human beings; compare "sons of the prophets," members of the prophetic order.

the human-like figure comes with the clouds of heaven. Finally, to this figure is given an everlasting dominion, in contrast to the earthly empires that rose and fell. The interpretive angel explains that those who are faithful to the end (the saints of the Most High) will receive a kingdom that cannot be destroyed, precisely because they are bearers of the dominion of God.

The Dominion Belongs to God
All of this means, in apocalyptic terms, that if there is hope for the future, it must be grounded in the mystery or secret of God's kingdom. Liberation must come from beyond this world, from above, not from below. In other words, the victory over tyrannical evil cannot come from any source within the historical process, for the world has been corrupted by violence. The victory will not come by repentance (change of lifestyle), by devotion to the Torah, or, we may add, by education, technology, social planning, or social revolution. The kingdom belongs to God, the cosmic King.

Here we can see a major difference between prophecy and apocalyptic. A prophet like Jeremiah, who announced the imminent judgment of God, perceived some continuity between the present and the future. Even when the Babylonian armies were pounding at the gates of Jerusalem, and all was lost, he bought a field, believing that there would be some continuity into the future (Jeremiah 32). But in apocalyptic thinking, the present age is rotten to the core; the whole structure of society is infected with cancerous evil. Hence the whole "system" must be destroyed. There will be radical discontinuity between "this evil age" and "the age to come," symbolized by a stone, not quarried by human hand, that struck the human kingdoms destructively and enlarged into the worldwide dominion of God (Dan. 2:31-35). In a later chapter we shall see how this apocalyptic view influenced, and was transformed by, Christianity.[13]

13. See fig. 8 describing the apocalyptic worldview, chapter 35.

34. LIFE, DEATH, AND RESURRECTION

We have seen that in the apocalyptic vision human history moves toward the inevitable triumph of the dominion of God over all the forces of evil. Discussion of the grand finale would be incomplete without considering one of the major contributions of apocalyptic literature to biblical theology: the hope for the resurrection of the dead. This theme, of course, dominates the whole New Testament. Indeed, the resurrection of Jesus Christ is proclaimed to be the sign of God's apocalyptic triumph over the powers of sin, darkness, and death, as we shall see later.

Apocalyptic interpreters announced that in the justice of God a place will be prepared for the martyrs who die before God's final triumph. They have not died in vain, for at the consummation God will raise them up in transformed bodily form to take part in a new community.

Making One's Grave in Sheol

This apocalyptic hope was a deviation from the traditional view in ancient Israel that there is no real life after death, except in the minimal sense of a shadowy existence in Sheol, the land of the dead. According to the ancient pictorial view of the universe, Sheol is located beneath the earth in the subterranean waters of chaos.[1] In Sheol there is no sense of community, no memory, no activity, and hence no praise of God (Ps. 115:17)—all that invests life with meaning. In a lament, where faith sinks into despair, a suppliant asks God:

> *Who among the dead celebrates*
> *Your miracles? Do shadows[2] rise*
> *to praise You?*
>
> *Do those in the Grave tell of*
> *Your kindness? Is Your love proclaimed*
> *in Ruin?*
>
> *Are your wonders declared in Darkness?*
> *Is Your justice announced in the Land*
> *of Forget?*
> —Ps. 88:10-12 (trans. Steven Bishop)

A psalm found in the book of Jonah (chap. 2) pictures the experience of approaching death as a person sinking into the deep waters of Sheol (vv. 3–6),

---

1. See the sketch of the ancient pictorial view of the universe by Joan Anderson in my *Understanding the Old Testament* (abridged paperback ed.; Englewood Cliffs, N.J.: Prentice-Hall, 1997), 408, and the adaptation of that sketch here, fig. 6 in chapter 23.

2. NRSV, NJPSV, and others translates "shades." A shade is a disembodied spirit or ghost—a shadow of one's former self.

when "life was ebbing away"; and other psalms describe deliverance from death as being rescued from the "mighty waters" (Ps. 18:16) and being restored to "the land of the living" (Ps. 27:13; 116:9). Psalm 18 (=2 Samuel 22), a royal thanksgiving, portrays deliverance from the threat of death in this powerful, mythopoetic language (vv. 4–18).

Among Israel's neighbors was a cult of the dead, including the practice of necromancy—communication with the spirits of the dead (Deut. 18:11). In the land of Israel necromancy was officially scorned, and was emphatically negated in the book of Ecclesiastes (9:5-6). There were, however, exceptions at the level of popular religion, as illustrated by the story of Saul's consulting the medium of Endor, who brought up the shade (ghost) of Samuel to forecast the outcome of the battle of Gilboa (1 Samuel 28). The description of Saul's visit as clandestine, by night, implies that such occult practices were banned (1 Sam. 28:3). Faith in Yahweh, the Lord of life, was characterized by a healthy this-worldliness. Death, especially at a ripe old age, was regarded as an aspect of the goodness of God's creation.

The Dynamic View of Life and Death

Some of Israel's psalms indicate that death is something more than a biological event that occurs when the heart stops beating and consciousness is extinguished. Life is constantly a struggle with the power of death, which threatens an individual and reduces the vitality of the *nephesh* ("self"—not "soul" in the Greek sense) almost to the vanishing point. Most people today think of death as an event that occurs at the end of life; but in the view of Israel's psalmists, death's power is at work in us now, during our historical existence. Death's power is felt in the midst of life to the degree that one experiences any weakening of personal vitality through illness, bodily handicap, imprisonment, attack from enemies, or advancing old age. Any threat to a person's welfare (Hebrew *shalom*), that is, one's freedom to be and to participate in the covenant community, is understood as an invasion of Death, regarded as a mythical Power, into "the land of the living."

In some of the psalms (especially individual psalms of thanksgiving), one can see how the experience of salvation from the power of death moves toward the experience of "resurrection," that is, being restored from death to life. "In rescuing people from affliction, healing serious sickness, or saving from enemies," writes Christoph Barth, an Old Testament theologian, "God truly raised them from the dead."[3]

One psalmist, for instance, portrays a "sickness unto death."

> *The snares of death encompassed me;*
> *the pangs of Sheol laid hold on me;*
> *I suffered distress and anguish.*

3. Christoph Barth, *God with Us: A Theological Introduction to the Old Testament* (Grand Rapids: Eerdmans, 1991), 277. On psalms of thanksgiving, see my *Out of the Depths* (Philadelphia: Westminster, 1983; rev. ed. forthcoming, 2000), chap. 4, where deliverance from death is discussed (121–27).

> Then I called on the name of the LORD [Yahweh]:
> "O LORD [Yahweh], I pray, save my life!"
>
> —Ps. 116:3-4

The prayer was answered, and the poet exclaims:

> For you have delivered my soul [nephesh] from death,
>   my eyes from tears,
>   my feet from stumbling.
> I walk before the LORD [Yahweh]
>   in the land of the living.
>
> —Ps. 116:8-9

In situations described in psalms of thanksgiving, "the believer was almost dead, and the liberation thus amounted almost to a resurrection."[4]

Life after Death

Now and then in the Old Testament there were attempts to rise above awareness of the limitations of mortal life, but they are few and far between. Recalling a beautiful solo in Handel's *Messiah*, some would think of a famous passage in which Job affirms that he knows that his Vindicator (Redeemer) lives. According to the Jewish translation, the Hebrew text, which is very problematic, reads:

> But I know that my Vindicator lives;
> In the end He will testify on earth—
> This, after my skin will have been peeled off.
> But I would behold God while still in my flesh,
> I myself, not another, would behold Him;
> Would see with my own eyes:
> My heart pines within me.
>
> —Job 19:25-27 (NJPSV)

Here Job expresses the confidence that after his death a redeemer will rise up to defend his cause. That would secure some justice for him, for it was the duty of the "blood redeemer" to avenge the deceased and gain vindication for him after his death. Here, however, Job is not concerned with a postmortem solution to his problem, though he is confident that he will ultimately be vindicated. He wants to see God now and have his case adjudicated fairly. This passage expresses the characteristic this-worldliness of the Old Testament.

Various psalms seem to express confidence that a person's life extends indefinitely into the future, such as Psalm 23, which concludes, according to the familiar translation: "I shall dwell in the house of the LORD [Yahweh] forever." But a close reading of the text indicates that the psalmist's confidence is limited to this life: "for many long years" (NJPSV) or "my whole life long" (NRSV).

---

4. Barth, *God with Us*, 217.

In the beautiful Psalm 139 the poet says, "if I make my bed in Sheol, you are there" (v. 8b), but here the psalmist is dealing with the theme of the inescapability of God. There is no hiding place, above or below, or in any extremity of the earth or heaven, where one can escape the God who knows a person intimately (see vv. 1–6).

Intimations of a Future Life
There are, however, three psalms, all of them wisdom psalms (37, 49, and 73), that may point beyond the horizons of mortality. Twice there is mention of persons' *aḥarith*, which means their "end" (73:17, NRSV) in the sense of "that which comes after"—variously translated as one's "future" (37:37-38, NJPSV), "posterity" (37:37-38, NRSV), "destiny" (73:17, REB), "fate" (49:14, NJPSV). Confronted with the injustice that sometimes the wicked prosper and the righteous suffer, the sage counsels us to look beyond the present to the future, when the outcome of a person's way of life will be manifest. This language may intimate vindication beyond death,[5] though this is doubtful. As in Job, the problem of suffering is heavy to bear precisely because a postmortem solution is not acceptable.

In Psalm 49 the horizon of life beyond death seems to be in view. The sage strikes one of the main themes of wisdom literature: it is foolish to boast of great wealth or glory in worldly success, because death comes inevitably, and "you cannot take it with you."

> *Such is the fate of those who are self-confident,*
> *the end of those pleased with their own talk.*
> *Sheeplike they head for Sheol,*
> *with Death as their shepherd.*
> —Ps. 49:14-15 (NJPSV)

Notice that in this translation Death (personified) is not just a biological event but a power that "shepherds" people toward their "end" or "fate."[6] Not so, however, in the case of the "upright."

> *But God will redeem my life from the clutches of Sheol,*
> *for He will take me.*
> —Ps. 49:16 (NJPSV)

In the judgment of Gerhard von Rad, the verb in the second line, variously translated as "take," "receive," or "snatch away," expresses "a life of communion with God which will outlast death."[7]

The matter is even clearer in the magnificent Psalm 73. Attempting to understand the perplexing injustices of the world, a poet goes to a worship service,

5. So Gerhard von Rad, *Wisdom in Israel*, trans. James D. Martin (Nashville: Abingdon, 1972), 203–4.
6. Reading the Hebrew word *aḥarith*, discussed above, though the Hebrew text is obscure at this point.
7. Von Rad, *Wisdom in Israel*, 204.

where things are seen in a new light. The poet's testimony begins with the great "nevertheless."

> *Nevertheless, I am continually with you;*
>   *you hold my right hand.*
> *You guide me with your counsel,*
>   *and afterward you will receive me with honor.*
> *Whom have I in heaven but you?*
>   *And there is nothing on earth that I desire other than you.*
> *My flesh and my heart may fail,*
>   *but God is the strength of my heart and my portion forever.*
> —Ps. 73:23-26

Unfortunately the meaning of the last part of v. 24 (sometimes translated, "afterward you will receive me to glory") is obscure in the Hebrew text. But the poet's sense of an unbroken fellowship with God seems to provide an intimation of future life. Other psalms may contain this hint too (Pss. 16:9-11; 17:15; 27:13).

Death Swallowed Up in Victory

What we have found so far are hints or intimations of life beyond death. As noted previously, it was in the apocalyptic literature of the Old Testament that a clear breakthrough into a hope for future life occurred. With the coming of God's kingdom, not only will the forces of evil be conquered but also the power of Death will be overcome.

This is the theme in a portrayal of "the eschatological banquet" in a section of the Isaiah Apocalypse (Isa. 24:21-23; 25:6-8). The consummation of "the last days" involves this scenario:

- After the cosmic catastrophe that shakes the earth, Yahweh will be enthroned in Zion—both the heavenly Zion and its earthly counterpart.
- The dispersed of Israel will be gathered to Zion with singing and rejoicing, and other nations will join them in the pilgrimage.
- On Mount Zion Yahweh will spread out a banquet, and invite all peoples to the celebration of divine triumph over evil and the dawn of peace.
- The peoples will join in a great hallelujah chorus to the King.
- The celebration "on this mountain" (25:9) will be joyful because, first, Yahweh will remove the veil that hides God's glory so that "all flesh" will behold the splendor of Yahweh, the Holy One of Israel; second, on Mount Zion "Yahweh will swallow up death forever."

What is involved in this "swallowing up" of death, a motif that is echoed in 1 Cor. 15:54-55? In Hos. 13:14 the language is rhetorical. Speaking of Ephraim, God's question is: "Shall I ransom them from the power of Sheol, shall I redeem them from death?" In other words, should God save the people from the destruction that they deserve as a consequence of their sins? In Isaiah 25, however, the apocalyptic writer is speaking of something far greater than the deliverance of the Israelite people from historical destruction. The poet's unusual language clearly has mythical overtones, for in Ugaritic (Canaanite) mythology, Baal—the lord of life and fertility—is opposed by Mot (Death), the god of darkness and death. What is at stake in this passage is God's victory over Death, "the last enemy" (1 Cor. 15:26), and therefore the complete transformation of the human condition. In the day of God's victory celebration, there will be no more death, and—like a tender parent—God will wipe away all tears from human faces and will remove the "reproach" of his people, Israel.

The Awakening

In an ensuing chapter this theme, the triumph over death, is picked up in an "apocalyptic psalm" (Isa. 26:7-21). The last line of the psalm is crucial for interpretation, but, alas, in the Hebrew the passage is difficult. A Jewish translation reads:

> *Oh, let Your [God's] dead revive!*
> *Let corpses arise!*
> *Awake and shout for joy,*
> *You who dwell in the dust!*[8]—
> *For Your dew is like the dew on fresh growth;*
> *You make the land of the shades come to life.*
> —Isa. 26:19 (NJPSV)

This is a cryptic passage. Some interpret it to be a figurative expression of the hope for a resurrection of the "body" Israel from the gloom of defeat and despair, as in Ezekiel's vision of the valley of dry bones (Ezekiel 37), where the people complain: "Our bones are dried up, and our hope is gone" (v. 11). In answer to the question, "Can these bones live?" the prophet envisions a resurrection of corporate Israel, "bone to its bone"—as pictured in the famous spiritual—and a "breath" or spirit (wind) blows into them new life or reanimates them.

There is a sense in which the view of corporate resurrection is true to this apocalyptic psalm in Isaiah. The poet is not speaking only about the resurrection of each individual after death but of the raising up of all the faithful dead in the end. But more is involved than corporate resurrection. When read in the previous context of the apocalyptic banquet and the announcement that death is swallowed up in divine victory, the passage contains an intimation of personal life beyond death. Early scribes must have viewed it this way, for the received text in Hebrew reads: "your dead will come to life, my body will arise." In any case, Paul quoted the passage about the "swallowing up of death" in 1 Cor. 15:54-55 to support the view of the continuation of personal life beyond death. (See the discussion of 1 Corinthians 15 below.)

---

8. That is, in Sheol, the land of the dead.

When Sleepers Awake

If there is any doubt about the eschatological significance of the passage from the Apocalypse of Isaiah, there is none in regard to a climactic passage in the book of Daniel. The reader is told that "a time of anguish" will come, such as has never before been experienced in the history of the nations.

> But at that time your people shall be delivered, everyone who is found written in the book. Many of those who sleep in the dust of the earth shall awake, some to everlasting life, and some to shame and everlasting contempt. Those who are wise shall shine like the brightness of the sky, and those who lead many to righteousness, like the stars forever and ever.
>
> —Dan. 12:1-4

Here the writer is speaking not about a general resurrection, but only of the "awaking" of those members of the community of faith whose names are enrolled in "the book of life" (cf. Exod. 32:32-33; Ps. 69:28), apparently an official register of members of the community of faith. "Many" will be brought back to life, and "some" of these will "live forever," shining like the stars of heavens. This passage is the clearest expression of future life—indeed, it contains the only mention of "everlasting life"—in the Hebrew Bible.

Resurrection of the Body versus Immortality of the Soul

In this apocalyptic way of thinking, the individual is raised to new life in the community that celebrates God's victory over the powers of evil, darkness, and death. This event occurs not after the immediate death of a person but at the end of history, the time when God's kingdom comes on earth as it is in heaven. People "sleep" until the final consummation, when they will be "awakened" to celebrate God's dominion with those who are alive.

The apocalyptic view of resurrection from the dead came to be a controversial issue among Jewish interpreters. One Jewish party, the Sadducees, denied the doctrine because it was not found in the Torah, while the Pharisees, more liberal in their interpretation, accepted it. On one occasion, according to the Gospels (Mark 12:18-23), some Sadducees questioned Jesus on the point, and Jesus gave an interpretation that sided with the Pharisees. In Paul's defense of the doctrine, he proved himself to be "a Pharisee, the son of a Pharisee" (Acts 23:6-8).

The Pharisaic resurrection view is alien to many modern people too, who prefer to think in terms of the immortality of the soul, if they believe in future life at all. Today the word "immortality" is often used loosely to refer to hope for a future life. Strictly, however, the term expresses a sharp dualism of a deathless soul and mortal body. Death is not real; at the end of life the deathless soul is merely freed from the corruptible body (prison) of flesh.

In the New Testament Jesus' triumph over death is, of course, expressed in terms of resurrection. Significantly, the earliest Christian confession of faith, the Apostles' Creed, does not affirm belief in the immortality of the soul but says: "I believe in the resurrection of the body and the life everlasting." The Nicene Creed, recited in many churches today, affirms belief in "the resurrection of the dead." In a famous sermon on "The Fulfillment of Life," Reinhold Niebuhr observed that the creedal affirmation, "I believe in the resurrection of the body," expresses pregnantly "the whole genius" of the biblical and Christian faith.[9]

Socrates and Jesus
In his celebrated Ingersol Lecture at Harvard University, the distinguished New Testament scholar Oscar Cullmann presented an impressive discussion of these two views by comparing Socrates drinking the hemlock, as set forth in Plato's *Phaedo*, to Jesus struggling with his impending fate in the Garden of Gethsemane, as portrayed in the Gospels of the New Testament.[10]

In the face of death, Socrates is calm, for death is not a significant event. In the Greek view, the soul is essentially deathless. It enters the body from a higher realm, the abode of eternal realities, and for a while suffers imprisonment. Death liberates the soul from the body, which has hindered it from performing freely, and it returns to eternity—beyond the boundaries of time and space. As Cullmann puts it, "the destruction of the body cannot mean the destruction of the soul any more than a musical composition can be destroyed when the instrument is destroyed."[11] Thus Socrates downs the poison calmly, knowing that death does not touch the soul but only liberates it to return to its true home, the realm of the Real and the Eternal.

By contrast, Jesus is confident that his life is enfolded in God's faithfulness and love, but death is a real experience. It means to be forsaken by God ("My God, why have you forsaken me?") and to be taken away from the covenant community, at least temporarily. The finality of death is expressed in the terse language of the Apostles' Creed: "crucified, dead, and buried." If there is a future, beyond the horror of death, it will result from God's act of grace, a new act of creation.

"I Believe in the Resurrection of the Body"

This language, derived ultimately from an apocalyptic worldview, is a *symbolic* expression of faith. It would be wrong to try to cramp the apocalyptic imagery into the exact limitations of literal prose. Moreover, both immortality and resurrection are symbolic modes of expression, neither of which can be proved beyond a shadow of doubt. But the apocalyptic symbolism has some advantages over the Greek doctrine of the immortality of the soul.

---

9. Reinhold Niebuhr, *Beyond Tragedy* (New York: Scribner's Sons, 1937), 42–52. See also Gabriel Fackre, "I Believe in the Resurrection of the Body," *Int* 46 (1992) 42–52.

10. Oscar Cullmann, "Immortality of the Soul or Resurrection of the Dead? The Witness of the New Testament," in *Immortality and Resurrection, Death and Resurrection: Two Conflicting Currents of Thought*, ed. Krister Stendahl (New York: Macmillan, 1965).

11. Ibid., 12.

Psychosomatic Unity of the Person

First, resurrection implies a different "anthropology," or view of human nature, than the one to which we are accustomed. Human nature is not a dichotomy—a body of mortal flesh and a deathless soul, as in some philosophies, but rather a unity of body and spirit, an animated body—*terra animata* (animated soul), as Augustine put it. This view is expressed classically in the creation story found in Genesis 2, according to which the Lord God infused "spirit" (life force) into a lump of clay and it "became a living *nephesh*" (Gen. 2:7; NRSV: "a living being").[12] The Hebrew word should not be translated "soul," if that means an immortal essence, but rather "person" or "self." The self is a unity of body and spirit, a psychosomatic unity. That humans are "embodied beings," not a duality of body and soul, is shown by recent research in genetics.[13]

In this view, death must be taken seriously. As a sage advises us, we should "count our days" (Psalm 90) and live life to the full while we are given time, a teaching of the book of Ecclesiastes.[14] When death comes, as it does to all forms of life that God has created, the self collapses, it dies. Death is a total event—there is no part of human nature, such as an immortal soul, that is untouched. The *nephesh* dissolves to the vanishing point. If, then, there is a continuation beyond this terminal point it will be a divine miracle.[15] The self must be given a new bodily form and the divine spirit or life force must be breathed into it (Gen. 2:7; cf. Ezek. 37:1-11). Future life, like the life we now experience, will be a gift from God, a new creation, not something that is ours by nature.

The Embodied Self

Second, resurrection imagery uses body language to depict the particularity and identity of the individual who has certain personal characteristics. Notice that "resurrection of the flesh" is not intended in this symbolism. The body is the form of our individuality, that which makes a person "somebody." Interestingly, when the medium of Endor, according to the biblical story (1 Samuel 28), "brought up" Samuel from Sheol, he appeared as "an old man wrapped in a robe" so that Saul recognized him. This, of course, reflects superstition that Israel's interpreters tried to prohibit, but it shows how hard it is for us to think of one's personal identity

---

12. Note that the same expression (*nephesh hayyah*) is used of the animals in Gen. 2:19.

13. The science of genetics, according to one study, indicates that "human personhood cannot be reduced to a purely immaterial or spiritual notion, as sometimes occurs when people identify themselves with souls. We are essentially and fundamentally embodied beings, with a genetic heritage from our parents, their parents, and so on. This genetic heritage affects all parts of us" (Bruce R. Reichenbach and V. Elding Anderson, *On Behalf of God: A Christian Ethic for Biology* [Grand Rapids: Eerdmans, 1995], 293; quoted in a paper presented to the American Theological Society [1998], "Theological Reflections on Genetics and Human Nature" by Audrey R. Chapman, Director Program of Dialogue Between Science and Religion, American Association for the Advancement of Science).

14. See above, chapter 31.

15. In the Old Testament this miracle is also expressed in terms of translation from earth to heaven, as in the cases of Enoch (Gen. 5:24) or Elijah (2 Kgs. 2:11).

apart from bodily form, even that of a spiritual body. "Spirit," without bodily manifestation, is vague and indeterminate. By contrast, body—especially a healthy body—images a concrete person, who belongs to a community, who has identifiable traits of personality, and who moves toward future fulfillment. The physical body makes possible dealing with others and thus expresses interpersonal (I-Thou) relationships.

A biblical view of the body (self) challenges the modern scientific worldview that rests on the subject/object or mind/matter dualism of the philosopher René Descartes (1596–1650). This rationalism, portrayed in the famous statue of "The Thinker" by Auguste Rodin (1840–1917), underlies the modern scientific worldview. By virtue of reason, human beings are able to control the material world through scientific know-how and technology. The great symbol is the computer, a creation of the human mind, which "thinks" logically and at times even seems to have a mind of its own! Medical science of the past has been too dominated by the view that the body is a complicated machine, ruled temporarily by a physical brain. But this reductionist view of personhood is inadequate, philosophically and theologically. The question "Who am I?" cannot be fully answered by the well-known Cartesian *"cogito ergo sum"* (I think, therefore I am).

The biblical view of the person as *terra animata* has implications for the care of the body and for medical treatment, to say nothing of issues of social welfare. According to Stephen Sapp it even has implications for Alzheimer's disease, "the disease of the century." In an incisive essay based on a biblical view of human nature, he argues that even when rational faculties fail or there is a tragic loss of memory, the "I," or the person who was made in the image of God, continues to exist.[16] The person's identity, expressed in his or her body, is remembered—and cared for—in the community and is "remembered" by God.

More than that, the person will be resurrected in a new bodily form to exist in eternal relationship with God and to take part in the redeemed community. If there is real future life for a person, beyond the mortal limitations of this life, there will be personal identity, personal recognition, and personal reunion. Thus body language has symbolic dimensions that are difficult to express in terms of a discarnate, immortal soul.

Life in the Redeemed Community

Also, the language of resurrection is based on the premise that life is given in community, as indicated above. Indeed, human life in isolation is not life in the full sense: "Ein Mensch ist kein Mensch," as the German proverb says.[17] That is why solitary confinement in prison, or the anonymity of the homeless, is so dehumanizing. "It is not good for the human being to be alone," says God in a biblical creation story (Gen. 2:18); so God overcomes this loneliness by providing a "partner," one who stands over against, vis-à-vis, in an "I-Thou" relationship. Human life is

16. Stephen Sapp, "Living with Alzheimer's: Body, Soul and the Remembering Community," *Christian Century* 115, no. 2 (1998) 54–60.

given in the context of interpersonal relationship. If "resurrection" during one's lifetime means restoration to the community, so that one may "walk before the Lord [Yahweh] in the land of the living" (Ps. 116:9), then the final liberation from death is appropriately portrayed as being raised to life so that one may take part in the redeemed community. It will mean extending the horizon of Psalm 23 beyond this earthly life and being invited to sit at the Lord's Table with others and to be a guest in God's house "forever," even beyond the limitations of mortal life.

Thus resurrection imagery emphasizes life in community, in contrast to the individualistic doctrine of the immortality of the soul. Indeed, these two ways of thinking yield important differences in ethics. "If Last Things are portrayed as the destiny of isolated persons," writes theologian Gabriel Fackre, "an individualistic ethic is predictable. In contrast, the resurrection of the *body* carries with it the mandate to care here and now for the hungry, homeless, and abused."[18] Moreover, when resurrection is seen in its apocalyptic context of a new creation, which includes the transformation of society and of nature, it has important ecological implications. As Paul said in a chapter that is indebted to the apocalyptic perspective, "the whole creation has been groaning in labor pains until now," waiting with human beings for the final consummation, namely, "the redemption of our bodies" (Rom. 8:22-23).

The End of History

Finally, resurrection imagery, when appearing in an apocalyptic context, implies movement toward the goal of history. Just as the life of the individual is a "pilgrim's progress," so the history of the world, from creation on, is understood to be a teleological movement toward the final event of the coming of the dominion of God on earth as it is in heaven. If the doctrine of immortality is unhistorical, promising to redeem individuals from the transience of time and the evil of history, the resurrection hope endorses the ultimate meaning of our historical life. In this view, there can be no divine justice if faithful individuals, who predecease the end, are denied access to the final consummation.

There are, of course, problems with this apocalyptic imagery. Questions inevitably arise: What happens to faithful individuals in the interim between their death and the final consummation? What continuity is there between the fleshly body that decays and the transformed spiritual body that is incorruptible? Is final salvation intended only for the righteous, the wicked being cast into darkness, or does it include all human beings universally? In facing these and other questions, interpreters must be on guard against turning the poetry of faith into the literalism of exact prose. The important thing is that the imagery of resurrection at the end emphasizes and endorses teleological movement, not only the destiny of individual life but the whole sweep of historical time. In apocalyptic imagination, at the great finale all faithful persons, living and dead, will take part in the eschatological victory banquet.

---

17. "One human being is not a human being at all."
18. Fackre, "I Believe in the Resurrection," 45–46.

The Metamorphosis

The best discussion of resurrection hope in the Bible is found in one of Paul's letters to the church at Corinth (1 Corinthians 15). The discussion is based on an apocalyptic perspective.

Here Paul divulges the apocalyptic "secret" or "mystery" (1 Cor. 15:51): the end is near, so near that not all alive will "sleep," that is, suffer death. Following the Jewish apocalyptic scenario, he declares that the end will be signaled by the sounding of a trumpet (see Joel 2:1; Zeph. 1:16). Then the dead will be raised to take part in the coming of God's kingdom. Their personal lives will be fulfilled in the ultimate goal of all history and creation.

In two respects, however, Paul departs from Old Testament apocalyptic. First, he insists that there will be a metamorphosis in which the physical body is transformed into a spiritual body, for "flesh and blood cannot inherit the kingdom of God" (1 Cor. 15:50). Notice: he does not speak of the release of the immortal soul from its bodily prison, but rather says that the mortal body must "put on immortality" as something that is added (v. 53). When this occurs, as an act of God's new creation, then the promise of the Isaiah Apocalypse (Isa. 25:8) will be fulfilled: "Death has been swallowed up in victory."[19]

Paul devotes considerable attention to the body of the resurrection (1 Cor. 15:35-49). Using various illustrations, he argues that there are different kinds of bodies, and that a spiritual body is one kind among these. His argument is that this physical body, which is now the form of a person's earthly existence, will be changed into a spiritual body or, as he says elsewhere, "a glorified body" (Phil. 3:21) suitable for the new conditions of life in the new age, the everlasting kingdom of God.

> Listen, I will tell you a mystery! We will not all die, but we will all be changed, in a moment, in the twinkling of an eye, at the last trumpet. For the trumpet will sound, and the dead will be raised imperishable, and we will be changed.
> —1 Cor. 15:51-52

To use a modern analogy, the metamorphosis is like that of the caterpillar that changes form and turns into a butterfly. This image has the advantage of portraying continuity and discontinuity: a different form, yet the same being.

The Dawning of God's Dominion

In the second place, Paul departs from traditional apocalyptic by making the bold announcement that the time of God's kingdom has already dawned. That is the meaning of Christ's resurrection, he says as he begins his discussion of the whole subject (1 Cor. 15:20-29). The resurrection of Christ is the "first fruits" of the harvest, showing that the full harvest is coming, namely, the general resurrection from the dead (v. 20). In the meantime, Christ is proclaimed the victorious king, who will continue his redemptive work until all powers hostile to God's purpose are overcome.

19. See the previous discussion in this chapter.

Notice that in this apocalyptic scenario, the "last enemy" to be overcome is Death (v. 26). In the present evil age Death is still an aggressive power, invading the land of the living and seizing its victims, as evidenced by violence, oppression, untimely death, and so on. But, according to Paul's proclamation, Death's power has been broken by God's raising Jesus from the dead. This divine victory is a foretaste of the final triumph over all powers that threaten to separate people from the love of God (Rom. 8:18-19). This event intensifies Christian hope for what is to come: "the liberation from mortality" (Rom. 8:23, REB) or better, "the redemption of our bodies."

> We know that the whole creation has been groaning in labor pains until now, and not only the creation, but we ourselves, who have the first fruits of the Spirit, groan inwardly, while we wait for adoption, the redemption of our bodies. For in hope we were saved.
>
> —Rom. 8:22-24a

Part of the apocalyptic scenario is that in God's plan Jesus Christ will reign as king until the time of the final victory, at which time he will hand over the dominion to God, who will be "all in all" (vv. 27-28). After the conflict is over, and Death is destroyed, the dominion of God will come in its full glory.

Be Steadfast!

As in the case of other apocalyptic literature, such as the book of Daniel, the primary purpose of this discussion is not to speculate about God's future timetable but to encourage people to be faithful in the struggles of daily life. Victory is on the way, and indeed we see its first signs already in Christ's resurrection. Accordingly, Paul ends the discussion of future resurrection with an exhortation to people caught in the midst of the historical struggle to hold on and act:

> Therefore, my beloved, be steadfast, immovable, always excelling in the work of the Lord, because you know that in the Lord your labor is not in vain.
>
> —1 Cor. 15:58

We have seen already, in the case of the book of Daniel, which was written for a revolution, that apocalyptic hope is not a "cop out" or a failure of nerve, but a motivation to stand firm against tremendous odds.[20] As Paul exclaims—to turn again to the magnificent eighth chapter of Romans:

> If God is on our side, who is against us?
>
> —Rom. 8:31 (REB)

20. See the discussion of the apocalypse of Daniel, above, chapter 33.

Conclusion

From the Old Testament to the New

The scriptures written long ago
were all written for our instruction,
in order that through the encouragement
they give us we may maintain
our hope with perseverance.

ROMANS 15:4 (REB)

35. The Apocalyptic Triumph
of Jesus Christ

In the Christian Bible, as we observed earlier, the Old Testament has a relative independence, justifying works on "Old Testament theology" or more properly, biblical theology of the Old Testament.[1] This point has been made forcefully by Brevard Childs in his *Biblical Theology of the Old and New Testaments.*[2] In the Christian Bible, he reminds us, Old and New Testaments have been linked as a unified composition; but this linkage "does not mean that the integrity of each individual testament has been destroyed." It is not justifiable to construct a biblical theology by considering how the New Testament interprets the Old; nor is it right to reduce the theological task to following certain lines of tradition from the Old Testament to their culmination in the New. "Both testaments make a discrete witness to Jesus Christ which must be heard, both separately and in concert."[3]

An exposition of New Testament theology lies beyond the purview of this study. Any consideration of the transition from the Old Testament to the New must, however, take full account of the fact that Christianity erupted out of the heart of Judaism. Contrary to earlier views, there was no such thing as a "normative Judaism." The Judaism of the time was very diverse: divided by parties (e.g., Pharisees, Sadducees), split by sectarian movements, and reactive to philosophies and religions of the Hellenistic world.

From the Old Testament several paths seem to lead to the New, at least from a Christian point of view. Two of these we have considered in the previous sections (III.A–B): (1) from torah to wisdom, and (2) from prophecy to apocalyptic.

The Persistence of the Wisdom Tradition

The wisdom movement continued vigorously into the opening of the Common Era, as evidenced by the presence of wisdom writings in the Greek Bible (Septuagint), writings considered deuterocanonical by Catholics and apocryphal by Protestants (see the books contained between the Old and New Testaments in some editions of the NRSV, REB, NJB, etc.). Since early Christians read Jewish Scriptures in the Greek translation (Septuagint), they were influenced by these extra wisdom writings (Wisdom of Ben Sira, Wisdom of Solomon) and others of the type. The cosmic dimension of wisdom, as found especially in Proverbs 8 and Wisdom of Solomon 8, was eventually emphasized in the Logos (Word) theology found in the prologue to the Gospel of John (John 1:1-18).

1. See above, chapter 2.
2. Brevard S. Childs, *Biblical Theology of the Old and New Testaments: Theological Reflection on the Christian Bible* (Minneapolis: Fortress Press, 1993), especially 77–79.
3. Ibid., 78.

A strong case could be made that a major road from the Old to the New Testaments was via torah and wisdom. Indeed, some scholars, participants in the so-called Jesus Seminar, maintain that "the historical Jesus" was originally a wandering Jewish sage whose image has been almost completely effaced by superimposed messianic interpretations. An analogy would be a palimpsest, a vellum or parchment document whose surface was used more than once, often leaving visible imperfectly erased writing. Some lost works of classical antiquity have been recovered by probing beneath the surface writing and recovering the earliest writing. Similarly, it is argued,[4] critical historical methodology enables scholars to recover the original sayings of a peasant sage, Jesus of Nazareth, who spoke in wisdom forms of speech, such as the parable of the shrewd manager (Luke 16:1-8a) or of the lost coin (Luke 15:8-9); or aphorisms, like the beatitude (congratulation) for the poor (Matt. 5:3 and parallels) or the beatitude for the hungry (Matt. 5:6 and parallels).

The view of Jesus as a wisdom teacher is, these scholars admit, a "reconstruction,"[5] accomplished by reading critically between the lines of the Gospels and by consulting other sources, such as the Gospel of Thomas, a collection of sayings discovered in 1945 in the ancient library of Nag Hammadi, Egypt.

In the judgment of many New Testament scholars, however, this bold reconstruction, which has attracted considerable public attention, rests on a questionable methodology.[6] It draws too sharp a contrast between ordinary "history" and the "story" of faith.[7] It ignores the resurrected Jesus, the foundation of the Christian gospel, in favor of a so-called pre-Easter Jesus. It sets up arbitrary ("scientific") rules to determine what evidence is acceptable.[8] In short, this is a "reductionism" that amounts to "the dismantling of Christianity," as Gordon Harland, a Canadian theological friend, has appropriately put it.

For the theology of the New Testament it is more important to give attention to that kind of wisdom, considered earlier (chapter 28), that comes from reflection on the texts of the Torah. Leaders of Judaism—scribes, Pharisees, Sadducees— who engaged in disputations with Jesus about interpretation of the Torah (e.g.,

---

4. See the book by Robert W. Funk, founder of the Jesus Seminar, *Honest to Jesus* (San Francisco: HarperSanFrancisco, 1996). A catalogue of the sayings, regarded as authentic by majority vote of members of the Seminar, is given in the appendix of his book, pp. 326–35.

5. See John Dominic Crossan, another leading member of the Jesus Seminar, *The Historical Jesus: The Life of a Mediterranean Jewish Peasant* (San Francisco: HarperSanFrancisco, 1991), especially his concluding remarks, pp. 424–26.

6. See Luke Timothy Johnson, *The Real Jesus: The Misguided Quest for the Historical Jesus and the Truth of the Traditional Gospels* (San Francisco: HarperSanFrancisco, 1996); also N. T. Wright, *Jesus and the Victory of God* (Minneapolis: Fortress Press, 1996), 29–35.

7. On this issue in the Old Testament, see above, chapter 1.

8. See the exchange on "Encountering Jesus" between William H. Willimon ("Modern Distractions") and Marcus Borg ("Postmodern Revisioning"), *Christian Century* 114, no. 31 (1997) 1009–13.

Mark 12:13, 18, 28), represented the wisdom of Torah study that was perpetuated in later rabbinic Judaism.[9]

Preaching the Kingdom of God

In his classic study, *The Quest for the Historical Jesus* (1906), one of the great books of the twentieth century, Albert Schweitzer was on firmer ground when he maintained that Jesus was an eschatological preacher who proclaimed the imminent coming of the final kingdom of God. The view that Jesus was an apocalyptic preacher has been strengthened by the discovery of the Dead Sea Scrolls at the headquarters of an Essenelike sect at Qumran, on the shore of the Dead Sea, not far from Jericho. There are striking affinities between this Jewish sectarian group and the early Christian community. Both were apocalyptic communities that awaited the dawn of the new age. Both regarded themselves as people of the new covenant—"the children of light" in conflict with "the children of darkness" (cf. Luke 16:8; John 12:36; 1 Thess. 5:5). Both shared messianic expectations. The Qumran community, however, awaited three figures: "a prophet like Moses," a Davidic king of Israel, and a priestly messiah of Aaron.[10] In the New Testament these three images—prophet, priest, and king—are combined in one messianic figure, as we shall see.

John the Baptist, who preached and baptized in the Dead Sea area (Mark 1:4-11), seems to have been an apocalyptic preacher. He preached that already the axe was laid to the root of the tree, that God was about to destroy the old order and make a new beginning, and that it was time to repent (Matt. 3:1-12). Jesus, who was baptized by John the Baptist in the Jordan River, must have been influenced by John's apocalyptic message when he announced the imminent coming of God's kingdom:

> The time is fulfilled, and the kingdom of God has come near; repent, and believe in the good news.
>
> —Mark 1:15

Mark's Apocalyptic Perspective

In any case, if we start with the New Testament Gospels in their canonical form, rather than going behind the text to recover a "historical Jesus," it is apparent that the Gospel writers perceived Jesus' message and career through an apocalyptic lens, as shown dramatically in the PBS television documentary, *From Jesus to Christ* (April 1998). That Jesus was an "apocalyptic prophet," has been demonstrated

9. See Michael Fishbane, "From Scribalism to Rabbinism: Perspectives on the Emergence of Classical Judaism," in *The Sage in Israel and the Ancient Near East*, ed. Leo G. Perdue and John G. Gammie (Winona Lake, Ind.: Eisenbrauns, 1990), 439–56.

10. See the article by Joseph A. Fitzmyer, "The Dead Sea Scrolls," in *Harper's Bible Dictionary*, ed. Paul Achtemeier et al. (San Francisco: Harper & Row, 1985), 982–88.

effectively by a leading New Testament scholar, N. T. Wright, in *Jesus and the Victory of God.*[11]

This apocalyptic perspective is evident from the earliest Gospel, the Gospel of Mark,[12] on which the other Gospels depend in some degree. In a book on Mark, *Community of the New Age*, Howard Kee observes that Mark shared with apocalyptic writings, such as the book of Daniel, "a set of convictions and expectations." He mentions several convictions held in common:

1. *Revelation of the Divine Secret.* Knowledge of God's purpose for the world, and especially for his people, has been revealed to them through visions and insights of his chosen agent.

2. *Martyrdom in the Face of Opposing Evil Powers.* The faithful must be willing to accept suffering or even death, in the face of fierce opposition from the religious and political powers that are presently in control.

3. *The Apocalyptic Dawn of a New Age.* Beyond the present time of testing and martyrdom lies a new age, in which God's purpose in and for the creation will be achieved, and his people will be fully and eternally vindicated.[13]

Also the letters of Paul, which come from approximately the middle of the first century, are heavily influenced by apocalyptic thinking.[14]

To underscore the future vindication of the faithful, early Christian interpreters, particularly Paul, employed the apocalyptic theme of resurrection from the dead (1 Corinthians 15). As we have seen earlier,[15] in apocalyptic prophecies resurrection is an end-time event, which makes it possible for faithful martyrs, who have predeceased the arrival of God's dominion, to take part in the final consummation.

Continuity and Discontinuity

At the beginning of our study, we found that the relation between the testaments, the Old and the New, is one of continuity and discontinuity.[16] The relationship is not a simple continuity, as though the stream of Jewish tradition flowed smoothly into the New Testament; Jewish tradition actually flows past the New Testament into the Talmud and rabbinical Judaism. Nor was there a sharp discontinuity, as though the stream issued in a waterfall that plunged to make a radically new beginning, as advocated by Marcion, who held that the Old Testament is non-Christian scripture (a view still shared by many today). Rather, the relationship is a dialectic of continuity *and* discontinuity. Both dimensions must be taken into account, as

---

11. See Part II of Wright's book (Fortress Press, 1996).

12. Probably written in the late 60s of the first century.

13. Howard C. Kee, *Community of the New Age: Studies in Mark's Gospel* (Philadelphia: Westminster, 1977), 12.

14. This is demonstrated by J. Christiaan Beker in *Paul the Apostle: The Triumph of God in Life and Thought* (Minneapolis: Fortress Press, 1980).

15. See above, chapter 33.

16. See above, chapter 2.

we have seen when considering such matters as the ancestral promise of land or the ethical demands of the Holiness Code.[17]

In the usual apocalyptic scenario there is sharp discontinuity between the old and the new. The old age must pass away; the new age will supervene. Paul seems to be saying something like this when he speaks of the dawning of God's new creation:

> If anyone is in Christ, [that person] is a new creation: everything old has passed away; see, everything has become new!
>
> —2 Cor. 5:17

When one compares Jewish and Christian apocalyptic, however, one finds not only striking similarities but also significant differences.

Apocalyptic Dimensions of the Christian Gospel

Consider three basic convictions that the Christian proclamation shares with Jewish apocalyptic.

The Kingdom of Satan vs. the Kingdom of God. Like apocalyptic, the early Christian gospel makes a radical distinction between the dominion of God and the rule of evil powers that attempt to usurp control of God's creation. In this view the problem of evil cannot be reduced to sin, that is, betrayal of covenant relationship with God; rather, people are victims of oppressive powers that are at work in human history, and even in the cosmos. Indeed, there is a kind of dualism—a conflict between the kingdom of God and the kingdom of the evil one (Satan), though one should add that this is a postcreation conflict, not one rooted in the creation itself. As in the conclusion of the Lord's Prayer, faithful people pray to be delivered from the sinister power of the evil one (Matt. 5:13).

The Present Age and the Age to Come. In the New Testament, as in apocalyptic literature, these two spheres of sovereignty (kingdoms) are depicted as two ages: "the present age," in which God's sovereignty is hidden except to eyes of faith, and "the age to come," in which the glory of God will be revealed for all to see. The present evil order, corrupted by sin and violence, stands under God's judgment and must pass away in order that the new creation may appear (see fig. 7).

Therefore, as Paul advises in correspondence to the church at Corinth, Christians should sit loosely to the present world:

> The appointed time has grown short; from now on, let even those who have wives be as though they had none, and those who mourn as though they were not mourning, and those who rejoice as though they were not rejoicing, and those who buy as though they had no possessions, and those who deal with the world as though they had no dealings with it. For the present form of this world is passing away.
>
> —1 Cor. 7:29-31

17. On the former see above, chapter 22; on the latter, chapter 15.

FIGURE 7. *The Two Ages*

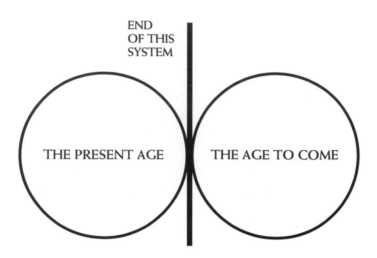

The Assurance of God's Ultimate Triumph. As in apocalyptic, the Christian gospel antic-ipates the coming triumph of God over the powers of evil and the imminent com-ing of an age in which there will be justice, well-being, harmony—everything ignified by the word "peace" (Hebrew *shalom*, Greek *eirene*). As Paul writes in 1 Corinthians 15, a chapter heavily influenced by an apocalyptic perspective,

> Then comes the end, when he [Christ] hands over the kingdom to God the Father, after he has destroyed every ruler and every authority and power.
>
> —1 Cor. 15:24

Reinterpreting the dominion God has given "the son of man" (human beings) according to Ps. 8:6, Paul goes on to say that Christ must reign until he has put all "his enemies" under his feet, those enemies being the demonic powers of evil that dominate the present age, including "the last enemy," Death. Apocalyptic prophecy, as we have seen, envisioned a great eschatological banquet, celebrating God's victory over powers of violence, oppression, and chaos, when death will be "swallowed up" forever (Isa. 24:6-10a).[18]

The Nearness of God's Dominion. As in apocalyptic, the Christian gospel announces that God's eschatological triumph is near. The kingdom of God is not that "one far-off divine event toward which the whole creation moves" (Tennyson); rather, it is "at hand." According to the Gospel of Mark, Jesus said to his listeners:

---

18. See above, chapter 33.

Truly I tell you, there are some standing here who will not taste death until they see
that the kingdom of God has come with power.

—Mark 9:1

In view of the nearness of God's kingdom, the faithful know that the present crisis
is urgent and they wait and pray in intense hope.[19]

Christian Transformation of Apocalyptic

The Christian gospel, however, has transformed the apocalyptic view because of
the announcement that God has done something totally and radically new
through the life, death, and resurrection of Jesus Christ. A "new creation" has
begun to appear (1 Cor. 5:7). This *novum* has changed people's whole outlook (2
Cor. 5:16), even the way they hear prophecies found in Jewish Scripture. Notice
some of the new accents of Christian apocalyptic.

Jesus as Aggressor against Satan's Kingdom. Jesus is not portrayed merely as an apocalyptic visionary who announces the mystery of God's kingdom to a select few;
rather, he himself is the sign of God's kingdom in the present historical age when
evil powers are at work, making people victims of structures of oppression or
threatening health and wholeness with invasive evil spirits. In the Gospel of Mark,
for instance, Jesus is portrayed as God's agent who, as the Divine Warrior, goes out
to fight against Satan's kingdom, which overpowers people and inflicts suffering
and bondage on them. Jesus' exorcisms are understood to be the Messiah's warfare
against Satan's kingdom for the purpose of freeing people from the power of evil
(or the evil one). Jesus' crucifixion, crowned with resurrection, signifies to
Christian faith that Jesus is the victor in the long struggle with evil. The Festival
of Christ as King, the last Sunday of the season of Trinity, is an occasion for celebrating his royal triumph, although the worshiping community knows that his
crown, his throne, and his dominion are not like that of the rulers of this world.

Martin Luther's famous hymn of the Reformation, "A Mighty Fortress Is Our
God," uses this mythopoetic language, though one fears that it may be excised
from some future hymnals owing to "the war on metaphors."[20]

> And though this world, with devils filled,
>   should threaten to undo us,
> We will not fear, for God hath willed
>   his truth to triumph through us.
> The Prince of Darkness grim,
>   we tremble not for him;
> his rage we can endure,
>   for lo, his doom is sure;
>   one little word shall fell him.

---

19. See N. T. Wright, "What Time Is It?" in *Jesus and the Victory of God*, 467–72.
20. Referring again to Kathleen Norris's essay in *The Cloister Walk*, see above, chapter 21.

That "word above all earthly powers," according to Luther's hymn, must be spoken by "the man of God's own choosing," for "he must win the battle."

God's Dawning New World. The Christian gospel announces that the period of waiting (Advent) is over, for the king has come and the dominion of God has already been inaugurated. In other words, the Christian gospel has broken the time scheme of apocalyptic, with its sharp separation of "the present [evil] age" from "the age to come." No longer are these two ages like circles that touch each other only tangentially (see fig. 7), so that the old must pass away before the new can come; rather, the two ages are like overlapping circles (see fig. 8), for already God has introduced the new age through Jesus Christ even while the old age persists.

Thus people of faith find themselves living in the zone where the circles overlap, "tasting the power of the age to come" (Heb. 6:5), even while the temptations and influence of the present world exert their power. The ethical problems of the Christian community arise from this double involvement: one foot in the present evil age, so to speak, and the other in the new age that has already dawned through Jesus Christ.[21]

Christ's Resurrection. In the Christian reinterpretation of apocalyptic, the supreme sign of the new age is the resurrection of Christ from the dead. As Paul argues effectively in 1 Corinthians 15, this end-time event has already occurred in the

FIGURE 8. *God's Dawning New World*

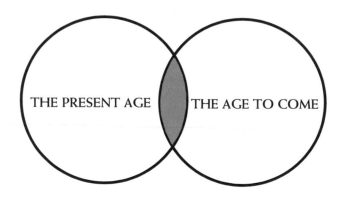

THE PRESENT AGE   THE AGE TO COME

21. See the relevant discussion by J. Paul Sampley, *Walking between the Times: Paul's Moral Reasoning* (Minneapolis: Fortress Press, 1991).

midst of the present age. Christ's resurrection, Paul declares, is "the first fruits" (1 Cor. 15:20) that gives promise of the "harvest" that will come in the end, when there will be a general resurrection of the predeceased to share the victory celebration of God's kingdom.

So near and certain is God's apocalyptic triumph that Paul can go so far as to say that not everyone will die, but for all there will be a metamorphosis, as there was in the case of Jesus, so that the present form of the self (body) will be transformed. In Handel's *Messiah*, the apocalyptic scenario is portrayed in the solo, "The Trumpet Shall Sound."

> Listen, I will tell you a mystery! We will not all die, but we will all be changed, in a moment, in the twinkling of an eye, at the last trumpet. For the trumpet will sound, and the dead will be raised imperishable, and we will be changed. For this perishable body must put on imperishability, and this mortal body must put on immortality.
>
> —1 Cor. 15:51-53

To be sure, the Christian community lives in the tension of "already" and "not yet." Using the symbolic language of apocalyptic, the trumpet signalizing God's final triumph has not yet sounded. There is still a period of waiting for the final consummation, the coming of God's kingdom fully on earth as it is in heaven or, in christological terms, the appearance (*parousia*) of Jesus Christ in glory. But this waiting is not the expectation of counting the days or speculating on an apocalyptic timetable. For already God's triumph has been manifest in the resurrection of Christ, the end-time event that gives a foretaste of the final consummation. This foretaste of God's kingdom is a summons to responsibility: "Be steadfast, immovable, always excelling in the work of the Lord, because you know that in the Lord your labor is not in vain" (1 Cor. 15:58).[22]

More Than Conquerors. Finally, apocalyptic has given to the early Christian community a profound grasp of the meaning of God's triumph in Jesus Christ. In one dimension, God's victory is liberation from the power of sin through divine forgiveness displayed in the vicarious and atoning death of Jesus. The apocalyptic perspective, however, pushes Christian interpreters to go beyond this prophetic message of sin and forgiveness and to proclaim God's triumph over all the powers of darkness, chaos, evil, and death. Paul lists some of those powers in his great victory proclamation at the end of Romans 8, where he declares that through Christ we are "more than conquerors."

> Who will separate us from the love of Christ? Will hardship, or distress, or persecution, or famine, or nakedness, or peril, or sword? . . . No, in all these things we are more than conquerors through him who loved us. For I am convinced that neither death, nor life, nor angels, nor rulers, nor things present, nor things to come,

---

22. Recall the discussion of 1 Cor. 15, above, chapter 34.

nor powers, nor height, nor depth, nor anything else in all creation, will be able to separate us from the love of God in Christ Jesus our Lord.

—Rom. 8:35-39

Christian liturgy ought to take this proclamation more seriously. Our usual liturgy has been heavily influenced by the prophetic and priestly message of sin and forgiveness. Toward the beginning of the service, worshipers usually engage in a general confession of sin, which is followed by an announcement of God's forgiveness, to which the congregation responds with the *Gloria Patri*. The celebration of God's victory, however, is incomplete unless the liturgy goes beyond the forgiveness of sins into the wider dimension of Christian apocalyptic: God's victory over all powers of darkness, evil, and death that oppress people.

Christian communities are called to be "beachheads of God's dawning new world," as J. C. Beker has nicely put it.[23] God has introduced the new creation in Christ; its powers are already at work in the world. The Christian community is summoned to be part of God's healing and saving work, not in some secure place of refuge in the desert or not just in the privacy of one's personal life, but in this world that is torn apart by conflict, violence, and war. To be "in Christ," that is, in the community that is his body, is—to quote the great prayer of Francis of Assisi— to be "an instrument of God's peace."

> *Lord, make us instruments of Thy peace.*
>   *Where there is hatred, let us sow love;*
>   *where there is injury, pardon;*
>   *where there is doubt, faith;*
>   *where there is despair, hope;*
>   *where there is darkness, light;*
>   *where there is sadness, joy.*
> *O Divine Master, grant that we may not so much seek*
>   *to be consoled, as to console;*
>   *to be understood, as to understand;*
>   *to be loved, as to love;*
> *For it is in giving that we receive;*
>   *it is in pardoning that we are pardoned;*
>   *and it is in dying that we are born to eternal life.*[24]

---

23. Beker, *Paul the Apostle*, 313.
24. I have adapted this, by changing singular pronouns to plural, so that the Christian community speaks.

36. Jesus Christ as Prophet, Priest, and King

In the light of God's "apocalyptic triumph" in Jesus Christ, the Christian community rereads the Scriptures of Israel: the Torah, the Prophets, and the Writings. These Scriptures "were written down to instruct us," Paul wrote to the Christian community at Corinth, "on whom the ends of the ages have come" (1 Cor. 10:11). New Testament writers frequently cite the Old Testament, usually in the Greek version (Septuagint), finding new meaning in the scriptural heritage. While the Old Testament can stand by itself, speaking with its own independent voices, the New Testament is "incomprehensible apart from the Old," as Brevard Childs rightly observes.[1]

God's Covenants with Israel Endorsed

Early Christian interpreters affirmed that God's covenants with Israel have been "fulfilled," or better, "validated," by God's new covenant instituted through Jesus Christ. To speak of the "fulfillment" of God's covenant promises is perhaps inadequate; for the verb "fulfill" means to carry out or realize something promised or expected. In one sense, God's new revelation did not realize the promises of the covenants with Israel but introduced a deep discontinuity with Israel's traditions, as we have seen. In another sense these traditions were received and transformed, enriching the content of the Christian gospel.

The relationship between the old and the new is not a dichotomy—a division into two mutually exclusive parts—but a dialectic of continuity and discontinuity. In this relationship of continuity/discontinuity, God's covenants with Israel were not abrogated or superseded; rather, they were transformed and endorsed by Christ. In him they received their "Yea and Amen" (2 Cor. 1:20).

The Covenants of Promise

Christian interpreters preferred the promissory covenants associated with Abraham and David—the "covenants of promise" as they are termed in Eph. 2:12. The Mosaic covenant of obligation was suspect in some circles (especially Pauline), for it was feared that the emphasis on obedience to the "law" might put one's relationship with God on a basis of merit rather than freely offered grace. Accordingly, Paul traced God's promises of grace back before the giving of the law at Sinai to Abraham, who heard "the gospel beforehand" (Gal. 3:8) and who put his faith in God's promises (cf. Gen. 15:1-5).

---

1. Childs, *Biblical Theology of the Old and New Testaments* (Minneapolis: Fortress Press, 1992), 77.

Some years ago J. C. Rylaarsdam, a scholar at the University of Chicago, wrote an illuminating essay, "Jewish-Christian Relationships: The Two Covenants and the Dilemmas of Christology."[2] He provided an excellent discussion of two of the symbolic trajectories that we have considered: the Mosaic pattern of symbolization that moves in the horizontal dimension of history, from promise to fulfillment; and the Davidic symbolization that moves in the vertical dimension of the cosmic and the mundane, heaven and earth. He maintained, on the one hand, that the Jewish community gives priority to the conditional Mosaic covenant of obligation, with its demand for obedience under the sanctions of the blessing and the curse, and subordinates the Davidic covenant with its cosmological symbolism of temple and king. On the other hand, the Christian community gives priority to the unconditional royal covenant in which the king is perceived to be the Son of God, who represents God's cosmic rule on earth and in which the Mosaic covenant of law is subordinate. Rylaarsdam proposed to understand the coexistence of the Jewish and Christian communities by considering these two covenants, the Davidic and the Mosaic, which belong together dialectically in the economy of God's purpose.

This was a bold and provocative attempt to understand theologically the separateness of these two communities and their essential partnership in God's purpose. The thesis, however, is challenged by the witness of both testaments. The two patterns of symbolization are present, and interact, in both testaments: it is not a matter of one or the other. In the New Testament, for instance, Jesus is perceived to be a prophet like Moses as well as a king like David. In the final analysis, all the covenants of grace—Mosaic, Abrahamic, Davidic—are necessary for expressing the presence of the holy God in our midst.

Old Testament Traditions and the Shaping of the Gospel

Careful study of the Synoptic Gospels discloses that Israel's major traditions have had a great influence in the literary expression of the Christian gospel. This is the conclusion of Willard M. Swartley, who, in a fascinating study, shows that major Old Testament streams of tradition have helped to shape the content and structure of the three Gospels, Matthew, Mark, and Luke.[3] The traditions of exodus, torah-teaching (Sinai), way in the wilderness—in other words, what we have called the Mosaic covenant trajectory—were influential in shaping the account of Jesus' Galilean ministry. Further, Israel's traditions of temple and kingship (i.e., the royal covenant trajectory) have helped to shape narratives about Jesus in Jerusalem and vicinity.[4] It is noteworthy, however, that in the Synoptic Gospels what we have

2. J. Coert Rylaarsdam, "Jewish-Christian Relationships: The Two Covenants and the Dilemmas of Christology," *JES* 9, no. 2 (1972) 249–70; discussed above, chapter 24.

3. Willard M. Swartley, *Israel's Scripture Traditions and the Synoptic Gospels: Story Shaping Story* (Peabody, Mass.: Hendrickson, 1994).

4. See chap. 7 in ibid. for a synthesis of his study.

designated as the Priestly trajectory is subordinated. To be sure, the temple figures prominently in them, but lacking are typically Priestly concerns: sacrifice, priesthood, the tabernacling presence, and the life of holiness.[5]

One of the important aspects of Swartley's study is that he emphasizes the dimensions of continuity and discontinuity (or "transformation") in the appropriation of Old Testament traditions. For instance, Jesus is portrayed as the Divine Warrior, as in Mosaic tradition (e.g., Exod. 15:1-18), but he liberates people from bondage to the oppressive kingdom of evil; moreover, the saving benefits are not limited to "God's own people" but are extended to the poor, Gentiles, women, and others "outside the boundaries."[6] Further, Jesus is portrayed in the colors of royal tradition, but his humble and vulnerable kingship, which is not "like the nations," is freed from all nationalistic interpretation.[7]

God with Us

To echo the opening theme of our exposition of Old Testament theology: the Bible, from beginning to end, bears witness to the incredible and startling good news that the holy God, who is completely beyond our world of experience and beyond the reach of our conceptualization, has come into this world supremely through Jesus Christ. To portray the meaning of the coming of Jesus, religious imagination soars beyond the prosaic realities of history and employs imagery or patterns of symbolization that we have found in the Old Testament. In the New Testament Jesus is portrayed in the symbolic vistas of at least three major images, all derived from the Old Testament. He is a prophet like Moses, though one greater than Moses; he is a priestly mediator of an everlasting covenant, though not standing in the succession of Israel's priests; and he is a king of the Davidic line, but his royalty is not like that of worldly rulers.

As we noticed previously, in the Qumran covenant community these three roles were represented in the expectation of three different messiahs (prophetic, royal, priestly), whereas in the New Testament Jesus, the Messiah, performs all three.

A Prophet Like Moses

Jesus Christ is, first, the eschatological prophet whom, according to the witness of Deuteronomy 18, God would raise up to speak God's words to the people. In the book of Acts, one of Peter's sermons portrays Jesus as the prophet like Moses whom God would raise up at last (Acts 3:12-16). Indeed, he specifically quotes the key passage from Deuteronomy:

---

5. Ibid., 266–68. He observes (p. 192) that the Synoptic tradition "did not undertake a theological assessment of priestly theology as did the book of Hebrews."

6. Ibid., 263–64.

7. Ibid., 268–69.

> Moses said, "The Lord your God will raise up for you from your own people a prophet like me."
>
> —Acts 3:22; (Deut. 18:15)

Here, however, the verb "raise up" is a double entendre, referring also to Jesus' being raised from the dead (v. 26). Despite this discontinuity, the sermon portrays Jesus as standing in a succession of prophets, beginning with Moses and including Samuel (v. 24)—and we could add, Elijah, who appeared with Moses on the Mount of Transfiguration (Mark 9:1-8).

Significantly, some people of the time supposed that Jesus might have been another Jeremiah (Matt. 16:14). As we have seen earlier,[8] Jeremiah also was regarded as a prophet like Moses, only with this difference: the prophet who speaks God's words to the people suffers in performing his task. This view of a "suffering prophet," not found in the original Mosaic tradition, was something new in Jeremiah's time. The view probably influenced the portrayal of the suffering servant of Isaiah, and it certainly influenced the prophetic image of Jesus in the New Testament. In the story of the walk to Emmaus, for instance, Jesus is portrayed as "a prophet mighty in deed and word before God and all the people" who "must suffer" before "entering into his glory" (Luke 24:19-27). In this view, Jesus is the suffering servant who performs the twofold role of covenant mediator: speaking God's words to the people and representing them before God. He is a prophet like Moses, yet much greater.

Mediator of an Everlasting Covenant

The priestly imagery of the temple and God's tabernacling presence among the people have had a great influence on the message of the New Testament. As we have seen, in the Synoptic Gospels the royal imagery of temple and throne was influential in the narration of Jesus' Judean ministry. But Priestly theology, which dominates the Pentateuch in its final form, comes to expression above all in the Epistle to the Hebrews, which draws on the ancient mythology of the relation between macrocosm and microcosm, celestial and terrestrial.[9] There Jesus is portrayed as the great high priest, of the order of Melchizedek (Ps. 110:4), who performs his sacrifice not in an earthly temple but in its heavenly prototype, and whose sacrifice is "once for all," not subject to cyclical repetition. In this view, which draws deeply on the Priestly theology of Exodus and Leviticus, Jesus is the mediator of an "everlasting covenant" (Heb. 13:20) that reconciles people to God and enables them to live in the presence of the holy God.

Jesus Christ as King

Finally, Jesus Christ is king, the "son of God" of royal messianic tradition. In the Gospel of Luke, an angel tells Mary that the child to be born to her will be called the Son of God.

---

8. Above, chapter 22.
9. On this heaven-earth correspondence, see above, chapter 13.

He will be great, and will be called the Son of the Most High, and the Lord God
will give to him the throne of his ancestor David.

—Luke 1:32

Joseph Fitzmyer points out that almost the same language is used in one of the
Dead Sea Scrolls, indicating that "such titles were not the product of the hell-
enization of the Christian gospel as it was carried by early missionaries from
Palestine into the Greco-Roman world," but belongs firmly in Jewish tradition.[10]

The Matthean version of Peter's confession at Casaerea Philippi: "You are the
Christ, the Son of God," echoes the Davidic covenant, which portrays the king in
these terms: "I will be a father to him, and he shall be son to me" (2 Sam. 7:14). At
first glance, Peter's testimony seems to go beyond the functional meaning of
Hebrew *mashiah* (anointed one), a term used of one anointed for a task. "Messiah"
(Greek *christos*) is basically a term of agency or function, not of ontological relationship with God. In this instance, the term "Son of God" seems to echo exalted
language used in ancient Israel of the king. In royal psalms the anointed one is
declared to be God's son "this day," originally the day of coronation (Ps. 2:7); he
is portrayed as seated at the right hand of God, sharing the divine rule (110:1); and
in one instance, if we follow "the difficult reading" of the received text rather than
sidestepping it (as in some modern translations), the king is addressed as divine:

> *Your throne, O God, endures forever and ever.*
>
> —Ps. 45:6

Most scholars understand this poetic language as the hyperbole of Eastern
"court style." The king was extolled in extravagant terms, especially on festival
occasions (enthronement, royal wedding). In the Old Testament there was no
serious departure from the view that the king was God's agent, anointed for a task.
This is undoubtedly true in the well-known messianic passage in Isaiah 9 ("unto us
a child is born, a son is given"), where the coming king is given the most glorious
throne titles: "Wonderful Counselor, Mighty God, Everlasting Father, Prince of
Peace" (Isa. 9:6). The king, even the one who was to come, was not regarded as
divine, "consubstantial" with the Deity.

The theologian Elizabeth Johnson is right in saying that "Jewish scriptural
symbols," such as "messiah" and "son of God," do not "connote divinity." A significant step, she adds, was made when interpreters used wisdom categories (e.g.,
Prov. 8:22-31) to explore the messiah's "ontological relationship with God" and the
cosmic status of the messiah, who is active with God in the creation.[11]

It was not in the Old Testament but in the New that a momentous theological
shift took place: from a functional Christology inherent in the word "messiah" or
"Christ" to an ontological Christology concerned with the being of Christ in

10. Fitzmyer, "The Dead Sea Scrolls," in *HarperCollins Bible Dictionary*, ed. Paul Achtemeier et
al. (rev. ed.; San Francisco: HarperSanFrancisco, 1996), 987. He cites and translates 4Q246
1:7—2:1.

11. Elizabeth Johnson, *She Who Is: The Mystery of God in Feminist Theological Discourse* (New York:
Crossroad, 1994), 98. On the wisdom categories see the discussion above, chapter 30.

relation to God. This shift is evident when one moves from the symbolic world of the Synoptic Gospels, deeply rooted in Israel's covenant traditions, to the quite different symbolic world of the Fourth Gospel, which is introduced by identifying Christ with the Logos (Word) that in the beginning was "with God" and "was God." This shift to ontology is also evident in post-Pauline writings such as the Epistle to the Colossians, which declares that God created the world in Christ (Col. 1:15-17) and that in him "all the fullness of God/deity" dwells (1:19; 2:9). Statements like these have no real parallels in the Old Testament but move in the direction of the trinitarian discussions of the early Christian church.

In Conclusion

To sum up, just as in the Old Testament the various covenants, interacting with one another, present patterns of symbolization that express God's relation to the people and the presence of the holy God in their midst, so in the New Testament these covenant perspectives are employed to confess our faith in Jesus, the Christ, whose life, death, and resurrection signify that "God is with us." Jesus stands in the succession of the prophets, especially those in the Mosaic tradition (Hosea and Jeremiah), yet he is more than a prophet. Jesus has a priestly role, like the priests who ministered in the Jerusalem temple, yet his priestly ministry is unique. And Jesus is king, a ruler like David who is called the Son of God and who bears the throne name Immanuel, yet a king whose dominion is unlike that of David.

From the standpoint of biblical theology, then, it is appropriate that in the church's theological traditions, especially the Reformed tradition,[12] the work of Christ is portrayed as a threefold office (*manus triplex*): prophet, priest, and king.[13]

---

12. John Calvin, *Institutes of the Christian Religion*, ed. John T. McNeill, trans. Ford Lewis Battles; Library of Christian Classics 20 (Philadelphia: Westminster, 1960), 494–503. Chapter 15: "To Know the Purpose for Which Christ was Sent by the Father, and What He Conferred upon Us, We Must Look above All at Three Things in Him: The Prophetic Office, Kingship, and Priesthood." On the threefold office, see further Geoffrey Wainwright, *For Our Salvation: Two Approaches to the Work of Christ* (Grand Rapids: Eerdmans, 1997), the second set of lectures.

13. On the threefold office see Geoffrey Wainwright, *For Our Salvation: Two Approaches to the Work of Christ* (Grand Rapids: Eerdmans, 1997) Part 2. He displays an edited version of Isaac Watts' hymn, "Join All the Glorious Names" (1709), which celebrates in three successive verses (p. 98) the three roles of Christ: "great prophet of God," "great high priest," and "our conqueror and king."

APPENDIX 1

BIBLICAL THEOLOGY OF THE OLD TESTAMENT
A COURSE PRÉCIS*

The title of this study (echoing earlier formulations in the history of the discipline) intends to emphasize that "Old Testament theology" belongs within the larger framework of biblical theology. This, of course, is a Christian formulation, just as "Old Testament" is Christian language for the Scriptures of Israel. Yet within the Christian Bible the Old Testament has its own integrity in relation to the New.

Various approaches to Old Testament theology have been used: *Heilsgeschichte* (in the sense of Oscar Cullmann), "cross-sectional" study of the covenantal structure of Israel's faith (Eichrodt), history of traditions (*Heilsgeschichte* in the sense of Gerhard von Rad), thematic, doctrinal, and so on. The approach used in this work is different from all, though influenced somewhat by von Rad and Eichrodt. The work begins with an exposition of Israel's experience of the holy (the *revelation* of the Holy One), not just as impersonal power but as personal power of concern and ethical demand, that is, the "root experiences" (Emil Fackenheim) of exodus and Sinai. This fundamental experience, which comes to expression in the symbolism of language and cultic practice, is seen against the background of, and in the context of, the religions of the ancient Near East.

Israel's experience of "the Holy One in our midst" is expressed in and refracted through major patterns of covenant symbolization, associated with Abraham, Moses, and David, respectively. Each attempts to bring to expression the fundamental confession that Yahweh (the personal name of the Deity) is the Holy One who has entered into the human world and is present in the midst of Israel. Each covenant symbolization is related to particular sociological circumstances in which the original formulation was socially meaningful (e.g., Mosaic covenant theology in the social setting of the tribal confederacy, Davidic covenant theology in the time of the rise of the monarchy), but the power of the symbolization outlasted the social setting and formed a major "trajectory" that became meaningful in other social settings and persisted into the New Testament.

These covenant symbolizations ("theologies" is too abstract a term), however, did not do full justice to the "dialectical contradictions" in the root experiences of the Holy God in the midst of a people and in the world. These polarities (e.g., universalism and particularism, divine sovereignty and human freedom, divine transcendence and immanence), treated differently in each of the covenant symbolizations, exploded the various covenant formulations, especially under the impact of the gravity and enormity of the problem of evil as experienced at the fall of the

*Presented April 2, 1982 at Princeton Theological Seminary.

nation and the exile of the people. Various attempts were made to synthesize covenant theologies (e.g., in the Deuteronomistic history, Second Isaiah, the Chronicler's history). In general the postexilic period was dominated by two movements: one torah and wisdom, the other apocalyptic ("prophecy in a new key").

The course ends by considering how these two major lines, torah/wisdom and prophecy/apocalyptic, lead into the New Testament, and how the covenant "theologies" associated with Abraham, Moses, and David are picked up in the New Testament formulations of the gospel that centers in Jesus, the Christ (Messiah). The relation between the testaments is considered to be a dialectical continuity/discontinuity.

Appendix 2
The Relevance of Archaeology
to Biblical Theology

A Tribute to George Ernest Wright

One way to sharpen our understanding of the task and method of Old Testament theology is to consider the relation of this discipline to so-called biblical archaeology.

At one time the two disciplines, biblical archaeology and biblical theology, were held to be essentially related. Back in the 1950s and 1960s, the days of the biblical theology movement, they were united in one person, George Ernest Wright, to whom this book is dedicated. Wright was a unique figure in the history of twentieth-century scholarship: he was both a leading archaeologist and a recognized biblical theologian.[1]

In the latter part of the century, however, this union dissolved, to be superseded by a nonbiblical enterprise, broadly called Syro-Palestinian archaeology. Indeed, "biblical archaeology" has been pronounced dead, although perhaps, as in the case of Mark Twain, the death notice may have been exaggerated. The interest in biblical archaeology still survives, for instance, in the Biblical Archaeology Society founded by Hershel Shanks.[2] Today, however, the two disciplines—Palestinian archaeology and Old Testament theology—are absolutely separate. The most recent book on Old Testament theology, the magnum opus by Walter Brueggemann, "brackets out" all historical issues, a far cry from the heyday of the biblical theology movement.[3]

I am neither an archaeologist nor the "son" of an archaeologist (i.e., member of the Albright school), but rather a disciple of James Muilenburg, a gifted scholar who displayed a deep interest in the historical situation of ancient Israel and even was involved in the archaeology of the Israelite center at Gilgal, but who, under the influence of Hermann Gunkel, moved more toward the poetic, stylistic criticism now called rhetorical criticism. In the early part of my career, however, I was influenced by Wright's work, beginning with his little book *The Challenge of Israel's Faith* (1944); then in the 1950s I joined with him in directing the Drew-

---

1. See the essay by one of his students, William G. Dever, "Biblical Theology and Biblical Archaeology: An Appreciation of G. Ernest Wright," *HTR* 73, nos. 1–2 (1980) 1–15; also his history and critique of biblical archaeology in *The Hebrew Bible and Its Modern Interpreters*, ed. D. A. Knight and G. M. Tucker (Chico, Calif.: Scholars Press, 1985), 31–74.

2. This essay is substantially a lecture given under the auspices of the Biblical Archaeology Society, Orlando, Fla., November 1998.

3. Walter Brueggemann, *Theology of the Old Testament: Testimony, Dispute, Advocacy* (Minneapolis: Fortress Press, 1997); see the long footnote, 118–20.

McCormick reexcavation of the biblical city Shechem.[4] In those summers "on the dig," while bearing "the burden and heat of the day" as a trench supervisor, I began to reflect on archaeological method and the relevance of archaeology to biblical theology. That question has haunted me down through the years. In this essay I continue those reflections, speaking primarily as a biblical theologian.

Biblical Theology and Historicity

First, it is clear to me that biblical archaeology forces upon the biblical theologian willy-nilly the problem of historicity, that is, the rootage of biblical texts in the historical experiences of ancient Israel. From the very first, Israel was inescapably involved in world politics. Significantly, the earliest reference to this people is found outside the Bible, in a stele set up by Pharaoh Merneptah in about 1207 B.C., celebrating his victories in Syria and Canaan, including defeat of the *people* Israel.[5] That inscription anchors the Israelite story firmly in history. To be sure, Israel's witness to the presence and activity of God in the world is written in such a manner as to appeal to our poetic sense and religious imagination; but the Israelite story is not a poetic construct or fictitious account. In many down-to-earth ways, archaeology has demonstrated that, as William Dever says in a helpful discussion,

> The Bible is about real, flesh-and-blood people, in a particular time and place, whose actual historical experience led them irrevocably to a vision of the human condition and promise that transcended anything yet conceived in antiquity.[6]

This inescapable point, however, only raises the question of the relation of the Israelite story to history in the modern sense. The distinguished American orientalist, William F. Albright, who dominated biblical studies in the mid-twentieth century, particularly in the United States, maintained that biblical archaeology and biblical history go hand in hand. Against skeptics who maintained that the biblical traditions are late and of little value historically, he insisted that archaeology and the study of the ancient Near East demonstrate "the Bible's substantial historicity." He was a conservative—not a Bible-believing fundamentalist, to be sure, but nevertheless a conservative—who defended the substantial accuracy of the biblical history against skeptical liberals (i.e., the so-called Julius Wellhausen school of higher criticism).[7]

While Albright emphasized the value of archaeology for biblical studies, it remained for one of his brilliant students, George Ernest Wright, to work out the

4. See George Ernest Wright, *Shechem: The Biography of a Biblical City* (New York: McGraw-Hill, 1964).

5. See *ANET*, 376–78. The translator observes that in this Egyptian text the word "Israel" is the only one written with the designation for people rather than land.

6. William G. Dever, *Recent Archaeological Discoveries and Biblical Research* (Seattle: University of Washington Press, 1990), 32.

7. See the critical evaluation by William G. Dever, "What Remains of the House That Albright Built?" *BA* 56 (1993) 25–35.

relation between biblical archaeology and biblical theology. This he did in his famous monograph, *God Who Acts*,[8] in which he maintained that the Bible bears witness to the "mighty acts of God" on behalf of Israel and that "historical recital"—not abstract "ideas of God" or "doctrines about God"—constitutes the basis of biblical theology. Accordingly, he spent much exegetical time and space, to say nothing of archaeological work, defending the substantial historicity of the biblical story: the ancestors of Israel, the exodus and Sinai covenant, the conquest of Canaan, and so on. It is doubtful whether Wright ever intended to say that archaeological research *proves* the Bible to be true (as a good Presbyterian he knew that faith is not based on proof or any other "works"). But he would surely say that those who stand within the believing and worshiping community, hearing and celebrating the "old, old story," are urged by faith to seek understanding of the "historical recital" with the help of archaeology and studies of the ancient Near East. In this way, biblical theology is "faith seeking understanding," to allude to Anselm's formula.

Archaeology, however, proved to be a very frail reed for the theologian to lean on. Here we need not rehearse the weaknesses of the biblical theology movement, which took as one of its premises the revelation of God in history.[9] Biblical archaeology itself proved to be the problem, for too often it failed to substantiate the biblical record, in fact at times it contradicted it. The parade example is the account of the fall of Jericho in Joshua 6. Kathleen Kenyon's careful excavation of the city showed no evidence of a violent attack in the thirteenth century when, according to the well-known biblical story, "the walls came tumblin' down."[10] We have been forced to conclude that this is a cultic story, composed imaginatively to celebrate the victories of Yahweh, the Lord of hosts (or Divine Warrior). It probably has no more historical value than the account of the symmetrical arrangement of the tribes while on the march or encamped around the tabernacle (Num. 2:1-31; 10:11-33). Many scholars who take historical method and archaeological research seriously have expressed radical skepticism about "the Bible's substantial historicity." As Hershel Shanks observes in a perceptive discussion, "these biblical minimalists have attempted to expunge ancient Israel's past."[11]

Other things have contributed to this skepticism. There can be no doubt that the Old Testament, in many and diverse ways, testifies to the presence and activity of God in human history, and particularly the history of Israel, the people of God. Today, however, God's action in the world is not just "a strange work" (Isa.

8. George Ernest Wright, *God Who Acts: Biblical Theology as Recital*, SBT 1/8 (Chicago: Regnery, 1952).

9. The theological assumptions of biblical theology championed by Wright were challenged by Brevard Childs in *Biblical Theology in Crisis* (Philadelphia: Westminster, 1970), a turning point in twentieth-century biblical theology.

10. The conflict between story and excavation is evident also in the case of Ai (Joshua 8). See the report of the excavator, J. A. Callaway, "Excavating at 'Ai (Et-Tell), 1964–1972," *BA* 39 (1976) 18–30.

11. Hershel Shanks, "The Biblical Minimalists: Expunging Ancient Israel's Past," *BRev* 13, no. 3 (1997) 32–39, 50–52.

28:21)—it is unbelievable in a century when people have experienced the threat of chaos, in the face of the most horrible acts of violence and of impending ecological disaster. The optimistic view of the Enlightenment, based on faith in reason and inevitable progress, has been shattered, preparing the way for the philosophy and hermeneutic of postmodernism.[12]

It is understandable then that, in the face of the "collapse of history" as a theological foundation,[13] biblical theologians have tried to flee into the "safe haven" of the text, and have disavowed attempts to go "behind the text" into the real historical experiences that generated it, for example, the fall of Jerusalem in 587 B.C. and the exile. This approach, however, goes too far. Admittedly, the biblical account does not conform to our standards of historicity (its purpose was to confess faith in God, not just to write history). Moreover, the evidence from archaeology is, at best, ambiguous and inconclusive. This only shows that faith that is based on the biblical witness is not subject to proof but is vulnerable to doubt and uncertainty. Nevertheless, biblical texts are illuminated again and again by the historical concreteness and cultural context that archaeology provides. Once we surrender the notion that archaeology proves the "substantial historicity" of the biblical account, we are free to "revisit" the whole question of "the acts of God" in history.[14] It would be a great irony if at this time, when some scientists are beginning to consider whether God acts in the physical world,[15] theologians were to continue to "expel God from history."[16]

Biblical Theology and the History of Israel's Religion

Second, biblical archaeology, as I see it, forces on the biblical theologian the problem of the relationship between biblical texts, regarded as authoritative (canonical) in the community of faith, and the religion as actually practiced by the people. The question of the relationship of Old Testament theology to the history of religions, specifically the religion of Israel, has been a major subject of theological discussion for years.[17] Which should it be: the religion of Israel, or the theology of the Old Testament? Or are both somehow interrelated?

12. For a general discussion of the postmodern age, see Stanley J. Grenz, *A Primer on Postmodernism* (Grand Rapids: Eerdmans, 1996). The underlying philosophy is discussed in Allan Magill, *Prophets of Extremity: Nietzsche, Heidegger, Foucault, Derrida* (Berkeley: University of California Press, 1985).

13. See Leo G. Perdue, *The Collapse of History* (Minneapolis: Fortress Press, 1994).

14. See the editorial by Patrick Miller, "Revisiting the God Who Acts," *TToday* 54, no. 1 (1997) 1–5.

15. John Polkinghorne, *Belief in God in an Age of Science* (New Haven: Yale Univ. Press, 1998), Chapter 3: "Does God Act in the Physical World?"

16. Emil L. Fackenheim, *God's Presence in History: Jewish Affirmations and Philosophical Reflections* (New York: New York Univ. Press, 1970), 5. Note that this book was written in the shadow of the Holocaust, the terrible event that seems to negate God's presence and activity in the world.

17. See, e.g., Ronald E. Clements, "The Old Testament and the History of Religion," in *Old Testament Theology: A Fresh Approach* (Atlanta: John Knox, 1978), Chapter 7.

The "new archaeology," as it is called, is not interested in confirming the reliability of biblical texts. Its limited task is to investigate the everyday life of the people: the structure of their buildings, the artifacts that they made, their economic livelihood, the culture they shared, and so on. Written texts may help us to understand how people—at least those educated enough to write—thought about life or viewed the world in mythical symbolism. But only fragments of Israelite writing have been discovered in Palestinian sites, in contrast to the wealth of material found elsewhere, especially in Babylonia and Egypt. The new archaeology deals primarily with artifacts and other tangible evidence. With the help of anthropology and sociology, it helps us to understand how the people lived and how they practiced religion.

William Dever, a vigorous defender of the new archaeology, proposes that archaeology enables the interpreter to go behind the biblical texts and recapture their original contexts. He points to a couple of inescapable issues. First, the biblical texts are "elitist" in that they reflect the views of "the intelligentsia" who could compose and appreciate such great literature, whereas archaeology enables us to understand the religion of the masses, religion as practiced outside the established centers of power (priesthood, royal court, wisdom circles). Second, the biblical texts are given to us in a literary context, perhaps that imposed by the final redactors, whereas archaeology enables us to read these texts in their original social or cultural context and thus to appreciate folk religion and even hear the voices of the counterculture. Seen in this perspective, the worship of Yahweh was not radically different from Canaanite religion. There is evidence that at the popular level Yahweh was invoked along with Asherah, the mother goddess of Canaanite religion, "possibly thought of as the consort of Yahweh, the god of Israel."[18]

Here we face a methodological question. It is doubtful whether a particular religious faith can be described or defined solely by studying the practices of the people, or only by considering the views of the majority. There must be some criterion for discrimination: a tradition of the elders, guiding creedal statements, a council discussion, canonical boundaries—whatever gives shape and identity to an otherwise amorphous whole.

I agree that there is a fundamental difference between the two disciplines. Dever puts it well: "Biblical theology . . . regards the Bible more as Scripture [sacred writings]," whereas archaeology ignores this canonical context and "seeks to grasp if at all possible . . . the essential phenomenon, in its original context."[19] This statement, however, seems to establish an unnecessarily sharp division between the disciplines. In my judgment the religion of Israel, as reconstructed by archaeology, is the "infrastructure," to use a current expression, which is indispensable for interpretation. The study of the religion of Israel in its popular manifestations helps us to understand the theological and social struggles that went on in the community as the biblical texts were handed on and reinterpreted. Even in

18. Dever, *Recent Archaeological Discoveries*, 140–49.
19. Ibid., 125–26.

the final form of Scripture, evidences of these struggles (e.g., between the worship of Yahweh and Baal, or over the question of who speaks for God) still survive. These theological tensions and "marginal voices" must be taken into account in biblical theology.

It is true, however, that biblical theology concentrates on biblical *texts* in their various literary forms, on "what is written," that is, Scripture. In this sense, it is based on *sola scriptura* (scripture alone). Therefore, biblical theology goes "hand in hand" not with archaeology, to which we must turn for the reasons given in this essay, but with hermeneutics, the "science" of interpretation that enables us to read and understand biblical texts in their various literary forms.

Biblical Theology and Historical Criticism

So we come finally to the inescapable question: the role of historical criticism in biblical theology. In the so-called postmodern age in which we now find ourselves, literary critics say, with a special accent, that the function of religious language, whether found in the Bible or other great literature, is "to create worlds" that we may "inhabit" existentially. Paul Ricoeur, a major philosophical advocate of this hermeneutic of language, maintains that the task of biblical interpretation is not to penetrate the historical situation of authors or to grasp their intention, but to hear the poetic testimony of the text that projects "a new world of being" different from "the world of ordinary experience." Poetic imagination enables one to "inhabit" that new world and to find "a new being" within it.[20]

Historical criticism has been the whipping boy of postmodern critics because, allegedly, it projects on biblical texts the philosophy of the Enlightenment, rooted in the view of René Descartes (1596–1650) that a human being is a thinker who cogitates an external world that may be rationally (mathematically) measured and scientifically explained. Cartesian philosophy, which underlies our scientific worldview, is said to be manifest in historical criticism that subjects biblical texts to rational analysis and historical verification.

There are already signs, however, even among those who appreciate a postmodern hermeneutic, that historical criticism may be evaluated more positively. As Margaret Odell observes in her perceptive review essay, "History and Metaphor," the aim of historical criticism was not to advocate a worldview. An important paragraph in her essay deserves quotation:

> It has never been the task of historical criticism to construct uniform worldviews. If anything, historical criticism is uniquely qualified to destroy them. Ever since Lorenzo Valla asserted, on the basis of methods that would come to be associated with historical criticism, that the Donation of Constantine was a forgery, historical criticism has exposed the problematic foundations of the critics' own worldviews.

20. See above, chapter 3, where I discuss Paul Ricoeur's contribution. Three leading advocates of postmodern understanding are Michel Foucault, Jacques Derrida, and Richard Rorty; see the helpful introduction by Stanley J. Grenz, *A Primer on Postmodernism*, especially chapter 6.

Moreover, as she observes, definite gains have come from historical criticism, as in studies that have highlighted overlooked or neglected roles of women in biblical texts. In short, "historical criticism does not construct worldviews; it helps us to reconsider them."[21]

A major illustration of the critical role of historical criticism is evident in the case of the overthrow of the developmental (evolutionary) interpretation of the Bible, popularized in Harry Emerson Fosdick's *Guide to the Understanding of the Bible*, a book that was recommended to students brushing up in preparation for comprehensive exams when I attended the Yale Graduate School in the early 1940s.[22] This book, which eloquently summarized a whole school of biblical scholarship, purported to find in the Bible a unilinear evolution from the presumed low religious level of early Israel in the Mosaic period, to the so-called ethical monotheism of the great prophets, and on to the lofty heights of the New Testament gospel of the universal "fatherhood of God and the brotherhood of man," as it was put in those days. Walther Eichrodt, the eminent Old Testament theologian, observed in a trenchant critical review that Fosdick wrote "the obituary of a whole scholarly approach and method of investigation, making both their inherent merits and their limitations clear to the thoughtful reader."[23] This judgment on "evolutionary historicism," however, was based not on a rival scholarly approach but on a "scientific" method that tested the subjective premises of the developmental approach and found them wanting, in the light of our increasing knowledge of the religions of the ancient Near East and of the early sources of Israelite traditions. It is significant that Eichrodt's review, delayed in reaching the United States because of World War II, was introduced with an English abstract by the distinguished American archaelogist, W. F. Albright. As we well know, Albright maintained, on the basis of historical and archaeological study, that in the Middle Bronze period (2000–1500 B.C.) the religions of the ancient Near East had already attained a high level of sophistication and that Israel's religion in the Late Bronze Age (1500–1200 B.C.) was no exception to the general rule.

"The time cometh and now is," to lapse into King James English, when historical criticism should receive more positive evaluation. Postmodern critics reap its benefits and, in some instances, presuppose its findings. This is evident in Walter Brueggemann's postmodern theology, which, though spurning historical criticism and bracketing out questions of historicity, emphasizes the importance of the exodus and the exile in Israel's religious testimony. As said earlier, even the question of "the God who acts," the theological theme associated preeminently with George Ernest Wright, deserves to be revisited and reconsidered. In the hermeneutical tumults of the twentieth century, it has been impossible to escape

---

21. Margaret S. Odell, "History or Metaphor: Contributions to Old Testament Theology in the Works of Leo G. Perdue," *RelSRev* 24, no. 3 (1998) 241–45, quotation 244.

22. Harry Emerson Fosdick, *A Guide to the Understanding of the Bible: The Development of Ideas within the Old and New Testaments* (New York: Harper, 1938).

23. Walther Eichrodt, review of *A Guide to the Understanding of the Bible*, (trans. W. F. Albright), *JBL* 65 (1946) 205–17.

the fundamental historical dimension of Israel's faith—or the faith of the New Testament for that matter.[24] As long as this historical rootedness is recognized as a fundamental theological concern, biblical interpreters will continue to debate the relevance of archaeology to biblical theology; and, I might add, biblical archaeology will survive as a valuable asset for biblical theology.

24. See N. T. Wright, *Jesus and the Victory of God* (Minneapolis: Fortress Press, 1996), e.g., 60–62.

Index of Subjects

Index of Authors

INDEX OF ANCIENT SOURCES